ESSENTIAL PUBLIC HEALTH

Essentials of Managing Public Health Organizations

James A. Johnson
Kimberly S. Davey

Series Editor: Richard Riegelman

James A. Johnson, PhD, MPA, MSc

Medical Social Scientist and Professor
School of Health Sciences
Central Michigan University
Mount Pleasant, Michigan
and
Visiting Professor
St. George's University
Grenada, West Indies

Kimberly S. Davey, PhD, MBA, MA

Associate Professor
Public Health and
Director of the Undergraduate
   Public Health Program
School of Public Health
Samford University
Birmingham, Alabama

JONES & BARTLETT
LEARNING

World Headquarters
Jones & Bartlett Learning
5 Wall Street
Burlington, MA 01803
978-443-5000
info@jblearning.com
www.jblearning.com

Jones & Bartlett Learning books and products are available through most bookstores and online booksellers. To contact Jones & Bartlett Learning directly, call 800-832-0034, fax 978-443-8000, or visit our website, www.jblearning.com.

18853-0

Production Credits

VP, Product Management: Amanda Martin
Director of Product Management: Cathy Esperti
Product Manager: Sophie Fleck Teague
Product Specialist: Sara Bempkins
Project Specialist: Jamie Reynolds
Digital Project Specialist: Rachel Reyes
Director of Marketing: Andrea DeFronzo
Senior Marketing Manager: Susanne Walker
Manufacturing and Inventory Control Supervisor: Amy Bacus
Composition: codeMantra U.S. LLC

Project Management: codeMantra U.S. LLC
Cover Design: Kristin E. Parker
Text Design: Kristin E. Parker
Senior Media Development Editor: Troy Liston
Rights Specialist: Maria Leon Maimone
Cover Image (Title Page, Chapter Opener):
© KTSDESIGN/Science Photo Library/Getty Images.
Printing and Binding: LSC Communications
Cover Printing: LSC Communications

Library of Congress Cataloging-in-Publication Data
Names: Johnson, James A., 1954- author. | Davey, Kimberly S., author. | Riegelman, Richard K., editor.
Title: Essentials of managing public health organizations/James A. Johnson, Kimberly S. Davey; editor, Richard Riegelman.
Other titles: Essential public health.
Description: Burlington, MA: Jones & Bartlett Learning, [2021] | Series: Essential public health | Includes bibliographical references and index.
Identifiers: LCCN 2019036546 | ISBN 9781284167115 (paperback)
Subjects: MESH: Public Health Administration
Classification: LCC RA418 | NLM WA 525 | DDC 362.1—dc23
LC record available at https://lccn.loc.gov/2019036546

6048

Printed in the United States of America
23 22 21 20 19   10 9 8 7 6 5 4 3 2 1

Dedicated to:

*My parents, Drs. Tom and Nena Sanders, for
their unconditional love and support*

*My husband, Ian Davey, for walking every mile with me
and helping me make my dreams come true*

*My daughter, Eva Davey, for being my sunrise,
sunset, and everything in between*

*My mentor, Dr. Thomas L. Powers, for being an
exceptional academic role model and colleague*

*My chair, Dr. Melissa Lumpkin, for her daily encouragement
and contagious passion for public health*

My students, for inspiring me everyday

Contents

THE ESSENTIAL PUBLIC HEALTH SERIES

From the impact of AIDS to the cost of health care, this unique series will introduce you to the full range of issues that impact the public's health.

Current and Forthcoming Titles in The Essential Public Health Series:

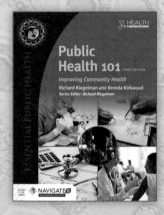
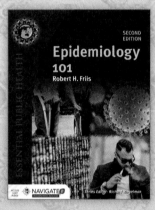
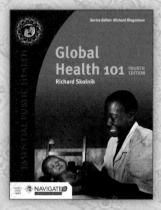
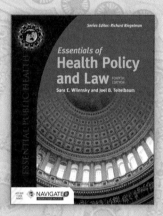

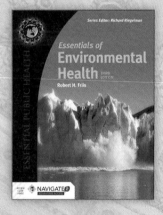
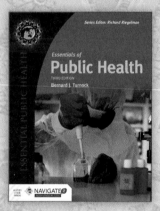
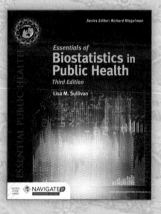

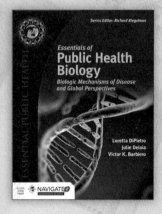

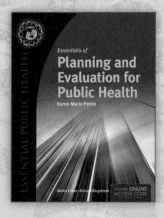

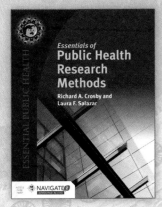

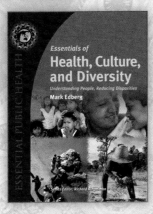

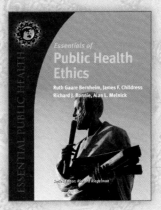

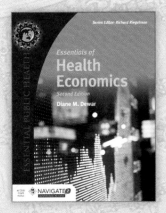

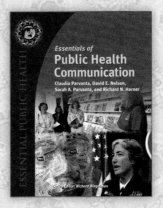

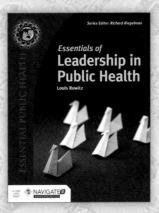

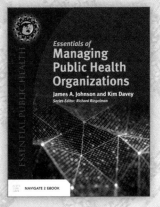

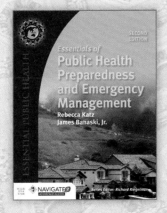

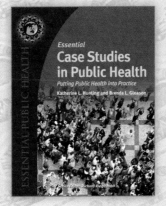

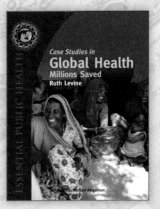

ABOUT THE EDITOR

Richard K. Riegelman, MD, MPH, PhD, is Professor of Epidemiology-Biostatistics, Medicine, and Health Policy, and Founding Dean of The George Washington University Milken Institute School of Public Health in Washington, DC. He has taken a lead role in developing the Educated Citizen and Public Health initiative which has brought together arts and sciences and public health education associations to implement the Institute of Medicine of the National Academies' recommendation that "…all undergraduates should have access to education in public health." Dr. Riegelman also led the development of The George Washington's undergraduate major and minor and currently teaches "Public Health 101" and "Epidemiology 101" to undergraduates.

Foreword

This book is a timely addition to the growing body of works dedicated to preparing undergraduate students for meaningful careers in public health. Although traditionally taught at graduate institutions, the reach of public health education in recent years has expanded in recognition of the need for a public health workforce well equipped to address some of the more complex challenges facing the world today. In fact, public health agencies and organizations themselves are complex human systems, as described throughout this book. Countless organizations at every level have emerged to confront daunting challenges, such as climate change, health disparities, and an uneven distribution of economic resources and social capital that greatly impact this health of individuals and communities. For such organizations to successfully carry out their mission, competent managers and leaders are crucial. A solid educational foundation, as in many other cases, is key to this success. With 62% of the public health workforce with no postgraduate education,[1] the need to prepare students in college for such careers is invaluable and will help to strengthen our capacity as a society to further build upon the gains we have made in public health over the many decades? As a professor at a liberal arts college, undergraduate education is particularly well suited for public health education. The ethos of the liberal arts is to provide a well-rounded education challenging students to think critically and preparing them to actively engage in the world in meaningful ways. Thus, such institutions are particularly well suited to prepare students for careers navigating the complexities presented by public health challenges and the deep level of critical thinking and creativity needed to address them. According to the Association of American Colleges and Universities (AAC&U), a leading voice for education in the liberal arts:

> An understanding of public health is a critical component of good citizenship and a prerequisite for taking responsibility for building healthy societies. At its best, the study of public health combines the social sciences, sciences, mathematics, humanities, and the arts. At the same time, it serves as a vehicle for the development of written and oral communication skills, critical and creative thinking, quantitative and information literacy, and teamwork and problem solving. It incorporates civic knowledge and engagement—both local and global—intercultural competence, and ethical reasoning and action, while forming the foundation for lifelong learning. The study of public health, in other words, models a capacious vision of liberal education.[2]

Essentials of Managing Public Health Organizations is a welcomed addition to the limited number of textbooks to improve a foundation for such undergraduate learning in public health and preparing future leaders to improve health and reduce human suffering.

Allen Johnson, DrPH, MPH
Director, Master of Public Health (MPH) Program
Rollins College, Winter Park, FL

► References

1. Leider JP, Harper E, Bharthapudi K, Castrucci BC. Educational attainment of the public health workforce and its implications for workforce development. *J Public Health Manag Pract*. November 2015;21(Suppl 6):S56–S68.
2. Association of American College & Universities. The educated citizen and public health. March 2019. https://www.aacu.org/public_health.

Editor's Preface

Essentials of Managing Public Health Organizations is an important addition to the *Essential Public Health* series. It addresses basic principles of organizational management and applies these principles to the unique opportunities and challenges of managing public health organizations.

Written specifically for an undergraduate audience, the textbook assumes no prior knowledge or experience in management roles or knowledge of the complex organizations that make up the public health system. This book is written to tie together key knowledge and skills required for graduates to enter the public health workplace.

The authors James A. Johnson, PhD, MPA, MSc, and Kimberly S. Davey, PhD, MBA, MA, have worked together to produce a book with one voice and a step-by-step set of chapters that provide an ideal textbook for an introductory course in a public health major or minor. Dr. Johnson is a prolific and highly successful author whose books on management and health systems organization are widely used and widely acclaimed. Dr. Davey brings a new perspective drawing on her teaching of leadership, management, strategy, and health policy, at the undergraduate level.

The authors use a range of teaching methods to bring the textbook to life, including interviews, cases, exercises, and class discussions. Likewise, their book is written to stimulate critical thinking and in-depth understanding. This textbook includes a range of online resources for students and faculty that are provided through the publisher.

The authors specifically aim to satisfy the accreditation criteria for public health management and the basic organization of the public health system. They incorporate concepts of systems thinking and stimulate students to think about the complex challenges of dealing with workplace diversity, public health emergency management, and organizational change.

I am confident that you will find *Essentials of Managing Public Health Organizations* to be a key textbook in the *Essential Public Health* series. Take a look and see for yourself.

—*Richard Riegelman, MD, MPH, PhD,*
Series Editor, Essential Public Health series

Author's Preface

This book was written to address a significant need in public health education. While there are many graduate level textbooks available for courses in public health, there are only a few that address public health management and organizations in a comprehensive way. One such book is Shi and Johnson's *Public Health Administration: Principles of Population-Based Management, 4th ed.* (formerly Novick and Morrow), which is very comprehensive, over 700 pages, and the most widely used textbook on this topic in graduate schools of public health. However, the Shi and Johnson book is too advanced for undergraduate students. As a result, undergraduate instructors have been hesitant to embrace it as a primary text. This book you are about to read, *Essentials of Managing Public Health Organizations* by myself and co-author Kimberly S. Davey, does indeed combine the scope and the context of public health while also addressing key management topics, processes, and emerging issues. Furthermore, this book links its various chapters to core competencies that are increasingly expected by the American Public Health Association (APHA) and public health accrediting commissions. This is especially timely for undergraduate programs, many of which are newly established and seeking recognition concurrent with their desire to offer students learning resources in the form of textbooks that are written for their audience.

This book comprises key chapters that address foundations, practical applications, and new directions in public health management. The goal is to enhance the student's knowledge, skills, and abilities in ways that help them become more effective in their careers in public health. This book will be especially useful to those who are at the early stage of their education or new to their jobs in public health organizations.

Public health agencies and organizations are complex human systems that have evolved over time and continue to do so. There are many of these organizations that exist at every level of society. These include large federal agencies and research centers, state health departments and regulatory agencies, and county and local public health agencies.

Public health organizations also have, by virtue of their distinct mission, unique qualities. These organizations consist of highly credentialed professionals who function under considerable scrutiny within many prescribed guidelines. The challenge of managing in this environment can be daunting unless one has a basic understanding of individual, group, and organization behavior. Additionally, public health organizations are not static, and managers are tasked to facilitate the change that is inevitable. This can be done in a systematic planned way utilizing approaches found in management practice, including team building and the examination of power, influence, conflict, motivation, and leadership in the context of public health services. This book will help the student better understand public health organizations and gain knowledge of management in ways that foster change in productive and sustainable ways.

Essentials of Managing Public Health Organizations

About the Authors

James A. Johnson, PhD, MPA, MSc, is a full professor in the School of Health Sciences at Central Michigan University where he teaches courses in comparative health systems, organizational behavior, and health systems thinking, as well as a course in international health systems and policy. Dr. Johnson is the former Chair of the Department of Health Administration and Policy at the Medical University of South Carolina and former associate professor of family medicine.

He is a very active researcher and health science writer with over 100 journal articles and 19 books published. One book that is read worldwide is titled *Comparative Health Systems: Global Perspectives* where he and co-researchers analyzed the health systems of 20 different countries. He is also the co-author and editor with Leiyu Shi, Johns Hopkins University, of the 4th edition of *Public Health Administration: Principles for Population-Based Management* and the recently published *Health Systems Thinking*. Eighteen of Professor Johnson's books have been selected for the permanent collection of the National Library of Medicine.

Dr. Johnson is an elected Member of the Governing Council of the American Public Health Association (APHA). He is past-editor of the American College of Healthcare Executives (ACHE) *Journal of Healthcare Management* and is currently a contributing editor for the *Journal of Health and Human Services Administration*, and global health editor for the *Journal of Human Security and Resilience*. He works closely with the World Health Organization (WHO) in Geneva, Switzerland, and ProWorld Service Corps in Belize, Central America, on international projects and student involvement. He is a regular delegate to the World Health Congress and a member of the Global Health Council. His work and travels have taken him to over 45 countries thus far.

Dr. Johnson has been an invited lecturer at Oxford University (England), Beijing University (China), University of Dublin (Ireland), University of Colima (Mexico), St. George's University (Grenada), and University of Pretoria (South Africa), as well as universities, associations, and health organizations within the United States, including visiting or adjunct professorships at University of Michigan, Auburn University, and St. George's University (Grenada).

Additionally, he has served on many boards, including the Scientific Advisory Board of the National Diabetes Trust Foundation, American Public Health Governing Council, Board of the Association of University Programs in Health Administration (AUPHA), Advisory Board of the Alliance for the Blind and Visually Impaired, Board President of Charleston Low Country AIDS Services, Advisory Board of the Joint Africa Working Group, Advisory Board of the Center for Collaborative Health Leadership, and Board of Advisors for Health Systems of America. Dr. Johnson completed his PhD at Florida State University where he specialized in health policy and organization development.

Kimberly S. Davey, PhD, MBA, MA – Associate Professor of Public Health, Samford University, Birmingham, Alabama

Dr. Kimberly S. Davey is an Associate Professor of Public Health and Director of the Undergraduate Public Health Program in the School of Public Health at Samford University in Birmingham, Alabama.

Dr. Davey has extensive teaching experience in the areas of management, leadership, health systems, health policy, marketing, and strategy at both the undergraduate and graduate level. A hallmark of Dr. Davey's teaching is the extensive interdisciplinary and interprofessional nature of her courses and teaching experience. At Samford, she has taught courses across four schools (School of Public Health, Ida V. Moffett School of Nursing, McWhorter School of Pharmacy, and the Cumberland School of Law). Prior to joining Samford, Dr. Davey served as a faculty member in the Department of Family, Community, and Health Systems at the University of Alabama at Birmingham (UAB) School of Nursing.

Dr. Davey is a member of the Health Administration Section of the American Public Health Association (APHA), the Southern Management Association (SMA), and Health Care Management Division of the

Academy of Management (AOM). She has received awards for her research including the SMA's Health Care Management, Hospitality, and Public Administration Track Best Doctoral Student Paper award and Best Track Paper Award. She has served as Chair of SMA's Health Care Management, Hospitality, and Public Administration Track, Chair of the Communications and Development Committee for the Alabama Health Action Coalition, and Co-Chair of the Communications Committee for the Health Administration Section of APHA. Dr. Davey is a reviewer for the APHA, AOM, and SMA. On campus, Dr. Davey serves as the co-faculty advisor of Samford's Circle of Omicron Delta Kappa, a prestigious national leadership honor society.

Dr. Davey earned a PhD in Health Services Administration from UAB, MA in Diplomacy and International Relations with specializations in International Economics and Development and International Negotiations and Conflict Management from Seton Hall University, and BS in Business Management, BA in Spanish, and MBA from Samford University.

CHAPTER 1

Public Health Today and Tomorrow

LEARNING OBJECTIVES

After reading this chapter, you should be able to:

- Describe public health from a population health perspective.
- Discuss the systems perspective in public health.
- Describe the core functions of public health.
- Identify the essential services of public health.
- Discuss public health management.
- Identify the core competencies of public health managers.
- Describe Public Health 3.0.
- Discuss the national health objectives from *Healthy People 2020* and *2030*.
- Discuss the social determinants of health in the context of the national health agenda.
- Describe the multidisciplinary nature of the public health workforce.

▶ Introduction

Public health continues to answer the call to promote the health, safety, and well-being of individuals and communities in the United States and around the world. The 21st century is an exciting, yet challenging, time. Advances in science, technology, and medicine have contributed to progress in all regions of the world. Such advances hold incredible promise for improving the health and well-being of all individuals in the future. This century has also been a perilous time due to radical and disruptive changes in every facet of the physical and social world—including the political, economic, cultural, technological, ecological, and legal. These global and national forces are interacting and producing complex interdependent systems at all levels from local communities to international organizations. There is now, perhaps more than ever, a need for smart organization and effective management in public health. A coordination of effort through **leadership** and **systems thinking** to meet these challenges and accomplish the requisite goals necessitate management knowledge, skills, and abilities, which will be explored throughout this text.

▶ Public Health as Population Health

As described in Leiyu Shi and James Johnson's book *Public Health Administration: Principles of Population-Based Management*, Fourth Edition,

Public health consists of organized efforts to improve the health of populations. The operative components of this definition are that public health efforts are directed to populations rather than to individuals. Public health practice does not rely on a specific body of knowledge and expertise, but rather relies on a dynamic, multidisciplinary approach that often combines the biological, medical, and social sciences. By extension, this must also include **management** as a body of knowledge and practice based on social and behavioral sciences. This definition of public health reflects its central goal, the reduction of disease and the improvement of health in a population.[1]

Thus, the fundamental mission of public health, both historically and currently, is to ensure the necessary conditions that promote the health of populations. To further elaborate, Richard Riegelman, founding dean of the School of Public Health and Health Services at George Washington University and Series Editor of the *Essential Public Health Series*, stated:

> Public health is about what makes us sick, what keeps us healthy, and what we can do TOGETHER about it. When we think about health, what comes to mind first is individual health and wellness. In public health, what should come to mind first is the health of communities and society as a whole. Thus, in public health the focus shifts from the individual to the population, from me to us.[1]

Shi and Johnson further describe these population-based strategies as improving health by including, but not limited to, efforts to control epidemics, ensure safe drinking water and food, reduce vaccine-preventable diseases, improve maternal and child health, and conduct surveillance of health problems. In addition to long-standing efforts to protect populations from infectious disease and environmental health hazards, the public health mission continues to expand to address contemporary health risks, such as opioids, tobacco use, obesity, physical inactivity, gun violence, substance abuse, sexually transmitted infections, natural disasters, and bioterrorism. To effectively address both current and emerging health concerns, public health approaches involve multilevel systemic interventions that address the individual, the community, and public policy. The importance of public health and population-based interventions is underscored by achievements in the 20th century during which individuals living in developed countries increased life expectancy from 45 to 75 years. Now in the 21st century, we have seen that life expectancy has increased to 78 years in the United States and 82 years in Japan.[1] The majority of this gain can be attributed to public health measures, such as better nutrition, improved air quality, sanitation, road safety, and clean drinking water. Both science and social factors form the basis for an effective public health intervention. For example, successfully eradicating a vaccine-preventable disease, such as measles, from a community requires more than the development of an effective vaccine. The acceptance and the widespread use of the vaccine in the community depend on a successful public health initiative providing public information and facilitating easy access and safe delivery of the vaccine. **Policies** in other domains, such as schools, to support the initiative further increase the likelihood of success. Unfortunately, many scientific advances are not fully translated into improved health outcomes. For example, in the United States, there is an opioid abuse epidemic. While medical science has developed medications to help mitigate opioid misuse and reverse overdose to prevent death, there are many social, behavioral, and cultural factors that must also be addressed. Thus, a public health approach must be comprehensive involving social determinants, epidemiology, harm reduction strategies, community education, and public policy changes, when needed.

▶ Public Health Functions

The Institute of Medicine (IOM) report, *The Future of Public Health*, defined three core functions that public health agencies should be performing.[2] While population health necessarily engages the full spectrum of stakeholders, it is the federal, state, and local public health agencies that are primarily responsible for accomplishing the essential health services. Although there is work that may be contracted out to other sectors, private and **nonprofit**, the fundamental responsibility remains with the government public health agencies.

These three core functions are defined as follows[1]:

- **Assessment** involves obtaining data to define the health of populations and the nature of health problems.
- **Assurance** includes the oversight responsibility for ensuring that essential components of an effective health system are in place.
- **Policy Development** includes developing evidence-based recommendations and analysis to guide public policy as it pertains to health.

TABLE 1.1 Essential Public Health Services

1. **Monitor** health status to identify community health problems.

2. **Diagnose and investigate** health problems and health hazards in the community.

3. **Inform, educate, and empower** people about health issues.

4. **Mobilize** community partnerships to identify and solve health problems.

5. **Develop policies and plans** that support individual and community health efforts.

6. **Enforce** laws and regulations that protect health and ensure safety.

7. **Link** people to the needed personal health services and assure the provision of health care, when otherwise unavailable.

8. **Assure** a competent public health and personal healthcare workforce.

9. **Evaluate** effectiveness, accessibility, and quality of personal and population-based health services.

10. **Research** new insights and innovative solutions to health problems.

Reproduced from the Centers for Disease Control and Prevention, Atlanta, GA. http://www.cdc.gov/nphpsp/essentialservices.html. Accessed February 1, 2019.

Building on the IOM recommendations, the U.S. Public Health Service (USPHS) and the **American Public Health Association (APHA)** advocate for a consistent and unified approach to public health. This is reflected in the widely accepted 10 essential services, as presented in **TABLE 1.1**. A hub and spoke chart, shown in **FIGURE 1.1**, enables us to better visualize how the core functions and essential services for public health fit together.[1] This framework is used by local, state, and federal agencies throughout the country and has been adapted for other countries as well. On a practical level, it serves as a guide and framework for public health organization design and development, workforce planning and staffing, strategic management, resource allocation, information systems design, and personnel training and development.

▶ Systems Perspective in Public Health

Today, most would agree that public health and the management of public health services and organizations are best understood from a **systems perspective**.[1,3] As described by health systems scholar, James Johnson, "Public health is highly interconnected and interdependent in its relationship to individuals, communities, and the larger society, including the global community. Using the language of systems theory, public health is a complex adaptive system. It is complex in that it is composed of multiple, diverse, interconnected elements, and it is adaptive in that the system is capable of changing and learning from experience and its environment."[3] As shown in **FIGURE 1.2**, the **Centers for Disease Control and Prevention (CDC)** provides an illustration that helps us to visualize some of the many interconnections that are commonly linked to a public health agency.[4]

In the book *Health Systems Thinking*, Johnson further explains that the systems approach in public health is not only the relationships that support and facilitate the **organization** and actions of public health but also "the mindset of public health professionals" that is salient in public health management, practice, and research.[1,3] It is useful to have a systems perspective when considering the causes of public health problems and challenges. Much of this can be attributed to deficits and poor quality in social areas of the society. These are referred to as social determinants of health (SDOH), some of which are shown in **FIGURE 1.3**.[5] Although this is not an exhaustive list, these determinants do show the interconnections that contribute to the larger system of public health in the society.

These SDOHs can also be used to design programs and address challenges before they happen, thus being instrumental in the prevention mandate of public and population health. **Social epidemiology,**

FIGURE 1.1 Core functions and essential public health services.

Reproduced from the Centers for Disease Control and Prevention, Atlanta, GA. http://www.cdc.gov/nceh/ehs/ephli/core_ess.htm. Accessed February 1, 2019.

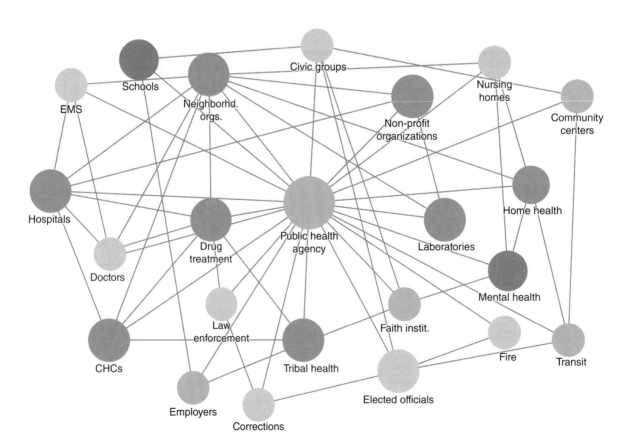

FIGURE 1.2 Public health agency interconnections.

Reproduced from The Public Health System & the 10 Essential Public Health Services. https://www.cdc.gov/publichealthgateway/publichealthservices/essentialhealthservices.html. Accessed February 5, 2019.

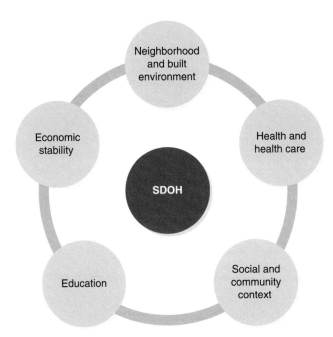

FIGURE 1.3 Social determinants of health.
Reproduced from Health People 2020.gov

a useful discipline, and its applications in **community assessment**, can also be employed to address or preempt many health issues.[1]

▶ Role of Public Health Managers

Public health managers and leaders are needed to help their organizations, agencies, and departments navigate the complex systems and constantly evolving culture and subcultures to enact change and influence health. Within the public health context, escalating costs, provider shortages, health disparities, obesity- and diet-related diseases, the opioid epidemic, climate change, resurgence of infectious diseases, demographic shifts, shrinking budgets, and numerous other challenges are threatening the health and the well-being of individuals and communities. These challenges require public health professionals who possess strong management knowledge, skills, and abilities. Public health professionals must be able to manage an evolving and expanding number of public health priorities, programs, professionals, organizations, interorganizational and multisector collaborations, population health activities, policy initiatives, and much more. Countries and communities around the world are looking to public health professionals and organizations for answers and innovative approaches to address health disparities and priorities. Furthermore, public health organizations and practice

must evolve to redefine and reinvent itself in response to environmental forces. Managers have a primary responsibility for enabling, implementing, and overseeing this evolution in public health organizations.

All organizations require managers who are essential for their **maintenance**, effectiveness, and sustainability.[5] Whether it be the management of **resources** (i.e., people, finances, buildings, and technology) or strategy (vision, mission, goals, and objectives) or behavior dynamics (motivation, conflict, change, and decision-making), or values (fairness, diversity, responsiveness, accountability, and social responsibility), the manager's role and effectiveness in that role are central to the organization's ability to exist and perform its mission and purpose. Public health managers are often leaders within their own professions, and many are leaders in their communities and in the world. In fact, public health, with its public service mission and global reach, is an ideal environment for managers who desire to have a positive and lasting impact. It is also a changing and sometimes demanding environment that offers many challenges and opportunities to grow professionally and personally and help others in large and small ways. **TABLE 1.2** identifies some of the ways public health managers make a difference.[6]

In public health, there is a considerable need for skilled and highly effective managers and leaders. The APHA, the Association of Schools and Programs in Public Health (ASPPH), and the **World Health Organization (WHO)** have all recognized the importance of management in public health systems, organizations, and programs. Furthermore, these groups have called for better management development and leadership if public health is to meet its greatest potential and achieve the goal of health for all. This is captured in the WHO perspective presented in **EXHIBIT 1.1**.[7]

As public health continues to advance, the role of the public health manager will likely expand. One such **vision**, as described by the CDC, has the public health leaders serving as *Chief Health Strategists* in their communities, partnering across multiple sectors, and leveraging data and resources to address social, environmental, and economic conditions that affect health and health equity.[8]

Core Competencies for Public Health Managers

The Council on Education for Public Health (CEPH) is the accrediting body for public health. This body oversees the criteria and process for accrediting

---

TABLE 1.2 Public Health Practice Profile for Public Health Managers

Public Health Administrators Make a Difference in the Following Ways:

Public Health Purposes
- ✓ Preventing epidemics and the spread of disease
- ✓ Protecting against environmental hazards
- ✓ Preventing injuries
- ✓ Promoting and encouraging healthy behaviors
- ✓ Responding to disasters and assisting communities in recovery
- ✓ Ensuring the quality and accessibility of health services

Essential Public Health Services
- ✓ Monitoring health status to identify community health problems
- ✓ Diagnosing and investigating health problems and health hazards in the community
- ✓ Informing, educating, and empowering people about health issues
- ✓ Mobilizing community partnerships to identify and solve health problems
- ✓ Developing policies and plans that support individual and community health efforts
- ✓ Enforcing laws and regulations that protect health and ensure safety
- ✓ Linking people with needed personal health services and ensuring the provision of health care, when otherwise unavailable
- ✓ Ensuring a competent public health and personal healthcare workforce
- ✓ Evaluating the effectiveness, the accessibility, and the quality of personal and population-based health services
- ✓ Researching new insights and innovative solutions to health problems

Reproduced from Turnock BJ. *Essentials of Public Health*. 3rd ed. Burlington, MA: Jones & Bartlett Learning; 2016.

EXHIBIT 1.1 WHO Perspective on Public Health Management

Effective leadership and management are essential to scaling up the quantity and quality of health services and to improving population health.

Good leadership and management are about:

- providing direction to, and gaining commitment from, partners and staff;
- facilitating change; and
- achieving better health services through efficient, creative, and responsible deployment of people and other resources.

Strengthening leadership and management requires the fulfillment of four main conditions: adequate numbers of managers deployed, managers with appropriate competencies, functioning management support systems, and a work environment that expects, supports, and rewards good management performance.

While leaders set the strategic vision and mobilize the efforts toward its realization, good managers ensure effective organization and utilization of resources to achieve results and meet the aims.

The WHO management framework proposes that good leadership and management at the operational level need to have a balance between four areas:

1. ensuring an adequate number of managers at all levels of the health system;
2. ensuring managers have appropriate competences;
3. creating better critical management support systems; and
4. creating and enabling the working environment.

The WHO is a strident advocate of systems thinking. These four conditions are closely interrelated. Strengthening one without the others is not likely to work.

Reprinted from Management for health services delivery, World Health Organization. URL: https://www.who.int/management/en

---

schools and programs of public health in the United States. The overarching goal of this organization is to prepare and equip students with the requisite knowledge, skills, and abilities to enter the public health workforce at all levels.[9] In 2016, CEPH updated the **accreditation** criteria for public health schools and programs by revising the core competencies to reflect a renewed emphasis on management and leadership as important elements of public health education and practice.[9] We are seeing public health curriculum moving toward content and concepts traditionally addressed in healthcare management and **administration** programs. Likewise, healthcare management and administrative programs are incorporating content and concepts traditionally addressed in public health.[5] This is an exciting time for all programs. The success of closing health gaps and achieving health goals relies on organizations with strong leaders and managers. To advance professionalism in management and leadership for public health, the ASPPH identifies the core competencies that can be used in curricular design.[10] These are organized in **TABLES 1.3** and **1.4**. The CEPH accreditation criteria and associated knowledge domains and competencies for public health programs have helped to guide the development of this text.[1,10]

▶ Emerging Role of Public Health

The National Academies of Medicine and the U.S. Department of Health and Human Services (HHS) promote an initiative called Public Health 3.0.[11] The third-generation model reflects the promise and perils of 21st-century public health in the United States.[2] Public Health 3.0, as profiled in **FIGURE 1.4**, is a model and a forward path in the field of public health. The model calls on public health to redefine and reinvent itself for the future. The model focuses on the SDOHs and the need for public health professionals and organizations to engage a broad range of community, industry, education, business, government, and other stakeholders to develop new models that make strategic investments in public health. The overarching goal is to shift the U.S. health system from focusing

TABLE 1.3 Management Competencies, Health Policy, and Management

D. Health Policy and Management*

Health policy and management represent a multidisciplinary field of inquiry and practice concerned with the delivery, quality, and costs of health care for individuals and populations. This definition assumes both a managerial and a policy concern with the structure, process, and outcomes of health services, including the costs, financing, organization, outcomes, and accessibility of care.

Competencies: Upon graduation, a student with a Master of Public Health (MPH) should be able to:

D.1 Identify the main components and issues of the organization, financing, and delivery of health services and public health systems in the United States.

D.2 Describe the legal and ethical bases for public health and health services.

D.3 Explain the methods for ensuring community health safety and preparedness.

D.4 Discuss the policy process for improving the health status of populations.

D.5 Apply the principles of program planning, development, budgeting, management, and evaluation in organizational and community initiatives.

D.6 Apply the principles of **strategic planning** and marketing to public health.

D.7 Apply quality and performance improvement concepts to address organizational performance issues.

D.8 Apply "systems thinking" for resolving organizational problems.

D.9 Communicate health policy and management issues using appropriate channels and technologies.

D.10 Demonstrate leadership skills for building partnerships.

*In this series, *health policy* is treated as a separate text and area of inquiry. As such, this text addresses only the health management competencies.

Reproduced with permission from Health Policy and Management, MPH Core Competency Model, Association of Schools and Programs of Public Health.

TABLE 1.4 Management Competencies and Leadership
H. Leadership

The ability to create and communicate a shared vision for a changing future, champion the solutions to organizational and community challenges, and energize a commitment to achieve these goals.

Competencies: Upon graduation, it is increasingly important that a student with an MPH be able to:

H.1   Describe the attributes of leadership in public health.

H.2   Describe alternative strategies for collaboration and partnership among organizations, focused on public health goals.

H.3   Articulate an achievable mission, a set of core values, and a vision.

H.4   Engage in dialogue and learn from others to advance public health goals.

H.5   Demonstrate team building, negotiation, and conflict management skills.

H.6   Demonstrate transparency, integrity, and honesty in all actions.

H.7   Use collaborative methods for achieving organizational and community health goals.

H.8   Apply social justice and human rights principles when addressing community needs.

H.9   Develop strategies for motivating others for collaborative problem solving, decision-making, and evaluation.

Reproduced with permission from Leadership, MPH Core Competency Model, Association of Schools and Programs of Public Health.

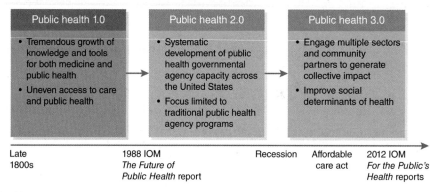

FIGURE 1.4 Public Health 3.0.

Reproduced from DeSalvo KB, Wang YC, Harris A, Auerbach J, Koo D, O'Carroll P. Public Health 3.0: A call to action for public health to meet the challenges of the 21st century. *Prev Chronic Dis.* 2017;14:170017. doi:10.5888/pcd14.170017

on sickness and disease to wellness and prevention.[11,12] The model was developed for the United States; however, it can be adapted and applied to other health systems around the world.[12]

Public health has evolved to reinvent and redefine itself with each iteration of the model. The Public Health 1.0 Model marked the birth and infancy of public health in the United States. The focus of public health was sanitation, safety, disease surveillance, and the discovery of prevention and treatment methods.

As mentioned earlier, in 1988, the IOM issued *The Future of Public Health* that served as an important inflection point for public health in the United States. The report served as a call to action and asked public health to consider what its role was in the face of a number of pressing health challenges.[2] In response, Public Health 2.0 marked the evolution of public health to a mature, refined, focused, and formalized system. The core functions and essential health services emerged from this period and provided considerable clarity to the role of public health.[1,2] Today, public health is yet again at another important inflection point.

The vision of Public Health 3.0 is to improve the population health by addressing upstream and social factors that influence health, such as working conditions, education, income and economic conditions, neighborhood conditions, and healthcare access. The model stresses the involvement of local communities and collaboration across sectors to enhance the contexts in which individuals live, learn, work, and play. The model's emphasis is consistent with the population health focus and priorities in *Healthy People 2020* and *2030*.[13,14]Both the model and the national health priorities emphasize the importance of local health departments in leading and managing initiatives and cross-sector collaboration to address the determinants of health and advance the population health and well-being. The Public Health 3.0 Model recommends the following[11]:

1. A strong public health workforce
2. Strategic, cross-sector partnerships
3. Expanded, flexible, and multisource funding
4. Timely and continuous data, metrics, and analytics to guide public health initiatives at all levels, especially at the subcounty or community level
5. A solid public health infrastructure

The recommendations speak to the essential roles and functions of public health, and the managers responsible for overseeing these responsibilities. Managers carry out a number of different functions, such as planning and decision-making, developing the organizational structure to deliver the organizational goals, hiring the right mix of professionals, coordinating the organization's resources, and finally evaluating individual, unit, and organizational performance. The Public Health Accreditation Board is further emphasizing the importance of strong management skills through the organization's public health department accreditation process.[15] Public health managers are pivotal to realizing the vision of Public Health 3.0, providing public health's core functions and essential services, and helping build a strong public health infrastructure through leading public health accreditation at their local and state health departments.

Not that Public Health 4.0 currently exists in any formal way, it is only natural for students of public health to wonder, What's next? When asked this very question, Jonathan Samet, Dean of the University of Colorado School of Public Health, replied that he sees:

Public Health 4.0 resting on "two pedestals," the first being the need to gather more and more data from increasingly sophisticated technology and figure out "the useful signals from that data." Second, we need to have extended interactions with communities in new ways, some of them data-driven. I think we will see that the public health community will recognize that a lot of the things we do are going to require greater engagement with communities.[16]

This perspective is consistent with the direction of public health as it continues to evolve in the 21st century while meeting the nation's health objectives in the coming decades.

National Health Objectives, *Healthy People 2020* and *Healthy People 2030*

Since 1980, the U.S. Department of HHS, in collaboration with community partners, has developed 10-year plans that outline key national health and health-related objectives to be accomplished during each decade. The current mission of this initiative is reflected in the most recent national health plan, *Healthy People 2020*.[13,17] Its vision, mission, and goals are shown in **TABLE 1.5**.

To be more comprehensive by looking at social and health systems as a whole, *Healthy People 2020* is differentiated from the previous *Healthy People* initiatives by including multiple new areas in its objective list, such as adolescent health; blood disorders and blood safety; dementias; genomics; global health; healthcare-associated infections; quality of life and well-being; lesbian, gay, bisexual, and transgender health; older adults; preparedness; sleep health; and SDOHs. This expansion of foci is demonstrated in **TABLE 1.6**. Of course, this will likely change or expand, at least somewhat, for *Healthy People 2030*.[14]

As shown in the Shi and Johnson's book, an action model, presented in **FIGURE 1.5**, was developed by HHS to assist public health managers and leaders accomplish these important national health goals.[1]

From the preliminary work on *Healthy People 2030*, we can anticipate even further evolution of systems thinking as well as innovation for the development and achievement of the next decade of national health goals and objectives.[14] The mission is "to promote, strengthen and evaluate the nation's efforts to improve the health and well-being of all people."

TABLE 1.5 *Healthy People 2020*

Vision

A society in which all people live long, healthy lives

Mission

Healthy People 2020 strives to:

Identify nationwide health improvement priorities
Increase public awareness and understanding of the determinants of health, disease, and disability and the
    opportunities for progress
Provide measurable objectives and goals that are applicable at the national, state, and local levels
Engage multiple sectors to take actions to strengthen policies and improve practices that are driven by the best
    available evidence and knowledge
Identify critical research, evaluation, and data collection needs

Overarching Goals

Attain high-quality, longer lives free of preventable disease, disability, injury, and premature death
Achieve health equity, eliminate disparities, and improve the health of all groups
Create social and physical environments that promote good health for all
Promote quality of life, healthy development, and healthy behaviors across all life stages

Reproduced from U.S. Department of Health and Human Services. (2016). About *Healthy People*. Available at https://www.healthypeople.gov/2020/About-Healthy-People

TABLE 1.6 *Healthy People 2020* Focus Areas

1. Access to Health Services	14. Mental Health and Mental Disorders
2. HIV	15. Diabetes
3. Adolescent Health	16. Nutrition and Weight Status
4. Immunization and Infectious Diseases	17. Disability and Health
5. Arthritis, Osteoporosis, and Chronic Back Conditions	18. Occupational Safety and Health
6. Injury and Violence Prevention	19. Early and Middle Childhood
7. Blood Disorders and Blood Safety	20. Older Adults
8. Lesbian, Gay, Bisexual, and Transgender Health	21. Educational and Community-Based Programs
9. Cancer	22. Oral Health
10. Maternal, Infant, and Child Health	23. Environmental Health
11. Chronic Kidney Disease	24. Physical Activity
12. Medical Product Safety	25. Family Planning
13. Dementias, Including Alzheimer's Disease	26. Preparedness

27. Food Safety	35. Health-Related Quality of Life and Well-Being
28. Public Health Infrastructure	36. Social Determinants of Health
29. Genomics	37. Healthcare-Associated Infections
30. Respiratory Diseases	38. Substance Abuse
31. Global Health	39. Hearing and Other Sensory or Communication Disorders
32. Sexually Transmitted Diseases	40. Tobacco Use
33. Health Communication and Health Information Technology	41. Heart Disease and Stroke
34. Sleep Health	42. Vision

Reproduced from U.S. Department of Health and Human Services. 2020 *Topics and Objectives—Objectives A–Z*. Available at https://www.healthypeople.gov/2020/topics-objectives, 2016.

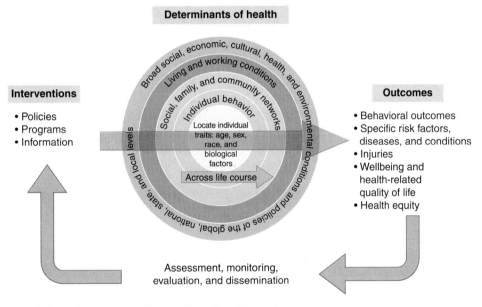

FIGURE 1.5 Action model to achieve overarching national health goals.
Reproduced from the Department of Health and Human Services.

Foundational Principles

- Promoting the health and well-being of all people and communities is essential to a thriving, equitable society.
- Promoting health and well-being and preventing disease are linked efforts that encompass physical, mental, and social health dimensions.
- Investing to achieve the full potential for the health and well-being of all provides valuable benefits to society.
- Achieving the health and well-being of all requires eliminating health disparities, achieving health equity, and attaining health literacy.
- Maintaining healthy physical, social, and economic environments helps to strengthen the potential for achieving the health and well-being of all individuals.
- Promoting and achieving the nation's health and well-being is a shared responsibility that is distributed across national, state, tribal, and community levels, including the public, private, and not-for-profit sectors.
- Working to attain the full potential for the health and well-being of the population is a component of decision-making and policy formulation across all sectors.

Overarching Goals

- Attain healthy, thriving lives and well-being, free of preventable disease, disability, injury, and premature death.
- Eliminate health disparities, achieve health equity, and attain health literacy to improve the health and well-being of all.
- Create social, physical, and economic environments that promote the attainment of full potential for the health and well-being for all.
- Promote healthy development, healthy behaviors, and well-being across all life stages.
- Engage leadership, key constituents, and the public across multiple sectors to take action and design policies that improve the health and well-being of all.

In order to accomplish these goals and objectives, public health managers and professionals at all levels will be needed for a wide range of roles and occupations. The workforce will necessarily expand and change as new health challenges continue to emerge.

▶ Public Health Workforce

For students studying public health and related fields, there will continue to be many opportunities for employment and career advancement. Some of these positions will be in managerial and administrative roles, whereas other positions will be technical or clinical in nature.

As stated by Turnock, "From a functional perspective, it is the individuals involved in carrying out the core functions and essential services of public health who constitute the public health workforce."[6]

Turnock clarified the multidisciplinary nature of the public health workforce by stating that there has never been any specific academic degree or unique set of experiences that distinguish public health workers from those of other fields. As he explained, many public health workers have a primary professional discipline in addition to their role in a public health organization.[6] There are accountants, economists, social workers, biostatisticians, physicians, nurses, lawyers, epidemiologists, urban planners, anthropologists, educators, nutritionists, data analysts, engineers, psychologists, dentists, policy analysts, and many other professionals and support staff who perform the work of public health. Most of these occupations and professions are identified in **TABLE 1.7**.[6] Although this is not an exhaustive list, it does demonstrate the range and professional diversity that is perhaps unique to public health.

This work is done in agencies and organizations throughout the country and the world—many of these will be identified and described in Chapter 2. Furthermore, Turnock saw a challenge and a benefit in this diversification, as he stated, "This multidisciplinary workforce, with somewhat divided loyalties to multiple professions, blurs the distinctiveness of public health as a unified profession. At the same time, however, it facilitates the interdisciplinary approaches

TABLE 1.7 Sample of Public Health Occupations and Careers	
Career Category with Examples of Titles Used in Public Health Organizations	**Bureau of Labor Statistics' Standard Occupational Categories Related to Public Health**
Public Health Administration - Health Services Manager - Public Health Agency Director Health Officer - Emergency Preparedness and Response Director	Professional Occupations - Emergency Management Directors - Medical and Health Services Managers - Social and Community Services Managers
Environmental and Occupational Health - Environmental Engineer - Environmental Health Specialist (entry level) - Environmental Health Specialist (midlevel) - Environmental Health Specialist (senior level) - Occupational Health and Safety Specialist	Professional Occupations - Environmental Engineers - Environmental Scientists and Specialists (including Health) - Health and Safety Engineers (except Mining Safety Engineers and Inspectors) - Occupational Health and Safety Specialists Technical Occupations - Environmental Engineering - Technicians - Environmental Science and Protection Technicians (including Health) - Occupational Health and Safety Technicians

Public Health Nursing
- Public Health Nurse (entry level)
- Public Health Nurse (senior level)
- Licensed Practical/Vocational Nurse

Professional Occupations
- Nurse Practitioners
- Registered Nurses

Technical Occupations
- Home Health Aides
- Licensed Practical and Licensed Vocational Nurses
- Nursing Assistants

Epidemiology and Disease Control
- Disease Investigator
- Epidemiologist (entry level)
- Epidemiologist (senior level)

Professional Occupations
- Epidemiologists
- Statisticians

Public Health Education and Information
- Public Health Educator (entry level)
- Public Health Educator (senior level)
- Public Information Officer
- Community Health Workers (and other Outreach Occupations)

Professional Occupations
- Health Educators
- **Public Relations** Specialists
- Technical Occupations
- Community Health Workers

Other Public Health Professional and Technical Personnel
- Public Health Nutritionist/Dietician
- Public Health Social, Behavioral, and Mental Health Worker
- Public Health Laboratory Worker
- Public Health Physician
- Public Health Veterinarian
- Public Health Pharmacist
- Public Health Oral Health Professional
- Administrative Law Judge/Hearing Officer
- Public Health Program Specialist/Coordinator
- Public Health Policy Analyst
- Public Health Information Specialist

Professional Occupations
- Audiologists
- Administrative Law Judges, Adjudicators, and Hearing Officers
- Dental Hygienists
- Dentists (General Dentist)
- Dieticians and Nutritionists
- Healthcare Social Workers
- Medical and Clinical Laboratory Technologists Mental Health Counselors
- Mental Health and Substance Abuse Social Workers
- Microbiologists
- Optometrists
- Pharmacists
- Physician Assistants
- Physicians (Family or General Practitioners)
- Substance Abuse and Behavioral Disorder Counselors
- Veterinarians

Technical Occupations
- Animal Control Workers
- Emergency Medical Technicians and Paramedics
- Medical and Clinical Laboratory Technicians

to community problem identification and problem solving, which are hallmarks of modern public health practice."[6]

For those who plan to seek management positions or engage in advanced leadership roles in public health agencies and organizations, there is increasingly a preference for pursuing additional management education, often beyond the undergraduate level, or to augment one's professional or clinical degree. Typically, public health managers have at least an undergraduate degree in fields such as public administration, business administration, behavioral or social sciences, accounting, engineering, life sciences, or a clinical field. However, as managers progress up the organizational ladder into higher-level administrative and leadership positions, they will almost always acquire a graduate degree. Most often, this will be a **Master of Public Health (MPH)** or **Master of Public Administration (MPA)**. To a lesser extent, other public health administrators acquire management-focused degrees, such as **Master of Health Administration (MHA), Master of Science (MS)** in administration or management, and the **Master of Business Administration (MBA)**. However, the largest number of senior administrators in public health agencies has either the MPA or the MPH degree. Within the scientific and clinical care units of the organization, there are also professionals with a PhD, MD, RN, DO, DDS, DNP, PsyD, PharmD, DVM, and ScD. At the policy and program management levels, there are professionals with DrPH, PhD, EdD, JD, and DHA. However, it is still quite beneficial for these individuals to also have management training or education.

Public Health Leader's Perspective from the Field

It is always important to hear from those who are working in the field being discussed. They are able to offer insight and sometimes advice that you usually cannot get otherwise. There will be several of these presented throughout this text from public health professionals working in a variety of agencies and organizations. The first one, presented in **EXHIBIT 1.2**, is an interview with a county health director in Florida.[3]

EXHIBIT 1.2 Interview with County Health Department Director

Sanford D. Zelnick, DO, MS
Director, Sumter County (Florida) Health Department
Florida Department of Health
Tallahassee, FL

Interviewed by Dr. James A. Johnson

Do you consider yourself a "systems thinker"? Please explain.

Dr. Zelnick: With all modesty, yes, I do. Again, this probably sounds immodest, but the first principle is the ability and will to think, meaning the ability/facility to develop an idea or concept, as opposed to merely following direction. Specifically, it was my occupational medicine training at the University of Cincinnati where I was strongly encouraged to do original research and where, for the first time, I truly began to think creatively in this sense. Meaning no disrespect, much of my career prior to this was the application of defined treatments to medical conditions as a family physician. It takes some thought obviously to make the correct clinical diagnosis, but, after that, the treatments are usually well defined. For example, you can look up how to treat high blood pressure, diabetes, depression, etc. When doing original research, you are frequently trying to answer a question that has not been asked. The skill set is quite different.

I will mention that the first idea or thought was the most difficult to come up with. Now, these ideas happen frequently, and I have come up with five to six major ideas regarding public health.

After one develops a skill to think in this way by creating an idea, the second step is to consider the possible ramifications, an important part of systems thinking, often considering the social and political context. This takes experience and judgment. There are some good ideas that may not be implemented for this reason. It takes judgment, timing, an ability to listen, and a little bit of self-created "luck" to bring a good idea to implementation in an operational sense.

How is systems thinking as a competency beneficial to the practice of public health?

Dr. Zelnick: If you do not understand the ramifications of an idea, you cannot serve as an effective advocate for health. In public health, there are many viewpoints, all of which must be respected and considered, when advocating for a specific approach to an issue, and sometimes I have been surprised by what I have heard at times, but again, all views must be valued and respected. Whatever the other opinions are, I feel better that I heard them at the onset. It is a collaborative function and one that values a sense of autonomy on the part of the public, even if you may disagree. I believe it was Stephen Covey who said, "First, seek to understand," referring to other viewpoints. When I develop an idea—an epiphany, as I jokingly mention it to my senior staff—I develop a wide circle of opinions, and I consider those opinions well before I embark on advocating a measure.

In what ways can systems thinking be integrated into program planning?

Dr. Zelnick: I believe a checklist or similar tool can be developed; although with experienced planners, much of this comes naturally. The initial considerations are the impacts—the measurement of any potential goods versus potential harms or risks—of any specific program on the population under consideration, including special or vulnerable populations. What evidence of effectiveness or of harm is there?

Is the thought under consideration something that would win public support? How would it be explained?

What resources are required, in terms of personnel, funds, training, and monitoring of effectiveness, of a specific program? Because this often competes with other priorities set either by the public or by higher headquarters, is this expenditure worth it?

How have you adopted systems thinking in your organization? Community? Describe an example you are proud of.

Dr. Zelnick: We have not developed a checklist, but the basic concepts I am describing are routinely followed in a successful public health program.

Often, the ideas that come to me happen, it seems, serendipitously (almost by accident, but I have come to realize, as I have stated, that it is no accident). A long time ago, I worked in Washington for the Air Force Surgeon General as chief of Occupational Medicine, and he told his staff then that if we just answered our email and responded to other inquiries that reached our desks, we really were not doing our jobs, and I took his point to what I do.

Shortly after I assumed my position here, I happened to be reading on the Internet an article in the West Orange County (Florida) newspaper about the problem of drowning deaths in children, and the much higher rate of drowning in black children, which is what this article was speaking to. I did additional research and found that the CDC supported the thrust of much of what was written in the article. I did additional research and located a book titled "Contested Waters" by Jeff Wiltse, which describes the experience of minority communities in a sociopolitical context (I would highly recommend reading).

I began to think about water safety programs, particularly in Florida, as we are surrounded on three sides by water and so much is defined by it, in terms of our recreation and economy.

In my small rural county, there were no such programs. I asked my staff, particularly my environmental staff, as they have a role in permitting public pools, to identify any pools that could be in our county and that could be used for training. At this time, I was developing a relationship with the local superintendent of schools. As luck would have it (and I don't mean to belabor this, but I believe you make your own luck), the local school board complex was once a former mental health treatment facility and they had a pool, which was rarely ever utilized.

After discussions with Sumter County Government and the Sumter County Schools, in 2012, we developed a 2-week program of instruction in basic swimming/water safety for children aged 3–12 years. Our water safety instruction team are all trained and certified by the American Red Cross. The program is extremely popular, training between 150 and 200 children every summer; in fact, 1 year, we trained 285 children in the summer. As the program matured, we found a second pool on the north end of the county, which we were permitted to use for free and which is closer to our urban center.

I am fortunate in that Sumter County Florida is an area of rapid economic growth, we are the seventh fastest growing county in the United States, and I was able to convince Sumter County Government to largely subsidize this program. We charge only $10.00 for 2 weeks of instruction, which is much less than what it costs to run the program but is what many families in the more rural parts of this county can afford.

As a health department (and a small one at that with only 40 people), again with all modesty, we directly train more children in water safety than any health department in Florida. We intend to publish our experiences about this in a peer-reviewed journal someday (we are gathering data in Excel and have received permission from the Florida Department of Health Institutional Review Board). Due to some creative work of one of my staff members here, we even have the possibility and the potential to develop a national data set regarding water safety training.

I have had several other ideas, some I have brought to fruition, some I am trying to bring about, but it would be too much to write about.

Why do you believe systems thinking has not easily been adopted more broadly in public health?

Dr. Zelnick: If you really want to accomplish something meaningful, you must understand the ramifications of your actions and garner support. So, I believe these processes are utilized among successful public health practitioners, but they are not standardized into a checklist or formal function perhaps to the extent that they should be. I think it would be useful for junior health officials and could be developed into a teaching/mentoring program.

Any ideas about how we can create a systems thinking culture in public and community health?

Dr. Zelnick: I think the first step is creating a supportive atmosphere—an atmosphere which stimulates thought and discussion. Ideally, systems thinking is something that should happen at the program level in a health agency, where program managers are encouraged to develop such a capacity/skill as they grow as health officials. In Florida, we have a mentorship program, understanding that every county is unique, in terms of its outlook, its priorities, and its challenges.

(continues)

EXHIBIT 1.2 Interview with County Health Department Director   *(continued)*

Often, I find that it is difficult for program managers to see beyond a somewhat constricted horizon. I am not sure why. Here, in this small health agency, I have strongly encouraged my staff to think in the ways I have written about and suggest their ideas. I solicit their thoughts about ideas I have come up with. Just last week, I had an idea about testing the well water consumed by persons diagnosed with *Helicobacter pylori* infection.

Conclusion

This chapter introduced public health from the perspectives of both population health and systems thinking. It also discussed the emergence of overarching public health goals and trends as shown in Public Health 3.0 and the *Healthy People* initiatives. The chapter identified the competencies for public health managers and some of the contextual aspects of public health organizations and the workforce, as well as occupational and career opportunities. Furthermore, the SDOHs were identified as part of the overall context of population health.

An interview with a practicing public health manager was presented to provide insights and advice from the field.

The next chapter will discuss and describe key public health organizations and agencies at the local, state, and federal levels. It will also identify public health and related associations and societies, many of which allow student memberships.

Discussion Questions

- Compare and contrast public health and population health.
- Discuss why public health benefits from a population health perspective.
- What are some examples of public health initiatives?
- What are the core functions of public health? Describe each one.
- What are the essential services of public health? How do they guide practice?
- Discuss why a systems perspective is so important in public health. Give several examples.
- Why is it important to consider social determinants of health when designing or implementing programs and initiatives?
- What is the role of the public health manager? What competencies should they have?
- What are national health objectives? Discuss them for the current decade.

- Identify various examples of roles and occupations that can be found in public health.
- Describe what most impressed you about the interview with Dr. Zelnick. What specifically did you learn?

Learning Activities

1. Do a search and read about Public Health 3.0. Is there likely to be a Public Health 4.0 any time soon? If so, why? If no, then why not? Discuss in class what this might look like for you in 10 years.
2. Review *Healthy People 2020* at the HHS website. In a small group in class brainstorm ideas about what should be included in *Healthy People 2030*.
3. Do your own personal inventory of skills and identify areas of weakness as it pertains to core competencies for public health.
4. Interview a public health manager and ask them how they developed the competencies needed in their position. Discuss how they continue to develop over time.
5. Interview a public health professional and ask how they use systems thinking in their organization. Ask for examples and perhaps get them to show you.
6. Make observations of social determinants of health in your own community at home and where your campus is located. Are there differences? How might these influence the health of each community?
7. Attend a local, state, or national meeting of a public health association. Make observations and participate in sessions. Meet others and network. Discuss with your class or in a journal what you saw, heard, and learned.

Note: The books in this list of suggested readings are available at many university libraries and can also be obtained through interlibrary loan. For those majoring in public health, purchasing is recommended, since they are all valuable resources for your various courses. The publishers' website is provided for each, and they are also available for rent or purchase through

book sellers, such as Amazon. The reports and online documents listed can be accessed for free through the links provided.

References

1. Shi L, Johnson JA. *Public Health Administration: Principles of Population-Based Management*. 4th ed. Burlington, MA: Jones & Bartlett Learning; 2020.
2. Institute of Medicine. *Future of Public Health.* Washington, DC: National Academies Press; 2002.
3. Johnson JA, Anderson DE, Rossow CC. *Health Systems Thinking*. Burlington, MA: Jones & Bartlett Learning; 2020.
4. CDC. Essential Public Health Services. https://www.cdc.gov/publichealthgateway/publichealthservices/essentialhealthservices.html
5. Johnson JA, Rossow CC. *Health Organizations*. 2nd ed. Burlington, MA: Jones & Bartlett Learning; 2019.
6. Turnock BJ. *Essentials of Public Health*. 3rd ed. Burlington, MA: Jones & Bartlett Learning; 2016.
7. World Health Organization. https://www.who.int/
8. CDC, Desalvo KB, et. al. https://www.cdc.gov/pcd/issues/2017/17_0017.htm
9. Council on Education for Public Health (CEPH). https://ceph.org/
10. Association of Schools and Programs in Public Health (ASPPH). https://www.aspph.org/
11. Public Health 3.0. https://www.cdc.gov/pcd/issues/2017/17_0017.htm
12. Johnson JA, Stoskopf C, Shi L. *Comparative Health Systems*. 2nd ed. Burlington, MA: Jones & Bartlett Learning; 2019.
13. Healthy People 2020. https://www.healthypeople.gov/
14. Healthy People 2030. https://www.healthypeople.gov/2020/About-Healthy-People/Development-Healthy-People-2030/Framework
15. Public Health Accreditation Board (PHAB). https://www.phaboard.org/
16. Samet J. What's in store for Public Health 4.0? https://www.cuanschutztoday.org/looking-ahead-to-public-health-4-0/
17. McKenzie JF, Pinger RR, Seabert DM. *Introduction to Community and Public Health*. 9th ed. Burlington, MA: Jones & Bartlett Learning; 2018.

Suggested Reading and Websites

American Public Health Association (APHA). https://www.apha.org/
Association of Schools of Public Health (ASPH). https://www.aspph.org/
Bernard T. *Essentials of Public Health*. 3rd ed. https://www.jblearning.com/catalog/productdetails/9781284069358
Council on Education for Public Health [CEPH]. https://ceph.org/
DeSalvo KB, Wang YC, Harris A, Auerbach J, Koo D, O'Carroll P. Public Health 3.0: A call to action for public health to meet the challenges of the 21st century. *Prev Chronic Dis.* 2017;14:170017. doi:10.5888/pcd14.170017.
Healthy People 2020. https://www.healthypeople.gov/
Healthy People 2030. https://www.healthypeople.gov/2020/About-Healthy-People/Development-Healthy-People-2030
Leiyu S, Johnson JA. *Public Health Administration: Principles of Population-Based Management*. 4th ed. https://www.jblearning.com/catalog/productdetails/9781449688332
Public Health 3.0. https://nam.edu/public-health-3-0-call-action-public-health-meet-challenges-21st-century
Richard R, Brenda K. *Public Health 101*. 3rd ed. https://www.jblearning.com/catalog/productdetails/9781284118445

CHAPTER 2
Key Public Health Organizations

▶ Introduction

The organizations involved in and responsible for public health in the United States are numerous. Although not all organizations involved in public health are public agencies, most are, as described by James Johnson in *Introduction to Public Health Management, Organizations, and Policy*.[1] This chapter will focus primarily on the governmental public health infrastructure at the federal, state, territorial, and local levels. However, to illustrate some of the complexity of this infrastructure, a systems perspective and population health are once again helpful. As shown in **FIGURE 2.1**, the public health system is multisectorial with influences, interactions, and partnerships from business, media, education, communities, healthcare delivery, and other public agencies.[2]

▶ The Public Sector

As we proceed in this chapter to gain a better understanding of the scope and scale of the public health organizational infrastructure, it is important to be aware of the distinctive issues that are at the forefront of these public sector organizations. Johnson explains, "while private businesses have some of the constraints, oversights, and pressures of public agencies, the fact is the influence is not as pervasive on a day-to-day basis."[1]

According to Christopher Pollitt, author of *The Essential Public Manager*, the public sector organization or agency faces the issues listed in **TABLE 2.1** more often or with more magnitude than private businesses.[3]

There are additional contextual, political, and cultural aspects that should be understood as the backdrop or foundation of the public sector's dominance in public health. In Leiyu Shi and James Johnson's book *Public*

FIGURE 2.1 Population health system.

TABLE 2.1 Issues and Challenges Facing Public Managers

Managing in a social-political system

Working with public pressure and potential protest

An ever-present sense of accountability

The need to understand public behavior

The challenge of rationing resources

Having to manage influence responsibly

Assessing multidimensional performance

Being open and responsive to the media

Understanding a wider responsibility to a changing society

Health Administration, Principles of Population-Based Management, this subject is discussed as follows.[4] The organization of governmental public health activities in the United States flows directly from the limited federalist system of government based on national, state, and local levels of **authority**. States occupy pivotal positions within this system because they maintain governmental authority that is not expressly reserved for the federal government. States may choose to exercise this authority directly or delegate it to local agencies and boards in accordance with state constitutional and legislative provisions. In the domain of public health, the federal government can exercise authority primarily through its constitutional powers to tax, spend, and regulate. By comparison, state government agencies typically play an even larger role in public health regulatory activities while also carrying out substantial responsibilities in public health program **administration** and **resource allocation**. States often delegate to local governmental agencies the primary responsibilities for implementing public health programs within communities. States vary considerably in the range of public health activities that they delegate to local governmental control. Federal agencies play an important role in the public health space because of their ability to formulate and implement a national health policy **agenda**, as seen with the *Healthy People* initiatives. Furthermore, they are able to allocate health resources across broad public priorities. Both executive agencies and legislative institutions engage in federal health policy and resource–allocation activities. As part of the policy development and administration process, many federal health agencies provide information and technical assistance to state and local agencies as well as nongovernmental organizations. In some cases, federal agencies also engage directly in implementing public health activities within specific communities or populations. Examples of these will be provided later in this chapter. Meanwhile, it is helpful to consider the political context of public health in the United States (**EXHIBIT 2.1**).[4]

Another way to help understand the context of public health today is to explore the history of the emergence of these various agencies at the federal, state, and local levels. A brief history is provided by public health scholar Richard Riegelman in **EXHIBIT 2.2**.[5]

EXHIBIT 2.1 Overview of U.S. Political System

As described in Johnson, Stoskopf, and Shi's book *Comparative Health Systems*, the federal government has three branches: **legislative** (the Senate and the House of Representatives), **executive** (the President and the cabinet departments), and **judicial** (federal courts and the U.S. Supreme Court). Each of the states also has its own constitution and its own legislative, executive (Governor and cabinet), and judicial branches.

In general, the states can do anything that is not prohibited by the U.S. Constitution or that is contrary to federal policy. Sometimes, a state might choose to embrace its own laws that do not necessarily align with federal policy; an example of this would be the regulation of recreational and medical marijuana. The major reserved powers of the state include the authority to regulate commerce within the state and exercise law enforcement. This gives states the right to pass and enforce laws that promote health, safety, welfare, and "morality." For example, in health promotion, you might see laws pertaining to the use of tobacco products. Elected politicians representing their constituents make decisions and take actions that are broadly referred to as **public policy**. Policies can take the form of new laws, repeals of existing laws, and interpretations and implementations of laws, executive orders, and court rulings. Throughout the policymaking process, the system of constitutional checks and balances prevails. The president (or governor) often plays an important leadership role in key policy issues. The Constitution grants Congress the power to make laws. The legislative process is often cumbersome as a bill (before it becomes law) goes through both houses of Congress, various committees, and subcommittees. Numerous organizations, called interest groups, which represent the common objectives of their members, try to influence policymakers to protect their members' interests. One example of a powerful interest group is the American Medical Association (AMA). Ultimately, if the president signs the approved bill, it becomes law. The president also has the power to veto (overturn) a bill passed by Congress. Unless a presidential veto is overruled by a two-thirds majority of Congress, it fails to become law. Even after a law has been passed, policymaking continues in the form of interpretation and implementation by the federal agency responsible for implementing the law. For example, the Department of Health and Human Services (DHHS) oversees more than 300 programs related to health and welfare services. It is responsible for 12 different agencies that deal with diverse areas related to public health, such as approval of new drugs and medical devices, health science research, services for children and the elderly, and substance abuse.

EXHIBIT 2.2 Brief History of Public Health Agencies in the United States

An understanding of the history of U.S. public health institutions requires an understanding of the response of local, state, and federal governments to public health crises and the complex interactions between these levels of government.

The colonial period in the United States saw repeated epidemics of smallpox, cholera, and yellow fever focused in the port cities. These epidemics brought fear and disruption of commerce, along with accompanying disease and death. One epidemic in 1793 in Philadelphia, which was then the nation's capital, nearly shut down the federal government.

These early public health crises brought about the first municipal boards of health, which consisted of respected citizens authorized to act in the community's interest to implement quarantine, evacuation, and other public health interventions of the day. The federal government's early role in combating epidemics led to the establishment in 1798 of what later became known as the U.S. Public Health Service.

Major changes in public health awaited the last half of the 1800s, with the enhanced understanding of diseases and the ability to control diseases through community actions. The Shattuck Commission in Massachusetts in 1850 outlined the roles of state health departments as being responsible for sanitary inspections, communicable disease control, food sanitation, vital statistics, and services for infants and children. During the next 50 years, the states gradually took the lead in developing public health institutions based on delivering these services.

Local health departments outside of the largest cities did not exist until the 1900s. The Rockefeller Foundation stimulated and helped fund early local health departments and campaigns, in part, to combat specific diseases, such as hookworm. There was no standard model for local health departments. By 1960, local health departments developed in at least 50 different ways in the 50 states and were chronically underfunded.

The federal government played a very small role in public health throughout the 19th century and well into the 20th century. An occasional public health crisis that was stimulated, in part, by media attention did bring about federal action. The founding of the Food and Drug Administration in 1906 resulted, in large part, from the journalistic activity known as "muckraking," which exposed the status of food and drug safety. The early 20th century set the

(continues)

EXHIBIT 2.2 Brief History of Public Health Agencies in the United States   (continued)

stage for expansion of the federal government's role in public health financed as the result of the passage of the 16th Amendment to the Constitution, which authorized federal income tax as a major source of federal government funding.

The Great Depression, in general, and the Social Security Act of 1935, in particular, brought about a new era in which federal funding became a major source of financial resources for state and local public health departments and nongovernmental organizations. The founding of what was then called the Communicable Disease Center (CDC) in 1946 led to a national and eventually international leadership role for the CDC, which attempts to connect and hold together the complex local, state, and federal public health efforts and integrate them into global public health efforts.

The Johnson administration's War on Poverty, as well as the Medicare and Medicaid programs, brought about greatly expanded funding for healthcare services and led many health departments to provide direct healthcare services, especially for those without other sources of care. The late 1980s and 1990s saw a redefinition of the roles of governmental public health, including the Institute of Medicine's definition of core functions and the development of the 10 essential public health services. These documents have guided the development of a broad population focus for public health and a move away from the direct provision of healthcare services by health departments.

The terrorism of September 11, 2001, and the subsequent anthrax scare moved public health institutions to the center of efforts to protect the public's health through emergency response and disaster preparedness. The development of flexible efforts to respond to expected and unexpected hazards is now a central feature of public health institutions' roles and funding. The success of these efforts has led to new levels of coordination of local, state, federal, and global public health agencies utilizing state-of-the-art surveillance, laboratory technology, and communications systems.

Reproduced from Riegelman R, Kirkwood B. Public Health 101. 3rd ed. Burlington, MA: Jones & Bartlett Learning; 2019.

► Federal Agencies Involved in Public Health

The Department of DHHS is the primary public health and social service agency of the United States. As described by Johnson, the Department has a long and rich history that began in 1789 with the passage by Congress of an act for the relief of sick and disabled seamen, thus establishing a network of hospitals for the care of merchant seamen. This became the forerunner of today's U.S. Public Health Service. In 1953, a Cabinet-level Department (Health, Education, and Welfare) was formed and reported directly to the U.S. President. Later, in 1980, the education function became its own **Department of Education (DOE)**, and the health and welfare functions were organized under the DHHS.[1] The current organizational chart, as shown in **FIGURE 2.2**, demonstrates the incredible expanse and range of agencies and programs within HHS.[2]

Many of these agencies comprise the functional units of HHS, known as the U.S. Public Health Service (USPHS). A description of this cluster of agencies is provided in **TABLE 2.2**.[2]

One of the influential positions in the USPHS is the SG. This individual is appointed by the President and serves to help frame and promote the national health agenda. For example, the SG is currently leading efforts to mitigate the opioid epidemic and the large number of unnecessary deaths due to opioid misuse. A description of the SG's role is provided in **EXHIBIT 2.3**.[6]

In 2018, HHS initiated its Strategic Plan that will run through 2022. This plan describes the

Department's efforts within the context of five broad Strategic Goals[7]:

- Strategic Goal 1: Reform, Strengthen, and Modernize the Nation's Healthcare System
- Strategic Goal 2: Protect the Health of Americans Where They Live, Learn, Work, and Play
- Strategic Goal 3: Strengthen the Economic and Social Well-Being of Americans Across Their Lifespan
- Strategic Goal 4: Foster Sound, Sustained Advances in the Sciences
- Strategic Goal 5: Promote Effective and Efficient Management and Stewardship

As seen in Strategic Goal 5, effective and efficient public health management is very important. So much of the work of public health requires the kinds of knowledge, skills, mind-set, and abilities that are addressed in this text.

One of the more high-profile agencies in HHS is the CDC.[8] Located in Atlanta, Georgia, it originally started there in 1946 as the Communicable Disease Center to combat a malaria epidemic in the southern states. Today, the agency has a global presence with personnel stationed in 40 different countries. The CDC workforce consists of nearly 200 different occupations with over half of the employees having advanced degrees, often in public health and related fields. The official mission of the CDC is as follows[8]:

The CDC works 24/7 to protect America from health, safety, and security threats, both foreign and in the United States. Whether the diseases start at home or abroad, are chronic or acute, curable or preventable,

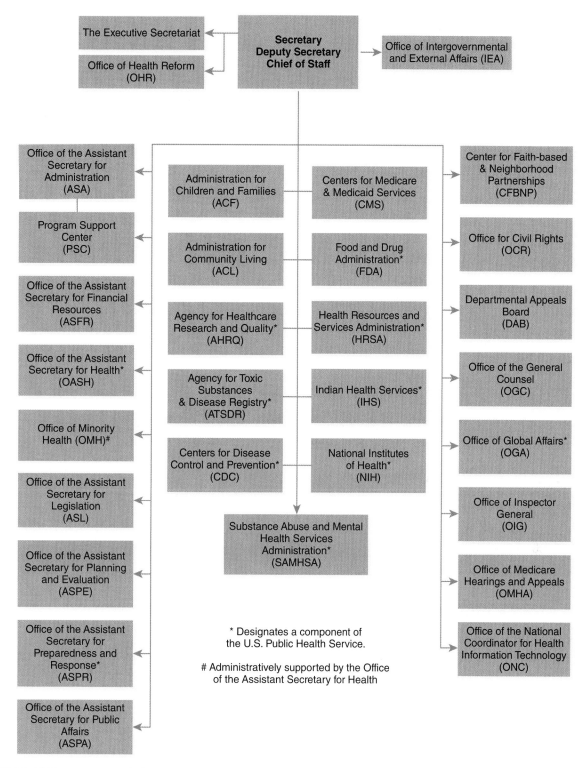

FIGURE 2.2 HHS organizational chart.

Courtesy of U.S. Department of Health and Human Services, 2014.

human error or deliberate attack, the CDC fights disease and supports communities and citizens to do the same.

The CDC increases the health security of our nation. As the nation's health protection agency, the CDC saves lives and protects people from health threats. To accomplish our mission, the CDC conducts critical science, provides health information that

protects our nation against expensive and dangerous health threats, and responds when these threats arise.

The organizational chart of the agency, presented in **FIGURE 2.3**, demonstrates much of the scope and the scale of the CDC's place in public health. Each state and territorial health department has strong relationships with the CDC and helps to form an interdependent system of public health surveillance, monitoring, and education.[9]

TABLE 2.2 USPHS Agencies

Health Resources and Services Administration (HRSA)

HRSA helps provide health resources for medically underserved populations. The main operating units of HRSA are the Bureau of Primary Health Care, Bureau of Health Professions, Maternal and Child Bureau, and the HIV/AIDS Bureau. A nationwide network of community and migrant health centers, augmented by primary care programs for the homeless and the residents of public housing, serve more than 10 million Americans each year. HRSA also works to build the healthcare workforce, and it maintains the National Health Service Corps. The agency provides services to people with AIDS through the Ryan White Care Act programs. It oversees the organ transplantation system and works to decrease infant mortality and improve maternal and child health. HRSA was established in 1982 by bringing together several existing programs. HRSA has nearly 2000 employees, most at its headquarters in Rockville, Maryland.

Indian Health Service (IHS)

IHS is responsible for providing federal health services to American Indians and Alaska Natives. The provision of health services to members of federally recognized tribes grew out of the special government-to-government relationship between the federal government and Indian tribes. This relationship, established in 1787, is based on Article I, Section 8 of the Constitution, and has been given form and substance by numerous treaties, laws, Supreme Court decisions, and Executive Orders. IHS is the principal federal healthcare provider and health advocate for Native Americans, and its goal is to raise their health status to the highest possible level. IHS currently provides health services to approximately 3 million American Indians and Alaska Natives who belong to more than 564 federally recognized tribes in 35 states. IHS was established in 1924; its mission was transferred from the Interior Department in 1955. Agency headquarters are in Rockville, Maryland. IHS has more than 15,000 employees.

Centers for Disease Control and Prevention (CDC)

Working with states and other partners, the CDC provides a system of health surveillance to monitor and prevent disease outbreaks, including bioterrorism events and threats, and it maintains the national health statistics. The CDC also provides for immunization services, supports research on disease and injury prevention, and guards against international disease transmission, with personnel stationed in more than 54 foreign countries. The CDC was established in 1946; its headquarters are in Atlanta, Georgia. The CDC has 11,000 employees.

National Institutes of Health (NIH)

Begun as a one-room Laboratory of Hygiene in 1887, the NIH today is one of the world's foremost medical research centers and the federal focal point for health research. The NIH is the steward of medical and behavioral research for the nation. Its mission is science in pursuit of fundamental knowledge about the nature and behavior of living systems and the application of that knowledge to extend healthy life and reduce the burdens of illness and disability. In realizing its goals, the NIH provides leadership and direction to programs designed to improve the health of the nation by conducting and supporting research in the causes, diagnosis, prevention, and cure of human diseases; in the processes of human growth and development; in the biological effects of environmental contaminants; in the understanding of mental, addictive, and physical disorders; and in the direction of programs for the collection, dissemination, and exchange of information in medicine and health, including the development and support of medical libraries and the training of medical librarians and other health information specialists. Although the majority of NIH resources sponsor external research, there is also a large in-house research program. The NIH includes 27 separate health institutes and centers; its headquarters are in Bethesda, Maryland. The NIH has approximately 19,000 employees.

Food and Drug Administration (FDA)

The FDA ensures that the food we eat is safe and wholesome, that the cosmetics we use will not harm us, and that medicines, medical devices, and radiation-transmitting products, such as microwave ovens, are safe and effective. The FDA also oversees feed and drugs for farm animals and pets. Authorized by Congress to enforce the Federal Food, Drug, and Cosmetic Act and several other public health laws, the agency monitors the manufacture, import, transport, storage, and sale of more than $1 trillion worth of goods annually. The FDA has more than 15,000 employees. Among its staff, the FDA has chemists, microbiologists, and other scientists, as well as investigators and inspectors who visit more than 16,000 facilities a year as part of their oversight of the businesses that FDA regulates. Established in 1906, the FDA has its headquarters in Silver Spring, Maryland.

Substance Abuse and Mental Health Services Administration (SAMHSA)

SAMHSA was established by Congress under Public Law 102-321 on October 1, 1992, to strengthen the nation's healthcare capacity to provide prevention, diagnosis, and treatment services for substance abuse and mental illnesses. SAMHSA works in partnership with states, communities, and private organizations to address the needs of people with substance abuse and mental illnesses, as well as community risk factors that contribute to these illnesses. SAMHSA serves as the umbrella under which substance abuse and mental health service centers are housed, including the Center for Mental Health Services (CMHS), the Center for Substance Abuse Prevention (CSAP), and the Center for Substance Abuse Treatment (CSAT). SAMHSA also houses the Office of the Administrator, the Office of Applied Studies, and the Office of Program Services. SAMHSA's headquarters are in Rockville, Maryland; the agency has about 600 employees.

Agency for Toxic Substances and Disease Registry (ATSDR)

Working with states and other federal agencies, ATSDR seeks to prevent exposure to hazardous substances from waste sites. The agency conducts public health assessments, health studies, surveillance activities, and health education training in communities near waste sites on the U.S. Environmental Protection Agency's National Priorities List. ATSDR also has developed toxicity profiles of hazardous chemicals found at these sites. The agency is closely associated administratively with the CDC; its headquarters are also in Atlanta, Georgia. ATSDR has more than 400 employees.

Agency for Health Care Research and Quality (AHRQ)

AHRQ supports cross-cutting research on healthcare systems, healthcare quality and cost issues, and effectiveness of medical treatments. Formerly known as the Agency for Health Care Policy and Research, AHRQ was established in 1989, assuming broadened responsibilities of its predecessor agency, the National Center for Health Services Research and Health Care Technology Assessment. The agency has about 300 employees; its headquarters are in Rockville, Maryland.

Reproduced from Turnock BJ. Public Health: What it is and how it Works, 6th Ed. MA: Jones & Bartlett Learning; 2016.

EXHIBIT 2.3 About the U.S. Public Health Service (USPHS)

Contributor: Douglas E. Anderson, Col (Ret), USAF, MSC, DHA, MBA, FACHE.

Legacy and Mission

Mission: To protect, promote, and advance the public health and the safety of the nation
People: 6000+ highly qualified healthcare professionals who are part of the DHHS are led by the U.S. SG.
Services: Largest public health program in the world. The mission is pursued through:

- Rapid and effective response to public health needs and emergencies
- Leadership and excellence in public health practices, advice, and response
- Advancing public health science through research and partnerships

The USPHS SG

- Oversees Public Health Service Commissioned Corps
- Is America's chief health educator on public health topics
- Is responsible for giving the best scientific information on how to improve health and reduce the risk of illness and injury
- Is the leading federal spokesperson on matters of public health
- Reports to the Assistant Secretary for Health, DHHS, and is the principal advisor to the Secretary on public health and scientific issues
- Appointed by the President with the advice and the consent of the U.S. Senate for a 4-year term of office

(continues)

EXHIBIT 2.3 About the U.S. Public Health Service (USPHS)   *(continued)*

Health and Healthcare Professions Within the USPHS

Physicians
Dentists
Nurses
Administrators
Pharmacists
Dietitians
Engineers
Environmental health officers
Mental health specialists

Optometrists
Physician assistants
Scientists/researchers
Therapists (including occupational therapy, physical therapy, speech language pathology, respiratory therapy, and audiology)
Veterinarians
Other health-related disciplines

USPHS Professionals Work in Most Federal Agencies at Multiple Locations

Disease control and prevention
Biomedical research
Regulation of food and drugs
Mental health care
Substance abuse treatment
Healthcare delivery
International health, and emergency and humanitarian response

For more information or career opportunities, the USPHS website is https://usphs.gov/

Courtesy of Douglas E. Anderson, Col (Ret), USAF, MSC, DHA, MBA, FACHE.

The CDC readily embraces systems thinking, collaboration, and partnerships to better serve the public.[8]

One of the world-class public health agencies with extraordinary influence in health science, biomedical research, and policy is the NIH, which works with universities and research centers throughout the country to understand the physiological and behavioral causes of disease. The many institutes and centers of the NIH are listed in **BOX 2.1**.[9] The NIH also houses a Clinical Center to test experimental therapies and the National Library of Medicine, which serves as a reference library for researchers around the world. It also makes itself accessible by **Internet** to the public.

Other Federal Agencies Involved in Public Health

In addition to HHS, there are various federal agencies that work to provide their own public health services or have a role in health policy and regulation. These agencies often work in partnership with HHS, but they have their own separate missions and responsibilities. These include the **Environmental Protection Agency** (EPA), the **Department of Labor (DOL)** that houses the **Occupational Safety and Health Administration** (OSHA), the **Department**

of Agriculture that does safety inspections and coordinates the Women, Infants, and Children (WIC) food program, the **Department of Homeland Security (DHS)**, the **Department of Veterans Affairs** (VA), the **Department of Defense (DOD)**, the **Department of Transportation** (DOT), and various other agencies and bureaus involved, at least partially, in public health.[1] Two of these, the DOD and the VA, are profiled in **EXHIBITS 2.4** and **2.5**.

▶ State Agencies Involved in Public Health

The historical and political context of the states' role and responsibilities in PH is described by James Johnson as follows:

From as far back as James Madison, the state governments have been characterized as 'laboratories of experimentation' where prospective public health policies may be tried out on a smaller scale and where existing federal programs can be adapted to the conditions and needs of individual states. The cornerstone of this approach is **fiscal federalism**,

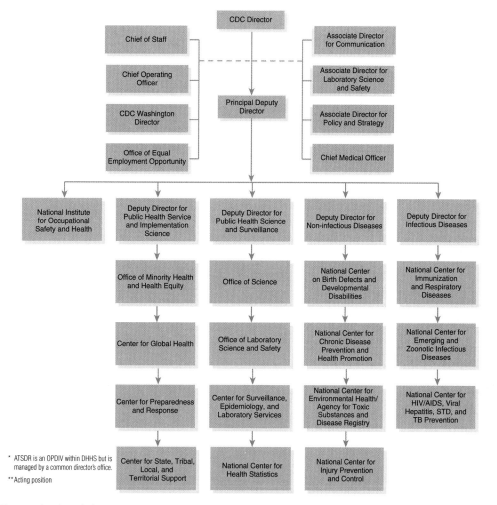

FIGURE 2.3 CDC organizational chart.

Reproduced from the Centers for Disease Control and Prevention, Organizational Chart. https://www.cdc.gov/about/pdf/organization/cdc-org-chart.pdf. Accessed October 01, 2015.

BOX 2.1 NIH Institutes, Centers, and Offices

- Office of the Director
- National Cancer Institute
- National Eye Institute
- National Heart, Lung, and Blood Institute
- National Human Genome Research Institute
- National Institute of Allergy and Infectious Disease
- National Institute on Aging
- National Institute on Alcohol Abuse and Alcoholism
- National Institute of Arthritis and Musculoskeletal and Skin Diseases
- National Institute of Biomedical Imaging and Bioengineering
- Eunice Kennedy Shriver National Institute of Child Health and Human Development
- National Institute on Deafness and Other Communication Disorders
- National Institute of Dental and Craniofacial Research
- National Institute of Diabetes and Digestive and Kidney Diseases
- National Institute on Drug Abuse
- National Institute of Environmental Health Sciences
- National Institute of General Medical Sciences
- National Institute of Mental Health
- National Institute on Minority Health and Health Disparities
- National Institute of Neurological Disorders and Stroke

(continues)

BOX 2.1 NIH Institutes, Centers, and Offices   (continued)

- National Institute of Nursing Research
- National Library of Medicine
- Center for Information Technology
- Center for Scientific Review
- Fogarty International Center
- National Center for Complementary and Alternative Medicine
- National Center for Advancing Translational Sciences
- NIH Clinical Center

National Institutes of Health.

EXHIBIT 2.4 The Defense Department's Role in Public Health

Daniel Wyman, MD, MPH, Brigadier General, USAF (ret).

The opportunities for military Public Health Officers (PHOs) are exciting and diverse. The duties and responsibilities of military PHOs include many of the same tasks accomplished within civilian public health departments, such as community health, health promotion, preventive medicine, disease surveillance, patient education, epidemiology, and outbreak investigation. Additionally, military PHOs may engage in a wide variety of other areas, including vector surveillance, occupational health, sanitation and food inspection, disease-specific programing (i.e., TB surveillance, treatment, and follow-up), research, and even veterinary medicine.

In garrison/at home base, the military Public Health (Public Health) section performs the same duties as a civilian community-based Public Health department and liaisons with the local Public Health department to ensure compliance with all local, state, and federal Public Health requirements. Across the United States and the globe, the U.S. military strives to be engaging partners within their communities, and Public Health plays a key role in the interactions between the military and civilian communities. In many healthcare settings, the PHOs represent the "face" of the military to the local community!

A significant responsibility for the military PHOs lies with ensuring the medical readiness of our forces. Prior to deployment, at home station, military PHOs conduct medical record reviews and member interviews (ensure fitness for duty), provide vaccinations and disease prophylaxis, and conduct predeployment education focused on disease and health threats and health maintenance. PHOs work closely with military commanders to ensure their soldiers/sailors/airmen/marines are "fit to fight"!

When military members deploy, the military PHOs lead the way! Typically, prior to a significant troop deployment, military PHOs comprise critical members of the advance team. The advance team is the "first boots on the ground," and the PHOs' role is disease/food/water surveillance and identifying/mitigating the health threats to our soldiers/sailors/airmen/marines. Additionally, the military PHOs establish communications with local healthcare authorities, assessing local capabilities and building positive relationships. After the troops arrive and throughout their deployment, the military PHOs stay very busy with the essential Public Health functions (health surveillance, disease/injury prevention, food/water safety/sanitation, vector surveillance/eradication, and education), as well as episodic tasks, such as outbreak and incident investigations.

And there a few skill sets within military Public Health that are unique. Some military PHOs are veterinarians! Military vets provide care for our military working dogs across the globe, they provide veterinary services for pets on base, and they are our experts on zoonotic diseases.

PHOs are also our bioterrorism experts. At home base or at deployed locations, military PHOs play a vital role in the defense of our forces! As bioterrorism SMEs, they develop exercise scenarios to assess military defenses and develop, employ, and maintain bioterrorism surveillance tools. And, as required, they are the military PHO liaisons with local, regional, and federal authorities to safeguard our soldiers/sailors/airmen/marines, their families, and their communities.

Truly, the military PHO career field is wide-ranging and extremely rewarding! Throughout his or her career, the military PHO will develop and use a broad and diverse set of skills and knowledge as a key member of the military healthcare team!

Courtesy of Daniel Wyman, MD, MPH, Brigadier General, USAF (ret)

EXHIBIT 2.5 The Veterans Affairs Role in Public Health

Richard G. Greenhill, DHA, MSc, MBA, FACHE.

Chief, Quality and Systems Improvement, Veterans Health Administration (VHA)

The VHA operates the largest integrated health system in the United States, offering care to eligible veterans who served (Evans, 2005). Within this behemoth of an entity, all aspects of health are managed (e.g., inpatient, outpatient, and PH). The focus on PH is as significant as the acute and postacute setting. This is illustrated in the VHA's creation of an entire service line dedicated to prevention. PH in the VHA is managed out of the Office of Patient Care Services (Public Health—VA, 2013). The Office of Patient Care Services has a host of responsibilities, including development of evidence-based PH policy, conducting operations research, and educational outreach (Public Health—VA, 2013). The evidence-based PH activities have two main dimensions: military exposures and health and wellness. Under military exposures, the VHA monitors and tracks the epidemiology of disease and the prodromal symptoms for those suspected of or who claim prior exposure. This dimension of the VHA's PH strategy aims to monitor and reduce determinants from prior exposures and minimize progression to disease or negatively impact the veterans and their families. Below is a list with brief descriptions of the veterans' health concerns that fit within the VHA's military exposure PH category (Public Health—VA, 2013):

Military Exposure

- Agent Orange-Related Diseases—These diseases are labeled "presumptive" and are associated with exposure to Agent Orange or other herbicides while in military service.
- Gulf War Veterans' Illnesses—These medically unexplained illnesses are associated with the Gulf War and service in the Southwest Asia theater from August 2, 1990 to present.
- Radiation-Related Diseases—Exposure to ionizing radiation may cause certain cancers. The agency assumes certain diseases may be linked to radiation exposure, and it tracks and treats these diseases as appropriate.
- Toxic Embedded Fragments—Veterans of certain wars may have shrapnel embedded in their bodies after certain injuries. The VA has a surveillance center where these individuals are under medical surveillance and, when appropriate, are referred for treatment.
- Traumatic Brain Injury (TBI)—TBI is caused by explosions and blasts disrupting normal brain function. Veterans of the Iraqi and Afghanistan Wars are screened, tracked, and treated.
- Birth Defects
- Infectious Diseases—The VA presumes that nine infectious diseases are due to service in the Southwest Asia theater of military operations during certain time frames. They are as follows: Brucellosis, Malaria, *Campylobacter jejuni*, *Coxiella burnetii*, *Mycobacterium tuberculosis*, nontyphoidal Salmonella, Shigella, visceral leishmaniasis, and West Nile virus. Veterans who served in those areas may be tracked and treated if they meet certain criteria.
- Vaccinations and Medications During Service—The VA conducts surveillance on the effects of certain vaccines and medications given to service members while on active duty: anthrax vaccine, pyridostigmine bromide, mefloquine, and smallpox vaccine.

Some of these categories have greater PH potential for concern, particularly infectious diseases and birth defects. The greater potential for these is linked to their propensity to spread to others in the veterans' home or family.

The other dimension of the VHA's approach to PH occurs in the traditional sense of disease prevention and management under the category health and wellness (Public Health—VA, 2013). Below is a list with a brief description of each:

- Tobacco and Health—VA offers programs (e.g., smoking cessation), individual counseling, medication, and therapy to assist veterans in quitting smoking.
- Vaccines and Immunizations—The agency is very focused on reducing vaccine-preventable diseases through immunization. Several vaccines are offered routinely and monitored based on age-appropriateness and other factors (e.g., influenza, pneumococcal infection, hepatitis A, hepatitis B, measles/mumps/rubella, varicella, shingles, tetanus/diphtheria/pertussis, and others).
- Hand Cleaning—There is an emphasis on reducing the spread of infection through ensuring proper use of hand sanitizers and handwashing.
- Education on Infection Reduction—The "Infection: Don't Pass It On (IDPIO)" is a PH campaign that involves staff, veterans, and their family members in preventing infections. Its education and communication touch on hand hygiene, annual influenza vaccination, use of personal protective equipment, pandemic influenza preparedness, and other basic PH measures to reduce transmission of infection.
- HIV/AIDS Daily Living—This area focuses on helping those living with HIV/AIDS learn about nutrition, exercise, and alternative therapies to live more comfortable lives.

(continues)

EXHIBIT 2.5   The Veterans Affairs Role in Public Health   *(continued)*

- Living with Hepatitis—Veterans can learn about managing their pain, nutrition, and alternative therapies to manage their hepatitis.
- Marijuana and Health—While the VA does not recommend medical marijuana, it does discuss options in those states where it is legal.
- Women's Health—The section on Women's Health includes a comprehensive guide on everything from vaccines to sexual safety.

The VHA is unique in that it focuses on the typical indicators for PH, but it also specializes in its niche for conditions of citizens who served our country.

References

Evans L. Recognizing the 75th Anniversary of the Establishment of the Veterans Administration. House of Representatives. Washington, DC: U.S. Government Printing Office; 2005.

Public Health—US Department of Veterans Affairs. (2013, August 15). Available at https://www.publichealth.va.gov/. Accessed February 17, 2019.

the pattern of taxation and grants provided by the federal government. This involves **block grants** and **categorical grants**, typically emanating from the U.S. Department of Health and Human Services (HHS).[1]

Johnson further explains,

> While the federal government often sets general goals and guidelines, individual states have a significant amount of discretion regarding the programs they implement. Most of the oversight, implementation, and enforcement of public health policy take place at the state level. Some states exceed federal requirements and often states have significant health programs and responsibilities of their own. One consequence of this type of state-based system is the wide variation in public health policy and organization we see in the United States.[1]

Concurrent with the influence of **federalism**, there are other factors that contribute to the differences among the states and territories in PH policy and the ways it is organized and implemented. In the *Handbook of Health Administration and Policy*, Anne Kilpatrick and James Johnson identify these factors as "determinants of state policy variation"[10]:

- **Economic determinants:** One example is variation in per capita income. There are high-income states like Connecticut and Massachusetts and others with low per capita incomes like Mississippi and South Carolina. This factor will likely influence how people vote.

  Another economic variable is the mix of industries and businesses in a state. California has a lot of tech businesses in Silicon Valley, whereas Florida and Hawaii have substantial tourism-related businesses.

- **Political determinants:** States with high citizen involvement and professional legislatures are more likely to support spending on PH programs. Examples of professional legislatures include California, Florida, and Massachusetts. Considerable grassroots citizen-initiated PH policies are seen in some states, such as Oregon, Vermont, and California, but not in others. Sometimes, a crisis will result in a PH initiative being supported more widely. An example of this is the opioid epidemic in Indiana, West Virginia, and Kentucky. Political party affiliation is also correlated with spending on PH. Generally, Democrats are more favorable than Republicans.

- **Interest Group determinants:** States may vary in interest groups due to their industries, religions, ethnicity, health patterns, and unique aspects of their local cultures. A dominant interest group in Arizona or Florida would be retirees; in heavy agriculture states like Kansas and Nebraska, it would be farmers; and in other states, such as Texas and California, there would be dominant Latino interest groups. Some states have more active environmental groups that the assert their influence; Oregon and Vermont are two examples.

State Health Departments

Given the variation in economic and political culture, the states and territories have developed different models of organizing their PH agencies. The Association of State and Territorial Health Officials (ASTHO) adopted the term *state health agency* to describe any agency of the state that is vested with primary responsibility for PH within that state. As described in their website, the ASTHO is the national nonprofit organization representing PH agencies in the United States, the U.S. Territories, and the District of Columbia, and

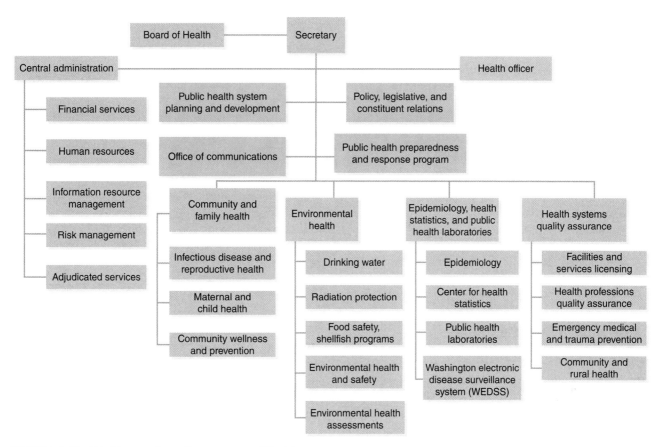

FIGURE 2.4 The Washington State Department of Health.

Washington State Department of Health. Available at: www.doh.wa.gov/AboutUs/ProgramsandServices/OrganizationChart.aspx

over 100,000 PH professionals these agencies employ.[11] The ASTHO members, the chief health officials of these jurisdictions, formulate and influence sound PH policy and ensure excellence in state-based PH practice. The ASTHO's primary function is to track, evaluate, and advise members on the impact and the formation of public or private health policy that may affect them and provide them with guidance and technical assistance on improving the nation's health.

As discussed in Shi and Johnson's book *Public Health Administration*, the organization of state PH agencies generally follows one of two basic models: a freestanding agency structure headed by an administrator who reports directly to the state's governor, or an organizational unit within a larger superagency structure that includes other functions, such as medical care and social services programs.[4] Approximately half of the states in the United States employ the freestanding agency model for their PH agency, in which the state agency is a cabinet-level unit within the **executive branch** of state government. For example, the state of Washington employs the freestanding structural model for its PH agency. An organizational chart of the Washington State Department of Health and its range of services and activities is presented in **FIGURE 2.4**.[12] This agency contains administrative units for core PH functions, such as epidemiology, health facilities licensing, infectious disease control, preventive health

care, and environmental health programs.[12] This agency is distinct, however, from the state departments that administer medical assistance (Medicaid) and social services programs, sometimes referred to as "umbrella agencies."[4]

In some states, the health agency is organized within a superagency structure or "umbrella" that also includes agencies that administer medical assistance, social services, and sometimes environmental programs. In these states, the PH agency does not occupy a cabinet-level position within the executive branch of government, but rather the superagency provides cabinet-level representation for PH issues, along with other issues within its purview.[4] Other states have superagencies that combine many other functions, such as social services, and environmental protection, such as the Colorado Department of Public Health and Environment. For example, the Michigan Department of Community Health has responsibility for PH, mental health, Medicaid, drug control, and aging services.

The variation in structure and scope across the 50 states and 5 territories is best described by the ASTHO in **EXHIBIT 2.6**.[11]

As articulated by the APHA, no single statement can provide a detailed blueprint for the structure and operation of state health departments in 50 states. The forces pressuring for diversity from state to state are myriad and infinitely complex.

EXHIBIT 2.6 State Health Agency Variations

There are 29 (58%) state PH agencies that are freestanding/independent agencies, whereas 21 (42%) are a unit of a larger combined health and human services organization—often referred to as an umbrella organization. Fifty state PH agencies report having a total of nearly 3000 local health departments and over 300 regional or district offices. Eighteen (36%) state health agencies reported having a state board of health. An additional nine (18%) states reported having an entity that performs similar functions. Approximately 25% of state health agencies share resources with each other, typically for all-hazards preparedness and response (67%) and epidemiology or surveillance (52%). Both of these trends have been steadily increasing since information collection began. Factors leading to this increase may reflect growing recognition of the importance of mutual aid agreements between states and incentives inserted in cooperative agreement objectives. State health agencies collaborate with many different entities, including local PH departments, hospitals, and healthcare delivery partners. Approximately 90% of state health agencies report exchanging information and working together on projects with hospitals, physician practices/medical groups, and community health centers. Most state health officers, about 66%, are appointed by the governor, 14% are appointed by a parent agency secretary, 10% are appointed by a board or a commission, and 10% are appointed by another entity.

Data from ASTHO Profile of State and Territorial Public Health. http://www.astho.org/Profile/Volume-Four/2016-ASTHO-Profile-of-State-and-Territorial-Public-Health/. Accessed February 15, 2019.

State Health Agencies' Roles and Responsibilities

The core PH functions (assessment, policy development, and assurance) discussed previously in Chapter 1 and presented in Figure 1.1, provide the overarching framework for PH policy in the state agencies. Each state health agency must assess the health status and the needs of the population, set goals to improve the health status of its citizens, secure the funding necessary to implement strategies designed to achieve the goals, set standards and enforce regulations, and provide assistance to local health departments and other agencies. Most states use the *Healthy People 2020* report when they are establishing their statewide goals and strategic plans.

As described by the APHA, the state health department's mission to advance community health is carried forward through four basic functions: (1) health surveillance, planning, and program development; (2) promotion of local health coverage; (3) setting and enforcement of standards; and (4) providing health services.[13] To further elaborate on the roles and responsibilities, there are the following:

Provision of Health Services: The state health department's responsibility for personal health services is to ensure that standards of care and completeness of service are adequate to the personal health needs of the citizens in every part of the state.

Control and Protection of the Environment: The state's obligation to maintain a wholesome living environment devolves largely on the state health department.

PH Research: Another tangible expression of state leadership is the encouragement and support of research on methods of quality control and improvement.

Education of the Public: A vigorous state health information and education program is essential because compared to the federal government, the state government is closer to the people, and it has more resources than the local government.

Education of the Health Professionals: The education of state health department personnel takes two essential directions—formal professional education and in-service training.

Administrative and Management Services: The successful execution of health programs demands the highest standards of administrative and management performance.

The perspectives of a state health department leader, a former Vermont health commissioner, are provided subsequently in an interview.

Local Health Departments

As described by Johnson, the first governmental PH departments in the United States were established in urban areas, usually seaports and river ports, in response to health issues associated with population density and immigration.[1] Local health departments were established along the east coast in Baltimore, Charleston, Philadelphia, Boston, and New York City, and along inland waterways in Louisville and Chicago. The west coast port of San Francisco also had an early health department as did the Gulf Coast port of New Orleans. The purpose then was primarily monitoring and addressing contagious diseases, enforcing quarantines, and eliminating environmental hazards through sanitation measures. As towns and cities grew, so did the scope of services with local health departments becoming involved in disease prevention by providing immunizations and health education.[1]

Today, there are approximately 3000 local agencies operating across the United States. The organizational structures and operational characteristics found among these local PH agencies are even more diverse than those observed at the state and federal levels. The local governmental entities that sponsor these agencies vary widely in their political authority and legal jurisdiction—including counties, cities, rural townships, and special districts. The local PH agencies vary widely due to the size and composition of the populations they serve. Needless to say, these agencies show considerable diversity in the political, economic, social, and intergovernmental environments in which they function. However, to get a visual depiction of what a local PH department might look like organizationally, **FIGURE 2.5** provides an example.[14]

The National Association for County and City Health Officials (NACCHO) sees the **local health department** (LHD) as a PH government entity at a local level, including a locally governed health department, state-created district, department serving a multicounty area, or any other arrangement with governmental authority and responsibility for PH functions at the local level.[15] The Association identifies common functions of an LHD, as shown in **EXHIBIT 2.7**.[4,15]

The standards were set forth by NACCHO to guide the fundamental responsibilities of LHDs (based on governance, staffing patterns, and size), recognizing that each LHD may have specific duties related to the

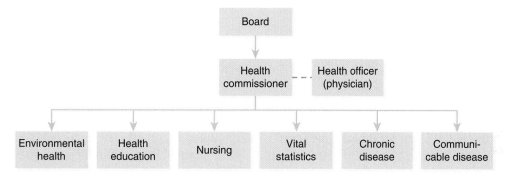

FIGURE 2.5 Organizational chart of a local health department.
Reproduced from McKenzie JF, Pinger RR, Seabert DM. Introduction to Community and Public Health. 9th ed. Burlington, MA: Jones & Bartlett Learning; 2018.

EXHIBIT 2.7 NACCHO: Local Health Department

A Functional LHD
- Understands the specific health issues confronting the community and how physical, behavioral, environmental, social, and economic conditions affect them
- Investigates health problems and health threats
- Prevents, minimizes, and contains adverse health effects from communicable diseases, disease outbreaks from unsafe food and water, chronic diseases, environmental hazards, injuries, and risky health behaviors
- Leads planning and response activities for PH emergencies
- Collaborates with other local responders and with state and federal agencies to intervene in other emergencies with PH significance (e.g., natural disasters)
- Implements health promotion programs
- Engages the community to address PH issues
- Develops partnerships with public and private healthcare providers and institutions, community-based organizations, and other government agencies (e.g., housing authority, criminal justice, and education) engaged in services that affect health to collectively identify, alleviate, and act on the sources of PH problems
- Coordinates the PH system's efforts in an intentional, noncompetitive, and nonduplicative manner
- Addresses health disparities
- Serves as an essential resource for local governing bodies and policymakers on up-to-date PH laws and policies
- Provides science-based, timely, and culturally competent health information and health alerts to the media and the community
- Provides its expertise to others who treat or address issues of PH significance
- Ensures compliance with PH laws and ordinances, using enforcement authority when appropriate
- Employs well-trained staff members who have the necessary resources to implement best practices and evidence-based programs and interventions
- Facilitates research efforts, when approached by researchers, that benefit the community
- Uses and contributes to the evidence base of PH
- Plans strategically its services and activities, evaluates performance and outcomes, and makes adjustments, as needed, to continually improve its effectiveness, enhance the community's health status, and meet the community's expectations

needs of the community it serves. These standards include the following[15]:

1. Monitor health status and understand health issues facing the community;
2. Protect people from health problems and health hazards;
3. Give people information they need to make healthy choices;
4. Engage the community to identify and solve health problems;
5. Develop PH policies and plans;
6. Enforce PH laws and regulations;
7. Help people receive health services;
8. Maintain a competent PH workforce;
9. Evaluate and improve programs and interventions; and
10. Contribute to and apply the evidence base for PH.

In addition to these standards, there are state-specific standards and National Public Health Performance Standards (NPHPS) for local health systems.[16] Using the NPHPS assessment can help ensure that health agencies can respond effectively to both day-to-day PH issues and PH emergencies by accomplishing the following[16]:

■ Improve organizational and community communication and collaboration
■ Educate participants about PH and the interconnectedness of activities
■ Strengthen the diverse network of partners within state and local PH systems
■ Identify strengths and weaknesses to address in quality improvement efforts
■ Provide a benchmark for PH practice improvements

The ASTHO and NACCHO maintain assessment instruments and supporting resources, available to three different audiences: state PH systems, local PH systems, and PH governing entities.[11,15]

Other Community Agencies Involved

Frequent contributors to PH activities include local social service agencies, elementary and secondary public schools, universities, housing departments, fire departments, law enforcement, city and county planning offices, parks and recreation departments, public libraries, public transit authorities, recycling services, waste management agencies, and water and sewer authorities. These organizations often maintain valuable resources for developing and implementing community-wide PH initiatives, such as support staff,

specialized expertise, building space and equipment, information and communications infrastructure, and public outreach mechanisms.

PH Leader's Perspective from the Field

As with Chapter 1, it is always important to hear from those who are working in the field being discussed. They are able to offer insights and sometimes advice that you usually cannot get otherwise, several of which will be presented throughout this text from PH professionals working in a variety of agencies and organizations. The second such interview with a former state health commissioner is presented in **EXHIBIT 2.8**.[1]

In her 13 years as the state health commissioner, Dr. Carney started an innovative PH program—*Healthy Vermonters*—which significantly reduced the levels of lead in babies' brains, made early baby visits almost universal, cut the rate of infant child abuse, increased childhood immunizations, and led to improvements in a number of other serious health issues, such as childhood obesity, breast cancer, HIV/AIDS, and smoking. U.S. Senator Bernie Sanders nominated Carney as Vermont's *Local Legend*, referring to her as a visionary leader who helped Vermonters experience extraordinary gains in their health and well-being.

Conclusion

This chapter identified and described a wide range of PH agencies and organizations seen in the federal government, as well as within the states and local communities. The context and political system that assures this demarcation was described as federalism. Organizational charts were presented for various agencies to help demonstrate the scope and the scale of their activities and responsibilities. The role of influential associations, such as ASTHO and NACCHO, was discussed and elements of the U.S. Public Health Service were described, including the role of the SG. Furthermore, an interview with a PH leader provided useful insights and advice from the field. Several examples of PH activities that take place outside of the official PH agencies were also provided. From reading this chapter, it should be evident just how large a presence PH has in the U.S. society, with a scale and scope of activity that are unsurpassed in the world.

Discussion Questions

■ Compare and contrast public health agencies at the federal, state, and local levels.
■ Discuss why federalism has an influence on the organization of PH.

EXHIBIT 2.8 Interview with Former Vermont Health Commissioner

Jan Kirk Carney, MD, MPH
Former Vermont State Health Commissioner and author of *Controversies in Public Health and Public Policy*
Interview by Dr. James Johnson

(Q): What is your own working definition of an effective public health leader?

Dr. Carney: An effective public health leader is credible, knows public health and how to figure out what needs to be done, sets measurable goals, and knows how to accomplish them by working with a wide range of people. I always remember (though I don't know who said it first …) that management is like climbing up a ladder, but leadership means knowing where to put the ladder. In order to achieve your vision, effective communication skills are critical, and you need to work well with people.

(Q): What skills and values are most essential for public health leaders like you?

Dr. Carney: Public health knowledge—from a broad general knowledge of public health to being able to become a "quick study," on a moment's notice on virtually any subject—is essential. Learning to make important decisions with less-than-complete information is another needed skill. Honesty, integrity, and truly believing in what you are trying to accomplish are at the core of daily values. I always felt that if I did my job in public health well, I could help many, many people, and nothing was more important or rewarding than that.

(Q): What advice do you have for students who plan a career in public health?

Dr. Carney: Expect hard work. It's not easy—there are never enough resources and too many public health needs. But the very things that make it so challenging also make it incredibly rewarding, and I can't think of a more important career. A small improvement in a public health issue means better health for many, many people.

- What are several examples of PH initiatives at HHS?
- Identify the many institutes of the NIH.
- What is the role of the U.S. SG? Who is the current SG?
- What are the services provided by the CDC?
- Discuss why there is a need for so much diversity in the way state health departments are organized. Give some examples.
- Discuss why there is a need for so much diversity in the way local health departments are organized. Give some examples.
- Are the *Healthy People* objectives discussed in Chapter 1 used by any of these agencies? If so, describe how.
- What are national health objectives? Discuss them with respect to the current decade.
- Identify various examples of roles and occupations that can be found in PH.
- What are the roles and responsibilities of PH professionals at the state and local levels?

Learning Activities

1. Do a search and read about the U.S. Public Health Service from its beginning to now. Try to identify some occupations in the USPHS that might interest you. Discuss in class and compare your interests to others in the course.
2. Review the HHS website. In a small group in class, discuss your favorite initiatives that are currently underway.
3. Review your state health department's website. In a small group in class, discuss your favorite initiatives that are currently underway. If you have a chance, go to a community forum on one of the initiatives.
4. Interview a PH manager and discuss why he or she chose to work in the federal, state, or local health agency.
5. Interview a PH professional and ask how he or she uses systems thinking in the organization. Ask for examples and demonstrations.
6. Make observations of local health department activities. Describe what they are doing and how these events assure or promote health.
7. Attend a local, state, or national meeting of a PH association. Make it a point to meet individuals from agencies. Describe the range of topics being discussed.

References

1. Johnson JA. *Introduction* to *Public Health Organizations, Management, and Policy.* Clifton Park, NY: Delmar-Cengage; 2013.
2. Turnock BJ. *Essentials of Public Health.* 3rd ed. Burlington, MA: Jones & Bartlett Learning; 2016.
3. Pollitt C. *The Essential Public Manager.* London: Open University Press; 2003.
4. Shi L, Johnson JA. *Public Health Administration: Principles of Population-Based Management.* 4th ed. Burlington, MA: Jones & Bartlett Learning; 2020.
5. Riegelman R, Kirkwood B. *Public Health 101.* 3rd ed. Burlington, MA: Jones & Bartlett Learning; 2019.
6. U.S. Surgeon General. https://www.surgeongeneral.gov/
7. U.S. DHHS Strategic Plan 2018–2022. https://www.hhs.gov /about/strategic-plan/index.html
8. CDC. https://www.cdc.gov/
9. Schneider MJ. *Introduction to Public Health.* 5th ed. Burlington, MA: Jones & Bartlett Learning; 2017.
10. Kilpatrick AO, Johnson JA. *Handbook of Health Administration and Policy.* New York, NY: Marcel-Dekker; 1999.
11. Association of State and Territorial Health Officers (ASTHO). www.astho.org/
12. Washington State Department of Health. https://www.doh .wa.gov/
13. American Public Health Association (APHA). https://www .apha.org/
14. McKenzie JF, Pinger RR, Seabert DM. *Introduction to Community and Public Health.* 9th ed. Burlington, MA: Jones & Bartlett Learning; 2018.
15. National Association of City and County Health Officers (NACCHO). https://www.naccho.org/
16. Public Health Foundation. National public health performance standards. http://www.phf.org/programs /NPHPS/Pages/default.aspx

Suggested Websites

a. ASTHO. www.astho.org/
b. CDC. https://www.cdc.gov/
c. HHS. https://www.hhs.gov
d. NACCHO. https://www.naccho.org/
e. USPHS. https://usphs.gov/

CHAPTER 3

Fundamentals of Management for Public Health

▶ Introduction

The need for management and managers has been around since the dawn of humankind. One could say that human societies created management and that management created societies through organizations. Early management was primitive, yet essential to building and advancing societies. Today, management and managers are still responsible for creating results that society values. Health is something society has valued historically and worked hard to protect and improve.[1] Management is important for public health professionals because it serves as a means to improve the health and the well-being of society. Public health has embraced management functions, skills, and roles arguably for centuries, even though management

as a discipline is only around 150 years old.[2] Today, as well as throughout history, public health has engaged in various forms of management and this has led to the recognition that public health managers are essential.

▶ What Is Management?

Management focuses on coordination within an organization. Daniel Wren, a famous management historian, states that management is the history of coordination.[2] Managers use a specific set of functions, skills, and roles to coordinate the resources, people, and processes within an organization to achieve the organization's priorities, plans, and goals. This text emphasizes management versus leadership concepts.

What Is the Difference Between Management and Leadership?

Management and leadership are distinct, yet related, concepts (**TABLE 3.1**). The duality of management and **leadership** is a source of confusion that results in the tendency to use the terms interchangeably. A manager can lead and a leader can manage. This is where conceptual confusion can emerge. We need both; however, each serves a different and distinct purpose. Management is often where potential leaders are first recognized and distinguish themselves. Management skills are vital at any stage of one's career; yet, early career professionals often find such skills particularly important to carrying out their daily work. Emphasis shifts from the need for management skills to leadership skills as individuals receive promotions and move up the organizational hierarchy. Then, what is the difference between management and leadership?

We can use additional questions to help us understand the difference. For example, we can ask, "What do managers do?" and "What do leaders do?" Peter Drucker, one of the seminal thinkers on modern management, answers these questions in his famous quote in which he differentiates management and leadership. Drucker states, "Management is doing things right; leadership is doing the right things."[3] John Kotter, another famous management scholar, answers the questions by stating:

> Management makes a system work. It helps you do what you know how to do. Leadership builds systems or transforms old ones. It takes you into territory that is new and less well known, or even completely unknown to you.[4(pvii)]

Managers and leaders must work together, but the roles of each are distinct and important to whether or not organizations achieve their goals—and, ultimately, survive. Management definitions focus on efficiency that is using organizational resource inputs to maximize results or organizational outputs. Managers are responsible for coordinating the transformation process of inputs into outputs within organizations. What is the transformation process? This process constitutes the activities, tasks, and work done in organizations each day. In contrast, leadership focuses on effectiveness, that is, making sure the results are what is needed in relation to the external environment or what is happening outside the organization. This makes a lot of sense to public health professionals who are watching population health trends and statistics

and then are responding to these needs through services, programs, projects, initiatives, partnerships, and other organizational activities to address these needs and thereby improve health.

Organizations have boundaries that distinguish an organization's internal environment from its external environment.[5] An organization's internal environment consists of the people, processes, and systems that perform work to accomplish specific activities within the organization. An organization's internal environment is the primary focus of management and managers. Managers are concerned with ensuring that an organization's internal people, processes, and systems are working and preforming as efficiently as possible to maximize organizational results.[6,7] In contrast, leadership focuses on what is happening outside an organization. Leaders are looking for trends, opportunities, and changes in the environment that impact the internal people, processes, and systems within the organization.[4] Organizational boundaries help differentiate management from leadership and vice versa.

> Management is a set of processes that can keep a complicated system of people and technology running smoothly. The most important aspects of management include planning, budgeting, organizing, staffing, controlling, and problem solving. Leadership is a set of processes that creates organizations in the first place or adapts them to significantly changing circumstances. Leadership defines what the future should look like, aligns people with that vision, and inspires them to make it happen despite the obstacles.[4(p28)]

The external environment consists of forces that are constantly changing and exerting influence on organizations. In turn, these external changes require changes within the organization. The external forces consist of changes in the political, economic, social, technological, and other external dimensions that the organization needs to respond to in order to ensure organizational effectiveness. There can be more than one force changing at any given time. Leaders actively scan and look for changes in the dimensions of the external environment to understand if the changes represent opportunities or threats to their organization. Leaders develop plans, along with managers in their organizations, about how to respond to these changes in the organization's external environment. Managers are responsible for consulting with the leader on organizational plans. More importantly, however, managers are responsible for putting these plans into action.[4] Leaders can miss organizational threats and opportunities if they focus too much on what is happening inside the organization.

TABLE 3.1 Common Descriptions of Managers and Leaders	
The Traditional View of Managers	**The Traditional View of Leadership**
Is mission- and purpose-oriented	Is vision- and goal-oriented
Is internally focused on status quo and rules	Is externally focused on strategic change and taking advantage of possibilities and opportunities
Knows and has mastered many different subjects	Understands how to learn and is willing to learn about anything
Approaches all issues as technical problems initially	Distinguishes between adaptive and technical issues and is comfortable with ambiguity initially
Leads by authority and direction	Leads with vision and influence
Works within his or her span of control	Spans organizational boundaries
Develops individuals for line and supervisory positions within the organization	Develops others who can play a boundary-spanning role between the organization and community
Does things right	Does the right things
Fosters and manages incremental change, continuous quality improvement (CQI)	Leads disruptive, significant change processes
Supports the ideals and symbols of the organization	Epitomizes the ideals of and symbolizes the organization to internal and external constituencies
Works through contracts and other formal, narrowly demarcated exchange agreements	Works through interest and curiosity, fostering open and longer-term exchange relationships
Is an excellent linear thinker and accomplisher	Is an excellent systems thinker and strategic planner
Is most focused on maintaining order and consistency	Values creativity, inspiration, and collaborative change
Reinforces the values and guiding principles of the organization	Establishes and embodies the organization's values and culture
Follows protocols and formal guidance	Exercises judgment, discernment, and contextual wisdom in order to make sound decisions
Negotiates with others via a positional approach	Negotiates through a "win-win" appreciation of separate and shared interests
Is an active "doer"	Is a reflective learner who applies insights to actions

Modified Table 12-2 from Shi L, Johnson JA. *Novick and Morrow's Public Health Administration*. 3rd ed. Burlington, MA: Jones & Bartlett Learning; 2013.

Leaders must trust managers to implement agreed upon organizational plans, and managers should assist with helping formulate such plans.

Studying the concepts of management and leadership separately makes it easier to see the distinction between each of the concepts and their related functions. However, management and leadership operate concurrently in practice. Successful public health organizations must be effective in identifying important population health issues. Likewise, public health organizations must also be efficient in using their resources to address these issues. Management and leadership functions are both necessary in public health organizations.

▶ What Is Public Health Management?

Management is a vital and unifying concept for the field and the practice of public health. Public health is a unique field that draws on a broad body of scientific knowledge. Management science is one field that public health draws on and is used to unite the other sciences.[8] Hunter and Berman define public health management as "[…] the mobilization and management of society's resources, including the specific resources of the health service sector, to improve the health of populations through whatever means is most appropriate."[8(p346)] Public health management focuses on the structure and function of public health organizations, programs, and personnel. Alderslade and Hunter define public health management as "the optimal use of the resources of society and its health services toward the improvement of the health experience of the population."[9] This definition points to the role that managers play in helping an organization efficiently transform input resources into organizational performance results to promote and improve population health. These definitions point to the public and private nature of public health management, as well as the need for public health professionals to understand and possess strong management skills. Hunt notes that public health management:

> […] requires managers who understand the importance of population-based approaches to health and public health specialists who are not mere purveyors of knowledge. They are also change agents and must become skilled in managing change, and in building coalitions of support for change both within the health care sector and across and into other sectors that have a significant impact on health.[10(p342)]

In summary, public health professionals broadly manage resources (both financial and nonfinancial), data, personnel, and programs with the overarching goal of improving the health and the well-being of the populations served. Public health managers must be able to build coalitions to lead change. Epidemiology serves as the basis for public health managers to understand the health needs and the types of coalitions and changes that are needed. This also helps to ensure that resources are allocated in ways that will have the most significant impact on population health.

▶ Example: Public Health Management Versus Leadership

The Public Health Accreditation Board (PHAB) oversees accrediting tribal, state, local, and territorial public health departments and validates the need for strong public health managers and leaders.[11] The **accreditation** process focuses on conducting a thorough analysis of the population health needs within a health department's jurisdiction. Leaders within the health department begin by identifying health priorities and developing plans to address these priorities with stakeholders inside the health department as well as other stakeholders outside the organization.[12] The priorities and plans then become the primary work of public health managers within the health department. The accreditation process focuses on continuous quality improvement of processes, programs, and interventions.[13] The accreditation standards are used to measure management capacity and assess policies, procedures, organizational culture, human resources, information management, and other organizational subsystems.[14] The public health accreditation process illustrates the intersection of public health management and leadership, and the need for both.

▶ Organizations as Systems

Modern management theories view organizations as complex adaptive systems.[15] Organizations are situated within an external environment. The environment consists of many different forces, such as political, economic, social, technological, ecological, legal, and regulatory, among others. These forces are constantly changing, which require organizations to change in order to adapt. Organizations are also changing and exerting influence on the environment as well. Organizations must adapt to different realities that they face in order to be effective. Managers are integral to adaptation because they are primarily concerned with the internal efficiency of an organization as it changes in order to adapt.

Kast and Rosenzweig developed a system's view of organizations in their seminal text titled *Organization and Management: A Systems and Contingency Approach*.[16] This text provides a conceptual model of organizations and identifies different systems and subsystems that form organizations. These authors believed

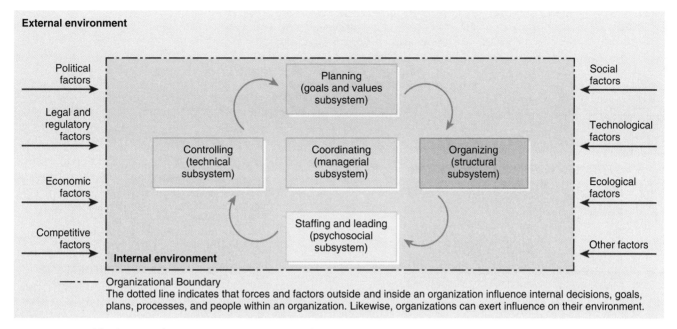

FIGURE 3.1 Modified Kast and Rosenzweig's organizational system.

Based on Kast FE, Rosenzweig JE. *Organization and Management: A Systems and Contingency Approach.* 4th ed. New York, NY: McGraw-Hill; 1985.

that a systems approach helps develop a common framework/model for understanding organizations. These authors identified five organizational subsystems (**FIGURE 3.1**): (1) goals and values subsystem, (2) structural subsystem, (3) psychosocial subsystem, (4) technical subsystem, and (5) managerial subsystem. The **goals and values subsystem** defines what the organization is trying to accomplish (or organizational goals) and identifies what the organization values. Organizational values serve to unite the organization and guide organizational thinking, decision-making, and activities. The **structural subsystem** refers to the way the organization divides tasks and responsibilities. An organizational chart, position descriptions, policies, and procedures all provide structure to the organization and those working in it. The **psychosocial subsystem** refers to the human resources within the organization. This subsystem also refers to both individuals and teams and other forms of interpersonal relationships and is concerned with behavior and motivation. The **technical subsystem** refers to the unique knowledge, processes, equipment, facilities, and techniques that the organization uses in its transformation phase. The **managerial subsystem** is responsible for coordinating all the other subsystems. Management is a process of coordination to create value by accomplishing organizational goals. The term process implies something that is continuous and ongoing within the organization, such as coordinating the organizational subsystems. Management coordinates by using the "management process," which

is made up of five functions: (1) planning (values and goals subsystem), (2) organizing (structural subsystem), (3) staffing (psychosocial subsystem), (4) coordinating (managerial subsystem), and (5) controlling (technical subsystem). Coordination is the key to value creation, efficiency, and effectiveness. Managers use the five managerial functions to coordinate the day-to-day activities within the organization through the five subsystems. The following sections provide a discussion of each of the five managerial functions.

▶ Management's Five Functions and the Managerial Process

In 1916, Henri Fayol wrote a book titled *General and Industrial Management*. The book identified the five functions of managers: planning, organizing, staffing, coordinating/leading, and controlling (**FIGURE 3.2**). Fayol believed that these tasks were universal to all managers, regardless of what industry or context they worked in. The five functions of management serve as the basic job description for managers and specify the activities in which managers engage on a day-to-day basis.[2] This text focuses on applying management principles to public health organizations. Understanding these five managerial functions helps us understand how management contributes to the field of public health.

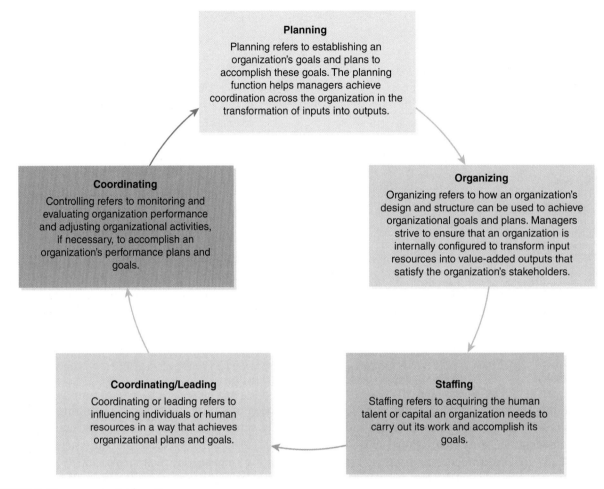

FIGURE 3.2 Five managerial functions.

Planning

Planning is a process that organizations use to establish direction, priorities, and goals. Planning relates to the goals and values subsystem previously discussed. Fundamentally, planning asks two questions. The first question is: "What is the organization going to do?" The next question is: "How is the organization going to do it?" These questions provide a common purpose for the organization. Managers formulate organizational goals and then develop specific action steps and plans to accomplish organizational goals. Communicating action steps and plans to employees is an important activity for managers and helps create a common purpose across the organization. Organizational values are the standards the organization uses to hold itself and its employees to as they work together to accomplish the goals of the organization.

Organizing

Organizing involves making decisions about what resources, processes, and structures organizations need to accomplish their goals. Organizing relates to the structural subsystem. Organizing activities include determining what types of resources (i.e., human, technology, material, and financial) are needed, as well as where these resources will come from. Next, this function determines what to do with the resources or what tasks need to be completed to accomplish the organization's goals. Tasks are identified and grouped into jobs, which is referred to as job design. Generally, similar tasks are grouped together into a job because they use similar resources and skills, which makes training easier and the work itself more efficient. Managers are also concerned with how teams, units, departments, and divisions within the organization are organized or designed. Organizational design groups individuals with similar jobs into teams and or types of organizational units. These individuals are grouped together because they often interact and work together to complete their jobs. Grouping jobs into teams, units, departments, and divisions promotes coordination and efficiency. An organization's goals and strategy should dictate its structure. The organizing function helps to coordinate organizational activities by systemically establishing key activity and communication patterns that are important to the organization's transformation process, value creation, and, ultimately, organizational outputs and goals.

Staffing

Staffing is concerned with the human resources that organizations need to achieve their goals. Staffing relates to the psychosocial subsystem. Managers must consider what types of tasks are going to be performed, as well as the knowledge, skills, and abilities needed to complete these tasks. Job descriptions are developed and used to recruit qualified candidates. Candidates are selected for interviews, and, ultimately, an individual is hired for a position. The candidates are then onboarded and orientated to the organization, department, and work they will be doing. Training and development are provided to enhance **employee** skills and capabilities for the future. Performance appraisals are used to identify training and development needs and, if necessary, for discipline and corrective actions. Compensation and benefit programs are used to motivate and reward employees, and employee relations processes are used to resolve workplace conflicts and engage employees in their work, teams, department, and the overall organization.

Coordinating

Coordinating or leading is the means by which management creates value in the transformation process. Coordinating relates to the managerial subsystem; it involves ensuring that all of the other subsystems work together to efficiently accomplish the organization's goal. This is where managers must lead by exerting influence on employees to shape their behavior to engage in helping the organization produce its outputs—whether that be goods, services, or some combination. Leading involves motivation, influencing attitudes, satisfaction, empowerment, and persuasion of people.

Controlling

Controlling refers to the process of monitoring and evaluating organizational activities and performance. Controlling relates to the technical subsystem. The technical subsystem refers to the methods, procedures, and processes to transform inputs into outputs. The feedback loop provides information about whether the organization is producing what the organization had planned on producing. The controlling function often reveals areas where adjustments or corrective action is

needed to assure that the organization accomplishes its goals.

Texts vary in the number of managerial functions they identify and discuss. There will be anywhere from four to six managerial functions typically identified, and sometimes more, as writers expand and contract the number of functions, depending on the level of the learner and the depth of discussion. Do not let the number or names of the functions confuse you. Planning and controlling are generally consistent across the various listings and discussions of managerial functions. Organizing often includes a discussion of the staffing function. Staffing is an area where many public health managers have little to no formal education. This text breaks out staffing to provide a more comprehensive overview of staffing in response to public health workforce needs. Many texts refer to coordinating as directing or leading. Directing was the term initially used by managers and management scholars. Leading is the term used today because it reflects the evolution of management thought and leadership theories concerning its importance today. This terminology shift also reflects the structure of the economy and types of jobs we have today. Knowledge workers dominate health care and prefer to be led (i.e., guided and persuaded) versus directed (i.e., told what to do). Directing reflects the time when manufacturing and unskilled workers dominated world economies. These workers were told what to do and how to do it. The five managerial functions are carried out at different levels of the organizations or at different management levels. Overall, the functions reflect tasks that are universal to all managers and provide insights into the work managers engage in on a day-to-day basis.

▶ Levels of Management

The levels of management in an organization are one way to begin studying management and understanding what managers do. The levels of management refer to a manager's position within the organizational hierarchy.[2] There are three levels of management in most organizations: top management, middle management, and first-line management (**FIGURE 3.3**).[2,5] Each of these levels require different skills. Organizational charts, as shown in **FIGURES 3.4** and **3.5**, provide an overview of an organization's structure and hierarchy at a specific point in time. **Organizational charts** provide insights into the levels of management, in addition to communication channels, key business units, departments, and functional areas, roles and responsibilities, and lines of **authority** within an organization.

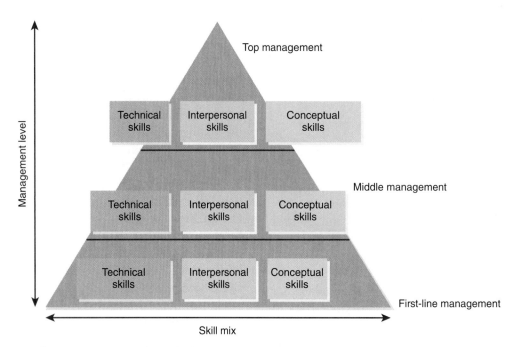

FIGURE 3.3 Levels of management and skills of effective managers.

Based on information from Katz R. Skills of an effective administrator. *Harv Bus Rev.* 1974; 52(5): 90–120.

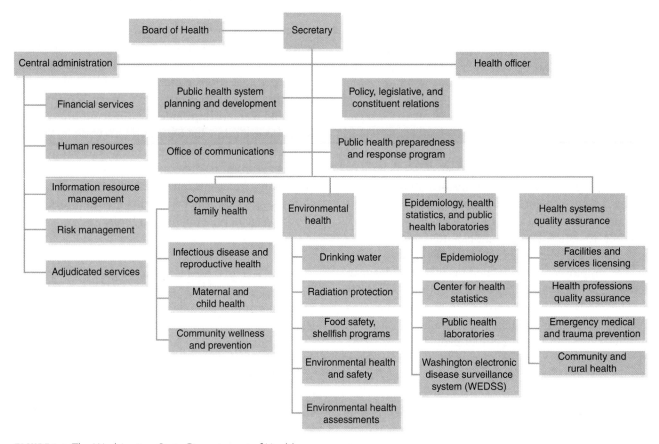

FIGURE 3.4 The Washington State Department of Health.

Washington State Department of Health. Available at: www.doh.wa.gov/AboutUs/ProgramsandServices/OrganizationChart.aspx

Top Management

Top management, also referred to as executive or senior management, consists of positions at the apex of the organization, as shown in Figures 3.4 and 3.5. Top management is responsible for overseeing the entire organization.[5] Top managers include positions such as the **chief executive officer**, **chief financial officer**, **chief operating officer**, chief medical director,

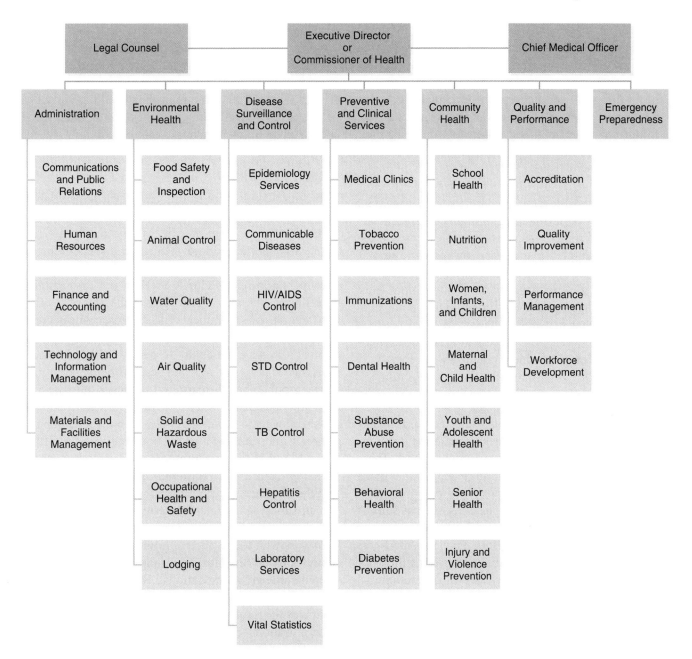

FIGURE 3.5 County health department organizational chart.

president, vice-president, director, executive director, and the board of directors or trustees. Most of the time, there is a top management team that consists of a group of top managers who work together to plan and evaluate organizational performance. For example, top management is responsible for developing strategic plans, priorities, and goals for the organization to ensure organizational effectiveness. These individuals are also responsible for assessing and evaluating organizational performance and making any adjustments necessary to ensure that organizational goals are accomplished. These individuals monitor what is happening outside the organization, as well as oversee operations inside the organization. Communication

skills are important to top managers because they are often communicating with key stakeholders outside the organization, as well as communicating organizational plans and priorities to middle managers inside the organization for the purpose of implementation.[2,5]

Middle Management

Middle management, also referred as mid-level managers, consists of positions in the middle of an organizational chart. These managers are below the top manager, to whom they report, and above the first-level managers who report to them. Middle managers include such positions as department or unit directors, regional managers, general managers, or divisional managers. Middle managers are responsible for implementing top management's plans to achieve performance goals. This requires middle managers to develop unit-, division-, and department-level plans based on top management's overall plans and performance goals. Middle management is responsible for overseeing their unit's functioning and performance. They also work with first-line managers, who report to them, to implement unit-level plans. Middle managers collect information and provide regular reports to top management on unit-level performance. Communication skills are important to middle managers because they are often interacting with top management on goals and results, as well as communicating organizational plans and priorities to first-line managers for implementation. Thus, middle managers provide information to top management, as well as first-line managers. Middle managers spend a lot of their time coordinating resources, people, and processes to achieve organizational goals.[2,5]

First-Line Management

First-line management, also referred to as frontline or supervisory-level management, is the positions toward the bottom of an organizational chart. These managers are below top managers and middle managers, and they generally report to middle managers. First-line managers include positions, such as shift or team supervisors, shift or team leaders, department supervisors, or unit supervisors. First-line managers are concerned with supervising or overseeing the work of employees on a day-to-day basis within a functional area of the organization to ensure that employees are productive. These managers assign work tasks, oversee the completion and the quality of work, train workers, resolve questions or complaints, evaluate suggestions or problems, communicate to middle managers, motivate employees, recognize employees, discipline employees, make hiring and firing decisions, and much more. First-line managers periodically collect information and provide reports to middle managers on day-to-day operations and performance. First-line managers spend a lot of their time directing and controlling the staff to ensure organizational efficiency.[2,5]

▶ Skills of Effective Managers

Robert Katz identified three skills of effective managers. The skills include technical skills, interpersonal skills, and conceptual skills, as shown in Figure 3.3.[17] Managers at different levels of the organization (i.e., top management, middle management, or first-line management) use all of these skills; however, the

management level emphasizes the need for different skills. Figure 3.3 illustrates the different mix of skills used by managers at different levels within the organization. Top managers need high levels of conceptual skills, whereas first-line managers need high levels of technical skills. All three levels of management need high levels of interpersonal skills.

Technical Skills

Technical skills refer to unique knowledge and abilities regarding techniques, processes, and tools within a discipline to perform specific tasks or functions.[17] This refers to specialized knowledge and understanding of the technology that organizations use to produce their outputs and relates closely to Kast and Rosenzweig's technical subsystem.[16] Managers at all levels of an organization possess technical skills, but to varying degrees. Technical skills are essential to first-line managers, who must also have the ability to carry out these services in their day-to-day role and responsibility. For example, a public health registered dietician must be able to understand the science behind nutrition and use this information to design diets for a diabetic population. Understanding how the body metabolizes certain foods and nutrients represents specialized knowledge that is required for registered dieticians to work with different clients and communities. The registered dietician supervising dietetic interns must have sufficient technical knowledge of nutrition to teach students how to work with clients and communities. Epidemiologists must possess technical knowledge of different types of epidemiologic investigations. They must also understand how to use visualization and analytic tools to convey the results of these investigations. Public health organizations are composed of an array of public health professionals who possess specialized skills and technical knowledge.

Interpersonal Skills

Interpersonal skills refer to a manager's ability to work with and through individuals inside and outside their organization to carry out plans to achieve organizational goals.[17] This is an important skill for managers because organizations are social systems or groups of individuals working together to achieve common goals. Managers all have a need to work and collaborate with others, as well as motivate employees, to accomplish organizational goals. A registered dietician relies on interpersonal skills to deliver food and nutrition education to specific populations. This requires strong communication skills related to motivational interviewing and behavioral change theories. The public health context also requires the registered dietician to recognize population health needs and provide culturally appropriate nutrition information and education. This could include recognizing and respecting dietary practices based on religion or the needs for nutritional information to be translated into different languages, for example. The Director of Nutritional Services for a state must work with registered dieticians across the state, different departments across the state health department, different state departments and agencies, community partners, and other stakeholders. Epidemiologists must be able to provide updates on investigations and communicate findings to diverse audiences from the public to the **Centers for Disease Control and Prevention** to departments within a **local health department**.

Conceptual Skills

Conceptual skills refer to a manager's cognitive ability to synthesize information, think critically, creatively, and logically.[17] Top managers in particular need these skills to align the organization with demands in its external environment. An example would be a manager's ability to make sense out of what is happening inside and outside the organization and what changes need to be made. A State Health Officer utilizes a different set of conceptual skills, such as policy analysis and strategic management skills, to ensure the health and the well-being of citizens within a state. Also, a State Health Officer relies on conceptual skills to manage the accreditation process. The officer must understand different types of assessment, planning, and reporting.

▶ Management Roles

In contrast to skills, managerial roles deal with the expectations that people—both inside and outside the organization—have of managers. Taking a closer look

at the different types of roles managers play within an organization helps to understand what public health managers do on a daily basis. Henry Mintzberg was interested in understanding the expectations of managers. He identified three broad categories and 10 specific management roles.[6] The three broad categories are interpersonal, informational, and decisional, as shown in **TABLE 3.2**. The interpersonal category includes three roles: figurehead, leader, and liaison. The informational category includes three roles: monitor, disseminator, and spokesperson. The decisional category includes four roles: entrepreneur, disturbance handler, resource allocator, and negotiator. These roles reflect the behavioral expectations of internal and external stakeholders. What is particularly interesting is the behavioral expectations that employees have for their managers. These three categories really reflect the definition of management by emphasizing the interpersonal aspect of management. The definition of management stresses the human element of work and that human relations are something a manager must master.

Interpersonal Roles

Interpersonal roles refer to the relationships that managers develop with individuals inside and outside the organizations. Managers form relationships inside their organizations with subordinates, mangers of other departments, superiors, and the board of directors. Managers also have a number of relationships outside their organization with patients, clients, the community, other organizations, and suppliers among others. Mintzberg identified three interpersonal roles managers fulfill, which include leader, liaison, and figurehead. In the **leader role**, managers are responsible for developing their employees. This requires a personal relationship to understand the unique skills, abilities, and growth potential of employees. Managers work with employees to

TABLE 3.2 Managerial Roles

Interpersonal Roles	Informational Roles	Decisional Roles
Figurehead	Monitor	Entrepreneur
Leader	Disseminator	Disturbance handler
Liaison	Spokesperson	Resource allocator
		Negotiator

Data from Mintzberg H. *Mintzberg on Management: Inside Our Strange World of Organizations.* New York, NY: Free Press: 1989.

develop growth and development plans that include training and educational opportunities. The **liaison role** recognizes that managers must work vertically and horizontally within an organization. This means managers serve as intermediaries between other departments within the organization, as well as intermediaries between subordinates and superiors. The **figurehead role** recognizes that managers officially represent their organization both inside and outside the organization. Internally, managers serve as agents or representatives for top management. They communicate top management's plans, priorities, and goals. Externally, managers network with those outside the organization and represent the organization at functions like dinners, ceremonies, meetings, or other business and professional activities.[6]

Informational Roles

Informational roles refer to the expectation of managers to be able to process and communicate information with stakeholders inside and outside the organization. Mintzberg identified three informational roles managers fulfill, which include: monitor, disseminator, and spokesperson. The **monitor role** recognizes the need for managers to gather information from inside and outside the organization to inform managerial decisions. Managers must be able to obtain, organize, and assess information. This could include information inside the organization, such as employee satisfaction, financial performance, and other operational metrics. Business intelligence, or information about what competitors are doing, provides an example of information managers must be able to obtain, organize, and analyze from outside their organization. The **disseminator role** recognizes the need for managers to transmit information obtained internally or externally within the organization to relevant individuals who need and can use this information for organizational purposes. The **spokesperson role** recognizes the need for managers to transmit information outside the organization. Managers serve as the official voice of their organization and speak on behalf of the organization to external stakeholders.[6]

Decisional Roles

Decisional roles refer to the expectation and the responsibility of managers to make decisions regarding organizational goals, priorities, and activities. Mintzberg identified four decisional roles that managers fulfill: entrepreneur, disturbance handler, resource allocator, and negotiator. The **entrepreneur role** requires managers to recognize new opportunities and initiate

organizational changes in response to forces in the organization's external environment to take advantage of these opportunities. The **disturbance handler role** requires managers to respond to interruptions to organizational activities. Interruptions can arise from inside or outside the organization. An example of an outside disturbance might be a public health manager who is unable to secure personal protective equipment from a third-party vendor to respond to an emergency. This inability of the organization to obtain the necessary equipment negatively affects its ability to respond to the emergency. The **resource allocator role** recognizes the control that managers have over organizational resources. Managers make decisions about how to best allocate resources based on an organization's plans, priorities, and goals. For example, the health officer for a state must make **budget** decisions about how money and other types of resources (e.g., equipment, facilities, and medications) will be used to achieve the state's health priorities. The **negotiator role** recognizes that managers negotiate inside and outside the organization. Externally, public health managers must be able to negotiate contracts for technology, supplies, services, partnerships, and other relationships with outside organizations, communities, and officials. Internally, public health managers often negotiate about new positions, employee salaries, equipment, and facilities.[6]

▶ Applying the Five Managerial Functions, Levels, and Roles to Public Health

Management is essential to public health and public health organizations. The 3 functions and the 10 essential services of public health, as shown in Table 1.1 or **FIGURE 3.6**, illustrate how important management is to the field of public health. Assessment requires considerable planning to understand what exactly it is that public health organizations need to do to enhance health. Policy development requires organizing, staffing, and leading different people and processes to impact public health. Assurance relates to the controlling function by ensuring that the organization's plans and processes achieve desired public health goals and results. To deliver on public health's core functions, public health managers must utilize the core functions of management.

The 10 essential public health services discussed earlier in Chapter 1 illustrate the many different levels of managers and the different roles that public health managers play. Monitoring health is an essential

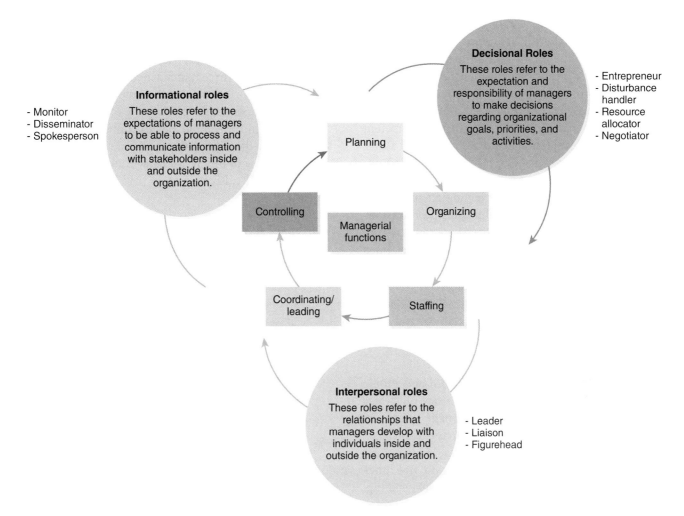

FIGURE 3.6 Comparison of managerial functions and roles.

Based on information from *Mintzberg H. Mintzberg on Management: Inside Our Strange World of Organizations*. New York, NY: Free Press; 1989.

public health service. This service reveals that public health managers have important informational and decisional roles within public health organizations. Managers must be able to monitor health trends to understand population health needs. Furthermore, public health managers must be able to disseminate information related to health. Public health managers often serve as spokespersons for public health organizations and communicate important health messages to ensure the public's safety and well-being. The spokesperson role of public health managers is often seen during emergencies, from weather-related emergencies (i.e., tornados, hurricanes, wild fires, earthquakes, blizzards, floods) to man-made emergencies (i.e., hazardous materials, terrorist attacks, biological weapons, nuclear power plants and blasts). Public health mangers often become a public voice and face for what to do during public health emergencies. Mobilizing communities is another essential service of public health. This service emphasizes how important interpersonal roles are for public health managers. Public health managers must serve as a liaison

between the community and the public health organization. This could include working with a local community to reduce the number of sexually transmitted diseases (STDs) in the area. Public health managers must establish relationships to be able to collaborate with the community as well as serve as knowledge experts within the public health department related to behavioral health and infectious diseases. Public health managers are also in a position where they can allocate resources to address an infectious disease outbreak, such as STDs. Management functions are essential to public health organizations because they provide a means for public health managers to coordinate inside and outside their organization to achieve the three core functions and 10 essential services of public health.

The core functions and essential services of public health also reveal the skills that managers need to be effective. Technical skills are important to be able to monitor health and diagnose and investigate diseases. Epidemiologists possess specialized technical knowledge to be able to perform the two essential services previously mentioned. Public health professionals need interpersonal skills to help inform, educate, and empower individual communities about matters related to their health safety and their well-being. The ability to mobilize community partnerships and develop policies that promote health and well-being require interpersonal skills. Assuring a competent workforce and evaluation requires conceptual skills, as well as technical skills. Conceptual skills help public health organizations to evaluate and understand if what they are doing is truly having an impact on health. These skills also help public health professionals to develop plans and make decisions that serve to guide the work that an organization is doing. Each of the core functions and essential services require a different mix of technical, interpersonal, and conceptual skills based on the level of the manager and the area in which the manager works.

Conclusion

Management is essential to public health and public health organizations. Public health history illustrates the important role that management plays in promoting health and wellness. Management and leadership are distinct, yet related, concepts. Management focuses on achieving efficiency through the five functions of management—planning, organizing, staffing, coordinating/leading, and controlling. In contrast, leadership focuses on effectiveness and ensures that the organization is doing the right things based on its external environment. This chapter also discussed the levels of management, important management skills, and managerial roles to help current and future public health managers understand the essentials of managing public health organizations.

Discussion Questions

- Compare and contrast the definitions of management and leadership.
- Define public health management.
- What are some examples of public health management?
- Describe an organization as a system. What are the subsystems of an organization?
- What are the five managerial functions? Provide an example of each function within the public health context.
- What is the relationship between the five managerial functions?

- What are the three levels of management? Provide an example of each level of management within the public health context.
- What are the three management skills? Which skill is important at each level of management? Provide an example of each type of management skills within the public health context.
- What are the different managerial roles? Provide an example of different managerial roles within the public health context.

Learning Activities

1. Write your personal definition of management and leadership. What managerial functions does your definition emphasize? What managerial skills does your definition emphasize? What managerial roles does your definition emphasize?

2. Exchange your definitions of management and leadership with a classmate. Compare and contrast the definitions. What managerial functions, skills, and roles does your classmate emphasize? Why?

3. Select a public health organization that interests you. Use Kast and Rosenzweig's Organizational System and Subsystems Model to identify examples of the following: (1) goals and values subsystem, (2) technical subsystem, (3) psychosocial subsystem, (4) structural subsystem, and (5) managerial subsystem.

4. Find an organizational chart for a public health organization. Identify the levels of management illustrated in the chart. What are the names of the positions at each level of the management levels? Use the organizational chart to discuss the management roles and skills at each level of management.

5. Interview a public health manager regarding his or her role and responsibilities within the organization. Provide an example of how the public health manager performs each of the five managerial functions. Assign a percentage to the managerial skills that the public health manager uses, and provide support for your scoring.

6. Interview a public health manager regarding his or her role and responsibilities within the organization. What managerial roles does the manager engaged in? Provide specific examples of the different managerial roles.

References

1. Porter D. *Health, Civilization, and the State: A History of Public Health from Ancient to Modern Times*. London, UK: Routledge; 1999.
2. Wren DA, Bedeian AG. *The Evolution of Management Thought*. 6th ed. Hobokan, NJ: Wiley; 2009.
3. Drucker PF. *The Essential Drucker: The Best of Sixty Years of Peter Drucker's Essential Writings on Management*. New York, NY: HarperCollins; 2009.
4. Kotter JP. *Leading Change*. Boston, MA: Harvard Business Review Press; 2012.
5. Mintzberg H. *The Structuring of Organizations*. Englewood Cliffs, NJ: Prentice-Hall; 1979.
6. Mintzberg H. *Mintzberg on Management: Inside Our Strange World of Organizations*. New York, NY: Free Press; 1989.
7. Mintzberg H. *Managing*. San Fransico, CA: Berrett-Koehler Publishers; 2009.
8. Hunter DJ, Berman PC. Public health management: Time for a new start? *Eur J Public Health*. 1997;7(3):345–349. doi:10.1093/eurpub/7.3.345.
9. Alderslade R, Hunter DJ. Commissioning and public health. *J Manage Med*. 1994;8(6):20–31. doi:10.1108/02689239410073411.
10. Hunt DJ. Public health management. *J Epidemiol Community Health*. 1998;52(6):342–343. doi:10.1136/jech.52.6.342.
11. Public Health Accreditation Board. About the Public Health Accreditation Board. https://www.phaboard.org/about-phab/. Accessed July 20, 2019.
12. Beitsch LM, Corso LC, Davis MV, Joly BM, Kronstadt J, Riley WJ. Transforming public health practice through accreditation (a user guide for the special accreditation issue). *J Public Health Manage Pract*. 2014;20(1):2–3. doi:10.1097/PHH.0b013e3182a8ea1e.
13. Public Health Accreditation Board. What is public health department accreditation? http://www.phaboard.org/accreditation-overview/what-is-accreditation/. Accessed July 20, 2019.
14. Public Health Accreditation Board. Standards and measures for initial accreditation. http://www.phaboard.org/accreditation-process/public-health-department-standards-and-measures/. Accessed July 20, 2019.
15. Johnson JA, Rossow CC. *Health Organizations: Theory, Behavior, and Development*. 2nd ed. Burlington, MA: Jones & Bartlett Learning; 2019.
16. Kast FE, Rosenzweig JE. *Organization and Management: A Systems and Contingency Approach*. 4th ed. New York, NY: McGraw-Hill; 1985.
17. Katz R. Skills of an effective administrator. *Harv Bus Rev*. 1974;52(5):90–102.

Suggested Reading

Journal of Public Health Management & Practice. https://journals.lww.com/jphmp/pages/default.aspx

CHAPTER 4

Planning and Decision-Making in Public Health Organizations

▶ Introduction to the Planning Function

Planning is a critical process for public health professionals and organizations today. Planning is a process that public health organizations use to establish direction, priorities, and goals. The process also outlines the steps, actions, and activities that organizations need to complete to accomplish their organizational goals. Robbins and Judge describe the planning function as "defining the organization's goals, establishing an overall strategy for achieving those goals, and developing a comprehensive set of plans to integrate and coordinate activities."[1(p6)] Managers at all levels of an organization participate in and often facilitate the planning process. Planning relates to the goals and values subsystem previously discussed.[2] The planning function provides the context in which the other managerial functions—organizing, staffing, coordinating/leading, and controlling—occur. The planning function helps managers achieve coordination within the organization in the transformation of inputs into outputs and guide the organization's and employees' daily work.

Fundamentally, planning asks two questions. The first question is: "What is the organization going to do?" This refers to the organization's goals. The next question is: "How is the organization going to do it?" This question refers to its the organization's plan concerning how to accomplish its goals. These questions reveal that planning is both outcome and process focused.[3] The answers to these questions provide a common purpose for the organization. Decision-making and planning go hand in hand. Planning reveals that there are many different ways to accomplish organizational goals and, therefore, relies on decision-making. Managers must first decide on the organization's vision, mission, and goals (i.e., organizational outcomes) and then develop plans (i.e., organizational processes) to accomplish the organization's outcomes. Managers must identify the different ways the organization can accomplish its goals and then select the best course of action from among all of the alternatives that are available. For this reason, goals are a critical starting point for organizational decision-making and planning.

The best course of action results in the plan that managers will use to accomplish the organization's goals in a coordinated and efficient manner. Managers are responsible for communicating goals and plans to employees throughout the organization or explaining what the organization will do and how it will do it. Managers translate organizational goals into department, unit, team, and individual performance goals and plans, depending on their managerial level within the organization. The controlling function assesses whether or not the organization has accomplished its goals or performance targets and provides feedback to managers on how well implementation plans are going. Managers are able to use this information to make decisions regarding current and future plans and organizational activities. This also highlights how the management functions work together from planning to controlling and ultimately provides managers with information about how well their decisions and related plans are working. The purpose of this chapter is to provide a general overview of planning and decision-making for entry- and mid-level public health managers to apply to their own personal practice and organizations.

▶ What Are Plans?

Plans outline the steps or activities that organizations should take to achieve their goals or desired results. Organizational plans are often referred to as roadmaps because they communicate where an organization is going. Maps clearly identify a starting point as well as an ending point (or goals). Plans provide details on how an organization is going to get from the starting point to the ending point or from point A to point B. This provides organizations and employees with purpose and focus. This also helps create cohesion and synergy, which reinforces organizational activities and goals. Planning is relevant to all types and levels of public health organizations. Therefore, public health managers must understand the planning process.

▶ The Planning Process

The **planning process** is the set of steps an organization follows to solve problems or take advantage of opportunities. Planning utilizes a systematic approach to develop goals, corresponding action steps (i.e., plans), and methods for monitoring and evaluating progress toward implementing plans and goal attainment. Managers must understand the planning process because they facilitate and participate in planning throughout the organization. Viewing organizations as systems helps when considering the planning process. The systems perspective helps organizations and managers consider the role that subsystems play in helping to accomplish the organization's goals and plans. Subsystems within organizations can develop specific action steps and tasks that can ultimately be associated with jobs that individual employees perform. The discussion on staffing demonstrates how managers develop job descriptions that consist of a group of tasks an **employee** performs, which are ultimately the result of organizational goals and plans. Managers are able to work with individual employees on training and development plans that support unit, department, and ultimately organizational plans. The managerial functions and, in particular, planning help to connect and coordinate organizational activities. Kaplan and Norton note that organizations often underperform or do not accomplish their goals because of poor planning.[4]

Planning includes internal and external stakeholders. **Stakeholders** are individuals, teams, groups, or organizations that are integral to accomplishing the organization's goals. Internal stakeholders include employees, teams, and departments/units within an organization, whereas external stakeholders are individuals, teams, groups, and organizations outside the organization. Stakeholders can vary based on the type of organization and the goals the organization is pursuing. Public health organizations engage stakeholders to fulfill their core functions and essential services. Stakeholders are diverse and depend on the purpose of the public health organizations. Stakeholders help public health organizations develop goals and corresponding plans for accomplishing their goals. Communicating organizational goals and plans to departments throughout an organization is an important part of leadership and communicating with key internal stakeholders. Managers then translate and communicate organizational plans into department-level goals and plans. Department managers then work to assign specific tasks and activities to employees. This connects the plans to the individuals who will be responsible for carrying out the plans. Managers also play a key role in monitoring activities and results, and they take corrective action, if necessary.

▶ What Are Goals?

The planning process results in **goals**, which are the results an organization is trying to achieve. Stated differently, goals are the outputs (i.e., services, products, or a combination) an organization is trying to produce. How does an organization decide what its goals should be? Organizations develop goals in relation to their external environment. How does an organization decide what its goals should be? The external environment influences an organization's goals, and goals represent the means by which an organization can align with its external environment. Goals help to ensure that an organization is effective and is creating value within its external environment.

Time is an important dimension when discussing goals. Organizations can have short-term goals and long-term goals. **Short-term goals** are generally goals an organization hopes to achieve in less than a year. **Long-term goals** are goals an organization hopes to achieve in over a year and might require several years. Organizations and textbooks use the term *goals* differently. Some organizations use the term *goals* to refer to long-term goals and use the term *objectives* to refer to short-term goals. Managers should ensure that the terminology is clear and that the time frame for accomplishing goals is clear. Labels can and often do vary between different organizations.

Regarding terminology, the important point is to ensure clarity and consistency within an organization. Goals also provide a clear purpose for an organization and its employees, and often goals motivate employees to contribute to something that they value. The more employees understand the organization's goals, and how the goals relate to their role (i.e., job) within the organization, the better able employees are to accomplish their individual goals and contribute to collective organizational goals. Goals provide a standard of performance to help organizations and managers determine if they are accomplishing the purpose of the organization. Individuals outside the organization understand an organization's purpose through its goals. Goals define the organization in the mind of external stakeholders. Goals also help managers understand how to allocate organizational resources across an organization and within departments.

▶ Goal-Setting

What makes a good goal? Managers face this question constantly as they work to develop, implement tasks, and evaluate goals. Edwin Lock articulated a goal-setting theory of motivation and found that employees achieved higher levels of task performance when goals are specific and challenging, as shown in **FIGURE 4.1**. This theory explains that higher levels of task performance and goal attainment result when employees believe they are capable of accomplishing the goals and managers provide regular feedback, resources, and rewards. The theory is helpful because it links

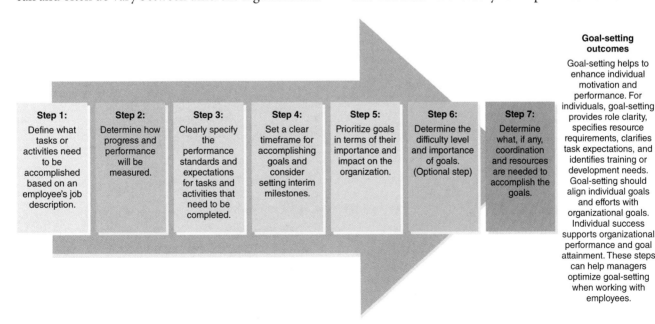

FIGURE 4.1 Locke and Latham's steps to goal-setting.

Based on information from Locke EA, Latham GP. *Goal Setting: A Motivational Technique That Works!* Englewood Cliffs, NJ: Prentice Hall; 1984.

an organization's goals to an individual's work and provides a role for managers in influencing this relationship.[5,6] Locke and Latham identified seven steps to optimize goal-setting (Figure 4.1): (1) specify the objectives or the tasks to be done, (2) specify how performance will be measured, (3) specify the standard to be reached, (4) specify the time frame involved, (5) prioritize the goals, (6) rate the goals in terms of difficulty and importance, and (7) determine the coordination requirements.[7]

Management by Objectives

Peter Drucker popularized the concept of **management by objectives** (MBO). This is another goal-setting approach, which seeks to align employee and organizational objectives or goals and, in turn, maximize performance. The popularity of MBO has resulted in planning and goal-setting being decentralized and diffused throughout organizations. The approach involves individual employees and managers working together to develop employee-specific objectives based on organizational objectives in an effort to enhance motivation and performance.[8]

The MBO process consists of five general steps, as shown in **FIGURE 4.2**. First, the organization sets strategic objectives or goals. Organizational objectives and goals are then broken down and translated into unit

level goals and objectives that are specific to the work the unit performs. Second, managers and employees develop individual-level objectives collaboratively that cascade down from and relate to the organization's goals or those of their lower level unit. This approach aligns employee goals with organizational goals to enhance coordination and performance across the organization. Third, managers and individual employees monitor performance and progress toward meeting the employee-level objectives identified in step 2. Managers are able to provide specific feedback to employees based on their objectives and their progress toward accomplishing them. Fourth, managers evaluate individuals based on their performance. This evaluation generally takes places as part of an employee's annual performance appraisal process. The employee's objectives and their attainment, or lack of attainment, are central to the evaluation process. Finally, managers are able to reward employees based on their performance and achievement of their objectives. The process then begins again, establishing or refining organizational objectives and corresponding employee-level objectives.[8]

MBO offers a number of benefits and has some drawbacks. The process promotes communication and participation in goal-setting across the organization. Managers and employees are able to communicate about goals, which helps to motivate and engage

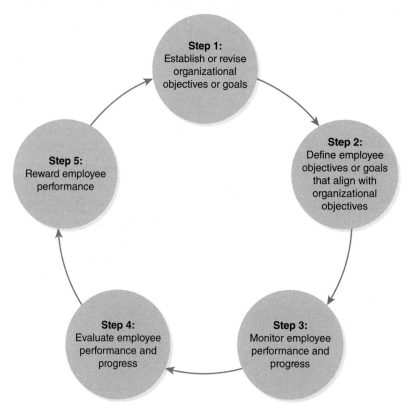

FIGURE 4.2 The management by objective process.
Based on Drucker P. *The Practice of Management*. New York, NY: Harper and Row; 1954.

employees toward the accomplishment of individual and organizational results. The performance appraisal process incorporates an employee's objectives, and the manager provides feedback to the employee. Managers are also able to recognize and reward employees for accomplishing their goals. Using this approach, organizations accomplish their goals as employees accomplish their performance objectives. This advances the employee and the organization and promotes coordination and synergy through a **means-end chain**. Organizational goals are the "ends" and employee performance objectives are the "means" to accomplish these ends. A drawback of this approach is that the goals cascade or flow down the organization, which can lead to organizational goals that do not always engage or incorporate feedback from individual employees. Goals can veer off course if employees and managers are not clear about the organization's goals and priorities. Additionally, this approach takes a considerable amount of time to implement and document. The process can also produce a set of static goals. Static objectives or goals do not serve an organization well when it is operating in a dynamic or constantly changing environment. Dynamic environments require organizational goals that are flexible and responsive to changes. Despite the drawbacks, MBO remains a popular goal-setting approach.

S.M.A.R.T. and S.M.A.R.T.E.R. Goals

The S.M.A.R.T. and S.M.A.R.T.E.R. acronyms stand for approaches to goal-setting that are widely used for personal and organizational goals. These approaches contain the elements of Locke and Latham's goal-setting approach[7] and Drucker's MBO approach.[8] Drucker developed the S.M.A.R.T. criteria as part of MBO. However, George Doran published an article in *Management Review* that helped popularize the S.M.A.R.T. acronym drawing on Drucker's criteria.[9] The S.M.A.R.T. acronym stands for **specific, measurable, attainable, relevant**, and **time-bound** (**FIGURE 4.3**). Goals should be **specific**, so that they identify a clear and desirable outcome. Answering questions like "What?," "Who?," and "Why?" help to avoid vague or ambiguous goals. Specific goals answer the following questions: What is the desired outcome? Who is involved? What resources are required? What are potential challenges? Why is the goal important? Goals should also be **measurable** and able to quantify desired outcomes. This dimension provides an end goal and speaks to milestones along the way. Articulating how much or how many is important. For example, how much should a clinic extend its operations in a geographical area? How many providers are needed to extend clinical operations to a new geographical area? Measurable goals help employees and managers know when goals are accomplished or how much progress has been made in relation to goal attainment. This dimension of goals provides a means for managers to monitor progress, take corrective action, and motivate employees. **Attainable** goals are ones that managers and employees believe are reasonable and something they are capable of achieving. This dimension looks at an organization's internal environment and assesses the

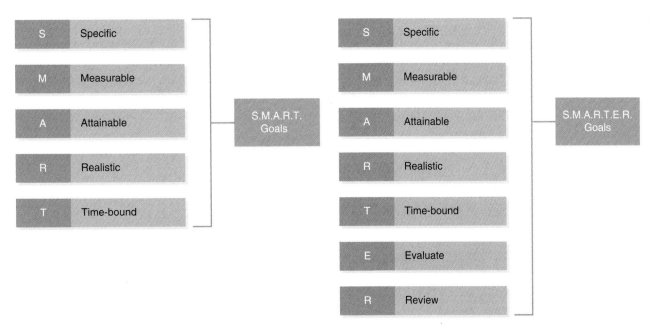

FIGURE 4.3 S.M.A.R.T. and S.M.A.R.T.E.R. goals.
Based on data from Doran GT. There's a S.M.A.R.T. way to write management's goals and objectives. *Manage Rev (AMA Forum)*. 1981;70(11):35–36. and Drucker P. *The Practice of Management*. New York, NY: Harper and Row; 1954.

abilities and resources an organization possesses and needs to achieve the desired outcome. If the organization has the abilities and resources, or can reasonably obtain them, the goal is attainable. Organizations and employees can quickly become demotivated if goals are unattainable because knowledge, skills, or resources impede their attainment. Managers can use this dimension to determine what training or other resources may need to be acquired to achieve the goal. Goals should be **relevant** and related to the organization's broader plans and strategic priorities. This dimension looks at an organization's external environment by asking if the organization is doing the right things in relation to what is happening outside the organization pertinent to accomplishing its purpose. Finally, goals should be **time-bound**. Deadlines help prioritize work and resources and serve as a motivating force for individuals and organizations. Organizations use short-term and long-term goals to help prioritize the actions or steps that need to be completed to achieve a specific outcome or goal.[9]

The S.M.A.R.T.E.R. acronym extends the S.M.A.R.T. approach to include **evaluate** and **reviewed** (or readjusted). The S.M.A.R.T.E.R. approach emphasizes evaluating progress and making any necessary adjustments to ensure progress and, ultimately, goal attainment. Managers must periodically **evaluate** progress and use the information to make adjustments. Regularly, reviewing goals and progress helps to identify plans and areas that are working well and identify areas where revising plans will help ensure goal attainment. Managers may need to adjust their plans to secure additional resources or provide additional training after evaluating progress. Listening is an important part of evaluating goals. Managers should communicate progress to stakeholders and listen to any feedback and insights they provide. Communication is important—whether things are progressing as planned or whether progress has veered off course. Managers play an important role in **reviewing and readjusting** goals. They also play an important role in communicating necessary changes and the rational for readjustments if an evaluation reveals that progress is not going to achieve the desired outcome. Finally, when goals are accomplished, employees and teams should be recognized and rewarded for their hard work. Managers play an important role in recognizing and rewarding employees who achieve the desired goals. Many managers and organizations overlook celebrating and rewarding the individuals, teams, or departments that meet goal expectations. This is an important motivator for employees.

The S.M.A.R.T. and S.M.A.R.T.E.R approaches to goal-setting do not guarantee organizational success or survival. The approach helps organizations write goals that are clear, actionable, and easier to communicate. Leaders and mangers in an organization must work to develop the organization's priorities and strategies. Managers must identify different options and plans through the planning process and select a plan that considers internal and external factors. These approaches do not help managers select between alternatives, but they do help organizations, managers, and employees write goals to essentially motivate employees and measure goal attainment.

▶ Levels of Planning and Plans

Plans and goals are important to organizations. The previous discussion alluded to the fact that goals and plans will vary based on the level of the organization. For example, organizational goals are broken down and assigned to different departments or units that develop plans to achieve these department- or unit-level goals. MBO illustrates that department- or unit-level goals can be further broken down into plans and goals for individual employees. Therefore, managers need to understand the different levels of an organization and the types of plans that are generally associated with each level (**FIGURE 4.4**). There are three general levels of plans and planning: strategic, tactical, and operational.

FIGURE 4.4 Organizational levels and plans.

Strategic Planning Process

The strategic planning process consists of a number of steps, as shown in **FIGURE 4.5**, which differentiate strategic plans from other types of organizational plans. An organization's mission, vision, and values serve as the starting point for the strategic planning process. An assessment of the organization's external and internal environment informs an organization's vision, mission, and values statements. These statements provide direction by communicating what the organization does and why, how the organization adds value to those it serves, and what makes the organization distinct from its competitors. Strategic plans focus on understanding how an organization fits or aligns with its external environment. **SWOT analysis** is a tool that organizations use to assess their internal strengths and weaknesses, as well as the opportunities and threats they face in their external environment. Organizations develop strategies that use their internal strengths to take advantage of external opportunities while avoiding threats and trying to remediate weaknesses. Organizations must assess forces outside the organization, such as political, economic, social, technological, ecological, and legal/regulatory changes. For example, public health organizations and managers must understand demographic trends, reimbursement models, health information technology, health policy, population health statistics, and environmental impacts on health, among other factors. Organizations must also assess their internal environment to determine their core capabilities. **Core capabilities** refer to the resources, processes, and knowledge or other distinctive competencies that organizations possess and use to attain their goals. Strategic planning considers how organizations can **leverage** their core capabilities to respond to opportunities and avoid threats in the organization's external environment. This assessment helps organizations determine what strategies are available to help them achieve their strategic goals and, indeed, what these goals should be.

Organizations then use the strategic planning process to translate strategic plans into tactical and operational plans to define goals and action plans for subdivisions of the organization, such as division, departments, and other work units. These lower level goals and plans are important because they help lower levels of the organization understand their role and the results they need to produce to attain organizational goals. Implementation plans include operational plans that provide very specific activities and goals for individuals and teams within departments to accomplish. Finally, the strategic planning process collects and analyzes information about progress made toward achieving the organization's strategic goals. This step is important and provides valuable feedback that the organization can use to set new strategic goals and associated strategies.

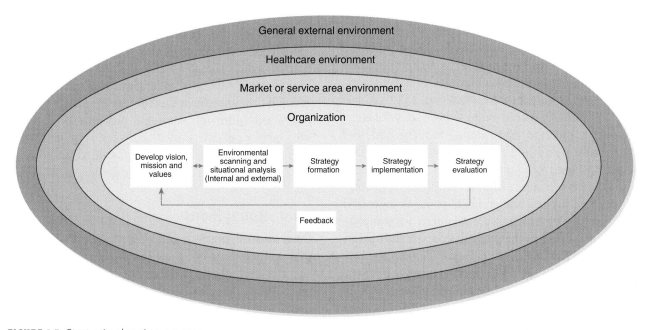

FIGURE 4.5 Strategic planning process.

Based on information and modifications from Daft RL. *Management.* 12th ed. Boston, MA: Cengage Learning; 2016. and Kaplan RS, Norton DP. Mastering the management system. *Harv Bus Rev.* 2008;86(1):62–77.

Strategic Plans

The strategic planning process generates a strategic plan that identifies an organization's purpose and direction. Top management develops the organization's strategic plan by engaging stakeholders inside and outside the organization. Strategic plans are future-oriented and focused on moving an organization from its current state to a desirable future state. The strategic plan serves as the basis for unit or departmental plans and even individual-level work plans. This plan also guides the process of allocating or acquiring organizational resources. The **strategic plan** contains the organization's vision statement, mission statement, values, goals, and strategies, which are sometimes referred to as directional strategies. Directional strategies communicate where an organization is going, and share the organization's common purpose with internal and external stakeholders.[10] Organizational members use directional statements and strategies to make decisions during the strategic planning process.

An organization's **vision or vision statement** communicates an organization's aspirations. The vision conveys what problem the organization is trying to solve, what change the organization is trying to inspire, and what the organization hopes to contribute to society and the greater good. An organization's **mission or mission statement** communicates its purpose. This statement also articulates how the organization is distinct from competitors. A strong mission statement conveys an organization's purpose, core customers, and the geographic areas served by the organization. An organization's **core values** state what the organization values and believes to be valid. Organizational values also communicate how the organization operates and how its employees will act, particularly concerning ethical issues. A strategic plan consists of a set of strategies and action plans to achieve its strategic vision, mission, and goals.[10,11] A **strategy** is a set of related decisions that help an organization achieve its goals and, ultimately, provide a competitive advantage.

Public health organizations have developed a number of different frameworks, models, and tool kits to help public health managers develop strategic plans at both local and state levels.[12] Public health organizations are increasingly emphasizing the strategic planning process and strategic plans as more and more health departments are required to complete such plans as part of the public health **accreditation** process. The National Association of County and City Health Officials (NACCHO) through funding from the **Centers for Disease Control and Prevention (CDC)** developed the Mobilizing for Action through Planning and Partnerships (MAPP) framework. The MAPP framework helps local health departments develop strategic plans at the community level. The MAPP framework includes the following: (1) engaging stakeholders; (2) visioning and systems thinking; (3) leveraging data; (4) establishing priorities; (5) communicating priorities; (6) developing objectives, strategies, and measures; and (7) implementing and monitoring.[13] The MAPP framework mirrors the strategic planning process previously discussed. The Association of State and Territorial Health Officials (ASTHO) through funding from the CDC's National Public Health Improvement Institute developed the State Health Improvement Planning (SHIP) framework that is a companion to the state health assessment.[13,14] The SHIP framework helps state health departments assess state health needs and develop a health improvement plan congruent with public health accreditation requirements. The SHIP framework provides another example of how the strategic planning process and strategic plans are used in public health.

Tactical Plans

Tactical plans focus on linking the organization's strategic plan to specific divisions, departments, or other units within the organization. These plans are primarily the concern of middle managers. Tactical plans also have shorter time frames than strategic plans and can be thought of as plans that help an organization set interim goals and build momentum, so that the organization can achieve its strategic goals. Setting smaller and more specific goals that are more easily attained help heighten motivation and, in turn, performance. The previous sections discussed how clear goals motivate employees. Similarly, tactical plans can motivate organizational members because these plans include specific steps targeted to achieve a more specific goal. Additional detail that is clear and more specific makes it easier for employees to understand. Employees are able to understand how the activities and jobs they perform contribute to smaller tactical goals and ultimately strategic organizational goals. This helps employees prioritize work activities, focus resources, accomplish work that is valued, and receive rewards for meeting performance goals.

Operational Plans

Operational plans break down tactical plans into daily activity schedules, such as production schedules and work schedules, for each operating unit and sub-unit. These plans clearly communicate: (a) what action needs to be taken, (b) who is responsible for taking a certain action, (c) a date when actions need to be started and completed, (d) resources that are required, and (e) challenges that could emerge and plans for addressing them. In contrast to strategic management and plans that focus on effectiveness, operational management and plans focus on efficiency or using the minimum resource inputs to produce the maximum product/service outputs possible.

▶ Types of Plans

Standing Plans

Managers create and utilize different types of plans for different purposes. Standing plans and single-use plans are two different types of plans that managers routinely develop and use. Managers use **standing plans** to reflect decisions that managers across an organization repeatedly and regularly make. These plans help the organization achieve its organizational goals in a consistent and coordinated manner. "Standard operating procedure(s)" is an another term used in organizations to refer to standing plans. Manuals and handbooks include policies and procedures regarding how to accomplish regularly occurring activities and decisions. A **policy** is a guideline or rule for organizational actions or behaviors. A **procedure** is a set of specific activities or steps to implement a policy. These plans guide managerial decision-making and ensure consistent decisions and uniformity across the organization. These plans also enhance efficiency as time does not have to be spent figuring out how to handle recurring activities. Standing plan examples include hiring and termination procedures. These plans also allow managers at one managerial level to delegate managerial decision-making and responsibility to lower levels of management while still exerting some degree of control.

Single-Use Plans

Managers develop **single-use plans** to accomplish specific organizational goals or results that are unique and are not regularly recurring. Goals, budgets, programs, and projects are examples of single-use plans. These plans are often single-use plans because they are specialized and used once to accomplish a specific goal or result. For example, accreditation is a goal of many state and local health departments. These departments develop single-use plans to detail the activities their organization needs to complete to successfully become **accredited**. Accreditation is generally for a specified period, such as 5 years. Reaccreditation would require the health department to develop another single-use

plan to ensure a successful reaccreditation because accreditation standards and practices change over time. This example illustrates how single-use plans help achieve specific and not regularly occurring goals. Budgets are another example of single-use plans because budgets are a financial plan that specifies how organizational resources will be used over a defined period. Budgets are generally adjusted each year to help the organization realize their goals.

▶ What Is a Decision?

Organizations face decisions every day. Managers are responsible for making decisions that affect all aspects of the organization. **Decision-making** is fundamentally making a choice or selecting between alternatives.[15,16] If there are no alternatives, then there is no need for a decision. The organizational subsystems coordinated by the managerial subsystem (i.e., planning, organizing, staffing, coordinating, and controlling) presents managers with different organizational decisions, as shown in **FIGURE 4.6**. Therefore, managers must possess decision-making skills and understanding of the decision-making process. Decision-making skills refer to "[…] the ability to conceptualize situations and select alternatives to solve problems and take advantage of opportunities."[17(p10)] Managers must be able to identify decisions that need to be made, generate alternatives or solutions individually or with a team, select the best solution/alternative, communicate the decision, implement the decision, monitor the decision, and evaluate the results of the decision. This section provides a general overview of decision-making.

Types of Decisions

Managers make two broad types of decisions—programmed and nonprogrammed.[15] First-line- and middle-level managers primarily make programmed decisions, whereas top management primarily makes nonprogrammed decisions.[16] **Programmed decisions** are those that managers have encountered and have made before. These are routine, defined, and structured types of decisions that managers make using budgets, project plans, policies, and procedures. Managers are able to make these types of decisions relatively quickly because there are policies, standards, and rules to help guide decision-making. **Nonprogrammed decisions** are those that managers have not made before. These decisions are ambiguous because they are nonroutine, undefined, and unstructured types of decisions. Nonprogrammed decisions

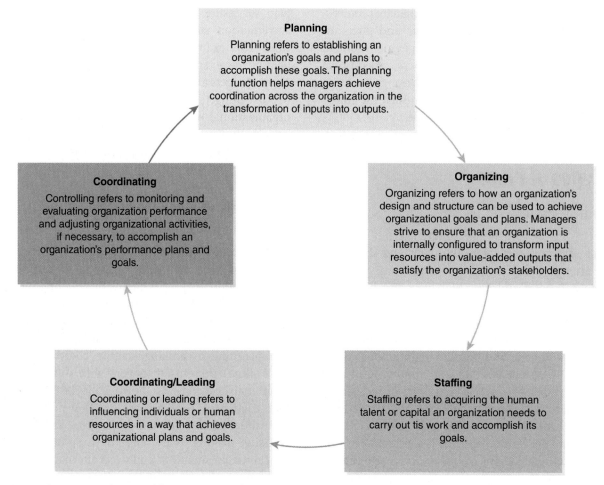

FIGURE 4.6 Decision-making and five managerial functions.

take longer and require higher levels of decision-making skills because there are no policies, standards, or rules to help guide decision-making. Nonprogrammed decisions take longer because more information usually has to be considered. This could mean that there are more individuals involved in the decision-making process and more alternatives to consider or the alternatives are not clear. Nonprogrammed decisions are riskier and have a significant impact on the organization, whereas programmed decisions are usually less risky and have a less significant impact on the organization.[15] As suggested earlier, decision-making can also be discussed based on the organizational level at which a decision is being made.

Levels of Decision-Making

Public health managers at every level of the organization make countless decisions each day. Therefore, the managerial level is an important decision-making dimension for managers to consider. Top management regularly makes strategic decisions. **Strategic**

decisions are significant decisions that affect the entire organization, such as the vision, mission, values, goals, and overall strategic direction of the organization. In contrast, first-line managers generally make operational decisions. **Operational decisions** affect individual employees and day-to-day operational activities, which affect a relatively limited number of individuals. Middle managers usually make **tactical decisions** at the unit or department level. Tactical decisions do not affect the entire organization, but they do affect the people and the processes of an entire department or unit. Middle managers can face both programmed and nonprogrammed decisions because they are supporting decision-making at both the strategic and operational levels. Decisions that will affect the entire organization usually require considerable time and resources versus those at lower levels.

Decision-Making Models

Decision-making models help managers navigate the decision-making process. Managers use different models based on the type of decision they face (i.e., programmed versus nonprogrammed), the amount of information they have, and the amount of time available to make the decision. There are three dominant decision-making approaches or models with which managers should be familiar: the rational decision-making process (rational model), the bounded-rationality model (administrative model), and the political decision-making model (political model).[15]

Rational Decision-Making Model

The rational decision-making or rational model provides a step-by-step approach to decision-making.[16] Daft outlines the approach in an eight–step process,[18(pp471-473)] as shown in **FIGURE 4.7**, and is discussed later. The first four steps relate to how managers can identify and define a decision. The last four steps relate to how managers can develop and evaluate alternative solutions and then select the best alternative (i.e., make a decision). The rational model often assumes that an organization faces a problem. Organizations frequently face problems; however, organizations also face numerous opportunities that require decisions. Managers face decisions about how to leverage organizational strengths and minimize organizational weaknesses. Daft's decision-making steps have been adapted to reflect both decisional problems and opportunities managers face. In particular, the decision steps can help managers make decisions about how to leverage organizational strengths and opportunities, as well as how

to mitigate organizational weaknesses and threats. The steps are:

- *Step 1. Monitor the internal and external decision environment:* Managers should be constantly scanning their internal and external environments. Conditions inside and outside the organization are common sources of managerial decisions. In response, managers are constantly trying to align what is happening inside the organization with what is happening outside their organization. Keeping a close eye on what is happening inside and outside the organization helps managers evaluate their performance, identify any areas for improvement, or anticipate organizational changes that are needed due to dynamics in their external environment.

- *Step 2. Define the decision problem or opportunity:* Managers are constantly scanning their environment for opportunities and threats in the external environment and strengths and weaknesses in their internal environment. Managers must make a decision regarding how to respond when their organization faces different opportunities or threats. Information gathering is key to helping managers define the decision that needs to made related to organizational problems and opportunities. This step illustrates how managers make sense of their internal and external environments. How managers interpret and make sense of their environment influences

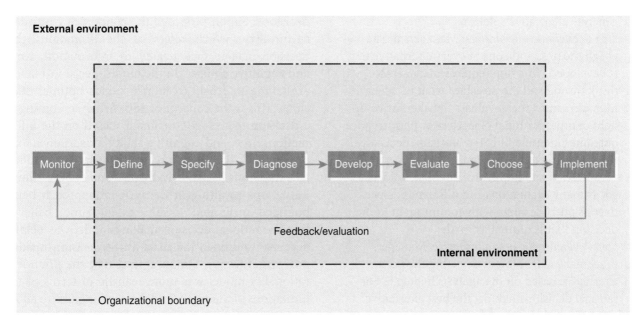

FIGURE 4.7 Steps in the rational decision-making approach.
Modified from Daft RL. *Management* 12th ed. Boston, MA: Cengage Learning; 2016.

how they define an organizational problem or opportunity.

- *Step 3. Specify decision objectives:* Managers must decide what type of outcomes they want for the organization. This includes some type of desirable organizational objective or performance outcome. The objectives are established based on the problem or opportunity the organization faces. This step highlights how an organization's external environment influences the internal objectives set by the organization.

- *Step 4. Diagnose the problem or opportunity:* Managers must analyze the problem or opportunity. This requires a close examination of all the information and may require the managers to do additional fact-finding to better understand the problems or opportunities the organization faces and required decisions. Managers are better able to generate alternative solutions if they have a thorough understanding of the issues the organization faces. Decisions that are complex or technical may require managers to involve others with the technical knowledge and expertise to ensure an accurate diagnosis.

- *Step 5. Develop alternative solutions:* Managers must develop a set of alternatives or different ways in which the organization could achieve their desired performance outcome. This is the idea generation stage of the decision-making process. Managers should challenge themselves to think of creative and innovative solutions. Decisions that are going to have a significant impact on the organization should involve key stakeholders and draw on their expertise to generate alternative solutions.

- *Step 6. Evaluate alternatives:* Managers must weigh the pros and cons of every alternative that is developed. This step requires managers to think through all the possible "what if" scenarios. Managers must then evaluate the alternatives in light of organizational objectives or performance outcomes identified in Step 3. Again, decisions that are going to have a significant impact on the organization should involve key stakeholders to get as many evaluations and different perspectives as possible along with commitment to the decision that is ultimately made.

- *Step 7. Choose the best alternative:* Managers must make a decision by selecting the best alternative based on the analysis in Step 6. For rational decision-making, the best alternative can frequently be identified based on objectives as complete or nearly complete information is frequently available.

- *Step 8. Implement the chosen alternative:* Managers must implement the decision to accomplish the desired objective. This requires managers to communicate the decision and persuade followers to help carry out the decision. Communication is vital at this stage in the decision-making process. Managers must clearly articulate the decision and the rationale for the decision to stakeholders inside and outside the organization. Decisions that are going to have a significant impact on the organization should reflect the decision-making process, as well as all of the pros and cons considered.[18]

Economic models serve as the conceptual foundation for the rational decision model. This model gives preference to economic, financial, operational, and other types of measurable information. This model assumes that the decision-makers possess complete information on alternatives and their consequences. A limitation of the model is that managers do not often follow this model in practice because they often lack complete information or the capacity to process the information they have in the time available to make a decision. Obtaining complete information is costly and time consuming to gather and analyze.[16] In response, the bounded-rationality model was proposed.

Bounded-Rationality Model

Herbert Simon developed the bounded-rationality model or administrative model of decision-making[19,20] to reflect the limitations of the rational decision model. He recognized that decision-makers often lack complete information on which to base their decisions. Simon proposed the concept of **bounded rationality**, which refers to the limitations that decision-makers face related to information, time, and cognitive ability.[20] In the model, decision-makers are trying to reach acceptable versus optimal decisions. This is the concept of **satisficing** or coming to a decision that is "good enough" based on the information, time, and cognitive ability a decision-maker possesses.[21] The model recognizes that individuals face trade-offs based on individual and organizational limitations resulting in the rational approach being bounded (or limited) to some extent. Simon believed that the rational decision-making model was helpful because it outlined the steps in the decision-making process. However, Simon argued that the bounded-rationality model was more realistic in terms of the limitations of managers and their willingness to adopt an acceptable versus an optimal decision. The model was more realistic because it is more reflective of the conditions managers face when trying to make a decision.[16,22] In response, the intuitive decision-making model was developed.

The **intuitive decision-making model** is an administrative model that focuses on an individual's experiences and judgment when making decisions versus quantifiable information. The model was developed in contrast to the systematic approaches advanced by the rational models. Nonprogrammed decisions lend themselves to this decision-making approach because they are ambiguous, nonroutine, undefined, and unstructured types of decisions. Decision-makers base their potential solutions on their experience by scanning their environment and looking for patterns to cue them into the solutions they should consider based on their prior experience. This helps the decision-maker begin to define the decision and generate alternative solutions. A decision-maker who has experienced a similar decision context can usually generate a number of potential options based on similarities in context and the success or failure of previous solutions. The intuitive approach, drawing on bounded-rationality, recognizes the cognitive limits of individuals. Decision-makers usually consider and evaluate one solution alternative at a time. If the alternative is not viable, the decision-maker will either reformulate it or disregard it completely. Considering and evaluating alternatives is an iterative process until an acceptable versus optimal solution is identified.[16,23] This approach to decision-making is most useful when there is incomplete information and it is difficult to identify all potential alternative and their consequences, but the goal of the decision is clear and decision-makers have relevant experience to draw upon.[15]

Political Decision-Making Model

The political decision-making model focuses on the personal interests and goals of key decision-makers or influential groups or coalitions within an organization. It is the only option for decisions where there is incomplete information, alternatives, and their consequences are not apparent, and there is not even agreement on the purpose of the decision for the organization.[15] This model does not view organizations as having a single unifying problem or opportunity but, instead, diverse interests because of differing interests and agendas of key decision-makers and dominant coalitions. Bargaining, negotiating, and making side deals are central to the political decision-making model, in contrast to the ordered steps of the rational model.[24] This leads to decentralized and incremental decision-making based on those who have power in the organization. This model considers few alternatives when a problem arises because powerful decision-makers do not

want to upset the balance of power among the dominant coalitions. This approach usually uses satisficing to come to a consensus on an acceptable decision for each of the dominant coalitions through negotiations and compromise.[18]

Decision-Making Styles

Rowe and Boulgarides developed the decision-style model, as shown in **FIGURE 4.8**.[25,26] The model identified four different styles that managers use when making decisions: analytical, conceptual, directive, and behavioral. Decision-making styles vary on two dimensions: value orientation and tolerance for ambiguity. Value orientation refers to how much concern a manager has for tasks or relationships when making decisions. Tolerance for ambiguity refers to how much ambiguity a manager can accept when making decisions. For most managers, one style of decision-making tends to predominate. The following are common managerial decision-making styles:

Directive Style

Managers with this dominant decision-making style are rational and autocratic decision-makers. They like structure, and they like to take control of decisions and the decision-making processes. Their focus during the decision-making process is concentrated on accomplishing tasks, being efficient, and achieving results. They excel at making short-range, internal organizational decisions in a quick and efficient manner. The downsides of this style are that they can be short-sided and tend to make decisions before they have a sufficient amount of information on which to base their decision.[16,25]

Analytic Style

Managers with this dominant decision-making style are task focused but have a higher tolerance for ambiguity in the decision-making process. They like to consider a lot of information (but in a structured way) and the fine details before making a decision. They excel at making long-range and important decisions. A downside of this style is that they can take a long time to make a decision.[16,25]

Conceptual Style

Managers with this dominant decision-making style are big, conceptual thinkers. They are eager to gather information and ideas from multiple sources. These decision-makers are relationship focused. This focus helps them obtain information as well as process the information. They draw on relationships with their

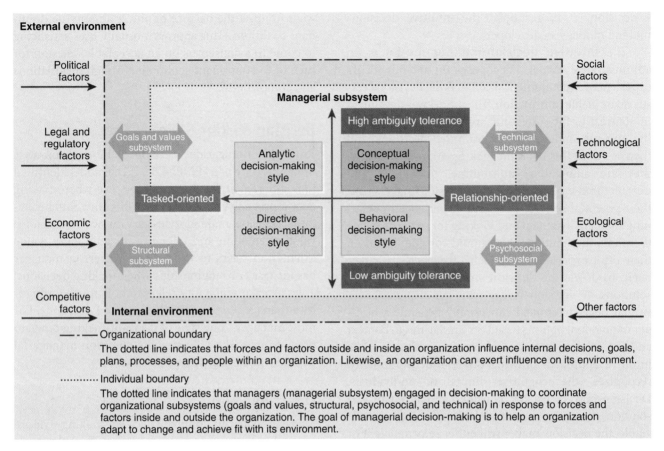

FIGURE 4.8 Decision-making styles.

Based on information from and modification of Kast FE, Rosenzweig JE. *Organization and Management: A Systems and Contingency Approach.* 4th ed. New York, NY: McGraw-Hill; 1985. and Rowe AJ, Boulgarides JD. Decision styles—a perspective. *Leadership Organ Dev J.* 1983;4(4):3–9.

subordinates and other organizational members for ideas and insights and will even involve them at times in the decision-making process. A downside of this type is that they tend to "think" more than "do," which can lead to limited results and perceived lower levels of performance.[16,25]

Behavioral Style

Managers using the behavioral decision-making style focus on the well-being of the organization and those working in it. These managers desire to minimize workplace conflict and maximize cooperation. Communication helps this style to build relationships. A drawback of this style is that users tend to make short-term decisions and to favor meetings.[16,25]

Conclusion

Planning is a critical process for public health professionals and organizations today. Planning is a process that public health organizations use to establish direction, priorities, and goals. The process also outlines the steps, actions, and activities organizations will need to complete to accomplish their organizational goals.

Managers are responsible for communicating goals and plans to employees thçroughout the organization by conveying what the organization will do and how it will do it. Managers translate strategic organization-wide goals into tactical goals for divisions, departments, and other organizational units and then to operational goals for smaller units and work groups depending on their managerial level within the organization. The MBO process is frequently used to link organizational goals through all of these levels down to individual performance goals. Decision-making is integral to the planning process. Understanding different approaches and decision-making styles helps organizations develop the appropriate type of plans to achieve their goals.

Discussion Questions

1. Why is planning important to an organization?
2. What are plans? Explain the difference between standing plans and single-use plans. Provide an example of each type of plan.
3. What are goals? How are goals and objectives related, and how are they sometimes considered to be different?

4. Compare and contrast goals and plans.
5. What is management by objectives (MBO)? How is MBO used to creative a means-end chain in organizations? Why is this important?
6. What are the elements of the S.M.A.R.T. and S.M.A.R.T.E.R. approaches to goal-setting?
7. Discuss the different types of plans developed at the different levels of an organization. Provide an example of each type of plan.
8. Discuss the decision-making process. Explain why decisions are important in an organization. How is decision-making related to planning?
9. What are the different types of decisions? Provide an example of each decision type.
10. Compare and contrast the rational, administrative, and political approaches to decision-making.
11. Compare and contrast the four basic styles of decision-making.

Learning Activities

1. Set a short-term and long-term personal or professional goal. Use the S.M.A.R.T. and S.M.A.R.T.E.R. approaches to goal-setting to develop and state your goals. What is the difference between the two approaches?
2. Select a public health organization that interests you and locate their strategic plan. Select an organizational goal that interests you and discuss whether the goal is a S.M.A.R.T. (or S.M.A.R.T.E.R.) goal. Why or why not?
3. Select a public health organization and locate their strategic plan. Analyze the elements of their strategic plan. What are strengths of the plan? What are weaknesses of the plan?
4. Analyze a good and a bad professional decision you have made or observed using each of the decision-making approaches that were discussed. For the good decision, what decision style was used? For the bad decision, what decision style was used? Why do you think the decision worked or did not work in each of the decisions?
5. Think of a manager you are currently working for or have worked for in the past. What was the manager's dominant decision-making style? Support your discussion with an example.

References

1. Robbins SP, Judge TA. *Organizational Behavior*. 14th ed. Upper Saddle River, NJ: Prentice-Hall; 2011.
2. Kast FE, Rosenzweig JE. *Organization and Management: A Systems and Contingency Approach*. 4th ed. New York, NY: McGraw-Hill; 1985.
3. Ledlow GR, Stephens JH. *Leadership for Health Professionals: Theory, Skills, and Applications*. 3rd ed. Burlington, MA: Jones & Bartlett Learning; 2018.
4. Kaplan RS, Norton DP. Mastering the management system. *Harv Bus Rev*. 2008;86(1):62–77.
5. Locke EA, Latham GP. New directions in goal-setting theory. *Curr Dir Psychol*. 2006;15(5):265–268. doi:10.1111/j.1467-8721.2006.00449.x.
6. Latham GP, Locke EA. New developments in and directions for goal-setting research. *Eur Psychol*. 2007;12(4):290–300. doi:10.1027/1016-9040.12.4.290.
7. Locke EA, Latham GP. *Goal Setting: A Motivational Technique That Works!* Englewood Cliffs, NJ: PrenticeHall; 1984.
8. Drucker P. *The Practice of Management*. New York, NY: Harper and Row; 1954.
9. Doran GT. There's a S.M.A.R.T. way to write management's goals and objectives. *Manage Rev (AMA Forum)*. 1981;70(11):35–36.
10. Ginter PM, Duncan WJ, Swayne LE. *Strategic Management of Health Care Organizations*. 8th ed. Hoboken, NJ: Wiley; 2018.
11. Society for Human Resourc Management. Mission & vision statements: What is the difference between mission, vision and values statements? https://www.shrm.org/resources andtools/tools-and-samples/hr-qa/pages/isthe readifference betweenacompany'smission,visionandvalue statements .aspx. Published March 5, 2018. Accessed July 23, 2019.
12. Centers for Disease Control and Prevention. Assessment & planning models, frameworks & tools. https://www .cdc.gov/publichealthgateway/cha/assessment.html. Published November 9, 2015. Accessed July 23, 2019.
13. National Association of County and City Health Officials and the Center for Disease Control and Prevention. Mobilizing for Action through Planning and Partnerships. https://www .naccho.org/programs/public-health-infrastructure /performance-improvement/community-health-assessment /mapp. Published 2001. Accessed July 23, 2019.
14. Association of State and Territorial Health Organizations and the Centers for Disease Control and Prevention. *Developing a State Health Improvement Plan: Guidance and Resources*. http://www.astho.org/WorkArea/DownloadAsset. aspx?id=6597. Published 2011. Accessed July 23, 2019.
15. Daft RL. *Management*. 12th ed. Boston, MA: Cengage Learning; 2016.
16. Borkowski B. *Organizational Behavior, Theory, and Design in Health Care*. 2nd ed. Burlington, MA: Jones & Bartlett Learning; 2016.
17. Lussier RN, Achua CF. *Leadership: Theory, Application, and Skill Development*. 6th ed. Boston, MA: Cengage Learning; 2016.
18. Daft RL. *Organization Theory and Design*. 12th ed. Boston, MA: Cengage Learning; 2016.
19. Simon HA. *Administrative Behavior: A Study of Decision-Making Process in Administrative Organization*. 4th ed. New York, NY: Free Press; 1997.

20. Simon H. Theories of bounded rationality. *Deci. Org.* 1972;1(1):161–176.

21. Simon HA. *Models of Bounded Rationality: Empirically Grounded Economic Reason.* Vol. 3. Cambridge, MA: MIT Press; 1997.

22. Johnson JA, Rossow CC. *Health Organizations: Theory, Behavior, and Development.* 2nd ed. Burlington, MA: Jones & Bartlett Learning; 2019.

23. Daft RL. *The Leadership Experience.* 7th ed. Boston, MA: Cengage Learning; 2018.

24. Nitta K. Decision making. Encyclopedia Britannica. https://www.britannica.com/topic/decision-making. Published January 24, 2014. Accessed July 23, 2019.

25. Rowe AJ, Boulgarides JD. Decision styles: a perspective. *Leadership Organ Dev J.* 1983;4(4):3–9. doi:10.1108/eb053534.

26. Boulgarides JD, Cohen, WA. Leadership style vs. leadership tactics. *J Appl Manage Entrepeneur.* 2001;6(1):59–73.

Suggested Readings and Websites

American Planning Association. https://www.planning.org/publications/document/9148247/

ASTHO. Evidence-based public health. http://www.astho.org/Programs/Evidence-Based-Public-Health/

CDC. Assessment and planning models, frameworks, and tools. https://www.cdc.gov/stltpublichealth/cha/assessment.html

CDC. Centers for disease control and prevention—Planning exercises. https://www.cdc.gov/aging/emergency/planning_tools/planning-exercises.htm

CDC. Community health assessment and health improvement plan. https://www.cdc.gov/stltpublichealth/cha/index.html

CDC. Contingency planning template. https://www2.cdc.gov/cdcup/library/templates/CDC_UP_Contingency_Planning_Template.doc

CDC. National health initiatives, strategies and action plans. https://www.cdc.gov/stltpublichealth/strategy/index.html

CDC. State and local planning examples. https://www.cdc.gov/aging/emergency/planning_tools/local.htm

Morbidity and Mortality Weekly. Evaluating the impact of national public health department accreditation—United States, 2016. https://www.cdc.gov/mmwr/volumes/65/wr/mm6531a3.htm

NACCHO. http://toolbox.naccho.org/pages/index.html

NACCHO. Resource center for community health assessments and community health improvement plans. http://archived.naccho.org/topics/infrastructure/chaip/chachip-online-resource-center.cfm

National Association of County and City Health Officials. Strategic planning. https://www.naccho.org/programs/public-health-infrastructure/performance-improvement/strategic-planning

The Community Guide. https://www.thecommunityguide.org/

Tools for Implementing and Evidence-Based Approach in Public Health Practice. https://www.cdc.gov/pcd/issues/2012/11_0324.htm

World Health Organization. National health policies, strategic and plans. http://www.who.int/nationalpolicies/resources/en/

CHAPTER 5

Organizing and Managing Change in Public Health Organizations

LEARNING OBJECTIVES

After reading this chapter, you should be able to:

- Define the management function of organizing.
- Identify the contingency factors and other factors that influence organization design.
- Discuss the differences between mechanistic and organic organizational structures.
- Compare and contrast the five general types of organizational structures.
- Define organizational change.
- Explain imitation and invention change strategies.
- Describe the different types of organizational change.
- Discuss the sources of organizational change.
- Explain why organizations resist change and strategies to overcome resistance.
- Compare and contrast the organizational change models.

▶ Introduction

The managerial function of **organizing** is concerned with how an organization's design and structure can be used to achieve organizational goals.[1] Managers strive to ensure that an organization is internally configured to transform input resources into value-added outputs that satisfy the organization's stakeholders. The organizing function is also important in controlling the transformation process and designing mechanisms that create value and contribute to achieving an organization's goals and objectives. The organizing function depends on the planning function to determine organizational goals that must be achieved to accomplish an organization's mission and realize its vision. These strategic goals must be translated into specific products, services, and other organizational outputs that will be produced to satisfy the organization's primary stakeholders, such as its customers, clients, patients, donors/funders, and so forth, depending on the type of organization.[2,3]

Managers must determine what resources are needed to produce these outputs, such as what personnel must be hired, what equipment and other technology will be used, what materials are necessary, what information and knowledge are required, among other resource inputs. Managers must also make decisions about creating the value chain within their organization. The **value chain** is the set of activities, processes, resources, and organizations use to assure that the necessary quantity and quality of outputs will be produced as efficient as possible to maximize value to stakeholders. (keep the superscript 4 for citation at the end of this sentence)[4] Managers create **organizational structures** to pattern and control these value-creating processes and activities. Managers must also constantly monitor the organization's external environment and its internal operations to identify problems and opportunities that might signal the need for **organizational change** to its structure, processes, and outcomes in order to assure ongoing value creation.[5,6] An organization's structure is a mechanism that can be used to help it adapt to its external environment by aligning its internal processes and systems through organizational change.[7,8] This chapter focuses on creating adaptive organizational structures that deliver and sustain value.

▶ Organizations and Organizing

Organizations can be thought of as goal-directed social systems. Organizations are considered social systems because they are comprised of people who are working together to accomplish the goals of the organization.[9] The complexity of organizations varies; however, organizations consist of a set of systems and subsystems, as we have seen and discussed.[10] **Organizing** is the process of creating the patterned relationships or social interactions and activities necessary for the organization to accomplish its goals.[11] This patterning of organizational activities is ultimately reflected in an organization's organizational structure.

Organizational Structure

The **organizational structure** reflects decisions regarding how activities will be coordinated, how **authority** and responsibility will be assigned, how information will flow, and how decision-making and control will take place across an organization.[5] An **organizational chart** depicts a specific organization's structure.[12] The organizational chart shows the number of levels of management, the functional activity centers (or departments), the key reporting relationships, and the delegation of authority (**chain of command**). An organizational chart is simply a snapshot of an organization's structure at a specific point in time. Organizational structure is constantly changing in most organizations as they adapt to the changes taking place in their external environment and to the needs for internal adjustments in how their activities are organized and coordinated throughout the transformation process.[5,8] For example, new technology influences organizational processes and structure as certain organizational activities are automated. Therefore, organizations must constantly consider how to design and redesign an organization to accomplish its goals.

Organizational Design

Organizational design is the process of deciding how best to structure an organization to accomplish its goals.[1] Organizational design begins during the planning process. An organization's goals must be translated into specific organizational products, services, or other outputs that will be produced to satisfy specific stakeholder needs. Organizational design takes these outputs and works backward to determine how they will be produced, what resources will be needed, and what transformation processes will be used. The concepts of differentiation and integration are used to create a division of labor to maximize efficiency in the production of outputs. **Division of labor** is assigning different tasks and activities to different individuals or groups of people/teams. **Differentiation** typically involves identifying the specific **tasks**, or units of activity, that must be accomplished to produce specific outputs. **Integration** involves putting together similar or related tasks or activities into **jobs** that require similar skills and technology, depending on decisions regarding how tasks will be performed. Then, similar or related jobs are typically assembled into **work units**, and related work units are typically grouped into **departments** that might be grouped into **divisions**, depending on the size of the organization, that ultimately comprise the overall organization. Through this integration process, an organizational structure is built from the tasks required to produce the organization's outputs as efficiently as possible.

Contingency Factors

There are a number of factors, termed contingency factors, that need to be considered in creating an organization's structure (as shown in **FIGURE 5.1**). **Contingency factors** are factors that influence an organization and are outside its control. Organizational design, as the particular structural design, is dependent, to some degree, on the decisions made about these factors. Daft identifies five factors that are important to consider when designing an organization, as shown in Figure 5.1.[9]

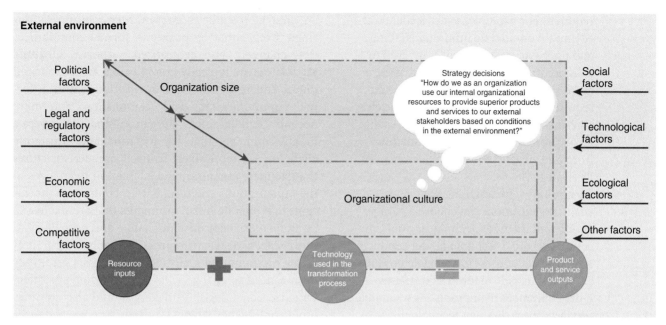

FIGURE 5.1 Contingency factors to consider when designing an organization.

Based on information from Daft RL. *Organization Theory and Design*. 12th ed. Boston, MA: Cengage Learning; 2016.

1. **Environment**—The external environment of some organizations is much more dynamic than that of others.[13] **Dynamism** refers to the rate of change in an organization's environment.[14] There are at least three aspects of dynamism in organizational environments: how many factors are changing, the degree to which they are changing, and how rapidly they are changing.[14,15] Some organizations may have multiple changes taking place simultaneously in their political, economic, social, technological, ecological, competitive, and legal/regulatory environments. Each of these changes could have different magnitudes of impact on the organization and could occur at different rates. Organizations in more dynamic environments face making decisions about needed changes more often than organizations in more stable external environments. Most healthcare organizations tend to be in very dynamic environments and need a more flexible organizational structure that allows them to adapt quickly to environmental changes.[13,16,17]

2. **Size**—Organizations vary in their size. Some organizations are small with only a few employees, whereas other organizations can be very large with thousands to hundreds of thousands of employees. Small organizations can operate with a very simple organizational structure. In contrast, large organizations require much more complex structures to coordinate their extensive operations. An organization's structure will become more complex as an organization increases in size to reflect the diversity of activities and units required in the transformation process. Organizational structures that are large and complex typically become more difficult to change.[6,8]

3. **Strategy**—Organizational strategy represents the set of related decisions an organization makes about how it will deliver superior value and outputs to its stakeholders. In competitive markets, this is referred to as achieving a **competitive advantage** relative to competitors. Some generic strategies that organizations can adopt include the following: **differentiation** where they seek to offer superior value in their outputs to create market preference; **cost leadership** where they seek to deliver a lower cost for their outputs; and **focus** where they might choose to limit their offering to some subset of a broader market while pursuing differentiation or cost leadership.[18] These are just a few examples of the myriad strategies organizations can pursue. The organizational structure for these different strategies can vary substantially due to the resources required for each strategy and the consequent value chain that is

required. For example, a cost-leader strategy might emphasize minimum staffing and tight **expense** control compared to a differentiation that might emphasize more services and amenities that would require more staff and resources. The clear consensus in organizational design is that an organization's structure should flow from and support the accomplishment of its strategy.[19]

4.   **Technology**—In designing their value chain, organizations can choose a number of different methods, techniques, tools, processes, and other technologies for producing their outputs.[4] Producing tangible products as outputs usually requires significantly more equipment than producing intangible services. These different technologies have implications for designing organizational structure. For example, if an organization decided to use robotics or other higher-level automation in its production process, it might need fewer operational-level employees, but more expensive knowledge workers. The production process of an organization that employs more sophisticated automation, as opposed to a more manual process, has implications for organizational design.

5.   **Culture**—An organization's culture consists of a shared set of beliefs, assumptions, and values that guide the social interactions in an organization.[7,20] The interaction of these elements creates a unique environment and context inside an organization. An organization's history, industry, employee mix, location, business markets, leadership vision, management styles, among other factors, also influence organizational culture.[5] For example, organizations operating in international or specific community contexts must consider local beliefs, assumptions, and values when designing an organization's operations and design.

These contingency factors have implications for organizational design. The factors influence the extent to which organizations adopt a rigid or flexible organizational structure. In the literature, two broad types of organizational structures are identified—mechanistic and organic.[13,16] Mechanistic structures are more rigid, whereas organic structures are more flexible (**TABLE 5.1** and **FIGURE 5.2**). **Mechanistic structures**

are characterized by more rigid hierarchical relationships, fixed duties by positions, formal communication channels, and centralized authority. **Organic structures** are typically more flexible, with expanded duties and responsibilities in positions, more informal communications and relationships, and more decentralized authority. Organizations that operate in environments that are dynamic and constantly changing are more likely to need organic structures that facilitate organizational adaptation to changes in the organization's environment. In contrast, organizations that operate in environments that are stable and do not experience constant change are more likely to utilize mechanistic structures. Mechanistic structures create economies of scale and reduce costs since they do not need to change what they are doing as often. Organizational decision-makers should also consider other contingency factors (i.e., size, strategy, and technology) to determine whether an organization's structure should be more rigid or flexible.[21,22] For example, a larger organization may find a more rigid structure useful, whereas smaller organizations may find a more flexible structure helpful.

▶ Structural Design Factors

When designing an organizational structure, a number of other factors that have important implications for the effectiveness, efficiency, and adaptability of the organization need to be considered. Daft identifies a number of factors that are important to consider when designing the structure of an organization.[23]

1.   **Centralization versus Decentralization**—The degree to which authority and responsibility in an organization are delegated determines who is involved in making decisions, how quickly decisions are made, and who holds the authority, responsibility, and accountability at each level in the organization. **Centralization** indicates that decisions are made at the higher management levels in an organization. **Decentralization** involves **delegation** or pushing authority, responsibility, and accountability down to lower levels of management and even to key employees. This allows for more flexibility and timely decision-making and action. However, decentralization can require more coordination to assure that actions are focused on accomplishing goals versus working against one another.

TABLE 5.1 Characteristics of Mechanistic and Organic Organizational Structures		
Characteristics	**Mechanistic Organizations**	**Organic Organizations**
Tasks	Rigidly defined and standardized	Redefined and revised as needed through teamwork and collaboration
	Broken down into smaller, specialized parts	Holistic view of activities that emphasizes how the whole consists of interdependent tasks
Organizational Structure	Strict organizational hierarchy	Less hierarchy
	Structure reflects hierarchy and chain-of-command to ensure control	Structure reflects less hierarchy and is configured to promote more collaboration
	Many vertical layers and levels	Less vertical layers which results in a flatter more horizontal organization
Roles	Detailed and clearly defined or fixed roles, which results in a taller more complex structure	Delegation of authority to enhance roles
Communication	Formal, top down (vertical) communication	Less formal communication with a mix of top down (vertical), bottom up, and horizontal communication
Specialization	Employees develop firm-specific expertise in their specialty	Employees are encouraged to develop expertise outside their specialty
Environment	Operates best in a stable environment	Operates best in a dynamic environment wither faster rates of change and greater uncertainty
	Slow rate of technological and market changes	Rapid rate of technological and market changes, often multiple sources of change and simultaneous changes
Control	Centralized at the top of the organization	More decentralized throughout the organization

Modified from Burns T, Stalker G. *The Management of Innovation*. 3rd ed. New York, NY: Oxford University Press; 1994.

2. **Line versus Staff**—Most organizations have two broad groups of employees—line and staff. **Line** employees are concerned directly with the production of an organization's outputs, and so their managers are known as line managers and their departments as line departments. Without line employees, outputs of the organization would not be produced and stakeholder's interests would not be satisfied. **Staff** employees provide support services to line employees to allow them to focus on producing outputs and are supervised by staff managers and work in staff departments. For example, in a public health clinic, the nurse manager would be a line **employee** overseeing the delivery of care to patients, whereas the human resources manager would be a staff employee relieving the nurse of some of the personnel

Positions on the Mechanistic and Organic Continuum

Burns and Stalker noted that there are stages on the continuum between the two extremes points (mechanistic and organic) and organizations may operate within both systems simultaneously.

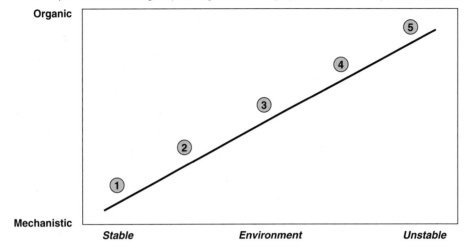

Position 1	Position 2	Position 3	Position 4	Position 5
Well-defined hierarchy, bureaucracy structure with high degree of formational, horizontal differentiation (i.e., task/job definitions) and positional terms of reference, downward communications with little participation in decision making.	Bureaucracy structure but with some flexibility to meet operational contingencies.	Bureaucracy structure but use of horizontal linkages (i.e., cross depart-mental meetings, teams and task forces) to facilitate communication and coordination of operational activities.	Matrix type organization relying on teamwork to accomplish goals.	Learning organization (flexible structure) using project teams to ensure goal attainment; low complexity and formalization, uses all types of communications (upward, down-ward, lateral) to coordinate activities with high degree of participation in decision making based on expertise rather than position.

FIGURE 5.2 Positions on the mechanistic and organic continuum.

Reproduced from Table 22-3 in Borkowski N. *Organizational Behavior, Theory, and Design in Health Care*. 2nd ed. Burlington, MA: Jones & Bartlett Publishing; 2016.

management work. The mix of line versus staff employees in an organization has implications for efficiently using key staff.

3. **Vertical versus Horizontal—Vertical structure** in an organization is concerned with the number of managerial levels in the organization. The more levels of man-agement, the "taller" the organizational structure and the fewer levels of manage-ment, the "flatter" the structure. **Horizontal structure** is concerned with the number of employees reporting to each manager,

sometimes referred to as **span of control**. The "wider" the horizontal structure, the more employees are reporting to each manager, and the "narrower" the struc-ture, the fewer employees are reporting to each manager. There is typically an inverse relationship between vertical and horizon-tal structure. That is, the taller the vertical structure, the narrower the horizontal structure, and vice versa. Generally, taller vertical and narrower horizontal structures tend to be more mechanistic, but can create more economies of scale, and, consequently, lower cost per unit of production. Flatter vertical structure and wider horizontal structures typically tend to be more organic and more flexible in response to change and adaptation.

4. **Knowledge versus Operative**—In recent decades, organizations in advanced economies and industries have shifted from predominately producing tangible products to producing more intangible service outputs. A consequence of these changes has been a shift in the composition of the workforce of modern organizations from primarily lesser skilled operative employees to more skilled knowledge workers. This shift has significant implications for the technology an organization adopts and the dynamism of its environment—two key contingency factors in organizational design.

While all of the contingency factors and other considerations in organizational design can be overwhelming, there are some clear trends emerging in the structuring of modern organizations. First, there is a decreasing division of labor. Modern organizations that employ increasing numbers of knowledge workers are engaging in **job enlargement** and **job enrichment**, adding more tasks and responsibility, respectively, to these workers' jobs due to their enhanced capacity to assume these responsibilities.[24] This enhances motivation and can increase the flexibility of the organization and the engagement of these employees. Second, modern organizations are clearly shifting from more vertical "command and control" to more horizontal "connect and collaborate" types of structures, with a corresponding decentralization of authority, responsibility, and accountability.[2] With the increasing numbers of knowledge workers and more rapidly changing external environments, most modern organizations have made this shift from more vertical to more horizontal structures to aid the organization in being flexible and adaptive to demands for change.[21]

Types of Organizational Structures

There is a wide variety of options for designing organizational structures with many possible variations, given the factors and considerations discussed earlier. How organizations decide to configure their structure depends on decisions about the factors discussed in the previous sections. The six types of organizational structures commonly used include: (1) simple structure, (2) functional structure, (3) divisional structure, (4) matrix structure, (5) team structure, and (6) virtual network structure.[6,9,20]

Simple Structure

Small organizations with only a few employees do not need much organizational structure. The **simple structure** is the default option for most small organizations where authority and decision-making are centralized with the manager, executive director or **chief operating officer**, and there are few to no departments, few formal work rules, and no levels of management (**FIGURE 5.3**). However, as organizations become larger, there is a need for more complex structures. Complex structures reflect organizations where decision-making is delegated throughout the organization, there are many departments, many formal work rules, and several levels of management.

Simple structures provide a number of advantages. Job enlargement and enrichment is an important advantage of this structure. Employees have a range of job duties and responsibilities. They are able to gain a diverse set of skills and experiences, which makes them valuable to their current organization and future employers. Communication can be easier in smaller organizations because there is not a rigid hierarchical structure in which information has to flow up and down. Generally, employees in small organizations know one another and are able to develop relationships across the organization. This facilitates communication and the flow of information. Simple

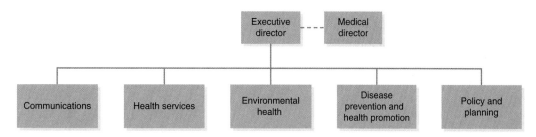

FIGURE 5.3 Simple organizational structure.

structures mean that the manager (or central decision-maker) can quickly make and implement decisions. Decision-makers can also obtain information relatively easily from stakeholders inside and outside the organization to inform decision-making. This allows organizations to respond to changes in their external environment.[5,6,23,25]

Simple structures can also have a number of disadvantages. Job enrichment can lead to frustration and overwork. This can lead to employee turnover and retention issues, which can adversely impact organizational processes and output. Employees can become confused over their role and responsibilities within the organization, which can lead to interpersonal conflict. This can lead to inefficiency and ineffectiveness. Centralized decision-making can be limited or one-sided because the organization does not have a management team that brings diverse perspectives to the table. This can limit the organization's strategy and negatively affect their organizational effectiveness. The lack of organizational formality can negatively impact organizational processes and outputs. Standardized policies, procedures, and processes promote consistency across an organization. Failure to have such standardization can influence an organization's ability to consistently generate high-quality outputs and organizational value.[5,6,23,25]

Functional Structure

The **functional structure** is probably the most widely used type of organizational structure. Department or business units are a hallmark of this organizational structure. This structure groups together common activities, skills, expertise, and resource usage into departments. Organizational charts reveal that functional structures utilize a vertical structure where authority, information, and communication flow up and down the organization (**FIGURE 5.4**). Employees are typically organized into organizational functions (or disciplines), such as finance, accounting, marketing, production, research and development, and human resources. Public health organizations often have departments or divisions dedicated to community health planning and evaluation, quality improvement and **accreditation**, health policy, community disease control and prevention, public health nursing, environmental health, school and adolescent health, overdose prevention, and sexually transmitted diseases, among others. Hospitals include nursing, surgery, environmental, nutrition, and other types of departments. Therefore, the type of organization determines what types of functional areas are required and reflected in the organizational chart.

Functional structures offer a number of advantages. First, the structure is easy and intuitive to design. This structure groups together employees who do similar or related jobs. Generally, these people and positions have similar training, perform similar work, and use similar types of technology and information systems. The functional structure groups these individuals together into a reporting unit or department. This structure facilitates communication because the department has a high degree of shared knowledge. People can learn from one another because their jobs are similar or interdependent. Additionally, functional structures allow organizations to realize economies of scale. Departments are able to synergize and share resources, which can help lower costs and create efficiencies. For employees, departments present a clear and progressive career path. Finally, functional structures clearly outline authority and the chain of command. This can help promote consistent communication and decision-making across a department, which can help promote individual and collective goal attainment.[6,20,23]

Functional structures also have a number of disadvantages. Functional structures focus the work of the unit internally. Employees can become exclusively focused on department goals and lose sight of an organization's broader goals. As a result, departments can be slow or reluctant to change to help meet broader organizational goals. This can also negatively impact interdepartmental relations. Departments that are internally focused may not meet the service or support needs of other departments. Diminished cross-functional communication and cooperation can cause working relationships, organizational performance, and morale to decline. Functional structures tend to concentrate authority and decision-making at higher levels of the organization. This can lead to slow decision-making and diminished initiative, creativity, and innovation. As functional organizations grow, each function tends to become larger and more complex. This complexity further complicates coordination and potentially diminishes performance of the function (or department) and overall organizational performance.[6,20,23]

Divisional Structure

The divisional structure (sometimes called a multidivisional or M-form structure) organizes units based on geographical, market, or product and service groups (**FIGURE 5.5**). The structure has evolved to overcome some of the disadvantages of the functional structure. Particularly, this structure emerged

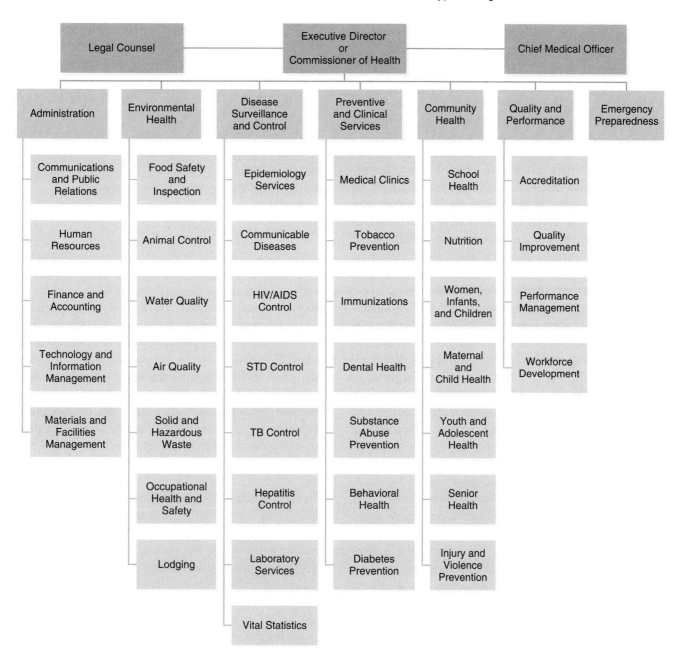

FIGURE 5.4 County health department organizational char.

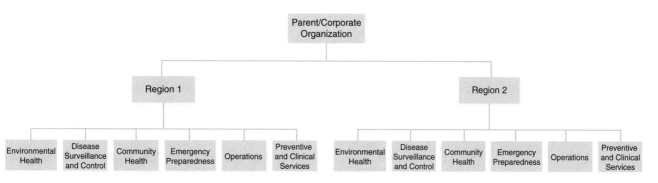

FIGURE 5.5 Divisional organizational structure.

to overcome challenges arising from size and to give a division more autonomy over decision-making and operations that are relevant to some group of customers, clients, or other external stakeholders. A top executive or director oversees and exerts strategic control over an operating division (that consists of a number of a different functional units or departments), such as setting major goals, allocating capital, and coordinating interdivisional issues to maximize overall organizational performance of the larger parent/corporate organization that controls the divisions. Typically, each operating division acts as a semiautonomous operating unit that makes decisions for all of the functional departments included in the division and operates as a self-sufficient entity within boundaries set by the larger parent/corporate organization.

Divisional structures offer a number of advantages. A major advantage is that it allows organizations to grow very large by simply adding new divisions or splitting existing divisions. For example, a divisional structure is appropriate if an organization grows to the point that its functional structure is inefficient. The divisional structure allows for more flexibility and faster responses by the parent/corporate organization in more dynamic external environments because it is made up of smaller, more nimble divisions. Divisional structures have the functional departments they need to meet their unique needs and compete more effectively. The division structure helps to coordinate activities and resources across the functional units that make up the division. This helps provide a greater degree of flexibility, so that the division can focus on meeting the specific needs of customers, products, services, geographic locations, or other groups. For example, a state department of public health could have a division dedicated to specific services like substance abuse and mental health, or specific age groups like children or older adults. The department could also have a division that focuses on specific communities within a broader geographic area.[6,20,23]

Divisional structures also have a number of potential disadvantages. For example, duplication of resources can occur. Each division in a larger multi-divisional organization may feel that it is necessary to have certain functional areas, such as human resources or finance or public relations versus centralizing these functions at the parent/corporate organization level and sharing staff departments. As a result, this can lead to duplication with each division having these departments. Additionally, this can lead to inefficient use of organizational resources and reduced economies of scale in the larger parent/corporate organization. This leads to another potential disadvantage where

divisions within a multi-divisional organization have limited technical specialization and expertise versus acquiring more extensive expertise from the parent/corporation organization. Finally, coordination can be difficult across multiple divisions, depending on their level of autonomy. This can lead to interorganizational competition for customers and resources from the parent/corporate organization, thereby generating significant levels of conflict that can diminish an organization's overall performance.[6,9,20]

Matrix Structure

The matrix structure combines multiple organizational structures to mitigate some of the major disadvantages and maximize the advantages of the functional and divisional structures. The matrix structure results in a dual chain of command—one at the parent organization's functional level and one at the division level. Matrix structures are useful for large-scale projects that span multiple disciplines, departments, and divisions[26,27] (**FIGURE 5.6**). The matrix structure tries to balance the advantages of high levels of functional expertise with responsiveness to each operating division or project. Typically, the functional representative reports to both the corporate-level functional manager vertically and the division-level (or project) manager horizontally. For example, each division might have a human resource director who reports to the president of the division and to the vice-president of human resources at the parent/corporate offices. The divisional human resource director would handle routine hiring and employee relations for the division and see that compensation and benefit needs are consistent across the multi-division organization by utilizing specialized staff at the parent/corporate offices.

Matrix structures provide a number of advantages. The major advantage of the matrix structure is the reduction in duplication of staff in functional departments across organizational divisions. This provides an opportunity to develop a deeper level of technical expertise at the parent/corporate level to support the operating divisions or large-scale projects. In addition, the corporate staff have the opportunity to work across the divisions and thereby learn and disseminate knowledge between divisions. This superior ability to acquire and spread knowledge can facilitate flexibility by anticipating issues and disseminate tested solutions among the divisions, along with marshaling interdisciplinary cooperation and expertise across the divisions.[9,20,27]

Matrix structures also have some significant disadvantages. Problems with the matrix structure include frustration, conflict, and confusion that can arise

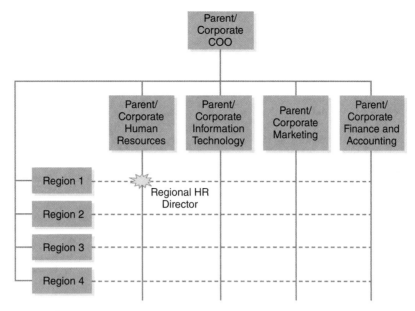

FIGURE 5.6 Matrix organizational structure.

from the dual reporting relationships. This can create very stressful situations for corporate and divisional employees and particularly for those in dual reporting positions. Employees who are trying to meet the expectations and the demands of two managers can find the experience very difficult. Managers who have conflicting goals for a project or division can negatively impact performance or can cause organizational resources to be used to rework a project or process. Meetings are a way to reduce and resolve organizational priorities and tensions. However, meetings can monopolize schedules and leave little time for getting work done. This can also be a source of significant frustration and contribute to underperformance and unmet organizational goals.[9,20,27]

Team Structure

The team structure brings together employees from across an organization with the knowledge, skills, and abilities to accomplish a shared goal (**FIGURE 5.7**). Organizations are increasingly utilizing team structures because they help flatten the organization and shift the structure from a vertical to a more horizontal orientation. This structure takes advantage of the contributions of knowledge workers by spurring organizational creativity, innovation, and adaption. This decentralized and nonhierarchical approach allows organizations to collaborate on ways to respond to environmental changes by bypassing hierarchy that is often rigid and more difficult to change and slow to respond. Team structures promote organizational flexibility

and adaptation because the structure brings together a diverse set of employees with a range of expertise. These teams are a strategy to delegate authority and push responsibility and decision-making to lower organizational levels. **Functional (vertical) teams** bring together the expertise of employees within one organizational function (e.g., department) that requires higher levels of specialized functional knowledge due to the complexity, scope, and time constraints inherent in accomplishing the shared task. **Cross-functional (horizontal) teams** bring together employees from multiple functional departments due to the breadth of expertise required for the shared task. **Autonomous or self-directed teams** self-organize and manage all team responsibilities with little outside direction.[9,28]

Team structures provide a number of advantages. The major advantages of the team structure are their flexibility and ability to generate creative and innovative solutions.[7,23] Team membership is fluid, and team members can be added or subtracted based on organizational needs. Likewise, organizations can form, merge, or dissolve teams based on needs. Teams provide a mechanism for organizations to adapt to the demands of a dynamic environment by making faster decisions.[29,30] Teams work to overcome barriers between departments, thus promoting faster decision-making. The team structure also allows the organization to assemble its best talent to concentrate on problems and opportunities as they arise.[31,32] This structure consequently promotes increased employee involvement with positive implications for engagement and morale.

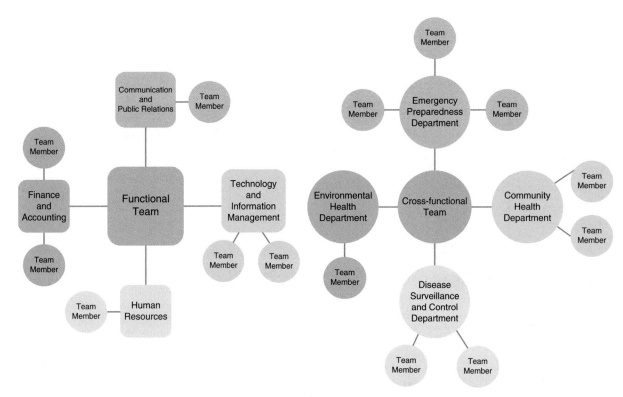

FIGURE 5.7 Types of organizational teams.

Team structures also have several disadvantages. Teams typically require many meetings with a significant amount of time spent in discussion. Dominant personalities can control meetings and even the direction of projects.[33] Conflict can arise and require negotiation to develop a resolution and safeguard team cohesion. As a result, decision-making can be time consuming and take a lot of effort on the part of the team. To facilitate productive teamwork, team members need training in team process skills. Carefully selecting team members helps to assure that teams have the right skill mix to be productive and successfully complete a team project. Teams can also make conflicting demands on team members if they serve on multiple teams, which can increase stress and affect morale.[34] Teams can also be difficult for upper managers to monitor and control in some cases.[23]

Virtual Network Structure

A virtual network structure "reduces the organization's functions down to its central competencies, and a network of suppliers and partners provide services that the organization does not consider central (or that are not cost effective to perform internally)"[20(p100)] (**FIGURE 5.8**). This is a relatively new approach to organizational structure made possible by information technology and advances in transportation and logistics. A network structure is one approach to what can be generally referred to as a virtual organization that uses technology to coordinate organizational operations among a number of separate organizations.[30,33] In these arrangements, there is typically a small group of employees who represent the core of the organization and concentrate on the key value-creating activities, with other major business resources or services being outsourced to other organizations that specialize in those functions.

Network structures have a number of advantages.[35,36] These structures are flexible and responsive to environmental changes.[36] By focusing on a core set of business activities, this allows them to detect subtle changes in the environment. This may mean that a different service supplier or partner needs to be engaged to help the organization adapt and respond to environmental changes.[37] Organizations can quickly **leverage** their resources to move in different directions based on customer feedback and environmental changes.[38] Network relationships also enhance interorganizational and organizational learning.[39] Organizations that are providing all functions in-house may not have slack resources to pivot in new directions without significantly disrupting their operations. Organizations are able to outsource functions locally or globally to the best suppliers and contractors to perform the required functions. Today, organizations can outsource almost anything and find

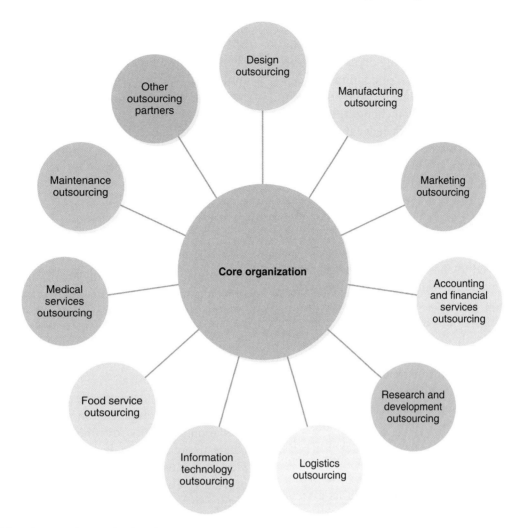

FIGURE 5.8 Virtual network organizational structure.

a number of potential suppliers to enhance the firm's capabilities.[40] With a number of suppliers, organizations can get competitive prices on the functions they need outsourced. This helps organizations minimize their overhead costs, which can go toward paying employees more, reinvesting in core operations, and upgrading technology, among other uses.[41]

Network structures have a number of potential disadvantages. An organization can lose control over part of the process used or needed to produce its output. Quality and timeliness are the two areas that can negatively impact an organization's offering.[36] Contracts become central to network relationships as the relationship is dictated by legal contracts, which can create a transactional versus a collaborative relationship. If contracts are incomplete, unclear, or otherwise insufficient, misunderstandings and disputes can emerge. Organizational resources, such as time and money, can be required to resolve these disputes. Legal action, which is costly, can be necessary in extreme cases.[42] Communication is also another

potential disadvantage of network structures.[43,44] Personalities can clash and information technology can fail. Important information can be missed because the organizations are physically separated, or the organizations do not have a strong relationship with regular communication. Irregular communication could result in a lack of trust and loyalty among organizations. Organizations that are looking for the cheapest option may see quality, customer service, and timeliness sacrificed. Developing a strong relationship with network members is important to ensure that an organization is able to obtain necessary resources and functions and deliver on its core business activities.

Emerging Issues in Organizational Design

The increasing complexity of organizational environments is continuing to drive the need for innovations in organizational design. This discussion has recognized the shift from more centralized, mechanistic, and vertical structures that are superior for producing economies of scale to more decentralized, organic, and horizontal structures that are more flexible and promote adaptive change. Learning organizations are one useful response to the need for continuous adaptation. **Learning organizations** develop the capacity to continuously learn, adapt, and change their behavior based on newly acquired knowledge through a set of practices that build on the capabilities of knowledge workers. These organizations are constantly seeking and sharing new knowledge about their environment. An organization's core competencies are central to what the organization is trying to learn about in order to adapt. Organizational members are constantly thinking about how the organization's core competencies might need to change or evolve in the future. Learning organizations realize that their knowledge workers are their greatest asset for value creation. As a result, learning organizations seek to acquire the best talent, constantly develop their capabilities, and engage them in creating value through collaboration, empowerment, and significant tangible and intangible rewards. This requires building organizational cultures with a meaningful vision, shared values, trust, and a sense of community. Some organizations have created **boundary-less** organizational structures that eliminate traditional barriers between departments (horizontal) and levels (vertical) within the organization and between the organization and its external environment. Self-directed (autonomous) work teams, virtual network structures, and strategic alliances with other organizations are steps in this direction.[45]

▶ Organizational Change

Change is central to an organization's performance and survival. Change is the means by which an organization responds or adapts to forces influencing its ability to function effectively and efficiently. Managers are responsible for monitoring external changes. They are also responsible for translating changes into specific internal actions the organization needs to take to assure it continues to produce outputs desired and valued by its external environment.[3,21,46] For this reason, managers must understand the nature of change, the issues that change presents, why organizations resist change, and potential responses. Organizations depend on managers who are able to help an organization successfully cope with change.

Definition of Organizational Change

Organizational change is the adoption of a new idea or behavior by an organization that results in a

difference in its organizational systems, processes, operations, and/or outputs.[47,48] Organizations require change to solve problems or take advantage of opportunities in order to improve organizational performance. The new idea or behavior adopted typically relates to one or more characteristics of the organization. For example, the change may result in some alteration in product or service outputs, technology (tools and techniques), people, culture, structure, goals, or other aspects. Organizations generally employ one of two strategies when they engage in organizational change—imitation or invention.

Change Strategies

Imitation occurs when an organization adopts and implements a specific change already practiced by another organization, even though the imitator may take the idea or behavior and alter (or reinvent) it to best fit the imitator's organization. Many public health organizations imitate one another. For example, a public health organization responding to an infectious disease outbreak may copy the practices and protocols used by another organization that has experienced a similar outbreak. **Invention** is another type of change where an organization develops an original (or novel) idea or behavior that other organizations have not previously identified or implemented.[49] This type of change may result in a dramatic impact on not just the organization but on the external environment and is sometimes referred to as a **disruptive innovation** due the scale and/or scope of its impact.[50] Public health is adopting a number of disruptive innovations to address the opioid epidemic. States that have allowed healthcare providers to prescribe the opioid overdose antidote to private citizens and drug users have disrupted health care in the United States.

Change can occur in different increments and over different time frames. **Incremental** (or **evolutionary**) **change** involves routine changes that occur on an ongoing basis and typically impact isolated parts of an organization or its activities; for example, implementing new work processes or new tools and techniques that improve efficiency in one or a few organizational units. These changes usually happen at lower levels of the organization. These **incremental changes** are slow to evolve, from a day-to-day perspective, and usually do not have a dramatic impact. However, if examined over time, these changes can be dramatic and can significantly influence the operation of the organization.[51] For example, updating policies and procedures following a public health exercise results in incremental changes. Public health organizations regularly exercise a variety of responses to ensure that the organization is ready in the event of an emergency. Exercises may reveal process improvement opportunities.

Transformational (or revolutionary) change is nonroutine and is revolutionary in its impact, in that it changes the organization dramatically, usually by impacting the entire organization.[50] Transformational changes often occur with a change in top-level leadership or ownership of the organization and frequently involve revisions in the organization's mission, goals, culture, structure, people, technology, resources, or core processes. For example, a sizeable change in state or federal budgets can significantly transform the services and programs a public health organization is able to offer. New laws can lead to transformational change to the public's health and well-being. Banning smoking in public spaces profoundly transformed entertainment venues that had historically had smoking and nonsmoking sections.

Sources of Change

The need for organizational change comes from both external and internal sources. Externally, the need for change typically arises from changes related to political, economic, social, technological, ecological, and legal/regulatory environmental shifts, as well as competitor actions, customer/stakeholder needs, among many other potential sources. External sources present the organization with threats and/or opportunities that have the potential to harm the organization or provide it with significant benefits. Internal sources of change come from issues related to the organization's goals, values, culture, employees, structure, technology, and value chain, among other sources. Internal sources typically emerge as organizational strengths and/or weaknesses in its various functional areas (e.g., departments). Analyses of external threats and internal weaknesses provide evidence of potential problem gaps the organization faces, while external opportunities and internal strengths can indicate potential opportunity gaps for enhancing performance. These gaps indicate what changes managers need to consider to ensure that the organization aligns effectively with environmental demands and is operating efficiently.[17]

Resistance to Change

Managers routinely encounter resistance in implementing change. This is hard to understand since the goal of organizational change is to create value for an organization, improve the organization's performance, and align and adapt an organization to its external environment, so that it can survive and thrive. However, resistance is a reality and a major challenge. Understanding why employees resist change is important to managers working to overcome resistance. Several major reasons are discussed below and are based on a number of sources:

1. **Self-interest**—Employees have a strong sense of self-interest in terms of how change may affect them personally. They want to know whether the change will affect their job, pay, workload, or other aspects of their work life. Employees particularly want to know whether the change will cause a real or perceived loss of power or status in the organization. Organizational managers who are open, honest, and transparent are able to minimize many employees' concerns. Communication from managers can help individuals understand change and any potential impact. Providing an opportunity for employees to voice concerns is important and can help mitigate resistance to change.[23,52,53]

2. **Lack of understanding**—A lack of understanding often emerges when there is a lack of trust between employees and managers. Employees who do not understand the reason for a change can harbor suspicion and question the motives behind the change. They can even sabotage change efforts. Sometimes, employees perceive the change will benefit the organization more than it will benefit them. Involving employees throughout the change process is crucial. Managers should involve employees during the decision and implementation stages of the change process. This helps employees better understand the problem or opportunity gaps the organization faces and the type of change needed. Employees can provide value in helping select and implement a change strategy. Distrust of management and the feeling that managers are not interested in the employees are often a source of unrest that can be a major impediment in change efforts.[20,47,52]

3. **Uncertainty**—The idea of uncertainty is rooted in a lack of information and the fear that comes from not knowing what is going to happen, as well as its consequences. This is particularly threatening for people who have a low tolerance for change and a strong need to be in control. Uncertainty causes employees to fear the unknown and be anxious about being harmed personally

or professionally. Most people are risk adverse and, in turn, prefer the known (or status quo) to the unknown. Managers must recognize this natural response to change. Frequent communication, coupled with coaching, is important for managers to provide to employees throughout the change process. Providing information that is factual versus speculation is also important. Facts help to build and reinforce trust between managers and employees. Speculation can result in gossip and continue to keep the level of uncertainty high among employees.[47,54]

4. **Different assessment of goals and benefits**—Managers and employees often have differing goals for the organization. This causes one group to resist the decisions being made by the other group. These differing opinions can be legitimate and well founded. Differences can also be rooted in variations in how one person or group perceives the benefits of the change and whether or not the change needs to be made or what the impact will be on the organization and/or employees. Again, managers

need to communicate with employees and involve them in the change process.[17,47]

Overcoming Resistance to Change

Resistance to change is natural and to be expected. Managers need to be prepared to address employee's concerns. Change models help managers conceptualize and implement organizational changes. Lewin's Force-Field Analysis[55] and Kotter's Change model[47] are the two well-known models for implementing organizational change. These models are closely related; however, they differ in the number of stages in the change process. Lewin's approach is conceptual and helps managers think about the change process in terms of three broad stages. Kotter's approach provides a more detailed, eight-step change process that provides a map to help managers implement change within their organization.

Lewin's Force-Field Analysis

Kurt Lewin was a distinguished social psychologist who proposed a conceptual approach to managing organizational change called **Force-Field Analysis** (as shown in **FIGURE 5.9**).[55] Lewin explained that there are three stages in the organizational change process, as shown in

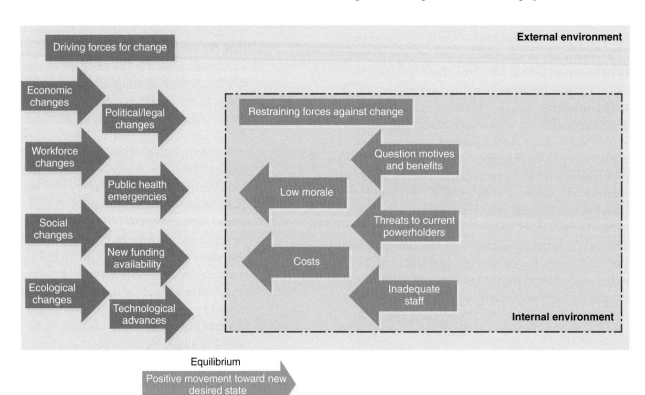

FIGURE 5.9 Lewin's Force Field Analysis.

Based Lewin K. *Field Theory in Social Science: Selected Theoretical Papers.* Cartwright D, ed. New York, NY: Harper and Row; 1951.

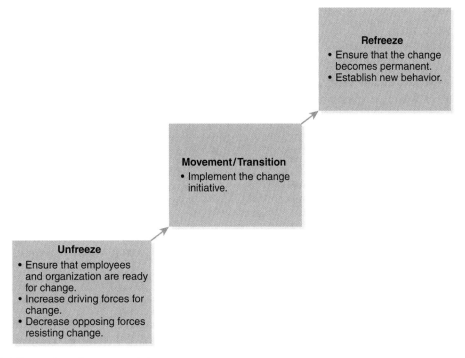

FIGURE 5.10 Lewin's three-step change model.

Modified Figure 19-4 from Borkowski, N. *Organizational Behavior in Health Care*. 3rd ed. Burlington, MA: Jones & Bartlett Publishing; 2016.

FIGURES 5.10. Change results from a problem or opportunity gap that an organization needs to respond to in order to adapt and align with its environment. Managers are responsible for identifying change strategies to help the organization respond to these gaps. This approach recognizes resistance to change and specifically works to address it. The three stages are:

Unfreezing—Lewin's Force-Field Analysis identifies two types of forces that influence organizational change: driving forcing and restraining forces. **Driving forces** are factors that promote, facilitate, or enable change. **Restraining forces** are barriers that slow and inhibit organizational change. Lewin explains that change takes place when driving forces pushing for change are greater than the restraining forces opposing it. Driving forces are derived from the problem and opportunity gaps that were identified and indicated the need for a change response from the organization. For problem gaps, the data and analysis supporting the identification of the performance problems can be used to support the need for the change, along with forecasted consequences of failing to respond. For opportunity gaps, the data and analysis can be shared and the potential benefits of a successful change can be communicated. Restraining forces are the various barriers that provide resistance to change such as those discussed earlier where some strategies for overcoming resistance were discussed. An organization will begin to shift from the status quo toward the desired future state when the strength of the driving forces is stronger than that of the restraining forces.

Moving/Transitioning—In this stage, efforts to sustain the driving forces and diminish the restraining forces must be intensified. This is the stage in which most of the change occurs and most of the problems arise. Managers and organizations must use different strategies to overcome employee resistance. Communication is central to this change step, particularly communication between managers and employees. Maintaining momentum is also important at this stage in the change process. Managers can explain benefits and answer questions about the proposed change. Including employees in decision-making and planning are ways to encourage participation. Managers can also provide education and training to help employees cope with the consequences of the change and help reduce their anxiety.

Refreezing—In this stage, the organization has successfully implemented the change, and efforts are focused on embedding and sustaining the change throughout the organization. It is critical to monitor and reinforce the change because previous practices and behaviors can easily reemerge and cause the organization to revert to the old status quo. Monitoring and reinforcement must continue until the change is widely accepted as the norm in the organization's operations and culture.

Many modern change management theories can be mapped back to Lewin's groundbreaking work.[1,56] However, some scholars believe that Lewin's approach oversimplifies the change process.[57,58] A number of subsequent change models were developed to provide more insights into the change management process.

Kotter's Leading Change Model

The distinguished Harvard Business School professor, John Kotter, expanded Lewin's three-stage model based on his experience consulting with firms around the globe.[47] Kotter's model has eight stages, but maps back to Lewin's approach, as shown in **FIGURE 5.11**. The stages are sequential, but can also overlap. Kotter believes organizations must complete all of the stages to achieve successful organizational change. Managers can use Kotter's model for more detailed guidance on how to lead and manage organizational change. The following discussion describes each of these stages in more detail.[47]

- **Stage 1: Establishing a Sense of Urgency—** Leaders and managers must clearly identify the issue that requires action by the organization.

They must also communicate with essential internal and external stakeholders by sharing information and imparting knowledge about the issue, related problems, and opportunities. Change leaders must convince employees that the issue requires their involvement. Complacency in involving people can undermine launching the change initiative.

- **Stage 2: Creating a Guiding Coalition—** Leaders must select individuals with enough influence to push the change forward. This means involving formal and informal leaders inside and key stakeholders outside the organization. These individuals are usually chosen to work together as a team to champion the change initiative. It is important that these leaders effectively communicate messages and model behaviors that support the need for change.

- **Stage 3: Developing a Vision and Strategy—** Leaders and the guiding **coalition** must create a new vision for the future to guide the change and develop a strategy to realize this vision. This needs to be a compelling future state that will engage and inspire participation in the change effort.

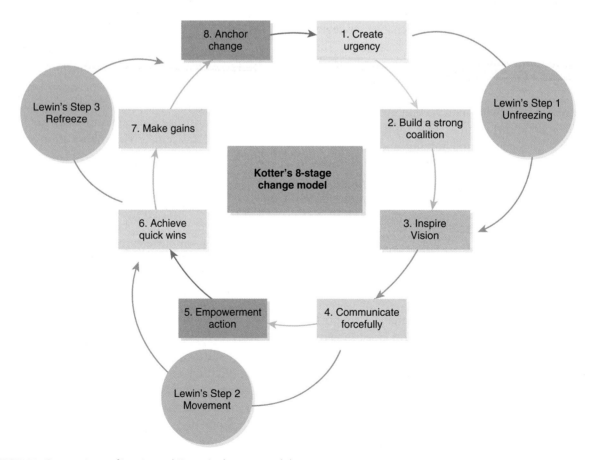

FIGURE 5.11 Comparison of Lewin and Kotter's change models.

Based on information from Kotter JP. *Leading Change*. Boston, MA: Harvard Business Review Press; 2012. and Lewin K. *Field Theory in Social Science: Selected Theoretical Papers*. Cartwright D, ed. New York, NY: Harper and Row; 1951.

- **Stage 4: Communicating the Change Vision**—Leaders, the guiding coalition, and all levels of management must communicate the change vision and strategy to everyone in the organization. Multiple channels of communication need to be used intensively. Recurring discussions of the vision and strategy are needed on an ongoing basis.

- **Stage 5: Empowering Employees for Broad-Based Action**—Systems, structures, and procedures must be modified to implement the change, along with changes in values, norms, and behaviors, as needed, to support the change. Obstacles must be removed. Leaders and managers must encourage employees to play a part in the change process by sharing new ideas and taking risks to move the change forward.

- **Stage 6: Generating Short-Term Wins**—Leaders and managers must segment the change process into achievable steps, so that participants can see progress in order to build momentum. Small successes in the beginning should be celebrated to encourage efforts to accomplish larger steps in the future to bring about the change. Visibility of progress and wins should be reinforced through employee recognition and rewards.

- **Stage 7: Consolidating Gains and Producing More Change**—Leaders and managers must consolidate and integrate achievements in each step into progress toward the overall change vision. As an organization sees many small advances accumulate toward the projected vision, the change process is strengthened and renewed. New, more challenging targets can be identified, further building momentum and sustaining enthusiasm.

- **Stage 8: Anchoring New Approaches in the Culture**—The change vision is not realized until the change becomes part of the ongoing operations and culture of the organization to assure that there is no regression to the old status quo. A plan needs to be put in place to ensure that new leaders and managers selected in the future support the change vision going forward.

Lewin and Kotter's models are interrelated and reinforce how to accomplish organizational change. While there are different approaches to aligning these models, one of the more common approaches is shown in Figure 5.11. The first three stages in Kotter's model provide a much more detailed set of action steps for "Unfreezing" the status quo in an organization initiating the change process. The next three stages in Kotter's model correspond to the "Movement/Transition"

phase in Lewin's model, with explicit steps for enabling and encouraging the actual tasks that have to be accomplished to realize the change vision. The final two stages in Kotter's model capture Lewin's concept of "Refreezing" the organization by confirming that the change is solidly embedded both operationally and culturally in the organization.

Underlying the stages in Lewin's and Kotter's models are a common set of managerial practices that are important for leading organizational change. First, top management must lead the change effort in word and deed by engaging all levels of management and other informal leaders throughout the organization to support the change. Second, all of these organizational leaders must constantly communicate and reinforce the change vision and strategy to everyone in the organization throughout the change process. Next, leaders need to proactively encourage participation by everyone in the organization. This means listening to feedback and providing training and other resources that are needed. Finally, leaders need to use persuasion and influence to change people in order to change the organization.

Conclusion

The managerial function of organizing is concerned with how an organization is configured internally. Organizing is the process of creating the patterned relationships or social interactions and activities necessary for the organization to accomplish its goals. Organizational design ensures an organization's internal structure is configured in a way that optimizes its transformation process. An organization's structure reflects decisions regarding how activities will be coordinated, how authority and responsibility will be assigned, how information will flow, and how decision-making and control will take place across the organization. Organizations use an organizational chart to depict an organization's structure at a specific point in time. The organizational chart shows the number of levels of management, the functional activity centers (or departments), the key reporting relationships, and the delegation of authority (chain of command). Common organizational structures include simple structure, functional structure, divisional structure, matrix structure, team structure, and virtual network structure. Contingency factors (i.e., environment, organizational size, organizational strategy, technology, and organizational culture) are important considerations when creating an organization's structure.

Organization's must change over time to enhance organizational performance and ultimately ensure an organization's survival. Organizational change is a continuous process of adopting a new idea or behavior that results in a difference in its organizational systems, processes, operations, and/or outputs. The need for organizational change comes from inside and outside the organization. Managers routinely encounter resistance to implementing change for a variety of reasons. Lewin's Force-Field Analysis and Kotter's Leading Change model help managers understand and implement change within their organization. Public health organizations are becoming increasingly complex, which is continuing to drive the need for innovations in organizational design and organizational change.

Discussion Questions

1. What is organizing?
2. What are the contingency factors that are important to consider when designing an organization?
3. What are the structural factors that are important to consider when designing an organization?
4. What is the difference between mechanistic and organic organizational structures?
5. Compare and contrast the different types of organizational structures (i.e., simple, functional, divisional, matrix, team, and virtual network).
6. What is a learning organization?
7. What is organizational change? Why do organizational need to change?
8. What is the difference between an imitation and an invention strategy? Provide an example of each strategy.
9. What are some of the internal and external sources of change?
10. What steps can managers take to respond to organizational change?
11. Why do organizations resist change?
12. What are some strategies managers can use to minimize resistance to change?

13. Explain the stages in Lewin's Force-Field Analysis.
14. Explain the stages in Kotter's Leading Change model. How do they relate to the stages in Lewin's model?

Learning Activities

1. Select a couple of public health organizations that interest you and locate their organizational charts. Classify the organizational charts based on the different types of organizational structures discussed in the chapter.
2. Interview a public health or healthcare manager. Ask the manager to share their experience about a time they needed to make a change in their organization. What opportunity or threat gap were they facing? What internal and external forces were creating the need for change? What type of strategy did the managers pursue—imitation or invention?
3. Interview a public health or healthcare manager. Ask the manager to describe an organizational change they implemented. Analyze the organizational change based on Lewin's Force-Field Analysis model or Kotter's Leading Change model. What challenges did they face? How did they overcome the challenges? What recommendations would you make based on the model you selected?
4. Visit the Case Consortium at Columbia University website, https://casestudies.ccnmtl.columbia.edu/. Select a case that interests you, https://casestudies.ccnmtl.columbia.edu/case/. (You could also select a public health organization in the news.) Now, envision you are a manager in the case. What type of change is the case trying to accomplish? Apply one of the organizational change models to analyze this change. What type of resistance to change do you think you will encounter? As a manager, how could you mitigate or overcome this resistance to change?

References

1. Robbins SP, Judge TA. *Organizational Behavior*. 14th ed. Upper Saddle River, NJ: Pearson Prentice Hall; 2011.
2. Miles RE, Snow CC. *Organization Strategy, Structure, and Process*. Tokyo: McGraw-Hill Kogakusha; 1978.
3. Miles RE, Snow CC, Pfeffer J. Organization-environment: Concepts and issues. *Ind Relat*. 1974;13(3):244–264. doi:10.1111/j.1468-232X.1974.tb00581.x
4. Porter ME. *Competitive Advantage: Creating and Sustaining Superior Performance*. New York, NY: The Free Press; 1985.
5. Borkowski B. *Organizational Behavior, Theory, and Design in Health Care*. 2nd ed. Burlington, MA: Jones & Bartlett Learning; 2016.
6. Galbraith JR. *Designing Organizations: Strategy, Structure, and Process at the Business Unit and Enterprise Levels*. 3rd ed. San Fransico, CA: Jossey-Bass; 2014.
7. Johnson JA, Rossow CC. *Health Organizations: Theory, Behavior, and Development*. 2nd ed. Burlington, MA: Jones & Bartlett Learning; 2019.

8. Galbraith JR. *Designing Complex Organizations*. Reading, MA: Addison-Wesley Publishing Company; 1973.

9. Daft RL. *Organization Theory and Design*. 12th ed. Boston, MA: Cengage Learning; 2016.

10. Kast FE, Rosenzweig JE. *Organization and Management: A Systems and Contingency Approach*. 4th ed. New York, NY: McGraw-Hill; 1985.

11. Godwyn ME, Gittell JH. *Sociology of Organizations: Structures and Relationships*. Thousand Oaks, CA: Sage Publications Inc.; 2012.

12. Buchbinder SB, Shanks NH. *Introduction to Health Care Management*. 3rd ed. Burlington, MA: Jones & Bartlett Learning; 2017.

13. Burns T, Stalker G. *The Management of Innovation*. London, UK: Tavistock Publications; 1961.

14. Sharfman MP, Dean JW. Conceptualizing and measuring the organizational environment: A multideminsional approach. *J Manage*. 1991;17(4):681–700. doi:10.1177/014920639101700403

15. Dess GG, Beard DW. Dimensions of organizational task environments. *Adm Sci Q*. 1984;29(1):52–73. doi:10.2307/2393080

16. Child J. Organizational structure, environment, and performance: The role of strategic choice. *Sociology*. 1972;6(1):1–22. doi:10.1177/003803857200600101

17. Ginter PM, Duncan WJ, Swayne LE. *Strategic Management of Health Care Organizations*. 8th ed. Hoboken, NJ: Wiley; 2018.

18. Porter ME. *Competitive Strategy: Techniques for Analyzing Industries and Competitors*. New York, NY: Free Press; 1980.

19. Chandler AD. *Strategy and Structure: Chapters in the History of the Industrial Enterprise*. Cambridge, MA: MIT Press; 1962.

20. Anderson DL. *Organization Design: Creating Strategic and Agile Organizations*. Thousand Oaks, CA: Sage Publications Inc.; 2019.

21. Lawrence PR, Lorsch J. Differentiation and integration in complex organizations. *Adm Sci Q*. 1967;12(1):1–47. doi:10.2307/2391211

22. Lawrence PR, Dyer D. *Renewing American Industry: Organizing for Efficiency and Innovation*. New York, NY: Free Press; 1984.

23. Daft RL. *Management*. 12th ed. Boston, MA: Cengage Learning; 2016.

24. Hackman JR, Oldham GR. Motivation through the design of work: Test of a theory. *Organ Behav Hum Perform*. 1976;16(2):250–279. doi:10.1016/0030-5073(76)90016-7

25. Mintzberg H. *The Structuring of Organizations*. Upper Saddle River, NJ: Prentice-Hall; 1979.

26. Stuckenbruck LC. The matrix organization. *Proj Manage Q*. 1979;10(3):21–33. https://www.pmi.org/learning/library/matrix-organization-structure-reason-evolution-1837. Accessed July 23, 2019.

27. Galbraith JR. Matrix organization designs: How to combine functional and project forms. *Bus Horiz*. 1971;14(1):37–45. doi:10.1016/0007-6813(71)90037-1

28. Anderson P, Tushman ML. Organizational environments and industry exit: The effects of uncertainty, munificence, and complexity. *Ind Corp Chang*. 2001;10(3):675–711. doi:10.1093/icc/10.3.675

29. Kozlowski SWJ, Bell BS. Work groups and teams in organizations. In: Weiner IB, Schmitt NW, Highhouse S, eds. *Handbook of Psychology (Volume 12): Industrial and Organizational Psychology*. 2nd ed. Hoboken, NJ: John Wiley & Sons, Inc.; 2013:412–469.

30. Ferrazzi K. Getting Virtual Teams Right. *Harvard Bus Rev*. https://hbr.org/2014/12/getting-virtual-teams-right. Published December 2014. Accessed July 23, 2019

31. Cohen SG, Bailey DE. What makes teams work: Group effectiveness research from the shop floor to the executive suite. *J Manage*. 1997;23(3):239–290. doi:10.1177/014920639702300303

32. Glassop LI. The organizational benefits of teams. *Hum Relations*. 2002;55(2):225–249. doi:10.1177/0018726702055002184

33. Hoch JE, Dulebohn JH. Team personality composition, emergent leadership and shared leadership in virtual teams: A theoretical framework. *Hum Resour Manage Rev*. 2017;27(4):678–693. doi:10.1016/J.HRMR.2016.12.012

34. O'Neill TA, McLarnon MJW. Optimizing team conflict dynamics for high performance teamwork. *Hum Resour Manage Rev*. 2018;28(4):378–394. doi:10.1016/J.HRMR.2017.06.002

35. Provan KG, Milward HB. A preliminary theory of interorganizational network effectiveness: A comparative study of four community mental health systems. *Adm Sci Q*. 1995;40(1):1–33. doi:10.2307/2393698

36. Popp J, MacKean G, Casebeer A, Milward HB, Lindstrom R. Interorganizational networks: A review of the literature to inform practice. http://www.businessofgovernment.org/sites/default/files/Inter-Organizational%20Networks.pdf; Published 2014. Accessed July 23, 2019

37. Barringer BR, Harrison JS. Walking a tightrope: Creating value through interorganizational relationships. *J Manage*. 2000;26:367–403. doi:10.1177/014920630002600302

38. Gulati R, Nohria N, Zaheer A. Strategic networks. *Strategic Manage J*. 2000;21(3):203–215. doi:10.1002/(SICI)1097-0266(200003)21:3<203::AID-SMJ102>3.0.CO;2-K

39. Ingram P. Interorganizational learning. In: Baum JAC, ed. *Companion to Organizations*. Malden, MA: Blackwell Publishers Ltd.; 2002:642–663.

40. Zaheer A, Bell GG. Benefiting from network position: Firm capabilities, structural holes, and performance. *Strategic Manage J*. 2005;26(9):809–825. doi:10.1002/smj.482

41. Zajac EJ, Westphal JD. Interorganizational economics. In: Baum JAC, ed. *Companion to Organizations*. Malden, MA: Blackwell Publishers Ltd.; 2002:233–255.

42. Williamson OE. Hierarchies, markets and power in the economy: An economic perspective. *Ind Corp Chang*. 1995;4(1):21–49. doi:10.1093/icc/4.1.21

43. Schilling MA, Phelps CC. Interfirm collaboration networks: The impact of large-scale network structure on firm innovation. *Manage Sci*. 2007;53(7):1113–1126. doi:10.1287/mnsc.1060.0624

44. Kraatz MS. Learning by association? Interorganizational networks and adaptation to environmental change. *Acad Manage J*. 1998;41(6):621–643. doi:10.5465/256961

45. Senge PM. *The Fifth Discipline: The Art and Practice of the Learning Organization*. New York, NY: Doubleday; 1990.

46. Child J. Strategic choice in the analysis of action, structure, organizations and environment: Retrospect and prospect. *Organ Stud*. 1997;18(1):43–76. doi:10.1177/017084069701800104

47. Kotter JP. *Leading Change:* Boston, MA: Harvard Business Review Press; 2012.

48. Kotter JP, Schlesinger LA. Choosing strategies for changes. *Harvard Bus Rev.* 2008;86(7-8):130–139.

49. Rogers E. *Diffusion of Innovations.* New York, NY: Free Press; 1962.

50. Christensen CM, Grossman JH, Hwang J. *An Innovator's Prescription: A Disruptive Solution for Health Care.* New York, NY: McGraw-Hill; 2009.

51. Rogers EM. *Diffusion of Innovations.* 5th ed. New York, NY: The Free Press; 2003.

52. Dent EB, Goldberg SG. Challenging "Resistance to Change." *J Appl Behav Sci.* 1999;35(1):25–41. doi:10.1177/0021886399351003

53. Ford JD, Ford LW, D'Amelio A. Resistance to change: The rest of the story. *Acad Manage.* 2008;33(2):362–377. doi:10.5465/amr.2008.31193235

54. Duncan RB. Characteristics of organizational environments and perceived environmental uncertainty. *Adm Sci Q.* 1972;17(3):313–327.

55. Lewin K. *Field Theory in Social Science: Selected Theoretical Papers.* Cartwright D, ed. New York, NY: Harper and Row; 1951.

56. Cummings S, Bridgman T, Brown KG. Unfreezing change as three steps: Rethinking Kurt Lewin's legacy for change management. *Hum Relations.* 2016;69(1):33–60. doi:10.1177/0018726715577707

57. Child J. *Organization: Contemporary Principles and Practice.* 2nd ed. Chichester, UK: Wiley; 2015.

58. Clegg SR, Kornberger M, Pitsis TS, Mount M. *Managing & Organizations: An Introduction to Theory and Practice.* 5th ed. London, UK: Sage; 2019.

CHAPTER 6

Staffing Public Health Organizations

▶ Introduction

Human resource management (HRM) is the process of acquiring, developing, and engaging the human resources (i.e., individuals, people, or organizational members) an organization needs to accomplish its goals. HRM primarily relates to the psychosocial subsystem in the systems model, which specifically deals with people within an organization.[1] Staffing is another name for the process of acquiring human resources. Managers must consider what types of tasks are going to be performed, as well as the knowledge, skills, and abilities needed to complete these tasks before hiring personnel to staff an organization. Managers develop job descriptions and qualifications that are used by managers to recruit qualified applicants for positions. Job descriptions help managers select qualified candidates to interview and ultimately hire. New employees are then oriented and onboarded to the organization and their work unit. Training and development are provided by organizations to enhance **employee** skills and capabilities. Performance appraisals are used to identify training and development needs and, if necessary, for coaching and counseling to improve performance. Organizations use compensation and benefit programs to motivate and reward employees. Various employee relations activities are used by managers to motivate employees and resolve workplace disputes, and increase employee engagement with the organization and their jobs. This chapter discusses how managers can use the human resource management process to acquire, develop, and engage employees to enhance individual and organizational performance.

Human Resource Management Process

Organizations have a human resource department or at least an individual focused on performing human resource activities and functions (**FIGURE 6.1**). The human resource department is responsible for overseeing the human resource management process, which consists of three broad activities: acquisition, development, and engagement of human resources. Employees, or human resources, are critical resources that managers are responsible for acquiring, developing, and engaging to perform jobs that contribute to accomplishing organizational goals. A number of activities fall under each of these categories, as shown in Figure 6.1. This chapter discusses the human resource acquisition or staffing process. Subsequent chapters focus on human resource development and engagement. Collectively, these chapters will help public health managers understand how the HRM process can be applied to public health organizations to enhance their performance. Public health managers should consult with their human resource department or representative in order to benefit from

the guidance and support they can provide on this important area of managerial practice.

Human Resource Acquisition or Staffing

Staffing, or talent acquisition, involves acquiring the human resources an organization needs to carry out its work and accomplish its goals. There are a number of steps in the acquisition process (**FIGURE 6.2**). The first step involves analyzing the work that needs to be done. Organizations and mangers must identify and group different tasks into jobs. Next, the organization must recruit qualified candidates who can potentially fill the jobs. The goal of recruitment is to source a pool of qualified candidates who will undergo further screening using applications, résumés, background verification, references, and selection testing, among other tools to identify the most qualified candidates to consider further. Usually candidates who best meet the job qualifications and requirements are invited to selection interviews. Organizations use different approaches to interviewing to make final selection decisions for job offers and hiring. This section provides a more detailed discussion of the steps in the human resource acquisition (staffing) process.

Job Analysis

A **job analysis** is conducted to better understand what types of human resources the organization needs to acquire to carry out its work activities to accomplish unit and organizational goals. Managers and the human

Acquisition
• Job description and qualifications
• Recruitment
• Selection
• Pre-employment screening
• Background verification
• Reference verification
• Interviewing
• Hiring

Development
• New employee orientation
• Onboarding
• Job training
• Professional development
• Performance appraisal
• Coaching
• Counseling
• Discipline
• Termination

Engagement
• Compensation
• Benefits
• Recognition programs
• Employee relations
• Labor relations
• Health and safety
• Wellness programs

FIGURE 6.1 Human resource management process and key activities.

Modified from Exhibit 4-2 Fallon LR, McConnell CR. *Human Resource Management in Health Care Principles and Practice.* 2nd ed. Burlington, MA: Jones & Bartlett Learning; 2014.

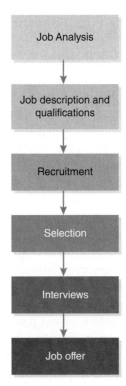

Job Analysis → Job description and qualifications → Recruitment → Selection → Interviews → Job offer

FIGURE 6.2 Human resource acquisition or staffing process.

resource department usually work together to complete a job analysis. The aim of a job analysis is to develop a **job description** that describes the specific duties the job will perform. Additionally, a **job specification** that describes the qualifications required to accomplish the job is developed as part of the job analysis. Managers conduct a job analysis before they write a job or position description.[2] Managers and organizations do this by analyzing the different types of tasks that need to be performed. Similar tasks are then grouped together into jobs. These tasks usually require similar types of knowledge and skills, use similar tools and technology, and are related to accomplishing a common work activity. In addition, grouping similar tasks together usually enhances efficiency. Information is collected from a number of sources to analyze a job, including information from employees currently in the position or in a similar position, information from employees who regularly work with the position, customers or clients, and research regarding similar positions in other organizations, among other sources of information. Collecting information from multiple sources helps to get an accurate picture of the types of tasks and activities that need to be performed in a job. Managers play an important role in identifying and grouping tasks into jobs. Usually mangers and human resource staff write job descriptions, or position descriptions, that describe the job duties and specify minimum job qualifications based on what are reasonable and appropriate duties for the job. Job descriptions must be reviewed and approved by upper management.[2] How a job description is written can make the difference as to whether a position is approved. Managers must demonstrate sufficient need for a position and communicate this to upper management in terms of how the position contributes toward accomplishing an organization's plans and goals.

Job Description and Qualifications

Job analysis helps managers understand what needs to be included in a job description. The job description is a key tool organizations use to match qualified candidates with jobs within the organization. Job descriptions include a number of important elements: job title, job status or grade, exempt or nonexempt status, wage rate or salary range, reporting relationship, summary of duties or responsibilities, job qualifications or specifications, skills required, effort required, working conditions/environment, general statement regarding additional job duties and responsibilities as assigned, company overview, and a contact name and information (**TABLE 6.1**). This section discusses each of these elements.

Job descriptions, often referred to as **position descriptions**, include specific information needed to

help match qualified candidates with jobs within an organization. Day-to-day activities vital to operations are detailed in job descriptions, and they become a vehicle for the organization to accomplish its goals. Job descriptions also help employees understand how they contribute to the organization's mission, vision, and goals through their daily activities. Job descriptions are an important tool for managers to link, engage, and integrate employees into the work, plans, and goals of an organization.[2] **EXHIBIT 6.1** provides an example of a job description. As previously stated, managers are responsible for developing job descriptions and identifying necessary job qualifications. Many organizations are moving toward descriptions that are broad and that include general core tasks, which may result in tasks and jobs that are not clearly defined for employees. Employees are depending on managers more than ever to clearly define the tasks that they need to accomplish and will be evaluated on. The failure of managers to clearly identify and communicate job roles and responsibilities can result in organizational inefficiency, lower levels of employee satisfaction and performance, and higher levels of turnover and attrition. Employees can also suffer negative consequences for poorly designed job descriptions, such as frustration, low morale, and poor performance reviews.[3] Job descriptions reflect the set of tasks a person will perform at a certain point in time. This can cause these descriptions to become outdated or even obsolete over time. Therefore, they need to be regularly reviewed and updated as necessary. The format of job descriptions can vary between organizations. However, organizations should have a standardized format. The human resource department usually prescribes and maintains this format, as well as a historical and current record of all positions within the organization.[2]

Job Title. **Job titles** provide a short description of an employee's role and responsibilities within the organization. The title helps in organizing an organization from a structural standpoint. Managers use jobs to assign certain tasks and work to accomplish work activities as well as operational and strategic plans. Titles provide a shorthand for delineating one job or set of work activities from another. Organizations can also use a combination of job numbers and titles to ensure each unique job is identified and that jobs with similar titles are not confused.

Job Status or Grade. Titles also communicate position and prestige within an organization.[3] Job titles correspond to **job status or grade** that indicates where a position is located within an organization's hierarchy and organizational chart. Jobs toward the top of the organization carry more duties and

TABLE 6.1 Job Description Elements

Element	Description
Job Title	Describes the key functions, responsibilities, and level of a job or a position within an organization
Job Status or Grade	Indicates where a position is located in an organization's hierarchy or organizational chart
Exempt versus Nonexempt	Exempt jobs are not eligible for overtime, whereas nonexempt jobs are eligible for overtime
Wage Rate or Salary Range	The minimum, midpoint, and maximum pay for a position
Reporting Relationship	Details who manages or supervises the position or what position the employee reports to in the organization
Summary of Duties or Responsibilities	Listing or description of the different tasks or functions an employee is responsible for performing in their position
Job Qualifications or Specifications	Minimum requirements necessary to perform a set of job tasks or functions
Skills Requirements	Specific knowledge, skills, and abilities required to perform a job
Effort Requirements	Mental and physical demands or requirements of a job
Working Conditions/Environment	Description of work environment, including location, hours, and hazards
General Statement	Statement that additional duties can and may be assigned
Company Overview	Description of the organization's history, mission, location(s), key business products or services, and any notable awards or recognition
Contact Information	Name, email, phone number, and address of the best person to contact regarding a position, which is typically the human resource department or a human resource representative

Modified from Exhibit 6-1 Fallon LR, McConnell CR. *Human Resource Management in Health Care Principles and Practice.* 2nd ed. Burlington, MA: Jones & Bartlett Learning; 2014.

EXHIBIT 6.1 Sample Job Description

Job Title: Community Practice Facility Controller
Unit or Section: Administration
Status: Exempt
Department: Finance
Salary Range: $65,000–$85,000
Basic Function: Plans, directs, and coordinates, on an efficient and economical basis, all facility accounting operational activities, including cost accounting, financial accounting, general accounting, information systems, and general office services
Scope: Work encompasses involvement in a broad range of accounting activities that are essential to the maintenance of facility operations and the dissemination of financial information to the board, senior managers, and owners

Summary of Duties:

1. Coordinates all essential accounting operational functions in a timely and accurate manner, developing methods geared to providing management with information vital to the decision-making processes.

2. Directs the development of methods and procedures necessary to ensure adequate financial controls within each of the facility's operational areas.
3. Performs analysis and appraisal of the facility's financial status.
4. Prepares recommendations with respect to future financial plans, forecasts, and policies.
5. Works closely with the chief executive officer on confidential financial matters and expedites such matters to conclusion.
6. Directs this operation within the accounting parameters established by facility, third-party provider, state, federal, and generally accepted accounting principles (GAAP), rules and regulations.
7. Manages the organizational area in a manner that fully complements and interfaces with all other coordinating agencies or business partners.
8. Performs other duties and responsibilities as directed by the Chief Executive Officer.

Supervision Exercised:	Yes
Employees:	
Direct: General supervisors in operational areas	2–3
Indirect: Other facility supervisors, administrativeand clerical personnel	15–20

Training and Education:
Certified Public Accountant (CPA) required; graduation from an accredited program with a bachelor's degree in accounting

Experience:
Must have at least 5 years of experience in accounting with some supervisory responsibility

Responsibility:
Budget of $3,500,000 per year
All required insurance for hospital
State and federal filings for tax and other financial purposes

Effort:
Minimal physical effort required; no lifting
Mental effort requires ability to concentrate on numbers for long periods of time and to occasionally work under severe deadlines

Working Conditions:
Well-lighted office; no exposure to hazards in the normal course of work
The above constitutes a general summary of duties. Additional duties may be required.

Approvals:
Supervisor: _____   Date: _____
Department manager: _____   Date: _____
HR Department: _____   Date: _____

Reviews:
Person: _____   Title: _____   Date: _____
_____   _____   _____

Modified Appendix 6-A from Fallon LR, McConnell. *Human Resource Management in Health Care Principles and Practice*. 2nd ed. Burlington, MA: Jones & Bartlett Learning; 2014.

responsibilities. Employees in these positions are usually compensated more in accordance with their degree of responsibility. A position's job status is one important factor used to determine wages, salary, and other forms of compensation.

Exempt Versus Nonexempt Positions. A job description also needs to specify if a position is exempt or nonexempt. **Exempt positions** are exempt from payment of overtime based on the Fair Labor Standards Act (FLSA) of 1938. **Nonexempt positions** are usually paid on an hourly basis, where any time beyond a 40-hour workweek is deemed as overtime. The FLSA protects nonexempt employees from working more than a 40-hour workweek without receiving additional compensation. Overtime for nonexempt employees is one and a half times their hourly wage rate for hours worked over 40 in a workweek. The FLSA provides guidance on what jobs are exempt and nonexempt, using a combination of salary, supervision, and responsibilities. Professional, managerial, and executive positions are usually salaried positions and exempt from overtime pay.[2]

Wage Rate and Salary Range. Job descriptions include a **wage rate or salary range** that usually provides the minimum, midpoint (or median), and maximum pay for a position. The range can be stated as an hourly rate or in terms of annual amounts. Wage and salary ranges help candidates and employees determine if an opportunity is worth their time and energy to pursue from a financial standpoint. Employers use pay ranges to control costs, ensure equity, and develop a viable **applicant pool** of qualified and interested candidates.[2]

Reporting Relationship. Public health organizations have a considerable range of job levels and different types of positions. **Reporting relationships** indicate who manages or supervises a position. This ensures that applicants and employees understand what position they report to in the organization.

Summary of Duties or Responsibilities. The **summary of duties or responsibilities** provides a listing that describes the different tasks or activities an employee is responsible for performing in their position. Generally, this summary includes five to eight tasks that are listed based on how frequently the tasks are performed. Tasks or functions that are regularly performed are listed toward the top of the duties section and those less regularly performed are listed toward the bottom. The list of duties should communicate information in a clear, descriptive, and concise manner using present tense, action verbs, and complete sentences to convey the core tasks and essential functions of a position.[2] The summary of duties section serves as the starting point for specifying qualifications required for the position.

Job Qualifications or Specifications. **Job qualifications**, also referred to as **job specifications**, are the minimum requirements necessary to perform a set of job tasks or functions. Qualifications typically include minimum requirements for education, credentials, licenses, skills, experience, effort, and other characteristics deemed necessary to successfully perform a job. Jobs may require different levels of education, such as a high school diploma or equivalent. Positions often require specific types of degrees. For example, the accounting and finance department of a public health organization might require a bachelor's degree in business, accounting, or finance. The director of medical services for a public health organization might need to possess a medical degree (i.e., MD or DO). Likewise, public health professionals often need professional credentials or licenses to perform certain job functions. The National Board of Public Health Examiners offers the Certified Public Health (CPH) credential to individuals who meet specified eligibility requirements. The Certified Health Education Specialist (CHES)

and Master Certified Health Education Specialist (MCHES) are additional examples of certifications that public health positions could require. The National Commission for Health Education Credentialing, Inc. (NCHEC) offers the CHES and MCHES credentials. Many public health positions require employees to possess licenses or certifications to operate certain equipment or machinery and perform various procedures and activities. Licenses might include a driver's license, medical licenses, or other types of licenses needed to practice or perform particular job activities.

Skill Requirements. Skill requirements are certain abilities that are important and helpful to performing certain job tasks. Job descriptions generally include a section that outlines key skills that are required for certain positions. Skills could include being proficient in using certain software or types of technology. Also, positions can require communication, customer service, **leadership**, and teamwork, among other skills.

Effort Requirements. **Effort requirements** specify the minimum physical requirements deemed necessary to perform a job. For example, lifting and standing are typical effort requirements that are included in job specifications. Other requirements can include essential abilities such as hearing, sight, dexterity and other motor abilities that are needed to successfully perform a job and comply with legal requirements.[2]

Working Conditions and Environment. The position description also includes information about **working conditions and environment**. This could include whether a position would be located in an office, clinic, laboratory, field, or some combination of locations, and other relevant information about these locations. Hazardous and atmospheric conditions might be present in some public health positions. Exposure to blood-borne pathogens, chemicals, and other potentially dangerous materials is important to include. This section of the job specification might also indicate the amount of travel required, along with travel areas or regions.[2]

General Statement. Job descriptions also include a general statement that additional job duties and responsibilities can be assigned by a manager or supervisor. This statement is included because jobs can change and require employees to take on new duties and responsibilities. Organizations need flexibility to address these changes. Some changes might be minor and temporary, while other might be substantial and enduring. This is why it is important to update job descriptions and specifications regularly. Other general statements may include different types of legal statements and disclaimers such as Equal Opportunity Employer and Non-Discrimination notices.

Company Overview. A **company overview** is a description of an organization's history, mission, locations, key business products or services, and any notable awards or recognitions. This gives job applicants an idea of what an organization does and values.

Contact Information. **Contact information** is also included in a job description. This provides a point of contact for applicants if they have questions or need assistance with the application process. Generally, the human resource department serves as the first point of contact.[2]

Recruitment

The human resource acquisition process includes utilizing a job description to recruit a pool of qualified candidates from inside and outside the organization. Usually, managers must request and receive approval from upper management and the human resource department before a position can be advertised and recruitment activities initiated. Managers work with the human resource department to identify qualified candidates. A qualified candidate is one who meets the minimum job qualifications or specifications listed in the job description. Managers should collaborate with their human resource department or professional to recruit for positions according to organizational policies. The human resource department develops recruitment strategies based on the type of position the organization is trying to fill. Managers should work with human resources to identify and suggest outlets to source applications as well as participate in recruitment activities, as appropriate.

Human resources works to recruit qualified applicants from inside and outside the organization. **Job postings** describe the process of letting internal employees know about open positions. Organizations have different practices when it comes to posting open positions. Some organizations give current employees, who meet minimum job qualifications, an opportunity to apply for a position before it is posted outside the organization. Open positions are typically advertised on an organization's intranet from a couple of days to a couple of weeks before the position is posted outside the organization. This allows time for existing employees to apply for the job and go through the selection process. While it can be good for morale if an internal candidate is selected; it will create another vacancy that will need to be filled. Ultimately, organizations have to recruit from outside the organization in the external job market.

There are a number of methods that can be used to recruit outside the organization. Online posts are the most popular and cost-effective way for an organization to advertise an open position. Organizations post open positions on their website and use social media networks and job posting sites on the **Internet**. In addition to the Internet, published advertisements, job fairs, networking events, recruiting trips, and search firms are strategies that can be used to recruit a qualified applicant pool. Professional organizations are particularly good sources for publicizing open positions with their members through networking events, publications, and websites. Job fairs, whether in conjunction with an organization or a standalone, can be a particularly useful method to recruit for entry-level positions. Recruitment trips that managers or recruiters make to conferences, university events, professional meetings, or other venues where there are a number of potential applicants are a valuable recruitment tool. Search firms can be used for positions that are hard to fill because they require specialized skills or there are not a lot of candidates available in the market. Other recruiting strategies include developing internship programs to create a pipeline of candidates; paying relocation expenses; helping spouses find employment; and offering signing bonuses, employee referral programs, or alternative work arrangements like telecommuting, to mention a few.[2,4] There are costs and benefits associated with any recruitment activity. Organizations and managers weigh the costs and benefits of strategies to meet their goals as cost-effectively as possible.

Why is finding the right job candidates so important? Managers will spend a significant amount of time dealing with training, discipline, and turnover, among other undesirable consequences if poor hiring decisions are made.[3] Recruiting creates the pool of candidates that the organization will choose from to fill open positions. A high-quality pool of candidates is a prerequisite for hiring quality employees. It is important to identify candidates in this step of the human resource acquisition process that at least meet, if not exceed, minimum job qualifications. Often, managers try to fill positions as quickly as possible. This can lead to a proper job analysis not being done or job descriptions and qualifications not being adequately reviewed and updated. This can attract candidates who are not suitable for the position. Managers need to take the acquisition process seriously and give it the time and attention it requires.

Selection

Selection is the next step in the human resource acquisition process and consists of choosing the best-qualified candidate from the applicant pool.

The human resource department and managers are able to initiate the selection process once there is a sufficient pool of qualified candidates. The first step in the selection process is screening the applicant pool to ensure that all the candidates meet the minimum job qualifications. Then other selection methods can be used, such as application and résumé review, selection testing, background verification, reference checks, and interviews. Not all organization use all of these techniques. The extent to which other selection methods are used varies and depends on an organization's assessment of the costs and benefits of each technique.

Applications Versus Résumés. Employment applications are an important part of the selection process. **Employment applications** solicit information from applicants that is used to evaluate candidates and make employment decisions. Applications should be created by the human resource department (or function) and reviewed by legal counsel to provide legal protections to managers and the organization when evaluating candidates' information and assuring it is credible. Well prepared employment applications provide uniform information about each candidate and include a number of legal releases a candidate agrees to, so that an organization can verify information provided in the application. Depending on the organization's policies, human resources and/or managers just use applications to screen candidate versus using résumés. Many times job applicants will submit a résumé that summarizes their qualifications for a position. Résumés should not be used in lieu of applications or be the only information used to screen candidates or make employment decisions. Candidates use résumés to paint the most favorable picture possible of their qualifications. However, this information is often grossly overexaggerated, factually incorrect, and sometimes entirely false. Managers should critically review résumés and look for fraudulent information or embellishment. For example, education and credential sections can include degrees or credentials that an applicant never received. Gaps in education or employment are always something a manger should question. Applicants will often try to shift dates to minimize or eliminate gaps. Titles, roles, responsibilities, salary information, honors, awards, memberships, publications, conference presentations, training, development programs, and certifications are the areas that managers and human resource professionals should verify as much as possible. The Internet provides a significant amount of information and makes verifying résumé information relatively easy.[2] Employment applications ask applicants for

permission to verify different types of information and legally protect organizations as they seek to do so. Organizations often include statements on the application that if applicants provide misleading or fraudulent information, they will not be considered for the position. Furthermore, applications often include statements that the applicant could be disciplined or even terminated if misleading or fraudulent information is subsequently discovered after being hired.[4]

Background Verification and References. Applications should include a statement that gives an organization permission to conduct a background verification or check. The purpose of a **background verification** is to confirm information provided on an employment application. Common types of background verification include employment dates, salary, professional credentials (i.e., certifications, licenses), education, and training programs. **References** are another form of background verification that sometimes solicits perceptual information about applicants in addition to factual information. There has been a trend for organizations not to provide references due to legal risks. For example, if a candidate does not receive a job offer, they may accuse a previous employer of providing information to a potential employer that hurt their employment chance. Prior employers will often only verify dates of employment, job titles, and sometimes salary information—all factual information—versus subjective information such as job performance, motivation, cooperation, and so forth. When doing reference checks, it is important that care is taken to avoid introducing subjectivity, judgments, and bias into the selection process. **Negligent hiring** occurs when an employee causes significant harm to individuals or property inside or outside the organization, because an organization did not reasonably verify background information prior to extending an employment offer.[2,4]

Pre-employment Selection Testing. Pre-employment selection testing is another selection method that can be used to identify qualified candidates. **Selection testing** involves administering various valid and reliable assessments to gain insights into a candidate's abilities related to key job activities. Selection tests are intended to predict successful performance on key job activities. **Reliability** means that a test consistently measures what it is intended to measure on repeated administrations of the test or on administering alternative forms of the test. **Validity** means that the test is really measuring what it is intended to measure. What a section test is intended to measure must be related to the job requirements. Managers must rely on their human resource professionals to oversee selection testing and assure that any tests used are valid, reliable, and job related and supported with appropriate documentation from credential professionals. There are serious potential legal liabilities if this is not the case and any tests are found to be discriminatory, as well, if test-takers privacy rights are violated. Tests should not be the sole information used in making hiring decisions. Testing should be used as another source of evidence about an applicant's ability to be successful in a job. Because of potential legal liability, costs, and the time required, many organizations may use limited, if any, testing in their selection process. However, advances in testing methods and decreasing costs due to online testing options are promoting wider use of selection testing. There is a wide array of selection tests that can be used.[3]

Selection tests can be categorized into several major categories that include cognitive tests, motor and physical ability tests, personality tests, achievement tests, and work sampling and simulation tests. **Cognitive tests** are used to measure mental abilities, reasoning, and memory. **Motor and physical ability tests** focus on a candidate's dexterity and physical strength, agility, coordination, and stamina when these are essential requirements for accomplishing key job duties. **Personality tests** focus on behavioral factors such as attitude, motivation, temperament, interests, and many other behavioral factors that are predictive of job performance. **Achievement tests** measure what a person has learned in a particular area from formal training, education, and experience. **Work sampling and simulation tests** assess candidates' proficiency on an actual sample of tasks from the job. Additional tests are specialized and can be used to assess a range of specialized knowledge, skills, and/or abilities. Again, consultation with trained professionals is vital in the use of selection testing as part of the selection process.[4]

Discrimination, Affirmative Action, and Equal Opportunity. When selecting qualified candidates, there are a number of legal considerations that managers must be aware of related to labor and employment law. The legal and regulatory environment continues to be complex and constantly evolving. Managers should always consult with the appropriate resource in their organization regarding legal matters. The following discussion provides a high-level overview of labor and employment law topics managers should be familiar with in relation to acquiring human resources. The following discussion does not constitute legal advice and should not be interpreted as such.

Discrimination and equal employment opportunity are recurrent themes in employment and labor law. Managers should understand what constitutes discrimination and other types of unfair employment practices. The discussion here is limited to laws that managers should consider during the employee selection process. The question a manager should constantly ask is, "Does the candidate meet the minimum job qualifications?" and "Can the candidate perform the minimum job requirements?" The following laws point managers back to these basic questions when considering candidates.

The **Equal Pay Act of 1963** requires employers to provide fair and equitable pay to men and women who perform the same job at the same organization. The **Civil Rights Act of 1964** and subsequent amendments in 1991 prohibit employers from discriminating in employment or other terms and conditions of employment on the basis of race, color, religion, sex, or national origin. This Act established the **Equal Employment Opportunity Commission (EEOC)** to investigate claims of employment discrimination. The **Age Discrimination Act of 1967** prohibits employers from using age as a basis to discriminate against candidates or employees. **The Pregnancy Discrimination Act of 1978** expanded the definition of sex discrimination to include employment practices that discriminate against women because of pregnancy, childbirth, or a related medical conditions. The **Immigration Reform and Control Act of 1986** requires employers to verify that job applicants are U.S. citizens or are legally permitted to work in the United States. This law created the Employment Eligibility Form or I-9 form to verify an applicant's identity and eligibility to work in the country. Employees must complete the form within three days of their hire date. The form becomes a part of the employee's employment record in human resources. The **Drug-Free Workplace Act of 1988** requires employers performing work for the federal government to make a reasonable effort to maintain a drug-free work environment through drug awareness and education programs. The **Americans with Disabilities Act** of 1990 extends protection provided under the Civil Rights Act of 1964 to disabled Americans. This Act prohibits potential employers from discriminating against disabled applicants or employees. Managers and potential employers are prohibited from asking about an applicant's health status or about any medical conditions that an applicant may have prior to an offer. The Act also requires employers to make reasonable accommodations for disabled employees. In addition, certain employers who **contract** with the federal government may be required to prepare an **Affirmative Action Plan** to promote hiring of females, minorities, and/or persons with disabilities who have historically faced discrimination.[2,3]

Interviewing. Managers regularly interview qualified candidates to aid in making a final selection decision to fill open positions. **Interviewing** provides an opportunity for managers and others involved in the hiring decision to ask questions to better understand a candidate's work experience, qualifications, and behaviors. There is no fixed rule about the number of candidates to interview. Generally, the human resource department screens applications and forwards around five applications for entry-level positions and three applications for executive-level or hard-to-fill positions.[2] Managers can participate in screening applications; however, staff from the human resource department are the experts. Organizations and managers should consider the costs associated with their time and the organization's time in making a decision. The purpose of the following discussion is to help managers understand the different interviewing approaches and the types of questions that are appropriate to ask in an interview setting.

Planning is essential to the interview process. The interview process typically begins with interviewers carefully reviewing the job description before an interview, so that the position duties and qualifications are fresh and easy to recall during the interview. Managers should also thoroughly review the application materials (i.e., application and résumé) before an interview. Interviewers who are trying to read an applicant's materials during an interview will be distracted and will not be fully engaged in the interview or able to actively listen to the interviewee's responses. Managers make an impression on applicants as well as applicants make an impression on managers and others making the hiring decision. Appearing to be unprepared and distracted is unprofessional and may result in a great candidate withdrawing their name for consideration or not accepting a position. Managers should consider where they conduct interviews and ensure that the area is private and free from disruptions. An office or conference room provides a comfortable, as well as a private, setting for interviews. Interviews will vary in length, depending on the type of position. Entry-level interviews are generally around 30–45 minutes. Mid-level interviews are generally a minimum of an hour and could last an entire day, depending on the position and organization. Executive-level interviews can vary from a couple of hours to multiday interviews. Managers and human resource staff should consider providing to candidates in advance an overview of what they should expect during an interview. Remember it is important to be fair and provide each candidate with the same information and schedule. Agendas with detailed meeting information are highly recommended for mid-level and executive-level interviews, especially when candidates participate in multi-department or multi-day interviews. This helps put the interviewee at ease and use the interview time as efficiently as possible. Entry-level position interviews often include a short tour of the workspace or environment where the candidate would work. Mid-level and executive-level interviews often include an in-depth tour, as well as breakfast, lunch, and/or dinner. A short tour is often a nice way for a manager to begin or end any interview. Managers should always be on time to interviews. In the event an emergency arises, the manager or interviewer should communicate why they are running late. Managers should remember that candidates are interviewing the organization. The manager is a representative of the organization and should always be professional, respectful, and courteous.[2]

Creating a positive environment for interviewees helps to facilitate their success. Interviewers should begin an interview in a way that creates a welcoming environment and puts the candidate at ease. An interview should open with the interviewer thanking the candidate for taking the time to interview for the position followed by introductions. The interviewer should know the candidate's name and address the candidate by name. This makes a good first impression, reassures the candidate, and communicates that the interviewer takes the interview seriously. The interviewer sets the tone for the interview. The interviewer and any additional interviewers should introduce themselves to the candidate by stating their name, title, department, and summary of their role in the organization. The interviewer should help the candidate feel at ease and provide an opportunity for the candidate to warm up, so that the interview is as productive as possible. Interviewers often ask candidates to provide a short summary of their education and work history.[3] Providing an overview of the interview is a nice way to transition to the interview process and the interview questions.

Types of Interviews. There are a number of different types of interviews, such as one-on-one, panel or team, mass or group, and virtual.[4] Managers who will supervise a position often lead interviewing efforts in consultation with the human resource department. The type of interview corresponds to both the number of interviewers and candidates, along with the type, level, and timeframe to fill the position. The interview type could also depend on typical organizational practices.

One-on-one interviews include one candidate and one interviewer. The advantage of this type of interview is that the interviewer is able to ask many questions and ask follow-up questions, as needed. Candidates often feel more relaxed when there is only one interviewer. The ability for both the candidate and the interviewer to ask questions and not feel pressured or rushed is important. A disadvantage of a one-on-one interview is that the candidate only gets to meet one current employee. Likewise, one person's assessment of the candidate is influencing the hiring decision.[2,4] Many organizations have moved to having a candidate complete several one-on-one interviews with different interviewers or utilize a team or panel interview.

Team or panel interviews include one candidate and multiple interviewers. Organizations use this approach if a position is part of a larger team or supervises a number of different departments or employees. Additionally, team or panel interviews can stem from an organization's values and culture that emphasize teamwork and collaboration. Team interviews offer a number of advantages. First, the candidate can get a better impression and sense of the organization by meeting more current employees and understanding what it is they do and how they relate to the open position. Second, the hiring decision considers input from multiple interviewers versus one interviewer. This is particularly important if the position oversees a department or multiple employees. This helps those being supervised or working with the individual in the position to feel like they were a part of the hiring decision. Team interviewers should use a standardized set of questions for all candidates. Team members should ideally work together to develop a list of important questions based on the job description and minimum qualifications. This provides an opportunity for team members to ask questions that are important to them and that demonstrate how they interact with the position. A drawback to this approach is the time it takes to schedule and participate in a group interview. Too many interviewers can leave little time for the candidates and the interviewers to get to know one another because one person dominates the conversation. Team interviewers can also have too many questions, which can rush the candidate's answers or interviewer's subsequent questions. Current employees can feel that they are not able to get their job done because they participate in too many interviews and become fatigued by the group interview. Group interviewers may not reach a consensus on the best candidate for a position. This can result in conflict and strain their work relationship.[3]

Mass or group interviewing is when more than one candidate interviews for a job at the same time. This interviewing approach has many advantages and disadvantages for those conducting and participating in the interview. The advantage for the interviewing organization or manager is that they are able to conduct multiple interviews simultaneously. This helps in terms of the time spent conducting the interviews. This approach drastically reduces the amount of time interviewers need to reserve for interviews and helps enhance organizational efficiency. This also helps an interviewer compare and contrast candidates and their qualifications and experiences. Interviewers can also observe how candidates interact not only with those conducting the interview but also with those who are participating in the interview. This gives the interviewer a better sense of how candidates will perform and work in teams. Ultimately, a group interview can help fill a position quickly. A drawback of group interviewing is that the interviewer or interviewers are unable to get to know each of the candidates very well. Additionally, a candidate who is great for a position may not stand out in a group interview because a handful of candidates dominate the interview. For candidates, the advantage of a group interview is that they are able to speak to why they are more qualified or experienced than another candidate. Candidates participating in a group interview should compare and contrast their experience and qualifications to other candidates. Candidates who are able to take control of a group interview may be noticed by those who are interviewing them and have a greater likelihood of being selected. Candidates, however, may not be able to ask specific questions that they have about a position. A group interview may lead a candidate to have a negative impression of the organization and may lead a highly qualified candidate to become disinterested in the position.[4]

Virtual interviewing utilizes technology to conduct an interview. This interviewing approach is growing in popularity. Interviewers and candidates connect over the Internet using video conferencing technology that utilizes a web camera and microphone. There are two general types of virtual interviews: one-way and two-way interviews. **One-way interviews** are an asynchronous type of interview and communication. With this approach, the employer sends a list of interview questions to potential candidates and the candidates video their responses to the questions and submits them to the organization. This approach allows candidates to develop and practice their responses. Candidates are also able to make multiple recordings and submit the best video for consideration. A major drawback to one-way interviewers is that candidates do not have an opportunity to interact with an interviewer or ask questions. Organizations may not view the submissions if they are pressed for time, which could mean that strong candidates are overlooked. A **two-way interview** is a synchronous type of interview where a candidate and an interviewer log on at the same time and have a real-time conversation that is much like a one-on-one interview. An advantage of this approach is that the candidate and the interviewer are able to interact in real time. This provides a more personal interview experience.[2,3]

There are a number of advantages to virtual interviewing for employers. First, virtual interviewing allows employers to draw qualified candidates from beyond a limited geographic region. Second, virtual interviewing is a great way to screen candidates to see if they have the requisite skills and qualifications for a specific position before a candidate is invited for an in-person interview and an organization incurs travel costs associated with bringing an applicant from out of town to the organization. Third, virtual interviewing is relatively inexpensive and efficient. Fourth, employers are able to assess candidates' comfort with technology, which is important if the job the candidate is applying for requires the candidate to utilize technology to work or collaborate virtually. The ability to virtually meet with an employer and consider a position that may be hundreds or thousands of miles from where a candidate lives is important. In contrast to phone interviews, candidates can see and better read the expressions of an interviewer. There are a number of disadvantages for employers. Employers may not be able to build a rapport or make a candidate feel comfortable. A potential benefit, however, is that the employers are able to read an interviewee's expressions and body language. Internet connections can vary. Candidates who have poor connections could limit the extent of interviews. For both the interviewer and the interviewee, virtual interviewing influences first impressions. Dressing professionally, being on time, and conducting the interview in a private setting are still important.

Types of Interview Questions. Interview questions are essential to the interview process. Managers should prepare interview questions based on the job description, qualifications, and in accordance with all applicable laws. Interview questions should remain focused on the job, qualifications, and activities performed as part of the job. There are a number of different types of interview questions that can be used during an interview. The type of questions again depends on the job and the organization. Two common types of interview questions are structured and unstructured. In practice, a combination of question types is used.

Structured interviews utilize a standardized set of interview questions for all candidates.[4] This helps remove bias because every candidate is being asked the same set of questions. They also help interviewers

ensure that they are asking legal questions that are relevant to a position. A list of questions also helps in efficiently conducting an interview and comparing responses after an interview. A drawback of structured interview questions is that they do not provide flexibility or opportunities for an interviewer to ask follow-up or probing questions.

Unstructured interview questions are open-ended questions that depend on the candidate to provide responses that direct the course of the interview.[4] Unstructured interview questions provide the advantage of being more flexible, which allows the question to be tailored to a candidate's specific qualifications and experience. This also allows the candidate to guide the interview, which can give an interviewer a better picture of a candidate's experience and qualifications. Drawbacks of this approach are that a standardized set of questions are not being asked across all candidates. This could potentially lead to discrimination or bias on the part of an interviewer and could present some legal risks to the organization. An unstructured interview approach means that the interview can take a number of different directions and a significant amount of time. If the candidate is guiding the interview, the interviewer may not get to ask important questions that can help make a determination about a candidate's experience and qualifications.

There are specific types of questions that can be used to ascertain different types of information from candidates regardless of whether a structured or unstructured interview format is used. **Background questions** are used to probe details about a candidate's experience and skills by asking for specific examples of how they have performed similar job duties and activities in the past. For example, "What experience have you had in recalibrating lab equipment like ours in the past"? **Situational questions** give applicants examples of actual situations that might arise in performing the job and then ask what they would do. For example, "Suppose you were conducting a public meeting and a difficult technical question arose that you did not know the answer to. What would you do?" **Job knowledge questions** ask about how to accomplish duties required in the position. For example, "Preparing a marketing plan for our outpatient clinics is one of the responsibilities in this position. How would you go about preparing a marketing plan?" **Behavioral questions** ask candidates to recall and relate past job-related behaviors to the vacant position. For example, "Please relate what you think is the most significant action you have ever taken to help out a fellow employee." These are just a few examples of different types of question that can illuminate different aspects of a candidate's capabilities.[4]

Interview Question to Ask and Avoid. Managers, particularly new managers, must take interviews seriously and understand what is legal and illegal to ask during an interview. This section will provide a discussion of interview questions managers should avoid. Legal questions to ask during an interview help assess what the candidate "knows, has done, can do, and would like to do."[3] [(p127)] **EXHIBIT 6.2** provides examples of legally permissible questions interviewers can ask during an interview. There are a number of interview questions managers and other interviewers should avoid because they are potentially illegal and/or discriminatory. Remember questions should always relate to the position description, qualifications, and ability of a candidate to perform job tasks. Hiring decisions made on personal information are usually illegal. **EXHIBIT 6.3** provides examples of illegal questions. Topics and questions to avoid during an interview include:

- Questions about a candidate's age, race, color, ethnicity, religion, sex, or national origin. For example, how old are you? What religious holidays do you celebrate? What is your gender? Are you a legal U.S. citizen?

- Questions about a candidate's marital status, pregnancy, childbirth, children, family plans, or about medical conditions related to pregnancy and childbearing. For example, are you married, single, divorced, or widowed? Are you pregnant or do you plan on becoming pregnant?
- Questions about a candidate's physical or mental disabilities. For example, what disabilities do you have and how severe are they?
- Questions about a candidate's health status or conditions. For example, are you a diabetic?

Managers should always consult with their human resource department if they have any questions about what to ask. There are often professional and legal ways to obtain information that is relevant to a job. For example, background verification could include checking an applicant's driving record or criminal record. Managers should prepare questions prior to an interview. This helps keep the questions focused on the position and ensures that illegal questions are avoided. Interviewers who fail to prepare questions in advance risk asking irrelevant and illegal questions.[3] Applicants will sometimes volunteer personal or illegal

EXHIBIT 6.2 Examples of Legally Permissible Pre-employment Questions

Concerning an applicant's personal information, in a pre-employment interview, a potential employer may legally ask the following questions or request the following information:

1. What is your full name?
2. What is your address and the telephone number at which you can be reached?
3. What is your prior work experience? For each prior employer, this may include:
   - Employer's name and address
   - Jobs or positions held
   - Duties performed
   - Skills needed to perform job duties
   - Tools, machinery, equipment, and vehicles used in job performance
   - Name of immediate supervisor
   - Rate of pay received
   - Length of time on the job
   - Reason for leaving
4. What do you know about the requirements of the job for which you are applying?
5. What skills, education, training, or experience have you had that is relevant to performing the duties of this job?
6. Do you hold the licenses or certifications that may be required for employment in the position in question (for example, a driver's license, an electrician's license, or a registered nursing license)?
7. What were the primary duties and the most important responsibilities of your most recent job?
8. What do you believe was the most difficult part of the job you have been most recently doing? Why?
9. What safety procedures were you required to follow at your most recent employment?
10. Are you applying for full-time, part-time, or temporary work?
11. Are you able to work the particular shift or shifts typical for this job?
12. Are you able to work overtime or weekends when it is necessary?
13. Are you able to meet this organization's attendance standard?
14. If hired, when are you able to begin work?

Reproduced Exhibit 13-3 from Fallon LR, McConnell CR. *Human Resources Management in Health Care Principles and Practice.* 2nd ed. Burlington, MA: Jones and Bartlett Learning; 2014.

EXHIBIT 6.3 Examples of Forbidden Pre-employment Questions

General

Concerning an applicant's general history, in a pre-employment interview, a potential employer may not ask the following:

1. Do you attend church regularly? What church do you go to, and who is the pastor?
2. What religious holidays do you observe?
3. What is your nationality, ancestry, descent, parentage, or lineage?
4. What nationality are your parents? Your spouse?
5. What is your native language?
6. Are you married? Divorced? Separated?
7. Where does your spouse work? What does he (or she) do for a living?
8. Do you have children? What are their names and ages? Do you have a reliable arrangement for childcare?
9. Was your name ever changed by marriage or court order? If so, what was your original name?
10. When were you born? How old are you?
11. Where were you born?
12. Where were your parents born? Where was your spouse born?
13. What country are you a citizen of?
14. Are you a native-born or naturalized citizen of the United States?
15. Do you own your own home or do you rent?
16. How did you acquire the ability to read, write, or speak English?
17. What kind of discharge did you receive from the U.S. military?
18. What clubs, societies, lodges, or fraternal organizations do you belong?
19. How many children do you plan to have?
20. Have you ever had your wages garnished?
21. Have you ever filed for bankruptcy, either personally or as a business owner?
22. Has your spouse ever worked here?
23. What is your height? Your weight?
24. Would your spouse approve of your employment here should you be hired?

Medical

Concerning an applicant's medical history, in a pre-employment interview, a potential employer may not ask the following:

1. How is your health in general?
2. Do you have any relevant medical problems or conditions?
3. Have you or any member of your family ever been treated for any of the following diseases or conditions? (This is followed by a checklist that may include: cancer, heart disease, high blood pressure, diabetes, epilepsy, AIDS, back problems, carpal tunnel syndrome, hearing loss, contact dermatitis, drug or alcohol abuse, tendonitis, arthritis, tuberculosis, sexually transmitted diseases, and mental illnesses.)
4. Are you taking prescription medication? Which medications are you taking and for what conditions are they prescribed?
5. Have you ever been hospitalized? For what conditions?
6. Do you have any disabilities or medical, physical, or mental limitations that could prevent you from performing the duties of the job in question?
7. Are you in any way disabled, or do you have a disability? If so, how did you become disabled?
8. What is the prognosis of your disability?
9. Will you require time off for treatment or medical leave due to anticipated incapacitation because of your disability?
10. Have you ever been injured on the job or had any other work-related accidents?
11. Check off on a list of potentially disabling impairments any physical limitations that you may have.
12. Is any member of your family disabled?
13. Have you ever filed a Workers' Compensation claim?
14. Have you received any payment for a Workers' Compensation claim?

Modified from Exhibit 13-2 from Fallon LR, McConnell CR. *Human Resources Management in Health Care Principles and Practice.* 2nd ed. Burlington, MA: Jones and Bartlett Learning; 2014.

information. This does not give managers permission to ask follow-up questions related to the information shared. Hiring decisions cannot be made based on personal or illegal information that was volunteered during an interview. Also, candidates can misinterpret a poorly worded or phrased question. Interviewers can redirect a candidate's responses by reiterating that the focus of the interview is on the position. Interviewers should have a couple of questions they can use to get an interview back on track when a candidate is volunteering too much personal or illegal information. Interviewers should consult with human resources on any aspect of an interview that is uncomfortable, inappropriate, or illegal. Human resources will have a procedure for documenting interviews. Reporting and documenting any incidents as soon as possible helps protect all parties, especially the interviewer and the organization. This also provides support for hiring decisions.[2]

Concluding an Interview. Interviewers should thank the candidate for their time and interest in the position. The interview should always conclude with the manager describing what the next steps are in the selection process. When possible, managers should provide a general timeline for when a decision will be made, what type of follow-up to expect, and who is likely to do the follow-up. Managers should not make any promises, official offers, or provide feedback on how the interview went with regard to the candidate (i.e., "You're the best candidate we've seen." "I can't wait for you to start!").[2]

Making an Employment Offer

Organizations vary in who is authorized to make an official employment offer. Frequently, the human resource department makes formal offers to a candidate who is selected for a position. The offer typically includes salary and benefit information as well as how long a candidate has to consider and respond to the offer. This information is generally communicated over the phone and then followed by a formal written offer. The candidate may negotiate salary and benefits based on the formal written offer. Usually, upper management and human resources must approve negotiated salaries and benefits. Managers are usually involved in salary negotiations within an established range. Managers are frequently involved in working out start dates.[2]

Most organizations ensure that unsuccessful candidates receive notification that a hiring decision has been made. Human resources is generally responsible for notifying unsuccessful candidates and thanking them for their time and interest. Unsuccessful candidates may contact managers or others who interviewed them to ask why they were not selected for a job. Managers, or anyone

who participated in an interview, should not disclose any information about why one candidate was selected over another. The best practice is to refer unsuccessful candidates to human resources. Human resource professionals are accustomed to responding to such inquiries and will ensure that the organization responds in a way that is appropriate and in compliance with all applicable laws.[3]

Conclusion

Staffing is concerned with acquiring the human resources or capital an organization needs to achieve their plans and goals. Managers play an important role in staffing. Conducting a job analysis reveals the types of tasks that need to be completed in an organization and serves as the starting point for developing a job description. Understanding the key elements of a job description is important to recruiting and ultimately selecting the best candidate for a position and organization. Public health managers must also be familiar with the selection process. Applications, résumés, and background verification are commonly used to help screen candidates for positions. Interviews are widely used to aid in making final selection decisions. One-on-one, panel (or team), and group interviews are used by public health organizations. Interviews can be conducted in person or virtually via video conferencing technology. Public health managers must comply with all applicable laws and regulations. Interview questions that are thoughtfully developed can help managers avoid legal issues and identify the best candidate for a position.

Discussion Questions

1. Explain the three major stages in the human resource management process. Staffing is related to what stage in the process?
2. What is the definition of staffing? What are the typical steps in the staffing process?
3. What is a job analysis? What sources of information should managers use to analyze tasks or functions performed in a job?
4. Describe important elements of a job or position description.
5. Describe important elements of job qualifications or specifications.
6. Why is the statement "Job descriptions are written for a position, not people" important?
7. Why is recruiting important to all the subsequent steps in the staffing process?
8. What is the difference between an employment application and a résumé? Why should organizations use applications for hiring versus résumés?

9. What are the major types of pre-employment selection tests?
10. What forms of discrimination do the major employment laws seek to prohibit?
11. Compare and contrast the different types of interviews discussed in the chapter.
12. What are some examples of legally permissible questions to ask during an interview?
13. What are some examples of illegal questions to ask during an interview?
14. Discuss how to make an employment offer.

Learning Activities

1. Find a public health position that interests you. You could select your current position if you are working in public health. You can also search the Internet or work with your Career Development Center to find a position that interests you. Analyze the position based on the important elements of a job description discussed in the chapter. Are all the position description elements reflected in the job posting? What is missing? What could be improved?
2. Select a public health organization that interests you. Imagine you are a manager in the organization. Create a position description for a job you are trying to fill. What would be your recruitment plan for recruiting internal and external candidates? What type of interviewing approach would you use?

3. Search the Internet to identify job applications used by a public health organization. Compare and contrast the applications based what was discussed in the chapter.
4. Search the Internet to identify job descriptions and qualifications used by a public health organization. Compare and contrast the job descriptions and qualifications based what was discussed in the chapter.
5. Develop a résumé that you can use to apply to public health positions. Research best practices in résumé writing. Check with your Career Development Center for resources and résumé templates. Consider inviting a professional career counselor from your Career Development Center to your class to discuss résumé writing and the basics of an internship or job search. Many Career Development Centers welcome students to make appointments to review and discuss their résumé during one-on-one counseling sessions. The centers often have an internship and job posting board or system, career fair, and other resources to help connect students with opportunities.
6. Find a public health position that interests you. Pretend you are the public health manager trying to fill the position. Research and develop a list of questions you would ask during interviews with candidates. Research and develop a list of questions that you would avoid asking during interviews because the questions are illegal to ask.

References

1. Kast FE, Rosenzweig JE. *Organization and Management: A Systems and Contingency Approach.* 4th ed. New York, NY: McGraw-Hill; 1985.
2. Fallon LR, McConnell CR. *Human Resource Management in Health Care Principles and Practice.* 2nd ed. Burlington, MA: Jones & Bartlett Learning; 2014.
3. McConnell CR. *Umiker's Management Skills for the New Health Care Supervisor.* 7th ed. Burlington, MA: Jones & Bartlett Learning; 2018.
4. Dressler G. *Human Resource Management.* 14th ed. Boston, MA: Pearson; 2015.

Suggested Readings and Websites

ASTHO. Human resources and workforce development directors peer network. Public Health Workforce Interests and Needs Survey. http://www.astho.org/phwins/

CDC. Workforce development resources. https://www.cdc.gov/ophss/csels/dsepd/resources.html

CDC. National public health workforce strategic roadmap. https://www.cdc.gov/ophss/csels/dsepd/strategic-workforce-activities/ph-workforce/roadmap.html

CDC. Strategic workforce activities. https://www.cdc.gov/ophss/csels/dsepd/strategic-workforce-activities/index.html

Global Health Workforce Alliance. http://www.who.int/workforce-alliance/knowledge/case_studies/en/

Human Resources for Health Journal. https://human-resources-health.biomedcentral.com/

Journal of Public Health Management and Practice Public Health Workforce Interests and Needs Survey (PH WINS). https://journals.lww.com/jphmp/pages/toc.aspx?year=2015&issue=11001

National Board of Public Health Examiners. https://www.nbphe.org/

National Commission for Health Education Credentialing, Inc. https://www.nchec.org/

Partners in Information Access for the Public Health Workforce. https://phpartners.org/workforcedevelopment.html

Society for Human Resource Management. https://www.shrm.org/

WHO. Global Strategy on human resources for health: Workforce 2030. http://apps.who.int/iris/bitstream/handle/10665/250368/?sequence=1

WHO. Health Workforce Newsletters. http://www.who.int/hrh/resources/en/

WHO. Human Resources for Health Observer. http://www.who.int/hrh/resources/observer/en/

CHAPTER 7

Human Resource Development and Engagement in Public Health

▶ Human Resource Management Process

The previous chapter discussed the first stage in the human resource management process—staffing. The staffing step was concerned with how public health organizations acquire human resources. This chapter discusses the second and third steps in the human resource management process—development and engagement. These steps are concerned with how public health managers develop and engage their staff or human resources once they have been acquired. Employees, or human resources, are critical resources that managers are responsible for acquiring, developing, and engaging to complete jobs that contribute to accomplishing organizational goals. **FIGURE 7.1** outlines the human resource management process and the activities that fall under each of the three stages.

Acquisition
- Job description and qualifications
- Recruitment
- Selection
- Pre-employment screening
- Background verification
- Reference verification
- Interviewing
- Hiring

Development
- New employee orientation
- Onboarding
- Job training
- Professional development
- Performance appraisal
- Coaching
- Counseling
- Discipline
- Termination

Engagement
- Compensation
- Benefits
- Recognition programs
- Employee relations
- Labor relations
- Health and safety
- Wellness programs

FIGURE 7.1 Human resource management process and key activities.

Modified from Exhibit 4-2 Fallon LR, McConnell CR. *Human Resource Management in Health Care Principles and Practice*. 2nd ed. Burlington, MA: Jones & Bartlett Learning; 2014.

EXHIBIT 7.1 Orientation Program Topics

- Overview of the organization's mission, vision, and values
- The organization's history and structure
- Overview of the compensation and benefits structure
- Blood-borne pathogens, TB control
- Confidentiality of patient information
- Cultural proficiency and diversity awareness
- Electrical safety, the Safe Medical Device Act
- Emergency preparedness, disaster plan
- Fire safety
- Hazardous communications, the Right-to-Know Law
- Improving organizational performance
- Risk management
- Incident reporting
- Infection control
- No-smoking policy
- Patients' rights
- Professional misconduct
- Security management
- General age-specific competencies
- Use of the organization's property and systems
- Internet, email, and social media use
- Overview of personnel policy manual
- Employee identification badge
- Confidentiality statement
- Employee handbook review

Reproduced from McConnell CR. *Umiker's Management Skills for the New Health Care Supervisor*. 7th ed. Burlington, MA: Jones & Bartlett Learning; 2018.

▶ Human Resource Development

Human resource development begins when an **employee** is hired and includes new employee orientation, onboarding, training, and development. Managers play an integral role in developing employees for performance in their current position and for future contributions to the organization. This section discusses managerial responsibilities after a candidate has accepted a position in a public health organization.

New Employee Orientation

Orientation is the process of introducing new employees to the organization and to their new job. The organization's human resource department usually conducts orientation for new employees. Orientation is for a defined period, which can range from half a day to a couple months, depending on the job and organization. Clinical positions often require a longer orientation period in comparison to nonclinical positions. Orientation typically focuses on introducing new employees to the organization's vision, mission, core values, organizational structure, and how all these elements work together to accomplish the organization's goals (**EXHIBIT 7.1**). Orientation also provides a review of important internal organizational processes and systems that are used to conduct business and manage the organization's employees. Orientation also reviews important policies and procedures that are contained in the employee handbook. New employees are often required to sign an acknowledgement that they have read and that they understand the handbook. This process makes expectations clear to new employees and provides some legal protections to an organization by assuring employees are aware of important organizational policies. New hires are able to complete required paperwork to receive benefits, such as **insurance**, retirement savings program, flexible spending accounts, employee wellness program, and other employee benefits. Also, employee IDs and parking permits are usually distributed at orientation.

For public health organizations, there are often certain types of training that must be completed before employees can begin work, such as sexual harassment training, CPR, basic first aid, Health Information Portability and Accountability Act (**HIPAA**) training, and blood-borne pathogen training, among others.[1-4]

Divisions, departments, or work units often have their own orientation to begin socializing the new employee and orienting them to their specific job duties. It is important that new employees are welcomed and introduced to their co-workers early on, particularly those that they will work with most closely. Managers must also set clear expectations for new employees. Orientations often have agendas and checklists to help ensure a thorough overview. Managers are responsible for developing unit- and job-specific checklists to facilitate orientation. Reviewing these checklists with new employees helps them to understand their role and performance expectations and allows managers to document that these were reviewed. Departmental orientations also focus on departmental policies and processes that a new employee needs to be aware of to accomplish their job. Managers review job descriptions, duties, responsibilities, and expectations. New employee should have an opportunity to ask questions and clarify any aspect of their new job. Managers should also review the work schedule with the new employee along with security information. Workplace safety and violence are changing the ways organizations and departments function. Increasingly, managers are responsible for communicating emergency preparedness plans and what employees should do in the case of an emergency. Overall, departmental orientations are important because they relate the employee's role to department and organizational goals.

Employee Onboarding

Employee onboarding refers to the process of socializing, integrating, and assimilating new employees to their role and to the culture of the organization. The goal or outcome of employee onboarding is to foster fit between the employee and the organization and, ultimately, attachment. **Attachment theory** serves as an undercurrent in onboarding because managers are working to develop relationships with new employees to motivate and engage them. Attachment helps promote employee motivation, satisfaction, productivity, and retention. This enhances individual employee performance and, in turn, organizational performance.[1,2] Onboarding is a process that can take anywhere from 6 to 24 months, depending on the job, experience,

education, organization, and other factors. Onboarding takes time because attachment requires interpersonal relationships, which take time to develop.

Onboarding begins during the human resource selection process and extends through the human resource development and engagement processes. Part of the selection process is communicating how a job contributes to the organization's vision, mission, and values. Managers play a pivotal role in communicating and helping candidates understand what the organization is about so candidates can assess whether they would be a good fit with the organization as well as the job. Indeed, the selection process focuses on how well a candidate fits with a job and with the larger organization. New employees begin to gain a sense of an organization's culture through the interview and selection process. New employee orientation sets the tone for what an organization values and is an integral part of the onboarding process.

Training

Training is an essential aspect of human resource development that focuses on providing employees with job-related skills. Training programs provide employees with skills necessary to accomplish their current job and enhance their performance in this position over time. Efficiency is one result of training. Different organizations have different equipment, systems, and processes, which require training, so that employees understand how such systems and processes relate to their job. Therefore, training tends to be focused on knowledge and skills needed for the job and lasts for relatively short periods of time. Managers are important in identifying training needs and providing opportunities for employees to participate in training activities. Typical types of training programs include on-the-job training, shadowing experienced workers, classroom instruction, online- and video-based learning, simulation and virtual technology, among many other options. Training enhances employee and departmental performance, which also enhances the organization's efficiency, effectiveness, and goal attainment.[3,4]

Development

Development focuses on building knowledge and capabilities for an employee to use in future jobs that can create value for the organization or other organizations. Building capabilities that enhance an employee's value and contribution to the organization is central to management responsibilities. Managers are responsible for identifying development opportunities and formalizing development plans for employees. An effective way to do this is in collaboration with employees. In contrast to training, development programs build a broader base of knowledge, skills, and abilities, which takes time and resources. Managers want to ensure that employees are committed to development and the types of contributions they can make to the organization after they complete professional development. Examples of development activities include university degree programs, professional certifications, continuing education workshops and seminars, job rotation, case studies, management games, simulations, leadership and management programs, corporate universities, coaching, and mentoring, among many other options.

Performance Appraisals

A **performance appraisal** is a tool that managers use to assess and enhance employee performance. **Performance management** is the process of using performance appraisal results to improve employee performance.[4] Performance management recognizes that managers play an active role in developing employees in addition to assessing their performance. Managers use performance appraisals to help employees understand how well they are doing in their current job. This process identifies areas that need improvement, as well as areas of exceptional performance. Appraisals also help employees understand what capabilities (i.e., knowledge, skills, or abilities) they need to develop to create additional value for the organization, which will also help them advance professionally. In many organizations, performance appraisal results serve as the basis for raises and other forms of compensation, as well as disciplinary action up to termination for poor job performance. Ultimately, the purpose of performance appraisal and management is to review job and performance expectations, evaluate past job performance, recognize an employee's accomplishments and contributions, and develop an action plan for enhancing future performance.[3] This process leverages the knowledge, skills, and abilities of employees in a way that links what they do to the organization's goals and strategy.

Managers are responsible for carrying out the performance appraisal process according to the organization's policies and procedures. The human resource department usually provides guidance to managers about when and how to complete appraisals and runs the overall program. Managers use an employee's job description and the organization's performance appraisal form to conduct an evaluation. Performance

appraisals become a part of an employee's permanent record. Since this process provides important feedback to employees about the work they are doing; therefore, new employees should receive frequent feedback from managers. Frequent feedback early in the job helps build rapport and reinforce performance expectations. Many organizations use 30-, 60-, 90-, or 120-day reviews for new employees or even existing employees. Formal performance evaluations generally occur at the 6-month mark or at the end of a new employee's probationary period. Usually existing employees receive at least an annual review, and some organizations require managers to conduct quarterly or biannual reviews. Performance appraisals take a lot of time for a managers that supervise a large department or multiple departments. Therefore, most organizations conduct annual performance evaluations. This does not mean that managers should not provide regular performance feedback that recognizes significant contributions or identifies areas for improvement in between these formal reviews. Managers should provide informal and formal feedback to employees throughout the year about their performance. Organizations are not legally required to conduct performance appraisals. However, performance appraisals provide a number of benefits to an organization. One of the primary benefits is that evaluations document an employee's job performance. Documenting poor performance provides the opportunity to develop improvement plans to help address and correct performance deficiencies. From a legal standpoint, this provides documentation for termination of employees who do not improve their performance. The next section discusses the different types of appraisals an organization might use.

Appraisal Methods

Organizations can use a variety of different appraisal methods to conduct performance appraisals. Appraisal methods vary in terms of the criteria used for the appraisal, the documentation and time required, and the level of detail and feedback provided. Outcomes and behaviors are the two major appraisal categories that are usually assessed. **Outcomes** are results produced from performing a job. **Behaviors** are actions that a person takes in doing their job. Appraisals can be unstructured or structured. **Unstructured appraisals** have a flexible and more open-ended flowing format. This design format elicits personalized information. In contrast, **structured appraisals** have a defined format. The design format elicits specific information in a standardized way. Common performance appraisal methods include narratives, checklists, rating scales, behavioral measures, objective measures, and critical incidents.

Narrative or Essay. This appraisal approach provides managers with a series of prompts or questions about an employee's performance. Managers can write a narrative or essay that describes an employee's performance using either an outcome or behavioral approach or a combination. A drawback of this method is that it can take a lot of time for managers to write up the assessment. The type and the amount of information included can vary significantly from manager to manager, which makes comparing employee performance for raises and promotions difficult. This approach can be cumbersome and time consuming for a manager with many employees. Also, the process is subjective and based on one person's assessment. This could lead to highly biased assessments. A manager has a significant amount of influence over an employee's performance rating with this type of assessment.[4,5]

Checklists. This appraisal approach provides managers with a series of statements. Managers select the statement that best describes the employee's behavior and performance. This approach provides the advantage of reducing the amount of time managers spend completing employee appraisals. A downside of this approach is that managers and employees may not recognize the unique contributions of employees.[4] Another major downside of this approach is that it provides limited feedback to employees concerning their performance. Managers may not provide specific feedback on areas where an employee is excelling or needs improvement.

Rating Scales. Rating scales can be qualitative (i.e., unacceptable, below competent, competent, very competent, or exceptional) or quantitative (i.e., 1–5 or 1–10). For quantitative rating scales, the higher the score, the more satisfactory an employee's job performance. An advantage of this approach is that it standardizes the performance appraisal process and reduces the amount of time it takes managers to complete performance reviews.[4] However, it has the same issues concerning the depth of feedback as the Checklist method.

Behavioral Measures. Behavioral measures focus on what employees do (or their behaviors) versus what they produce (or their outputs). Measures include such statements as "The employee shows up to work on time" or "The employee meets deadlines." An advantage of this approach is that it focuses on what employees do. A downside to this approach is that managers and employees may not recognize the unique contributions of employees. Also, an employee may have satisfactory behaviors but not meet key performance goals.[4]

Objective Measures. Management by Objectives (MBO) is a popular approach that uses performance objectives, or results, for an employee's job as the basis for the appraisal. The MBO approach involves both an employee and manager. Jointly, they develop performance objectives that are specific, measurable, attainable, relevant, and time-bound. Managers evaluate employees based on their progress toward meeting and achieving these objectives. An advantage of this approach is that it is tailored to individual employees and reflects goals employees have set for themselves. Likewise, they have set their goals in consultation with their manager. A drawback of this approach is that it takes considerable time for managers to help develop, monitor, and evaluate each employee's objectives.[4]

Critical Incidents. This assessment allows managers to provide feedback outside the formal performance appraisal. Feedback can relate to something that was outstanding or needs to be improved. Managers describe the incident in detail, and the documentation is included as part of the employee's permanent record and performance appraisal.

Managers complete employee appraisals and then schedule meetings to discuss the evaluations with them. In this session, the manager reviews the appraisal and provides feedback about both strengths and weaknesses in the employee's performance. If necessary, a plan is developed for improving performance and/or for other development activities. Performance appraisals use feedback from a number of different sources.

Feedback Sources

Feedback for appraisals can come from a number of different sources depending on the organization's practices. Common sources of appraisals include self, supervisor, team, and customers, or a combination. All evaluations should focus on job performance regardless of the feedback source. Each feedback source has advantages and disadvantages that managers should consider.[4]

Self

Self or personal appraisals consist of an employee evaluating and reflecting on their own job performance. Organizations would ask employees to use one of the assessment methods previously discussed. Employees often use the essay or narrative appraisal method to assess their performance. However, employees could rate their performance or use a checklist with short explanations, among other options, to evaluate their performance. Despite the approach, organizations usually standardize the form employees use to conduct their self-assessment. Managers also conduct a performance appraisal and use the same or a similar form to facilitate comparisons across employees, which helps to standardize the process. This helps foster and promote dialogue between the employee and the manager. Self-evaluations are appropriate for any employee. However, supervisors, managers, professional staff, technical positions, and upper-level management most often use this appraisal approach. The benefits of self-evaluation include personal investment in the process, increased motivation, satisfaction, controllability of situation, and input in the training and development process. This approach is also inexpensive and easy to do. The disadvantages of the approach are that employees may not honestly assess themselves because of fear. Employees may feel that managers or others within the organization could use the information as documentation against them at a future point in time. Self-evaluations are one sided and only include the employee's perspective, but this is an important perspective. A more comprehensive evaluation can be achieved by combining an employee's evaluation with a supervisor's evaluation or team members' evaluations to gain additional perspectives and develop a more complete picture of an employee's job performance.[3,4]

Manager/Supervisor

Managers are an important source of feedback regarding an employee's job performance. Managers often find performance appraisals time consuming and even uncomfortable. However, managers should keep in mind the purpose of performance appraisals when completing an evaluation. Evaluations and personal performance appraisal interviews provide an opportunity for the manager to review job expectations and an employee's progress toward meeting these expectations. Managers should reiterate the role that the employee's position plays in accomplishing the organization's goals. Managers should clearly communicate how well an employee is performing based on the job description and recognize an employee's accomplishments and contributions as well as any deficiencies. Managers should include in their performance evaluation a plan for enhancing an employee's future performance by including a training or development plan as

part of their evaluation. Employees should be able to provide input into any action plans that are developed based on their performance appraisal. The personal appraisal interview is an excellent time for managers to have a conversation with employees about ways to enhance their performance moving forward.[3]

Team or Peer

Public health and other health organizations are increasingly emphasizing the value and importance of teams to accomplish organizational goals. This emphasis on teamwork is making teams an important source of information that managers are using for performance appraisals. The advantages of team or peer evaluations include specific performance examples that highlight the unique contributions an employee makes to a team. A disadvantage of peer evaluations is that they can take a significant amount of time to complete and team members may be reluctant to complete the evaluations because they are not sure how the information will be used. Also, peer evaluations may undermine team cohesion and performance as individual performance is emphasized over that of the team. In addition, peers could collude and give a team member they do not like a bad evaluation in an effort to get the individual removed from the team or even terminated. This is probably an extreme case; however, managers should be aware of the likelihood of this situation as they consider using peer evaluations.

Customers

Organizations are ultimately trying to meet the needs or desires of their customers. Customers have a diverse meaning for public health and other healthcare organizations and could include patients, clients, community members, or other key stakeholders. Managers might ask customers to provide performance feedback.[5] The advantages of customer feedback include providing feedback from outside the organization about how employees are performing their job. The disadvantages center on customer feedback being more expensive and time consuming to collect for individual employees.[4,5]

Multisource Feedback

Multisource feedback is an evaluation approach that utilizes information from a variety of sources—self, manager, teammates, customer, and other relevant stakeholders. This feedback provides managers with a more well-rounded view of an employee's performance. An advantage of this approach is that it provides a more robust **account** of an employee's strengths and accomplishments or weaknesses. The information can highlight accomplishments that a manager was not aware of, as well as identify areas for further development. A disadvantage of this approach is that an employee's performance could be negatively assessed because evaluators do not fully understand the nuances of an employee's job. However, clear instructions can help overcome this drawback. Also, this approach can take considerable time for evaluators and the managers.[4,5]

Performance Appraisal or Evaluation Interview

Appraisals are generally not complete until the manager and employee have an appraisal interview. Appraisal interviews are an integral part of the performance appraisal process. These interviews provide an opportunity for managers to review an employee's performance and offer specific feedback to the employee regarding their performance. Managers spend a significant amount of time conducting appraisal interviews depending on the number of employees they supervise. Managers should ensure that appraisal interviews occur in a timely fashion and in accordance with organizational policies. Managers should also ensure that a sufficient amount of time has been scheduled for each employee. Likewise, managers should ensure that privacy and **confidentiality** are maintained at every step in the performance appraisal process. Managers and employees typically sign and date their performance appraisal at the end of the meeting. The signatures recognize that the meeting took place and that the employee's performance and any recommendations or plans were discussed. Managers may have employees who refuse to sign unfavorable performance appraisals. In such cases, managers should consult with human resources and note that the employee refused to sign the evaluation.[4]

Preparation before a performance appraisal is key for managers. Managers should review all performance appraisal materials prior to the appraisal interview to ensure they are ready to give specific feedback to employees. Managers should note examples of exceptional and unacceptable performance that specifically relate to an employee's job duties. Specific examples indicate to employees that managers recognize the many contributions they make to the organization through their job and can provide clear guidance on areas for improvement. Employees with more than one manager usually complete their interview with the manager who supervises their work the majority of the time. Additional managers should be asked to provide performance feedback to the manager conducting the interview and submitting the

appraisal to human resources. Employees typically receive a copy of their signed performance evaluation for their records, and the original is submitted to the human resource department.[4]

Appeals

Some organizations allow employees to appeal the results of their performance appraisal. An organization's employee handbook should clearly state the organization's appeal policy and process. Managers should avoid disputes with employees about their performance appraisal and, instead, refer employees to the appeal policy and process. Managers should also refer any employees to human resources if the employee is upset or the discussion escalates. Organizations generally require employees to submit a formal, written appeal request within a specified number of business days following a performance appraisal. The appeal asks employees to state the reason for the appeal and to provide any supporting evidence or materials. Human resources generally conducts a confidential investigation following a formal appeal request. The investigation includes an interview with the employee, supervisor, and any other relevant parties, as well as a review of any relevant documentation. Human resources can then make a recommendation, or the appeal may be referred to an employee appeals **committee** or panel that will make a recommendation. Managers, employees, and organizations should operate in good faith and in a confidential manner. Employee retaliation is illegal and should not be tolerated by any organization, manager, or employee during or after an appeal is made. A transparent appeal process is in the best interest of employees, managers, and organizations and helps to reduce employment-related **litigation**.

Legal Aspects

Managers must be aware of the legal implications of performance appraisals. Generally, organizations are not required to conduct performance appraisals. However, some public sector organizations like public health departments might be required to do so by state law or regulations. Performance appraisals are an all or nothing activity. Either all of the organization participates in an appraisal program or no one in the organization participates in the appraisal process because of the potential for discrimination. Organizations do have flexibility to tailor performance appraisal processes to employees based on their jobs or level. For example, executive directors may all use a narrative evaluation while hourly employees utilize a checklist evaluation. The important point for managers is to follow the organization's appraisal policy and procedures. Managers are responsible for helping ensure a fair and transparent process. Neither organizations nor managers can use performance appraisals as a tool to discriminate against employees, especially against protected classes. The performance appraisal process must be fair and equitable. The process must minimize bias and subjectivity. Discrimination and wrongful termination are the two common types of legal actions that can be brought against organizations and their managers. Performance appraisals can either support or refute a legal claim.

Performance Management

Employees and managers should identify areas for performance improvement based on feedback during the performance appraisal interview. Feedback is an important part of the appraisal interview and managerial role. Managers provide feedback related to how well the employee is performing the functions and responsibilities outlined in their job description. Based on the review, the employee and the manager identify areas for improvement or development and work with employees to develop action plans to enhance employee performance moving forward. This is an ideal time for a managers to gain insights into any challenges an employee is having or growth opportunities they are looking for.

Improvement Plans

Improvement plans are for employees who are underperforming in their current job and need to improve their performance. The goal of an improvement plan is to help employees successfully perform their current job and fulfill the essential job tasks and duties that are outlined in the employee's job description. Training is often included in employee improvement plans. Again, training is focused on helping an employee perform their current job successfully.

Development Plans

Development plans are for employees who are successfully performing their current job and are looking for additional growth opportunities within an organization. Development plans enhance the knowledge skills and abilities of employees and help to prepare them to be successful in future jobs or positions within the organization. Career preparation can help motivate employees and should be discussed during personal appraisal interviews.

Coaching, Counseling, Discipline, and Termination

Coaching, counseling, and discipline are additional tools for performance management. These are all strategies managers can use to help employees engage in their work and be successful in their jobs. Knowing how to support higher performers and help weaker performers is an important managerial responsibility that is discussed in this section. Many new and seasoned managers do not feel comfortable addressing areas of concern or improvement with employees. This section also discusses how to use coaching, counseling, and discipline to try to avoid the need for terminating an employee.

Coaching

Coaching is fundamentally about helping employees improve their performance and achieve results based on an employee's development plan. Managers use coaching as a way to enhance the value of human resources and, specifically, help employees develop new capabilities. **Capabilities** are new knowledge, skills, and abilities that serve both the individual employee and the organization. Employees can **leverage** new capabilities to advance professionally. At the same time, organizations are also able to leverage these new capabilities employees acquire to create organizational value. Coaching shapes not just an employee's performance but also their attitude and outlook.[3] Development plans identify growth opportunities for employees and detail the activities and experiences that will aid them in realizing these opportunities.

Coaching begins at orientation when new employees and managers begin to establish a working relationship. Regular and recurring interactions help foster this relationship. Early interactions include communication about expectations to ensure clarity about job expectations, as well as timely performance feedback. The coaching relationship should evolve over time. Effective coaches are dedicated, engaged, enthusiastic, encouraging, open, honest, and active listeners and role models; they are supportive and they recognize employees for a job well done. Coaches provide both positive and negative (or constructive) feedback. **Feedback**, whether positive or constructive, should be specific and timely. Specific feedback allows employees to know when performance expectations or results have, or have not, been achieved. Timely feedback provides employees with an opportunity to improve. The coaching relationship is all about professional growth and development through honest, open feedback, and development experiences.

Counseling

Counseling focuses on addressing performance deficiencies, so that an employee does not have to face disciplinary action or termination. Counseling is based on an employee's improvement plan. Employees receive counseling due to performance or behavioral deficiencies. Examples of performance deficiencies include not meeting deadlines or producing poor quality work, or other failures to appropriately complete job duties. Examples of behavioral deficiencies include tardiness, unexcused absences, violations of work rules, policies or procedures, a negative attitude, customer or peer complaints, or poor interpersonal skills, among others.[3] Either type of deficiency reduces an employee's performance, which, in turn, affects the organization's ability to accomplish its goals. Managers should approach counseling in a respectful and honest way and should not avoid issues because the topic is difficult. Delaying any identified performance issue only makes addressing the issue more difficult in the future.

Managers should understand the performance expectations of every position they supervise. Regularly reviewing the performance of each employee's work can help identify any deficiencies before they become major problems. Informal feedback often helps address such issues. This is why having healthy relationships with open communication matters. When managers notice sustained patterns of unacceptable behavior or performance, they must formally document this and identify corrective actions. **Corrective actions** are the steps an employee needs to take to address any deficiencies and improve performance. Managers should have specific examples of unacceptable behaviors or performance, so that corrective actions can be as detailed and specific as possible. Managers are responsible for developing improvement plans that specifically identify deficiencies, corrective actions, and steps the employee should take to address concerns. Managers should schedule a meeting with the employee to discuss improvement areas, and the details of the improvement plan. The plan should include any training or additional resources available to the employee, as well as a time line for assessing improvement. Managers often fail to address unsatisfactory performance because (a) they are not sure what to do, (b) they think the issues will resolve on their own, (c) they are too busy and do not have time to counsel an employee, (d) discussing poor performance can be uncomfortable, (e) they are not sure how their employee will react, or (f) they do not want to compromise their working relationship. This is not fair or helpful to the employee or the organization and often leads to chronic performance problems if managers fail to deal with issues. Managers must monitor and document performance and action steps after a counseling session. Counseling sessions, improvement plans, and follow-up reports typically become part of an employee's permanent record. If a manager has not monitored or completed follow-up reports, the manager exposes the organization to potential legal action. An employee could claim wrongful termination if a manager failed to document corrective action, counseling sessions, and how follow-up with the employee was handled due to poor documentation. Managers may need to discipline employees if performance does not adequately improve after counseling.[3,4]

Discipline

Discipline involves applying sanctions to correct an employee's ongoing behavior or performance problems. Managers work to shape employee behavior to be consistent with an organization's rules, policies, procedures, values, and performance expectations. The employee handbook usually explains policies and procedures related to discipline. Managers must decide if a behavioral or performance issue exists. Then, managers refer to the employee handbook and policies to determine the appropriate way to formally address this with an employee.[3] Discipline should be timely and occur shortly after performance or behavioral issues occur. **Progressive discipline** refers to a process that uses a systematic approach to address employee behavior or poor performance. There are times when progressive discipline may not be used due to the severity of misconduct or underperformance. Disciplinary sanctions include verbal warnings, written warnings or reprimands, suspensions, demotions, and pay reductions. **EXHIBIT 7.2** provides examples of behavior or performance issues and the types of disciplinary actions managers can apply. Formal disciplinary action should take place only after employees have received counseling related to performance and/or behavioral issues and a sufficient amount of time has passed for an employee to demonstrate improvement. Human resources should be consulted for guidance and assistance throughout the process.[4]

The severity of disciplinary sanctions increases if the employee's behavior and/or performance does not improve over a reasonable period of time using the progressive discipline approach. Progressive discipline usually begins with a **verbal warning**. This is the least severe form of discipline. An employee may receive a verbal warning for being late to work, wasting time, being uncooperative, poor quality work, or other unacceptable behaviors or performance results. The manager should immediately provide a

EXHIBIT 7.2 Guidelines for Disciplinary Action

Class I: Minor Infractions

Discipline

- First offense—oral warning
- Second offense—written warning
- Third offense—1-day suspension
- Fourth offense—3-day suspension

Typical Infractions

- Absenteeism
- Tardiness
- Discourtesy to patients, visitors, coworkers, etc.

Class II: More Serious Infractions

Discipline

- First offense—written warning
- Second offense—3-day suspension
- Third offense—discharge

Typical Infractions

- Failure to report when scheduled for work
- Unexcused absence
- Performance of personal business on hospital time
- Violation of smoking, safety, fire, or emergency regulations

Class III: Still More Serious Infractions

Discipline

- First offense—written warning
- Second offense—discharge

Typical Infractions

- Insubordination
- Negligence
- Falsification of records, reports, or information
- Unauthorized release of confidential or privileged information
- Sexual harassment

Class IV: Most Serious Infractions

Discipline

- First offense—discharge

Typical Infractions

- Absence without notice for 3 consecutive days ("3 days no-call, no-show")
- Fighting on the job
- Theft
- Being under the influence of alcohol or drugs on premises
- Willful damage to hospital property

Reproduced Exhibit 17-1 from McConnell CR. *Umiker's Management Skills for the New Health Care Supervisor*. 7th Ed. Burlington, MA: Jones and Bartlett Learning; 2018.

verbal warning to explain why the behavior is problematic. Managers should document the oral warning by including a short description of the warning and the reason for the warning, along with the date

and time.[3] The manager can reference the note in the future if the problem persists.

Written warnings are formal documentation retained in an employee's personnel file. Written warnings are usually issued when verbal warnings have not been effective in correcting the employee's performance problem or the performance problem is considered more serious based on the organization's policies. Managers should be specific about the problem and the reason for the written warning. The warning should clearly state performance expectations and the time frame for corrective action to take place. Furthermore, the warning should specify what will happen if these expectations are not met. It is important that managers follow up during the specific time frame to verify that the performance problem has been corrected. If a manager does not see performance improvement, more serious disciplinary action would be in order.[4]

Suspensions, demotion, and pay reductions are additional disciplinary actions to address poor performance. Organizations use suspensions to temporarily remove employees from the workplace for severe offenses, such as theft, threat of workplace violence, or violating important organizational policies.[3] Suspensions can be with or without pay based on an organization's policies. Demotions may be used when it is determined that an employee cannot adequately accomplish their job duties, but can potentially accomplish a job with lesser responsibilities. Demotions may include pay reductions due to moving to a less responsible position. Documentation is important from a legal perspective. Managers should ensure that they follow their organization's policies and that they provide a detailed record of the performance issues and necessary corrective actions. Failure to document corrective actions and discipline can open an organization and manager up to legal risks. Consultation with the human resource department is always prudent and may be required by policy before disciplinary action.

Termination

Termination refers to the separation of an employee from the employment relationship with an organization. Separation can be voluntary, involuntary, or because of the need to reduce the workforce. Retirement, a new job, or a partner relocation are examples of voluntary termination. **Voluntary termination** means that an employee decides to leave their position and initiates separation from the organization. **Involuntary termination** means that an employee is separated from their position due to a decision by the organization versus by the employee so the separation is involuntary on the employee's part.[3] Organizations typically initiate terminations due to performance problems that have not been corrected through the progressive discipline process or due to workforce reductions. Employees who are discharged, terminated, or fired leave an organization in poor standing and typically are not eligible for rehire in the future. Workforce reductions, sometime called layoffs or downsizings, are reductions in employment due to some changes in the organization's operations. Changes in demand for its products or services, consolidation with other organizations, reduction in funding allocations for public organizations, and so forth are typical examples of some factors that can lead to workforce reductions. In these cases, employees are typically dismissed because they are not needed or cannot be funded anymore, but leave the organization in good standing and are eligible for rehire in the future.

Terminating employees is never easy. Managers should ensure that the employee handbook and all policies and procedures have been followed and the human resource department has been consulted prior to terminating an employee. It is important that documentation supports involuntary terminations for performance issues. This provides a degree of protection if an employee decides to pursue legal action.

Exit Interview and Survey

Exit interviews and exit surveys are conducted when employees voluntarily leave an organization to determine their reason for leaving and other employment-related information. **Exit interviews** are generally in-person meetings between an employee and a human resources representative before an employee leaves the organization. The human resources representative asks the employee a series of questions related to the reason for the departure, experience while working at the organization, any areas of concern, and recommendations for improving the employment experience. **Exit surveys** are another method of collecting information about an employee's work experience. Many organizations combine an **exit interview** with an exit survey. The exit survey provides an anonymous mechanism for collecting information, usually electronically. Employees may be reluctant to share negative or unfavorable experiences during an exit interview because the employee would like to preserve their relationship with the organization. Exit interviews and surveys are useful tools to ascertain potential employee relations problems that need to be addressed to better engage employees within the organization.

▶ Human Resource Engagement

Human resource engagement also focuses on how organizations motivate employees to proactively contribute to accomplishing the organization's goals. Organizations design both economic and noneconomic reward systems to motivate employees along with systems for building and sustaining positive relationships. Managers are responsible for implementing these systems to motivate employees.[3] Increasing motivation and positive relationship provide a foundation for desirable workplace behaviors like regular attendance at work, attachment to the organization, productivity in accomplishing duties, a willingness to go beyond minimum performance requirements, lower levels of counterproductive behaviors, and higher levels of satisfaction, among other benefits.[5]

Rewards

Common rewards include compensation and benefits. **Compensation** refers to payments that employees receive in exchange for the work they perform in their job. Compensation includes monetary pay like an employee's hourly wage, salary, vacation pay, and bonuses. Hourly wages and salaries are based on an employee's time. Bonuses are a type of incentive pay. Incentive pay is based on some type of performance standard (i.e., quota, sales volume, and number of new clients) that employees must achieve to receive the bonus versus just the time they worked.

Benefits are another type of reward used by organizations to motivate employees. There are two types of benefits: nonvoluntary (or mandatory) benefits and voluntary benefits. **Nonvoluntary** or **mandatory benefits** are required by law.[3] Examples of mandatory benefits that employers pay for in part or in whole include social security, Medicare, unemployment insurance, workers' compensation insurance, family and medical leave, and health insurance (for organizations with more than 50 employees per the Affordable Care Act). Many public health organizations are public organization that are required to provide federal and state holidays to their employees.

Voluntary benefits are benefits employers are not required by law to provide. Voluntary benefits are used by organizations to attract and retain employees. Employers can offer a variety of voluntary benefits, such as vacation, holidays, a pension plan, retirement savings plans, life insurance, vision insurance, dental insurance, pet insurance, college loan consolidation programs, and long-term care insurance, among other options. Employees are demanding more and more voluntary benefits to the point where many voluntary benefits are becoming treated like mandatory benefits.[6]

Recognition Programs

Employee recognition programs are noneconomic rewards that provide acknowledgement, appreciation, gratitude, and esteem to employees for their efforts, achievements, and other contributions to the organization. Employees can be recognized for a variety of reasons, and strong recognition programs provide different ways to recognize as many employees as possible. Common recognition programs include employee service awards, customer/client service awards, employee appreciation day, gifts, peer recognition, manager recognition, employee of the month, employee of the year, handwritten thank-you notes, and employee profiles in company publications and social media, among many other options. Recognition can be as simple as a certificate or gift card for a free coffee or lunch or range up to valuable gifts, trips, or additional vacation. The important point of recognition programs is that they demonstrate the organization's appreciation for employees' contributions.

Employee and Labor Relations

Employee relations refers to an organization's efforts to build and maintain positive working relationships across the organization.[3] Organizations with well-written policies and procedures, handbooks, and dispute resolution programs have important building blocks to establish strong working relationships and an organizational culture that helps all employees thrive. The lack of these building blocks can frustrate employees and managers and leave an organization exposed to legal risks.

Labor relations refers to employee relations practices in a unionized setting. **Unions** are third-party organizations that represent the interests of employees who are members of the union in negotiating with an organization over the terms and conditions of their employment, including pay, benefits, work schedules, personnel policies and work rules, and so forth. The National Labor Relations Act of 1935, and its subsequent amendments, provides the legal guidelines for employees to form and join unions, collectively bargain to reach a **contract** that defines the terms and conditions covered by the contract, and human resource polices that must be administered in accordance with the terms of the **collective bargaining** agreement. Many states have laws that govern unionization and collective bargaining within their state and the right of public sector employees to unionize. Since many public health organizations are in the public sector, this is an important issue in managing employee relations in these organizations. Managers must work particularly close with their human resource department if their organization is unionized. Working with the human resource department helps ensure they are acting properly and within legal and regularly frameworks as well as the terms of any collective bargaining agreements.[4,5]

Employee Handbook

Employee handbooks provide a concise overview of important policies and procedures, work rules, and key information about the organization for employees. Many organizations have a separate policies and procedures manual that provides full copies of these documents for reference. Managers should be familiar with the employee handbook and policies and procedures. They should be able to answer questions about its contents. Employees are usually asked to sign a form that acknowledges that they have received and read a copy of the employee handbook and that they agree to work in accordance with its requirements. Typically, contents in an employee handbook include an overview of the company (i.e., history, mission, vision, core values, code of ethics, and code of conduct), general employment information (i.e., equal employment opportunity policy, disability accommodations, sexual harassment reporting and investigation process, and discrimination reporting and investigation process), work attendance (i.e., breaks, lunch, severe weather, telecommuting, and work hours), professionalism in the workplace (i.e., dress code, smoking, drug, and alcohol statements, workplace violence, parking, conflicts of interest, business travel, and mileage rates), payroll information, benefits information, employee time off (i.e., vacation, sick days, jury duty, military duty, and family and medical leave), use of company equipment, and performance evaluation information.[7] Employee handbooks provide employees with the rules of the workpace so that they know what is expected in terms of behavior and performance.

Policies and Procedures

Organizations develop **policies and procedures** to communicate to employees how they should conduct themselves, business activities, and situations that commonly arise in the workplace. Some examples of typical organizational policies related to human resources include employee attendance, progressive discipline, sexual harassment, and dress code. Procedures refer to the steps that employees should follow related to implementing policies. For example, if an employee is going to be late or tardy for work, the attendance policy would provide a set of steps that the employee should follow to notify their manager. Failing to notify one's manager per the policy and procedures may result in disciplinary action. Generally, procedures change more frequently than policies. This is because technology, work tasks and processes, and staffing change regularly, which can influence the steps that need to be followed. From a legal standpoint, policies and procedures help protect an organization and its employees from legal action. This is why organizations, managers, and employees should consult and follow these guidelines consistently.

Grievances and Dispute Resolution

Managers are often confronted with grievances (or complaints) and disputes arising in the workplace that need to be resolved to maintain a positive working environment. Employee handbooks and an organization's policies and procedures should include important information on how to handle different types of grievances (i.e., pay, working conditions, benefits, and performance appraisal) and dispute resolution (i.e., between peers and between managers and subordinates). The handbook and policies and procedures should outline how to file a formal complaint, the type of information that is needed, and a time line for investigating the complaint and the process for resolving the matter. Usually, the human resource department will investigate any issues and seek to resolve them and reconcile the parties. Sometimes, issues are so serious that the human resource department cannot resolve them. In these cases, depending on the organization's policies, a third-party mediator might be used to seek an agreement, or a panel of unrelated employees might be used to hear the issues and make a recommendation for resolution.

Some organizations require arbitration of disputes that cannot be resolved within the organization through mediation or negotiations because it has escalated to the point that it requires an impartial third party to help reach a resolution. Arbitration is an alternative to litigation, and many employees and organizations prefer arbitration because it is quicker and less expensive than litigation. The goal of arbitration is to reach a resolution. With arbitration, an impartial third party listens to all parties and makes a recommendation. The resolution can be nonbinding or binding. Nonbinding resolutions are recommendations from an arbitrator, whereas binding resolutions are a definitive decision (or ruling) that is imposed on all parties.[4]

Employee Health and Safety

Employers have a vested interest in keeping employees safe and healthy. Occupational health and safety are a particularly important consideration for public health managers because the nature of public health work can expose professionals to a number of hazards. The Occupational Health and Safety Act (OSHA) was passed in 1970 to address workplace hazards. This law prescribes standards that employers must meet in terms of assuring safe working conditions and protecting employees from harm. OSHA has significantly improved working conditions in the United States and reduced the number of work-related injuries and deaths. Prior to 1970, American workers had high levels of exposure to potentially harmful working environments, and they lacked the proper personal protective equipment to work in such conditions. OSHA provided worker protections and a mechanism for employees to report OSHA violations. The Occupational Safety and Health Administration investigates OSHA violations and can conduct inspections and take enforcement action if violations are found.[8]

Health screenings and wellness programs are additional ways that organizations are prioritizing employee health. Health screenings identify health conditions that need attention and could potentially affect an employee's ability to work. Employee wellness programs consist of health education and prevention activities. This could include walking clubs, group exercise, seminars on how to manage a chronic health condition, and prevention programs. Many organizations find that employee health influences motivation and performance. Health screenings and wellness programs also help to keep an organization's finances healthy. Addressing rising healthcare costs and providing health insurance are a significant part of an organization's **budget**. Healthy employees help to lower healthcare costs for employees and the organization. Wellness programs are also a great way to engage and retain employees.

Conclusion

Managers play an important role in developing and engaging human resources once they are hired. Public health managers are responsible for orienting and onboarding new employees after they are hired. Additionally, managers are responsible for assuring employees are provided with ongoing training and development to be successful in their current job and are prepared to advance in the future. The performance appraisal process provides an opportunity for public health managers to review employee performance and jointly prepare improvement plans with employees who need help and development plans for high performing employees that want to advance professionally. Coaching and counseling are proactive tools that public health managers can use to enhance employee performance to avoid the need for disciplinary action.

Progressive discipline provides employees with formal notice of performance problems and makes opportunities available to address these issues in order to avoid the need for termination. Managers must carry out these responsibilities in accordance with their organization's policies, procedures, and all applicable laws. If not, the manager and the organization could face legal liability. An organization's employee handbook and policies and procedures provide legal protection if followed and play an important role in fostering positive employee relations and engagement. Public health managers must continually motivate and engage their employees. Rewards, recognition, and other positive employee relations practices provide proactive approaches to enhancing motivation and engagement.

Discussion Questions

1. What is the difference between orientation and onboarding?
2. Compare and contrast employee training and development.
3. How can a manager use a job description during an annual performance appraisal?
4. What are the different performance appraisal methods? Which would be most appropriate for different categories and levels of employees?
5. What is the difference between an improvement plan and a development plan?
6. Distinguish coaching, counseling, and discipline.
7. What is progressive discipline? Why is it important for managers to be familiar with the concept as well as their organization's employee handbook, and policies and procedures?
8. Why should managers address a disciplinary issue as soon as possible versus waiting until it is time for an employee's annual performance appraisal?
9. Why is documentation important in the disciplinary process?
10. What are the types of rewards managers and organizations can use? Why might you use one versus the other?
11. What are mandatory and voluntary benefits? Provide an example of each.
12. Why is grievance and dispute resolution an important employee relations strategy?
13. Why are employee safety and health particularly important to public health organizations?

Learning Activities

1. Find a new employee orientation or onboarding program for a public health organization. How long does it last? What topics are covered? Are there any topics you would recommend including as part of the orientation program? Develop a list of questions that a new employee should ask during orientation.
2. Identify a public health position that interests you. Locate the compensation and benefits for the position. You may need to look on the organization's website or an online job posting site.
3. Find and analyze a performance appraisal policy and procedures for a public health organization. How often does the organization conduct performance appraisals? Does the organization have a standard performance evaluation form that managers must use to evaluate employees? What performance areas are employees assessed on? Does the organization have a specific performance evaluation form for probationary or new employees? What are the performance areas for probationary employees?
4. Think about different knowledge, skills, and abilities you would like to acquire as a student. Write a development plan for yourself. Research different development plan formats and select a format that works for you and your career goals. (Considering writing your development goals using the S.M.A.R.T. format from Chapter 4.)
5. Locate an employee handbook and policies and procedures for a public health organization or healthcare organization. Analyze the contents of the handbook and policies and procedures. Select some policies that you think are important. For example, you could look at policies and procedures related to employee orientation, sick time, holidays, leave, performance appraisals, discipline, resigning, termination, and grievance and dispute resolution. Discuss why these policies are important to public health managers and employees.

References

1. Wang S, Greenberger DB, Noe RA, Fan J. The development of mentoring relationships: An attachment theory perspective. In: Buckly MR, Wheeler AR, Halbesleben JRB, eds. *Research in Personnel and Human Resources Management*. Vol. 35. Bingley, UK: Emerald Publishing Limitied; 2017:53–101.

2. Yip J, Ehrhardt K, Black H, Walker DO. Attachment theory at work: A review and directions for future research. *J Organ Behav*. 2017;39(2):185–198. doi:10.1002/job.2204.

3. McConnell CR. *Umiker's Management Skills for the New Health Care Supervisor*. 7th ed. Burlington, MA: Jones & Bartlett Learning; 2018.

4. Fallon LR, McConnell CR. *Human Resource Management in Health Care Principles and Practice*. 2nd ed. Burlington, MA: Jones & Bartlett Learning; 2014.

5. Armstrong S, Mitchell B. *The Essential HR Handbook*. Newburyport, MA: Career Press; 2019.

6. Miller S. Voluntary benefits now essential, not fringe. Society for Human Resource Management. https://www.shrm.org/resourcesandtools/hr-topics/benefits/pages/voluntary-benefits-now-essential-not-fringe.aspx. Published April 13, 2018. Accessed July 26, 2019.

7. Heathfield SM. Employee manual handbook table of contents. The Balance Careers. https://www.thebalancecareers.com/need-to-know-what-goes-in-an-employee-handbook-1918308. Published June 25, 2019. Accessed July 26, 2019.

8. McKenzie JF, Pinger RR, Seabert D. *Introduction to Community and Public Health*. 9th ed. Burlington, MA: Jones & Bartlett Learning; 2018.

Suggested Readings and Websites

ASTHO. Human Resources and Workforce Development Directors Peer Network. Public Health Workforce Interests and Needs Survey. http://www.astho.org/phwins/

CDC Workforce Development Resources. https://www.cdc.gov/ophss/csels/dsepd/resources.html

Human Resources for Health Journal. https://human-resources-health.biomedcentral.com/

Journal of Public Health Management and Practice Public Health Workforce Interests and Needs Survey (PH WINS). https://journals.lww.com/jphmp/pages/toc.aspx?year=2015&issue=11001

Society for Human Resource Management. https://www.shrm.org/

CHAPTER 8

Organizational Dynamics for Public Health Managers

▶ Introduction

Organizational dynamics refers to how organizational members behave and interact with one another to accomplish the goals of the organization. Public health managers work to promote positive relationships and productive behaviors among organizational members. Power, motivation, teams, and conflict are important topics for public health managers to consider as they work to promote cohesion and collaboration across an organization versus conflict and counterproductive work environments.

▶ Sources and Types of Power

Power is "the potential ability of one person to influence other people to bring about desired outcomes."[1(p372)] Management and leadership are often associated with the concept of power because both are trying to influence the behavior of people in an organization to accomplish a particular purpose. However, power and influence are not the same thing. Power implies the ability to coerce others. Power generally shows little, if any, consideration for followers and does not seek consensus. In contrast, influence considers followers in decision-making and uses

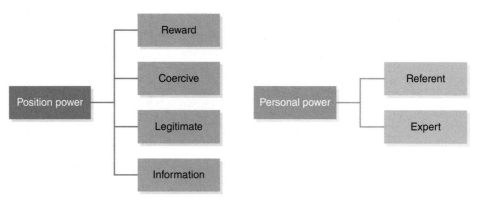

FIGURE 8.1 Types of power.

Information from French JRJ, Raven BH. The bases of social power. In: Cartwright D, ed. *Studies in Social Power*. Ann Arbor, MI: Institute for Social Research; 1959:259–269.

persuasion versus punitive threats to gain follower support. Leaders tend to use influence, whereas managers tend to use power.[2] Since managers and leaders have power in organizations, it is important that they understand what it is and how to use it responsibility in exerting influence. Likewise, they also need to understand the role of persuasion in influencing people in organizations.

French and Raven identified six bases of power. The two basic categories of power are position power and personal power. There can be different bases or sources for each type of power. The bases for position power are legitimate, informational, reward, and coercive. The bases for personal power are expert and referent power.[3,4] The following sections discuss the different types of power (**FIGURE 8.1**).

▶ Types of Position Power

The first category of power is position power. **Position power** comes from a person's formal **authority** or position within an organization and includes several types of power. The four types of position power include legitimate, informational, reward, and coercive.[1,3,4]

Legitimate Power

Legitimate power refers to formal power that flows from a person's position in an organization's structure as depicted by the organizational chart.[3] Positions toward the top of the chart have more position power, or formal authority, than positions toward the bottom of the organization. Each position in an organization has some degree of formal authority based on its job title, role, and responsibilities.[1]

Informational Power

Informational power refers to a position's ability to control knowledge and data that others want or need

to accomplish their work. Examples of how others can control information include withholding information or access to information. This could also include giving someone incomplete or entirely incorrect information.[3,4]

Reward Power

Reward power means that a person is in a position that provides them with the ability to give rewards to others if they comply with their instructions or wishes.[3,4] Rewards can consist of pay increases, bonuses, promotions, favorable assignments, training, and recognition, among others. This type of power serves as a powerful motivator. A downside of reward power is that what is valued can change, and rewards that do not provide value will not lead to compliance.[1]

Coercive Power

Coercive power is the opposite of reward power. Coercive power means that a person is in a position that provides them with the ability to penalize or punish others for not complying with their instructions or wishes.[3,4] This type of power relies on fear and threats of punishment to achieve compliance from subordinates. This type of power is also a powerful motivator. Examples of coercion include disciplinary actions, such as oral and written reprimands, suspensions, termination, pay reduction, withholding bonuses, and demotions. A downside of coercive power is that it is often not productive over the long term as it can lead to a lack of engagement and even retaliation. Also, communication is strained; so, innovative ideas or ways to improve may be withheld out of fear.[1,5]

▶ Types of Personal Power

The second category of power is personal power. **Personal power** comes from a person's unique or superior knowledge, skills, and abilities that the organization needs to accomplish its tasks and goals. Personal power also comes from others liking and respecting an individual. This type of power inspires and engages others. Interpersonal relationships are central to the concept of personal power.[1] The two types of personal power include expert and referent.

Expert Power

Expert power means that a person is competent and possesses some unique knowledge, skills, or abilities needed to perform and accomplish certain work.[3,4] Experts know what to do and how to do it, which draws other people to them. Organizational members have confidence in the expert's superior ability because they know that the expert's work complies with certain expectations. Examples of expert power include taking lead positions on projects, serving as a mentor, or helping others acquire knowledge, skills, and abilities as a trainer.[5-7]

Referent Power

Referent power means that power comes from others liking, trusting, or respecting another person. Interpersonal relationships and interactions are the foundation of this type of power because others admire and want to be like the referent person to some degree.[3,4] Individuals comply because they want to gain the approval, support, friendship, and respect of a manager or leader. Power comes from appealing to others in a way that inspires them to comply. Examples of referent power include role models and charismatic leaders.[1,5,7]

▶ Persuasion

Today, persuasion is replacing traditional command-and-control leadership styles.[8] Knowledge workers, in particular, do not respond well to leaders telling them what to do. **Persuasion** is the ability to influence or convince someone to believe or to do something. Leaders must persuade their followers to behave in ways that benefit the organization by appealing to their head and heart.[9] A leader must understand their followers by listening to their needs, wants, and desires. Understanding followers provides a starting point for identifying common interests and goals. This also facilitates negotiation between the leader and followers to reach mutually beneficial positions. Likewise, better understanding allows leaders to appeal to follower's needs and wants in ways that compel and persuade them to take action that is in their best interests and those of the organization. Positive and

meaningful contributions to organizational goals help ensure leaders move from telling their followers what to do to persuading them.[1,7,8]

▶ Motivation

Motivation relates to the psychosocial or people subsystem of an organization.[10] The coordinating or leading function primarily influences this subsystem. Leaders and managers try to influence followers to engage in behaviors that lead to individual as well as organizational goal attainment. They are concerned with motivation because motivated employees exhibit behaviors and create outputs that are critical to organizational success. Motivation increases desirable organizational behaviors that include attachment, attendance, productivity, satisfaction, organizational citizenship behavior, and nondeviant (or counterproductive) behaviors.[11] Managing motivation takes a lot of a time and energy because everyone in the organization is motivated in different ways and for different reasons. Therefore, leaders and managers need to understand motivation, so that they can influence employees. This section provides an overview of key motivation concepts and theories.

What Is Motivation?

Motivation is excitement or enthusiasm that causes an individual to take repeated action over time to accomplish a specific purpose or goal. Robbins and Judge define motivation as "the processes that **account** for an individual's intensity, direction, and persistence of effort toward attaining a goal."[11(p204)] Lussier and Achua define motivation as "anything that affects behavior in pursuing a certain outcome."[12(p79)]

There are two sources of motivation: internal or intrinsic motivation and external or extrinsic motivation.[7] **Intrinsic motivation** comes from inside a person. This is a person's internal desire to acquire or achieve something. Individuals who possess intrinsic motivation receive internal satisfaction from completing certain activities or achieving certain goals.[12] **Extrinsic motivation** comes from outside a person. This type of motivation comes from some external action, stimuli, or source. Receiving a reward for doing something can be a source of extrinsic motivation. Promotions, bonuses, time off, and raises are examples of external rewards that can serve as a source of extrinsic motivation. Despite the type of motivation, followers are driven to accomplish a goal and persist until the goal is achieved so that they can receive the external reward (intrinsic motivation) or the internal satisfaction (intrinsic motivation). Both types of motivation are important for leaders and managers to understand so they can enhance the motivation of their followers and encourage more of the desired organizational behaviors.[1,12]

Motivation Theories

Motivation theories developed alongside management theories. Early motivation theories that emerged from the scientific management era, in the early 20th century, believed that economic rewards were the way individuals were motivated. This was called the **economic man** view of motivation. The source of motivation was external (extrinsic) economic rewards, such as increased pay or financial incentives for performance that exceeded the established performance standards. Views of motivation expanded during the the human relations movement in the 1930s. Studies suggested that internal (intrinsic) satisfaction motivated some employees. This was called the **social man** view of motivation. Some employees experienced satisfaction from doing a good job or achieving certain performance goals. Other employees experienced satisfaction from the social ties and relationships they experienced with their supervisor or coworkers. Today, the **total man** view of motivation is used. This view says that both extrinsic and **intrinsic rewards** increase an employee's motivation. The type of motivation depends on the person and situation. Leaders and managers should use the best type of reward or combination of rewards based on the person and the situation.[13]

Motivation theories seek to explain what influences motivation and how to increase it. There are three major categories: content theories, process theories, and other theories[12] (**FIGURE 8.2**). **Content theories of motivation** deal with the intrinsic or the extrinsic needs an **employee** is trying to satisfy.[7] The role of leaders and managers is to identify the needs that employees have and then help employees satisfy their needs by providing rewards that employees need. These theories suggest that employees will be motivated to behave in ways that will fulfill their needs,

which will motivate employees. The content theories discussed include: Hierarchy of Needs Theory, ERG Theory, Two-Factor Theory, and Acquired Needs Theory. **Process theories of motivation** deal with how an individual tries to fulfill their needs. These theories are conceptually more complex because they consider how individuals identify their needs and then the behaviors they take to satisfy their needs.[7] This theory is focused on decisions and behaviors. The process theories discussed include Expectancy Theory, Equity Theory, and Goal-Setting Theory. There are a number of other types of theories that seek to explain motivation, but they are not considered content or process theories. These other theories include Reinforcement Theory and Job Design Theory. These theories look at how consequences can motive employee behavior and how designing jobs with certain characteristics can increase motivation.

Content Theories of Motivation

Maslow's Hierarchy of Needs. In the 1940s, Abraham Maslow developed the first major theory of motivation referred to today as **Maslow's Hierarchy of Needs Theory**.[14] This theory states that all humans have a hierarchy of needs they are trying to satisfy or fulfill. Maslow identified five levels of needs that include physiological, safety, belonging, esteem, and self-actualization needs. **Physiological or survival needs** are the most basic human needs and include food, water, sexual drive, and subsistence-related needs. Pay or compensation is the primary way organizations help employees satisfy these needs. **Safety needs** are the next need level and include clothing, shelter, safe home environment, employment, healthy and safe work environment, access to health care, money, police, and other necessities. In the work setting, this would include a safe work environment and fringe benefits like health insurance, life insurance, and retirement. **Belonging needs** are the next need level and refer to the desire people have for social interactions and connections with friends, family, community members, and other social groups. Social

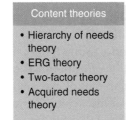
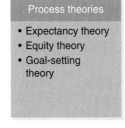
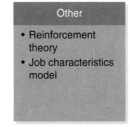

FIGURE 8.2 Major motivation categories, theories, and models.

contact provides opportunities for affection, networking, friendship, and support. From a workplace perspective, the ability to have productive relationships with coworkers, managers, and customers is typically important. **Esteem needs** are the next need level and refer to the desire people have for status, recognition, and a positive regard for one's self and from others. This need is typically met by factors such as recognition, awards, titles, promotions, and expanded roles and responsibilities in the workplace. Finally, the highest need level is self-actualization. **Self-actualization** refers to the human need for achievement, personal growth and development, and fulfillment. Essentially, these relate to dreams and aspirations individuals have for themselves. In an organization, this means that employees are looking for advancement opportunities, as well as opportunities to be innovative and produce value for their organization.[7,14] Maslow explained that the order in which these needs are met matters. The

lowest level of needs or physiological needs must be met first before the next level becomes a significant motivational influence. The higher level needs serve to motivate individuals to satisfy even higher level needs. Leaders and managers can use this theory to better understand the need level of each of their employees and motive them by helping them move to the next level. Needs toward the bottom of Maslow's hierarchy are primarily extrinsic, while the needs toward to the top of the hierarchy are primarily intrinsic (**FIGURE 8.3**).

Alderfer's ERG Theory. Clayton Alderfer developed the **Existence, Relatedness, Growth (ERG) Theory** of motivation in the 1970s.[15] Alderfer was trying to confirm Maslow's Hierarchy of Needs Theory. Alderfer's research did not verify Maslow's theory as it was originally stated, but he did identify three levels of needs that include the need for existence, the need for relatedness, and the need for growth (**FIGURE 8.4**).

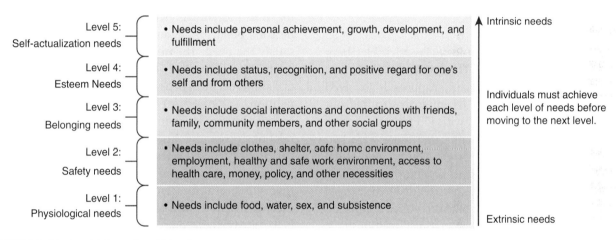

FIGURE 8.3 Maslow's Hierarchy of Needs.
Based on information from Maslow AH. A theory of human motivation. *Psychol Rev.* 1943;50(4):370–396.

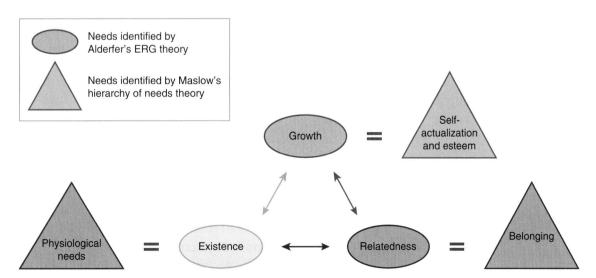

FIGURE 8.4 Comparison of Alderfer's ERG Theory and Maslow's Hierarchy of Needs Theory.

Existence needs relate to Maslow's first and second levels of needs or physiological and safety needs. These are needs that, when met, assure a person can survive and achieve some reasonable level of well-being. **Relatedness** needs correspond to Maslow's third level of needs or the need for belonging. This need centers on the desire individuals have for social interaction and relationships with others. **Growth needs** relate to Maslow's fourth and fifth levels of needs or esteem and self-actualization needs. Alderfer discovered that there was not the rigid hierarchy of needs like Maslow proposed. Instead, Alderfer observed that individuals could move between levels, depending on the extent to which their needs were being met. He referred to this as the **frustration–regression principle**. This means that individuals can regress back and focus on a lower level of needs if they become frustrated because they cannot achieve higher-level needs. The ERG Theory provides leaders and managers with a simpler and more flexibility theory than Maslow's to use in motivating their employees.[7]

Herzberg's Two-Factor Theory. Fredrick Herzberg developed the **Two-Factor Theory** in the 1950s and 1960s (**FIGURE 8.5**).[16] Hertzberg's approach involved interviewing a large sample of employees to find out what factors were associated with job satisfaction and dissatisfaction. His finding indicated there were two categories of factors. The first category was called **hygiene factors** (or dissatisfiers), which were associated with job dissatisfaction. These tended to be extrinsic factors such as supervision, pay, policies, working conditions, and some interpersonal relationships, among others. The second category was called **motivator factors** (or satisfiers), which were associated with job satisfaction. These factors tended to be intrinsic factors such as achievement, recognition, responsibility, advancement, growth, and the work itself.[11] Hertzberg found that motivation was a product of both hygiene and motivator factors.[6] Hygiene factors are important, but these do not actually satisfy employees so that they are highly motivated to contribute more. Instead, the absence of these factors reduces an employee's satisfaction and motivation.[7] Hygiene factors are needed to reduce dissatisfaction, but this only moves an employee to no dissatisfaction, or from being demotivated to not being demotivated. Motivator factors must be present

FIGURE 8.5 Herzberg's Two-Factor Theory.

Reproduced Figure 5-1 from Borkowski N. *Organizational Behavior in Health Care*. 3rd ed. Burlington, MA: Jones & Bartlett Learning; 2016.

to motivate employees from no satisfaction or motivation to being satisfied and motivated. The managerial implication is that motivation is dependent on two separate factors. First, dissatisfiers must be removed by providing equitable pay, reasonable benefits, fair work rules, safe working conditions, and good supervision. Then, satisfiers such as recognition, engaging work, responsibility, and advancement must be present to increase satisfaction and motivation.[6,7]

McClelland's Acquired Needs Theory. David McClelland developed the Acquired Needs Theory.[7] This theory gets its name from the idea that individuals acquire or develop needs over their life based on their life experiences. McClelland identified three needs that individuals try to satisfy, which motivate human behavior. The three needs are achievement, affiliation, and power. Most people have all three of these needs but to varying degrees. The theory suggests that one of these needs tends to be dominant for most individuals. The dominant need motivates a person's behavior because the individual is trying to satisfy the need. The **need for achievement** (nAch) refers to an individual's desire to be successful, master tasks, and perform better than his or her peers or competition. The **need for affiliation** (nAff) focuses on an individual's desire to belong and have meaningful relationships and connections with others. The **need for power (nPwr)** refers to an individual's desire for influence, control, and authority over others. This theory is useful for managers to understand because individuals are drawn to work and organizations that help satisfy their dominant need. This theory also helps managers match employees with work based on their dominant need or design the work in a way that responds to their dominate need. Managers can motivate employees who have a need for achievement by assigning them challenging but clearly defined tasks. Managers can motivate employees who have a need for affiliation by assigning them to work on teams or providing opportunities to collaborate with individuals inside and outside the organization. Finally, managers can motive employees who have a need for power by involving them in decision-making and planning. These employees frequently tend to prefer to work alone versus in a team, so that they can control tasks and assignments.[1,7,12]

Process Theories of Motivation

Vroom's Expectancy Theory. Victor Vroom developed Expectancy Theory in 1964.[17] The theory is an influential and highly regarded theory of motivation that focuses on an individual's expectation

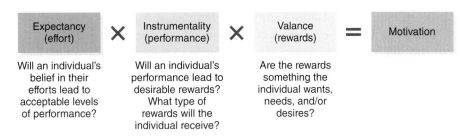

FIGURE 8.6 Vroom's Expectancy Theory.

Adapted from https://iedunote.com/expectancey-theory and Figure 6-1 from Borkowski N. *Organizational Behavior in Health Care*. 3rd ed. Burlington, MA: Jones & Bartlett Learning; 2016.

about their ability to perform a task and obtain a reward that they value.[6,7] The theory has four main elements: expectancy (or effort), instrumentality (or performance), outcome (reward), and valence (or value assigned to the reward). **Expectancy** refers to an individual's expectations that they can complete a task if they put in the effort. Individuals are more motivated to complete the task if they feel confident that they can and are able to complete the task. **Instrumentality** refers to an individual's expectation that their performance will result in a desired outcome or valued reward. Individuals are more motivated to complete a task if they feel they can meet performance expectations sufficiently to receive a desired reward. **Valence** refers to how much a particular outcome or reward is valued by the person. Valence can be positive or negative. Individuals can have strong positive or negative emotions regarding a specific outcomes.[7] Vroom expressed his theory of motivation in the form of an equation (**FIGURE 8.6**).

As the model indicates, motivation comes from an individual's expectation that they can perform a task (performance expectancy) and that their performance (instrumentality) will lead to an outcome or reward that they value (valence). The more an individual believes this relationship exists, the more they value the outcome or reward, and the more they will be motivated. Managers can use this theory to better understand the different elements of motivation, as well as how these elements relate to one another. Managers can influence motivation by determining what outcomes or rewards employees desire and then helping them recognize the linkage between performance, outcomes, and rewards. They can also help employees build confidence in their ability to perform and achieve certain outcomes. In addition, managers need to be aware of their employee's performance, so that they can provide the appropriate rewards when they are earned. Employees who feel their manager does not recognize their effort and performance will tend to reduce their effort and performance over time. Finally, managers play a role in providing rewards that are

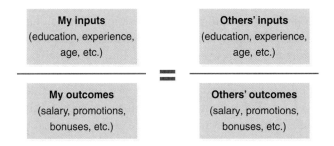

FIGURE 8.7 Adam's Equity Theory.

Reproduced Figure 6-3 from Borkowski N. *Organizational Behavior in Health Care*. 3rd ed. Burlington, MA: Jones & Bartlett Learning; 2016.

valued, desired, or needed and that are ultimately something employees want.[1,7]

Equity Theory. Stacey Adams developed Equity Theory in the 1960s.[18,19] This theory gets its name from an employee's perception of equity in the workplace (**FIGURE 8.7**). An employee's perception of how fairly or unfairly they are being treated influences their motivation. Employees provide inputs to their job, such as time, energy, creativity, and effort, among others, which produce outputs, such as completed tasks or projects. Employees are motivated if they perceive they are receiving outcomes such as pay that is fair, or more than fair, for the work they do. Employees are less motivated, or even demotivated, if they perceive they are not being fairly treated. The theory's name comes from the process of assessing the extent to which the employee perceives they are being treated equitably or not. Employees compare themselves to individuals inside and outside their organization that they believe have a similar job or responsibilities. Individuals then determine if they are being treated fairly based on this comparison. The comparison can either motivate or demotivate them. Employees are motivated if they perceive they are being treated more fairly than individuals in similar positions inside and outside their organization. Employees are demotivated if they perceive they are being treated less fairly. Employees are neither motivated nor demotivated if they perceive they are being treated similarly to individuals in comparable positions inside and outside their organization.[7]

Compensation is a great example of how Equity Theory influences motivation in the workplace. Employees who perceive they are paid less than others inside or outside the organizations will view this as inequitable. Consequently, employees might ask for a raise, put forth less effort, reduce performance, or look for another job. This will help restore the perceived imbalance between an employee's effort (input) and their reward (output). In contrast, employees who perceive they are paid more than others inside or outside their organization might be motivated to work harder to justify the additional compensation. This will help ensure the perceived imbalance between an employee's effort and their reward is adjusted. Employees who perceive they are being fairly compensated will be neither motivated nor demotivated in theory. Therefore, managers are instrumental in designing jobs and working with human resources to assure that compensation is equitable compared to similar positions inside and outside the organization. Managers may have a hard or easy time staffing positions, depending on compensation (i.e., pay and benefits). Positions with compensation perceived as low may be harder to fill. Managers should ensure employees feel equitably compensated and treated fairly to enhance motivation and, in turn, productivity, in the workplace. Managers should take corrective action if employees do not feel equitably compensated or fairly treated by their organization.[12]

Goal-Setting Theory. Edwin Locke[20] and Gary Latham[21,22] developed the Goal-Setting Theory of motivation over several decades of resarch.[21-24] **Goals** are seen as expected results, outcomes, or outputs. As such, goals can be used as a means for motivation for an individual's behavior just as organizational goals direct the activities of an organization. Locke and Latham's research compared the performance of employees who had stated goals with employees who did not have stated goals. They found that employees with goals had higher levels of performance than employees who did not have goals. These results indicate that individuals who know what is expected of them (i.e., goals) are more likely to meet these expectations.[21-23]

Goal-Setting Theory also provides insights into the characteristics of goals that promote higher levels of motivation and performance. Goals that are **clear**, **challenging**, and **mutually agreed upon** promote higher levels of motivation and performance. **Clear goals** are goals that are specific and measurable. These goals clearly communicate performance expectations. Employees are motivated because they know exactly what needs to be accomplished. **Challenging**

goals motivate employees because they want to meet expectations they have for themselves and the expectations others have for them. Goals must be realistic and something that the individual is capable of accomplishing and believes they can accomplish. **Mutually agreed upon goals** promote higher levels of motivation and, in turn, performance because individuals have input into the goals they are working to accomplish. This increases the likelihood that goals are developed in a way that motivates an individual, and it also increases an individual's commitment to goal. **Feedback** is key to helping individuals understand expectations and receive recognition for making progress toward or meeting goals. Consistent feedback on performance and progress toward goal attainment motivates employees because they receive recognition. Feedback also gives employees an opportunity to take corrective action if they need to or ask for help. This allows employees to change their behavior, which helps improve performance. **Task complexity** is also another aspect of goal-setting to consider. Goals should be challenging. However, goals should not be so complex that they are unattainable. Unattainable goals will not lead to motivation but, most likely, to stagnant performance.[21-23]

This theory has profound implications for modern management and organizations. Leaders spend a significant amount of time and energy developing organizational goals. Goal-setting Theory provides an opportunity to link individual-level goals with organizational goals to improve motivation and performance. The annual performance process serves as a time for managers and employees to review performance and jointly set goals for the next year (or performance period). Managers are able to provide ongoing feedback to employees about their performance, which helps to motivate individual performance and thereby enhance overall organizational performance (**FIGURE 8.8**).

Other Theories of Motivation

Skinner's Reinforcement Theory. B.F. Skinner popularized Reinforcement Theory[25]; however, many researchers contributed to building this theory. The Law of Effect is a central element of Reinforcement Theory. **The Law of Effect** states that individuals tend to repeat behaviors when they receive rewards, and tend to avoid behaviors when they receive no reward or a punishment. Reinforcement theory identifies four types of reinforcement (**FIGURE 8.9**): positive reinforcement, negative reinforcement, punishment, and extinction. **Positive reinforcement** refers to when an individual receives a reward (positive consequence) for desired behaviors, which encourages the individual to repeat

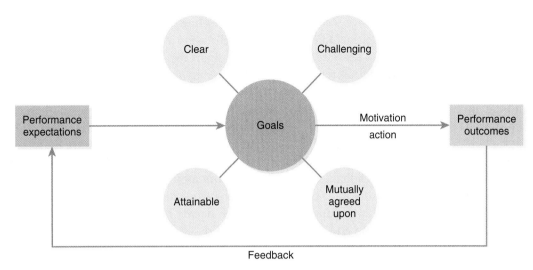

FIGURE 8.8 Latham and Locke's goal-setting model.

Based on information from and a modification of Latham GP, Locke EA. Goal setting – A motivational technique that works. *Organ Dyanmics*.1979; 8(2):68–80.

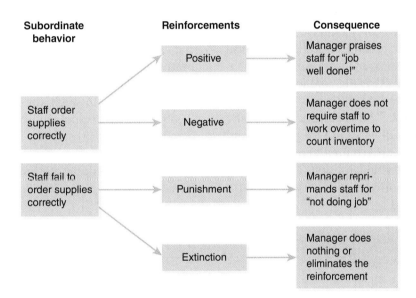

FIGURE 8.9 Skinner's Reinforcement Theory and types of reinforcements.

Reproduced Figure 6-6 from Borkowski N. *Organizational Behavior in Health Care*. 3rd ed. Burlington, MA: Jones & Bartlett Learning; 2016.

the behaviors. Rewards can be tangible incentives like bonuses or intangible incentives like recognition and awards. **Negative reinforcement** refers to when a negative consequence is removed once a behavior has improved, thereby encouraging the desired behavior. The idea is that removing the negative consequence, like a supervisor ceasing to caution a malingering employee once the behavior changes, encourages the employee to avoid this behavior in the future to avoid the hassle from the supervisor. **Punishment** refers to the application of undesired consequences in response to undesirable employee behavior. An example of punishment could be a verbal or written reprimand for being late to work, suspension from work for gambling or theft, or termination for more serious

deviant behavior. **Extinction** refers to when positive reinforcements are withheld from an employee. An example of extinction is when an employee with high levels of absenteeism no longer receives a bonus personal day at the end of the year. In this example, a positive reinforcement was withheld to encourage the employee to exhibit a desirable behavior (i.e., regularly showing up to work) to receive the positive reward in the future. [7,11]

Reinforcement Theory provides a number of practical implications for managers. Managers should use positive reinforcement or rewards to enhance employee performance. Positive reinforcement is preferred over punishment because it produces higher levels of performance and helps to sustain higher performance over time. Punishing employees can lead to deviant behaviors, such as sabotage, malingering, and other counterproductive behaviors. Rewards can help motivate behavior change, as well as reinforce desired behaviors. Managers should also consider the frequency and the timing of reinforcement. Generally, reinforcement should be prompt and consistent.

Hackman and Oldham's Job Characteristics Model. Richard Hackman and Greg Oldham developed the Job Characteristics Model of work motivation in the 1970s.[26] This model states that making jobs more meaningful can enhance motivation and, particularly, intrinsic motivation. **FIGURE 8.10** illustrates the Job Characteristics Model. Meaningful work results in a number of desirable organizational behaviors, such as higher-level performance, job satisfaction, and retention, and reduces undesirable behaviors, such as lower-quality work, absenteeism, and turnover. The model identifies a set of five core job characteristics to use when designing jobs that result in critical psychological states that influence personal and work outcomes.[26–28]

The model indicates that the core job characteristics are skill variety, task identity, task significance, autonomy, and feedback.[29] **Skill variety** refers to the different activities an individual uses in their job and the variety of skills that are required to perform these activities. The more activities and skills a job has, the more engaging and motivating it is. **Task identity**

refers to how much of a job an individual completes, as well as how easy it is for them to see their contribution as part of a larger work product. The more of a job that an employee does or the more they can see their contribution, the more engaging and motivating a job is. **Task significance** refers to the perceived importance of a job and its perceived impact. The greater the importance and impact, the more the job matters. Jobs with higher levels of perceived importance and impact are more motivating to employees. **Autonomy** refers to the degree of freedom and discretion an individual has to decide how to do their job. The more discretion and self-determination in accomplishing a job, the greater its motivating potential. **Feedback** refers to the information that individuals receive related to their work performance.[29] The more of these core characteristics designed into a job, the more employees will be motivated and the more performance, work quality, and satisfaction will be enhanced.[6]

The Job Characteristics Model identifies three critical psychological states that are key to creating motivation in a job. These three states are concerned with whether an individual is (1) experiencing meaningfulness through the work they are doing, (2) experiencing responsibility for the work they are completing, and (3) gaining knowledge about their performance. These psychological states contribute to a number of desirable individual and organizational behaviors (e.g., intrinsic motivation, quality

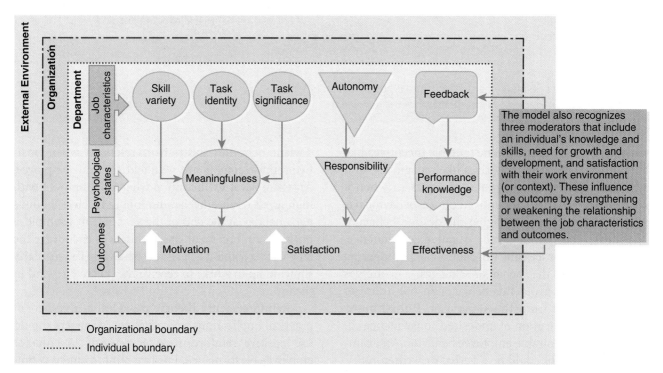

FIGURE 8.10 The Job Characteristics Model of work motivation.
Based on information from and modification of Hackman JR, Oldham GR. *Work Redesign.* Addison-Welsey: Reading, MA; 1980.

work, satisfaction, and retention).[29] Skill variety, task identity, and task significance contribute to the psychological state of **experienced meaningfulness**. Jobs that require employees to use a variety of different skills are more motivating because the job is more meaningful to them, whereas jobs that are repetitious or monotonous diminish interest and engagement. Therefore, jobs that require a worker to use a variety of skills are more motivating and satisfying than those that do not require skill variety. Jobs that require individuals to complete large parts or all of the tasks in a job have high task identity. Individuals identify with and attach themselves to tasks that take a significant amount of time to complete as this can be indicative of their importance and difficulty. The degree of importance or perceived importance gives meaning to the work individuals do and, in turn, motivates them. Individuals are not motivated to complete tasks if they believe that what they are doing does not matter. Autonomy contributes to the psychological state of **experiencing responsibility** for the work they are completing. Jobs that allow individuals to decide what needs to be done, how it needs to be done, and when it needs to be done result in a greater likelihood of satisfaction and motivation. Feedback contributes to the psychological state of **knowledge about their performance** and the outcomes they are producing through their work. Individuals who receive regular and constructive feedback related to their job performance experience higher levels of job satisfaction and motivation.[28,29] Managers should work with their human resource department to design and redesign jobs to maximize motivating potential.

▶ Teams and Teamwork

Public health is complex and often requires teams to accomplish tasks and achieve goals. Leaders and managers serve as catalysts and coaches for teams and "teaming"[30] within organizations. Kozlowski and Bell have looked at a number of definitions of teams and found that they emphasize several common characteristics. First, a team is composed of two or more individuals who work in a coordinated and interdependent way to achieve a common purpose or shared goal(s). Second, team members hold each other accountable for different roles and responsibilities assigned to the various team members by the team. Third, teams are evaluated based on the team's collective performance.[31] The terms team and group are often used interchangeably; however, there are distinctions between the two concepts. Understanding the difference is helpful and

important. Teams are a type of group; however, not all groups are teams.[32] Groups differ from teams in the way the members work together. Groups are composed of individuals who are working independently and toward individual goals. Group members are not holding one another accountable because they may not be aware of someone's personal performance goals. In contrast, teams are working on a common goal and trying to achieve the goal through coordination and synergy.[7]

In health care, there has been a push toward the concept of "teaming" versus teamwork.[33] The concept of teaming builds on the classical definitions of teams and the idea of teamwork. Amy Edmondson defines teaming as "fluid, collaborative, interdependent work across shifting products and a shifting mix of partners, often across organizational boundaries."[33(para2)] Teaming emphasizes action and recurring interactions, so that the team accomplishes their common purpose and goal(s) and creates value. To create value, healthcare organizations and teams must continuously respond to health priorities and adapt to environmental realities. Team members must adopt a mind-set of continuous collaboration because the context in which the team is operating and trying to achieve its common purpose and goal(s) is constantly changing. Roles, boundaries, and tasks are not static or always clearly defined when a team uses a "teaming" approach to their work. Teaming places the team in a constant state of teamwork, which is a new way of viewing teams.[34] Within health care, teams help promote higher levels of care coordination, patient satisfaction, provider satisfaction, productivity, and clinical outcomes. Society is demanding more from public health professionals and organizations. To respond, public health organizations and teams must continue to embrace the concept of teaming as a strategy to help meet society's increasing public health needs.

Types of Teams

There are a number of different types of teams utilized in public health organizations. Fried and Fottler discuss six types of healthcare teams that include cross-functional, project team (or temporary team and task forces), self-directed (or self-managed), task force, process improvement, and virtual.[35] Functional and global are additional types of teams that are used and will be discussed.[1] Organizations often utilize different types of teams simultaneously. Public health professionals can find themselves leading or serving on multiple teams at any given time. Understanding the structure and purpose of different types of teams can help enhance team effectiveness or the ability of the team to accomplish their common purpose or goal(s).

- *Functional Teams*: These teams consist of team members from one functional area in an organization. Members of the team are all performing similar tasks and functions. However, they could be performing functional tasks at different levels (e.g., Director, Assistant Director, Coordinator, and frontline staff) within the organization.[1] The organizational chart identifies functional areas within an organization. For example, a public health department could have a functional team dedicated to community assessment and evaluation, aging, population health, disease prevention, or youth wellness. The team would most likely be composed of the director and key frontline personnel within the department. These teams focus internally on work and projects within their functional areas.[12]

- *Cross-Functional or Interprofessional Teams*: These teams consist of team members from different functional units or departments. Organizational charts help identify different functional areas. Team members are selected to join the team based on their functional knowledge and expertise. Team members consider how the team's work will influence their functional unit, as well as how the work will influence other functional units and the broader organization.[1,12] Cross-functional teams are often interprofessional teams in health-related organizations. Interprofessional teams are composed of two or more members from different health professions. Teams can consist of both clinicians and non-clinicians.[36] The goal of interprofessional teams in health care is to provide patient-centered care that is high quality and cost effective. Team members use their assessments and expertise and communicate with other providers to develop the best care plan for the patient. This approach keeps the patient central in decision-making and draws on a wider body of knowledge and expertise to treat the patient.[37]

- *Project or Temporary Teams*: Teams are formed for a specific purpose and for a defined period. Team members can consist of members from one or multiple functional areas within an organization. Management generally selects team members based on their knowledge, skills, and abilities that will be valuable to accomplishing a specific project. The project team is dissolved once the project has been completed.[32]

- *Task Forces*: These teams solve complex problems. Team members work together to develop an implementation and evaluation plan to address the problem. Task force members are appointed based on their knowledge, expertise, interest, or influence as it relates to the purpose of the task force.[35] Public health organizations at all levels utilize task forces. For example, the U.S. Preventive Services Task Force provides "evidence-based recommendations about clinical preventive services."[38(para1)] This organization develops task forces around specific preventive topics, such as screenings for bladder cancer in adults, autism spectrum disorder in young children, celiac disease, and cervical cancer, among other topics.[39] Members have clinical knowledge specific to the topical area but come from diverse public health and health-care organizations and settings. The task force reviews the scientific evidence and provides recommendations along with implementation plans and evaluation metrics. The task force stops meeting after its final recommendations have been issued.

- *Self-Directed or Self-Managed Teams*: Self-directed, or self-managed, teams manage themselves based on goals assigned to the team. These team are relatively autonomous and do not have a leader constantly involved in guiding the team's work or providing performance feedback to the team. Team members provide team leadership, which generally rotates from one team member to another over time. The team develops an action plan and assigns roles and responsibilities without input from formal leadership within the organization. The team becomes a cohesive and coordinated unit focused on accomplishing its common purpose or goal(s). Public health organizations use self-directed teams. For example, emergency and disaster relief teams rely on real-time planning and decision-making. These teams have a common purpose and specific team goals that are broadly defined by their organization(s). These teams are also under considerable pressure and must constantly adjust to achieve their goals because their work is time sensitive.[12] Self-directed teams would not be successful if they had to constantly consult with organizational leadership on every plan and decision as an emergency unfolded.

- *Process Improvement Teams*: These teams focus on improving some aspect of a workplace and consist of members from one or more departments. These teams can improve processes related to quality, safety, efficiency, and productivity, among other topics. Clearly, defining and studying the process that needs to be improved is integral to the team's work. Understanding the steps in the process and root causes of any process issues allows the team to create a detailed action plan for process improvement. Teams also create measures to determine if the team's improvement plan is working along with metrics for monitoring the process over time.[35]

- *Virtual Teams*: Virtual teams are geographically dispersed and use technology to collaborate or meet.[35] Physical separation requires team members to use electronic forms of communication, such as email, text messaging, video conferencing, teleconferencing, and cloud-based project management platforms.[40] Public health organizations often rely on virtual teams to provide core and essential public health services. A state health department can use virtual teams to help manage disease outbreaks or coordinate statewide emergency responses.

- *Global Teams*: Global teams are separated by international boundaries and often include team members with different cultural and ethnic backgrounds, as well as language proficiency.[6] There are a number of public health organizations that are composed of multinational actors and organizations. The World Health Organization utilizes global teams to address a number of regional, as well as global, health concerns ranging from climate change to infectious diseases to poverty. Global teams work to address the health, safety, and well-being of citizens worldwide.

Teambuilding and the Team Development Model

Bruce Tuckman developed the Team Development Model that identifies a set of developmental stages for teams. The initial model developed in 1965 included four stages of team development.[41] A revised model was developed in 1977 that included a fifth stage.[42] The developmental stages include (1) **forming**, (2) **storming**, (3) **norming**, (4) **performing**, and (5) terminating or **adjourning**. Leaders and managers can use this model, as shown in **FIGURE 8.11**, to better understand and guide how teams develop.

- Stage 1, **Forming**: During this phase, team members are familiarizing themselves with their common purpose or goal(s) and with one another. Conflict among team member is low during this stage. Team members are worried about whether they will fit in with the team. Team members are also concerned with why they are on the team and what the team is expected to accomplish. Team performance is also low because the team is in the start-up phase of team development.[41,42]

- Stage 2, **Storming**: During this phase, conflict and disagreement can emerge as team members begin to vie for leadership and status within the group. Personalities and work styles begin to emerge, which can cause conflict and tensions within the team. This is natural but something that the team needs to resolve, so that the team can move forward with its work. The team begins

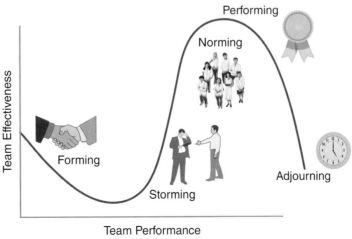

FIGURE 8.11 Tuckman's Team Development Model.

Information from Tuckman BW. Developmental sequence in small groups. *Psychol Bull.* 1965;63(6):384–399. doi:10.1037/h0022100; Tuckman BW, Jensen MAC. Stages of small group development revisited. *Group Organ Stud.* 1977;2(4):419–427. doi:10.1177/105960117700200404

to develop a project plan and assign different roles and responsibilities. Team performance is still low because the team is still in the start-up phase of team development.[41,42]

- Stage 3, **Norming**: During this phase, the team resolves previous conflicts and begins to work as a cohesive unit. The team focuses on defining desirable team behaviors and mutual expectations for performance. The team also decides how the team will work together. Team performance begins to accelerate.[41,42]

- Stage 4, **Performing**: During this phase, the team becomes effective and performance levels are high. The team is exercising the structures it developed during the storming and norming phases of team development. Team members are carrying out their plans to achieve their purpose. Individual team members carry out specific tasks, roles, and responsibilities. Conflicts and disagreements can arise during this phase. However, the team works to resolve these issues through problem solving, dialogue, and cooperation to achieve their common purpose or goal(s). Team performance is at its highest level during this stage.[41,42]

- Stage 5, **Terminating or Adjourning**: During this phase, the team celebrates their victories and debriefs on areas for improvement. Performance levels are low as the team winds down their work together. This phase focuses on finishing and submitting any final tasks or work products. For standing or ongoing teams, new members may join the team. This will lead the team to revisit the developmental stages although the stages will generally be shorter since the team is established with a defined purpose and norms.[42]

Team Roles

Despite the type of team, all teams have different roles that are fulfilled by different members on the team. Roles help the team achieve higher levels of team effectiveness and performance. Understanding the different types of team roles helps leaders assemble teams with the right mix of members. Team roles vary based on the degree to which the roles focus on tasks or relationships. Optimal teams are composed of a diverse set of members who have roles focused on both tasks and relationships to varying degrees.

Meredith Belbin began conducting research in the 1970s on team roles, and formalized his research by defining the nine Belbin Team Roles in the early 1980s.[43] These roles characterize an individual's behaviors and contributions to a team. These roles also emphasize tasks and relationships to varying degrees

and illustrate that teams need an optimal mix of team members focused on both tasks and relationships. Teams do not require all the roles to be successful. Also, most team members are comfortable with more than one team role and are able to shift in the different roles over time to meet team needs. Belbin believed that individuals had "preferred," "manageable," and "least preferred" roles based on their natural behaviors and tendencies. The nine Belbin Team Roles are categorized into one of three categories (**FIGURE 8.12**).[44] The "thinking or cerebral" category includes the team roles of Plant, Specialist, and Monitor Evaluator. The "social" category includes the roles of Coordinator, Resource Investigator, and Team Worker. The "action" category includes the roles of Shaper, Implementer, and Completer/Finisher.[44,45]

Thinking Roles

- *Plant Role*—Plants infuse teams with creative and innovative ideas. They help jump-start teams and projects. This role often likes to work independently to reflect and develop new ways of doing things. This role thinks outside the box and challenges team members to work and solve problems in unconventional and novel ways. Plants are creative, and too many plants on a team can prevent the team from accomplishing the team's goal(s). They may also become obsessed with the creation and perfecting process. Some plants may not be able to accept constructive criticism since they have invested a significant amount of time, energy, and creativity in developing their ideas. Some plants may be weak communicators and need help translating or communicating their ideas to the team.[44,45]

- *Specialist Role*—Specialists have a deep passion for learning. They are able to research topics and quickly become experts. Teams can appreciate their ability to find technical information and translate it into a solution. Specialists prefer to work alone because it is easy to dig deep and find answers alone. Teams should assign specialists a topic and time line and then let them become an expert. Mentorship is a strength of many specialists. They have a passion for learning, and they find that they also have a passion for sharing or teaching others what they have learned. These team members earn respect because of the deep and diverse knowledge they possess.[44,45]

- *Monitor Evaluator Role*—Monitor evaluators provide analytical and critical thinking to teams. They are able to synthesize large amounts of information and provide a detailed analysis of the

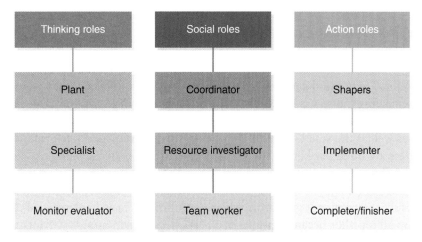

FIGURE 8.12 Belbin's team roles.
Based on information from Belbin RM. Team Roles in a Nutshell. https://www.belbin.com/media/1141/belbin-uk-2011-teamrolesinanutshell.pdf. Published 2011. Accessed July 29, 2019.

benefits and challenges associated with problems, ideas, and solutions proposed by team members. Evaluators are thoughtful and thorough. This makes them valuable decision-makers and "devils advocates." Their systematic approach to team matters can make them slow and a target for team members that are more action oriented. Conflict can emerge within teams because of their critiques.[44,45]

Social Roles

- *Coordinator*—Coordinators are able to organize the work to accomplish the team's goals. They are able to create synergy among team members. This role is also able to assess the personalities, strengths, and weaknesses of team members and assign tasks that utilize a member's strengths. Coordinators prefer to work through team members. They are able to answer and resolve questions that members may have about their individual work and how it contributes to the team's goals. If left unchecked, coordinators can use their influence in a counterproductive and manipulative way.[44,45]
- *Resource Investigator*—Resource investigators help teams acquire resources to carry out the team's work plan. This role likes to work with individuals inside and outside the team and organization to promote the team's plan and purpose. Resource investigators are outgoing and strong communicators, and they are good at developing relationships. Teams need to keep resource investigators engaged in the team by putting their networking and negotiation skills to good use.[44,45]
- *Team Worker*—Team workers provide the team with strong psychosocial connections

and support. They are the "glue" that holds the team together. This role works to safeguard the social and psychological well-being of team members individually and collectively. They are often popular and well thought of by their team members because they ensure that concerns are voiced and addressed. They work to promote respectful dialogue among group members and resolve conflict, when necessary. Appreciation and recognition are something these team members do naturally. This helps team members feel appreciated and helps enhance satisfaction, motivation, and engagement among team members.[44,45]

Action Roles

- *Shapers*—Shapers provide teams with momentum by pushing team members and projects toward their goal. This role leverages relationships to keep team members focused on their individual tasks and collective goals. Shapers are decisive and direct communicators. They make decisions and waste no time in communicating the decision. Shapers can become impatient if the team is not progressing toward their goal in a timely manner. An overly direct communication style can be abrasive to some team members and result in team conflict.[44,45]
- *Implementer*—Implementers provide teams with activators and put a team's plan into motion. They value the plan the team has developed and work to systematically implement it. Implementers like to follow a plan or rules because they see these as serving the organization and its success. This can make implementers inflexible at times and unable to "troubleshoot" solutions if plans do not work exactly as envisioned.[44,45]

■ *Completer/Finisher*—Completers or finishers provide teams with a detail-oriented eye. They value high quality and correct work. They are able to pick up the last-minute details that need correcting. Completers are methodical and systematic when reviewing the team's work. They are also patient and they have an ability to look at the big picture, as well as the small details of a project. Completers are often perfectionists, which can cause conflict in teams. Team members may feel they are unable to achieve perfection. As a result, they may not give projects their best or give up all together because they feel their work is not good enough. Completers can become frustrated with team members when they perceive that low-quality work has been "dumped" in their lap at the last minute.[44,45]

There are several important takeaways for managers related to teams. First, managers need to be sure that teams are the right answer. Team are expensive because they require the time of a number of people. Team members dedicate time to the team in lieu of doing other work for the organization. Organizational costs increase as teams add additional members and meetings. Managers should consider the cost versus the benefits of using a team and determine if there are other suitable options. Second, if a team is the answer, managers should ensure the proper type of team is utilized. This decision is important to determining team size and membership. Third, managers should consider team roles when selecting members. Ensuring a team has the right mix of members helps promote efficient and effective teams. Finally, team development needs to be taken seriously so that the team has the best chance of being an effective team. This may require facilitation and training to help a new team transition through the developmental stages and members to assume appropriate roles.

▶ Conflict

Teams and workplaces are prone to conflict. There are a number of potential sources of conflict such as resource competition, unclear goals, roles, responsibilities, different personalities, mergers, acquisitions, workforce reductions, generational differences, organizational change, poor management or mismanagement, high turnover, and poorly designed jobs.[46] Understanding the sources of conflict helps teams, leaders, and organizations avoid, minimize, manage, and resolve conflict. Unresolved conflict often escalates if leaders do not appropriately manage it. This can damage relationships between co-workers and diminish organizational performance. However, conflict in organizations is not always bad.

Extensive research has been done on organizational conflict in recent decades.[11] The earliest views on organizational conflict were that all conflict was bad for the organization. The rationale was that conflict diverted attention away from doing work, which, in turn, diminished performance. Research indicates that the type and level of conflict influences whether or not conflict is detrimental to performance. Team conflict can stem from relationships (or interpersonal conflict) or task performance. Interpersonal conflict is often detrimental to performance because it leads to people spending time on negative interactions versus collaborating and accomplishing work goals. Task conflict stems from conflict about how best to accomplish tasks and processes. This type of conflict can be useful because it can lead to new ideas and efficiencies that can improve performance.[6] The level of conflict is also important. Interestingly, studies have found that low levels of conflict are associated with low levels of performance. This is the relationship one would expect to find for high levels of conflict. In the case of low levels, the motivational benefit of conflict can be lost as some conflict can engage and stimulate people to contribute and collaborate. However, high levels of conflict usually diminish performance as the conflict versus the work becomes the focus of attention. Moderate levels of conflict have been associated with the highest level of performance. So, a moderate level conflict can be beneficial if it is focused on improving the tasks that need to be accomplished. Otherwise, conflict can be detrimental to organizational performance.[7,11]

Conflict can escalate to violence if it is not properly addressed and dealt with. Workplace violence is a growing concern in health care.[47] Violence can stem from conflict between employees or those they serve. Leaders and managers are responsible for developing reporting systems, conducting safety audits and violence surveys, consulting with local law enforcement to promote workplace safety,[48] and providing counseling and support for victims of workplace violence.[47] Conflict can have negative and costly consequences for individuals, teams, and leaders. The negative consequences of conflict can result in a hostile workplace that talented employees leave, resulting in employee turnover. This strains staffing, which can further exacerbate and reinforce a poor work environment. Verbal and physical assault, injury, and death can also occur if workplace and emergency response plans are not in place.[48,49] Understanding the source of conflict and how to resolve conflict is paramount for public health managers and organizations.

Conflict Styles

Resolving conflict is important for individuals, teams, and organization. Individuals handle conflict in different ways or have different conflict management styles. These styles relate to differences in a person's preference for assertiveness in getting their way versus their preference for cooperativeness (or cooperation) in letting others get their way.[32,50] Kenneth Thomas and Ralph Kilmann identified five conflict management styles that include accommodating, avoiding, compromising or negotiating, collaborating or problem solving, and competing or forcing.[51] These conflict management styles differ based on an individual's "concern for self" or "concern for others."[32] A two-dimensional graph, as shown in **FIGURE 8.13**, helps visualize these conflict management styles and associated behaviors based on the degrees to which an individual is concerned for self or others. The degree to which an individual is concerned for self will influence how assertive they are. Similarly, the degree to which an individual is concerned for others will influence how cooperative they are. Discussing the following conflict management styles in terms of the degree of assertiveness and cooperativeness provides insights into the behaviors each style exhibits. The following conflict management style discussion draws on insights from a number of authors (**BOX 8.1**).

- *Accommodating*—The accommodating style shows more concern for others than self. This style exhibits a high level of cooperativeness and a low level of assertiveness.[32] This can be thought of as the "your way" conflict style.[1(p314)] With this style, an individual yields to another person or party. The individual may provide input, but they ultimately defer to the other person. This

approach helps to preserve relationships. However, it can lead to suboptimal decisions and outcomes. Individuals can become frustrated over time as a result. This approach is best when decisions are time sensitive and the decision is more important to one party than the other.[12] This approach can help build social capital and maintain positive working relationships.[1]

- *Avoiding*—The avoiding conflict management style shows lower concern for both self and others. This style exhibits lower levels of cooperativeness and assertiveness.[32] This can be thought of as the "no way" conflict management style.[1(p314)] Individuals who use this style may be withdrawn, unengaged, and even physically absent. This approach helps to preserve relationships like the accommodating style. However, it can lead to unresolved conflict that can escalate over time. This approach is best when preserving the relationship is more important than making a decision or when emotions are high.[12] This approach can help build social capital and maintain positive working relationships. However, the short-term and long-term impact of avoiding conflict is an important consideration.[1] Will avoiding conflict do more harm than good?

- *Compromising or Negotiating*—The compromising or negotiating[12] conflict management style shows moderate concern for others and self. This style exhibits moderate levels of cooperativeness and assertiveness.[32] This can be thought of as the "half way" conflict management style.[1(p314)] Individuals who use this style are committed to finding a mutually beneficial decision or outcome that all parties can live with. This approach works to build relationships through

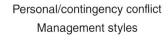

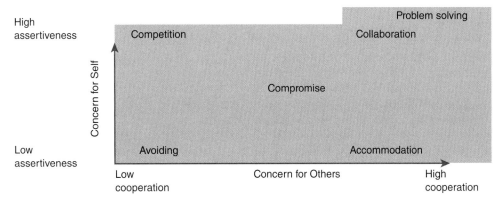

FIGURE 8.13 Conflict management styles regarding concern for self and others.

BOX 8.1 Conflict Management Styles

Accommodating

- When you find you are wrong, to allow a better position to be heard; to learn; and to show your reasonableness
- When issues are more important to others than to you, to satisfy others and maintain cooperation
- To build social capital for later issues
- To minimize loss when you are outmatched and losing the conflict
- When harmony and stability are especially important
- To allow subordinates to develop by learning from their mistakes

Avoiding

- When an issue is trivial or more important issues are pressing
- When you perceive no chance of satisfying your needs
- When potential disruption outweighs the benefits of resolution
- To let people cool down and regain perspective
- When gathering information supersedes immediate decision-making
- When others can resolve the conflict more effectively
- When issues seem a result of other issues

Collaborating

- To find an integrative solution when both sets of concerns are too important to be compromised
- When your objective is to learn
- To merge insights from people with different perspectives
- To gain commitment by incorporating concerns into a consensus
- To work through feelings that have harmed an interpersonal relationship

Competing

- When quick, decisive action is vital (e.g., emergency situations, such as a disaster, terrorism incident, or accident)
- On important issues where unpopular actions need implementing (e.g., cost-cutting, enforcing unpopular rules, and discipline)
- On issues vital to company welfare and survival when you know you are right
- Against people who take advantage of noncompetitive behavior

Compromising

- When goals are important, but not worth the effort or potential disruption of competing
- When opponents with equal power are committed to mutually exclusive goals
- To achieve temporary settlements to complex issues
- To arrive at expedient solutions under time pressure
- As a backup when collaboration or competition is unsuccessful

Problem Solving

- May not always work (it takes two to make this style work)
- Requires the identification of a broader range of strategies
- Points for problem solving
  - Both parties must have a vested interest in the outcome (the resolution)
  - Both parties feel a better solution can be achieved through problem-based collaboration
  - Both parties recognize the problem is caused by the relationship, not the people involved
  - Focus is on solving the problem, not on accommodating differing views
  - Both parties are flexible
  - Understanding that all solutions have positive and negative aspects
  - Both parties understand each other's issues
  - Problem is looked at objectively, not personally
  - Both parties are knowledgeable about conflict management
  - Allows everyone to "save face"
  - Celebrates successful outcomes openly

iterative interactions or negotiations. However, it can lead to suboptimal decisions and outcomes because the mutually agreed upon decision may not be the optimal decision. This approach works best when there is not a power differential or each side has equal power. Individuals can become frustrated if the process takes too long or one side does not appear to be dealing honestly or in a "give and take" manner. As a result, parties to the conflict may question each other's motives. The outcome is rarely optimal for either side, as each side gives up something to come to an agreement. Frequently, this outcome is viewed as a zero-sum game, which creates some losses for each person or party.[12]

- *Collaborating or Problem Solving*—The collaborating conflict management style shows high concern for others and high concern for self. This style exhibits high levels of cooperativeness and assertiveness.[32] This can be thought of as the "our way" conflict management style.[1(p314)] Individuals who use this style are committed to working together to achieve an optimal outcome. In contrast to the compromising style, the outcome benefits each side. This style uses a non-zero sum versus zero sum perspective when working toward an outcome. This style works best when there is open and honest communication. Understanding how to identify shared interests, common goals, and a mutually beneficial outcome takes time and practice. The collaborating style is best for complex issues because this style considers multiple viewpoints. This style can often lead to creative and innovative solutions that build social capital and strengthen relationships in the process.[12]
- *Competing or Forcing*—The competing or forcing conflict management style shows low concern for others and high concern for self. This style exhibits a low level of cooperativeness and a high level of assertiveness.[32] This can be thought of as the "my way" conflict management style.[1(p314)] Individuals who use this style are often aggressive and domineering. Ensuring a personal win or outcome that is personally beneficial is important to them. This style shows little regard for relationships and will often use intimidation, threats, dominance, and force to get their way. A downside of this style is that individuals can develop a reputation for not being able to work with others. They can become a target for "payback" from others because of their selfish and aggressive methods.[12]

Conclusion

Organizational dynamics refers to how organizational members behave and interact with one another. These interactions are important and influence an organization's ability to accomplish its goals. This chapter discussed a number of different topics, concepts, and theories that can help managers understand relationships and interactions within an organization. The goal for managers is to make relationships and interactions as positive and productive as possible.

Power is present in all organizations. Personal and position power are the traditional types of power present and used in organizations to exert influence. In addition to power, persuasion is a way managers can exert influence. Increasingly, understanding persuasion is important as knowledge workers and knowledge-based organizations dominate the public health landscape. Motivation is also a means to exert influence and engage employees in their work. There are many different motivation theories that reveal just how complex and challenging motivating employees can be. The content theories of motivation identified a set of needs that employees are trying to fulfill. These theories also reveal how managers can influence employee motivation by helping employees satisfy their needs. The process theories of motivation provide insights into how individuals are motivated versus what motivates them. Other motivation theories explored how goals, reinforcement, and job design can influence motivation.

This chapter concludes with a discussion of teams. Understanding the different types of teams and the important roles that members must assume is important to team effectiveness and performance. Assigning work based on a team member's strengths and preference helps **leverage** the diverse knowledge, skills, abilities, and experiences of team members. Understanding the developmental stages of the teams helps enhance their effectiveness. Conflict often arises in teams and organizations and can diminish both team and organizational performance. Understanding the different conflict management styles can help managers analyze, channel, and resolve conflict.

Discussion Questions

1. What is power? How is power different from influence?
2. What is persuasion? How is persuasion different from power and influence?
3. What are the key differences between leaders and managers regarding power and influence?

4. What are the different types of power? Provide an example of each type.
5. What is motivation? Why is motivation important in organizations?
6. Compare and contrast the different theories of motivation.
7. What is a team? How is a team different from a group?
8. What are the different types of teams discussed in the chapter? Provide an example of each type of team.
9. What are the different stages of team development?
10. What are the different team roles?
11. What are the different types of conflict? Provide an example of each conflict management style.
12. What is the relationship between the level of conflict and team performance?

Learning Activities

1. Think about a work experience you have had. Provide an example of the different types of power you witnessed.
2. Provide a short summary of a time when you had to work with someone who lacked motivation at school or work. Now, imagine you are that person's manager. Discuss what motivation theory you would use to motivate the individual.
3. Think about a team you have worked in at school or work. What type of team was it? Discuss the stages of team development you experienced. Did the team skip any stages? Did the team spend too long in any of the stages? What was the most challenging stage? Why?
4. Think about a team you have worked in at school or work. Assign each team member a role based on Belbin's team roles. Provide support for why you assigned the role to the team member.
5. Identify a team-building exercise you would use as a manager. Come to class ready to lead the class in the team-building exercise. Compare and contrast your team-building exercise with other exercises presented by your classmates.
6. Think about a team you have worked in at school or at work where you experienced conflict. Provide a summary of the conflict and identify the different conflict management styles that were used by team members. Respect privacy and confidentiality by not using personally identifiable information (i.e., names, organizations, etc.).

References

1. Daft RL. *The Leadership Experience*. 7th ed. Boston, MA: Cengage Learning; 2018.
2. Liebler JG, McConnell CR. *Umiker's Management Principles for Health Professionals*. 7th ed. Burlington, MA: Jones & Bartlett Learning; 2017.
3. French JRJ, Raven BH. The bases of social power. In: Cartwright D, ed. *Studies in Social Power*. Ann Arbor, MI: Institute for Social Research; 1959:259–269.
4. Raven BH. Social influence and power. In: Steiner ID, Fischer M, eds. *Current Studies in Social Psychology*. New York, NY: Holt, Rinehar, & Winston; 1965:371–382.
5. Northouse PG. *Leadership: Theory and Practice*. 8th ed. Thousands Oaks, CA: Sage Publications Inc.; 2019.
6. Daft RL. *Management*. 12th ed. Boston, MA: Cengage Learning; 2016.
7. Borkowski B. *Organizational Behavior, Theory, and Design in Health Care*. 2nd ed. Burlington, MA: Jones & Bartlett Learning; 2016.
8. Conger JA. The necessary art of persuasion. *Harv Bus Rev*. 1998;76(3):84–97.
9. Ellett W. The practical art of persuasion. *Harv Bus Rev*. https://hbr.org/2011/03/the-practical-art-of-persuasio. Published 2011. Accessed July 26, 2019.
10. Kast FE, Rosenzweig JE. *Organization and Management: A Systems and Contingency Approach*. 4th ed. New York, NY: McGraw-Hill; 1985.
11. Robbins SP, Judge TA. *Organizational Behavior*. 14th ed. Upper Saddle River, NJ: Pearson Prentice Hall; 2011.
12. Lussier RN, Achua CF. *Leadership: Theory, Application, and Skill Development*. 6th ed. Mason, OH: Cengage Learning; 2016.
13. Wren DA, Bedeian AG. *The Evolution of Management Thought*. 6th ed. Hobokan, NJ: Wiley; 2009.
14. Maslow AH. A theory of human motivation. *Psychol Rev*. 1943;50(4):370–396. doi:10.1037/h0054346.
15. Alderfer C. *Existence, Relatedness, and Growth*. New York, NY: Free Press; 1972.
16. Herzberg F. *The Motivation of Work*. New York, NY: Wiley; 1959.
17. Vroom VH. *Work and Motivation*. New York, NY: Wiley; 1964.
18. Adams JS. Toward an understanding of inequity. *J Abnorm Soc Psychol*. 1963;67(5):422–436. doi:10.1037/h0040968.
19. Adams JS. Inequity in social exchange. *Adv Exp Psychol*. 1965; 2:267–300.
20. Locke EA. Toward a theory of task motivation and incentive. *Organ Behav Hum Perform*. 1968;3(2):157–189. doi:10.1016/0030-5073(68)90004-4.
21. Locke EA, Latham GP. *A Theory of Goal Setting and Task Performance*. Englewood Cliffs, NJ: Prentice Hall; 1990.
22. Locke EA, Latham GP. Building a practically useful theory of goal setting and task motivation: A 35-year odyssey. *Am Psychol*. 2002;57(9):705–717.
23. Locke EA, Latham GP. New directions in goal-setting theory. *Curr Dir Psychol*. 2006;15(5):265–268. doi:10.1111/j.1467–8721.2006.00449.x.

24. Latham GP, Locke EA. New developments in and directions for goal-setting research. *Eur Psychol.* 2009;12(4):290–300. doi:10.1027/1016-9040.12.4.290.

25. Skinner BF. *Science and Human Behavior.* New York, NY: Macmillan; 1953.

26. Oldham GR, Hackman JR, Pearce JL. Conditions under which employees respond positively to enriched work. *J Appl Psychol.* 1976;61(4):395–403. doi:10.1037/0021-9010.61.4.395.

27. Hackman JR, Lawler EE. Employee reactions to job characteristics. *J Appl Psychol.* 1971;55(3):259–286. doi:10.1037/h0031152.

28. Hackman JR, Oldham GR. *Work Redesign.* Reading, MA: Addison-Wesley Publishing Company; 1980.

29. Hackman JR, Oldham GR. Motivation through the design of work: Test of a theory. *Organ Behav Hum Perform.* 1976;16(2):250–279. doi:10.1016/0030-5073(76)90016-7.

30. Edmondson AC. *Teaming: How Organizations Learn, Innovate, and Compete in the Knowledge Economy.* San Fransico, CA: Jossey-Bass; 2012.

31. Kozlowski SWJ. Work groups and teams in organizations. In: Weiner IB, Schmitt NW, Highhouse S, eds. *Handbook of Psychology: Industrial and Organizational Psychology.* Vol. 12. 2nd ed. Hoboken, NJ: John Wiley & Sons, Inc.; 2013:412–469.

32. Johnson JA, Rossow CC. *Health Organizations: Theory, Behavior, and Development.* 2nd ed. Burlington, MA: Jones & Bartlett Learning; 2019.

33. Edmondson AC. The kinds of teams health care needs. *Harv Bus Rev.* https://hbr.org/2015/12/the-kinds-of-teams-health-care-needs. Published December 16, 2015. Accessed July 26, 2019.

34. Edmondson AC, Harvey JF. *Extreme Teaming: Lessons in Complex, Cross-Sector Leadership.* Bingley, UK: Emerald Publishing Limited; 2017.

35. Fried BJ, Fottler MD, eds. *Human Resources in Healthcare: Managing for Success.* 4th ed. Chicago, IL: Health Administration Press; 2015.

36. Institute of Medicine. *Health Professions Education: A Bridge to Quality.* Washington, DC: The National Academies Press; 2003. doi:10.17226/10681.

37. Bridges DR, Davidson RA, Odegard PS, Maki IV, Tomkowiak J. Interprofessional collaboration: three best practice models of interprofessional education. *Med Educ Online.* 2011;16(1):6035. doi:10.3402/meo.v16i0.6035.

38. U.S. Preventive Services Task Force. About the U.S. Preventive Services Task Force. https://uspreventiveservicestaskforce.org/Page/Name/about-the-uspstf. Updated 2019. Accessed July 28, 2019.

39. U.S. Preventive Services Task Force. Published Recommendations. https://www.uspreventiveservicestaskforce.org/BrowseRec/Index/browse-recommendations. Updated 2019. Accessed July 28, 2019.

40. Ferrazzi K. Getting virtual teams right. *Harvard Business Review.* https://hbr.org/2014/12/getting-virtual-teams-right. Published December 2014. Accessed October 14, 2018.

41. Tuckman BW. Developmental sequence in small groups. *Psychol Bull.* 1965;63(6):384–399. doi:10.1037/h0022100.

42. Tuckman BW, Jensen MAC. Stages of small-group development revisited. *Group Organ Manage.* 1977;2(4):419–427. doi:10.1177/105960117700200404.

43. Belbin RM. *Management Team: Why They Succeed or Fail.* London, UK: Heinemann; 1981.

44. Belbin RM. *Team Roles at Work.* 2nd ed. New York, NY: Routledge; 2010.

45. Belbin RM. Team Roles in a Nutshell. https://www.belbin.com/media/1141/belbin-uk-2011-teamrolesinanutshell.pdf. Published 2011. Accessed July 29, 2019.

46. Society for Human Resource Management. Managing Workplace Conflict. https://www.shrm.org/resourcesandtools/tools-and-samples/toolkits/pages/managingworkplaceconflict.aspx. Published 2017. Accessed July 26, 2019.

47. The Joint Commission. Physical and verbal violence against health care workers. *Sentin Event Alert*; https://www.jointcommission.org/assets/1/18/SEA_59_Workplace_violence_4_13_18_FINAL.pdf. Publish April 17, 2018. Accessed July 28, 2019.

48. Whitman E. Quelling a storm of violence in healthcare settings. *Modern Healthcare.* http://www.modernhealthcare.com/article/20170311/MAGAZINE/303119990. Published March 11, 2017. Accessed July 26, 2019.

49. Mays GP, Halverson PK, Kaluzny AD. Collaboration to improve community health: trends and alternative models. *Jt Comm J Qual Improv.* 1998;24(10):518–540. doi:10.1016/S1070-3241(16)30401-1.

50. Ledlow GR, Stephens JH. *Leadership for Health Professionals: Theory, Skills, and Applications.* 3rd ed. Burlington, MA: Jones & Bartlett Learning; 2018.

51. Thomas KW. Conflict and conflict management. In: Ed. D, ed. *Handbook of Industrial and Organizational Psychology.* Chicago, IL: Rand McNally; 1976:889–935.

Suggested Readings and Websites

Agency for Healthcare Research and Quality. https://www.ahrq.gov/teamstepps/index.html

Belbin. https://www.belbin.com/about/

CHAPTER 9

Coordinating and Leading Public Health Organizations

LEARNING OBJECTIVES

After reading this chapter, you should be able to:

- Define the management function of coordinating/leading.
- Explain the relationship between management and leadership.
- Compare and contrast the major trait theories.
- Compare and contrast the major behavioral theories.
- Compare and contrast the major contingency theories.
- Compare and contrast the major transactional theories.
- Explain the role of followership.
- Compare and contrast the major transformational theories.
- Explain substitutes and neutralizers of leadership.

▶ Introduction

The coordinating function is the process of influencing human resources or in a way that achieves organizational goals. The modern term for coordinating is leading. As previously mentioned, this text emphasizes management versus leadership concepts. The two concepts are distinct, yet related. Thinking back to the organizational systems model, the coordinating or leading function primarily influences the psychosocial subsystem. The psychosocial subsystem deals with people or employees.[1] **Leadership** is a reciprocal relationship between a leader and a follower. Leaders use their relationships to influence followers toward a common goal.[2] The common or shared goals that the leadership definition

is referring to are an organization's goals. Leadership works to influence followers to behave in desirable ways that enhance organizational performance and goal attainment.

Kotter advanced the idea that leadership and management have distinct and different foci.[3] Leaders focus on effectiveness, whereas managers focus on efficiency. Leadership focuses on effectiveness, that is, making sure that the organization's results are what is needed in relation to the external environment or what is happening outside the organization. This makes a lot of sense to public health professionals who are watching health trends and statistics and then responding to those needs through services, programs, projects, initiatives, partnerships, and other organizational activities to address needs and improve health.

Management definitions focus on efficiency, that is, using organization resource inputs to maximize results or organizational outputs. Managers are responsible for coordinating the transformation process of inputs into outputs within organizations. Leaders actively scan and look for changes in dimensions of the external environment to understand if these changes represent opportunities and/or threats to their organization. Leaders develop plans, along with managers, in their organizations about how to respond to these changes in the organization's external environment. Managers are responsible for consulting with the leader on organizational plans. More importantly, however, managers are responsible for putting these plans into action. Leaders can miss environmental threats and opportunities if they focus too much on what is happening within the organization. Leaders must trust managers to enact agreed upon organizational plans, and managers should be involved with helping formulate such plans.[3]

▶ Overview of Leadership Theory

A plethora of leadership perspectives, approaches, concepts, and theories has developed over the last 100 years to explain leadership.[4] There is not one universally accepted definition or theory of leadership. However, consensus has developed over time around key leadership characteristics and concepts. Leadership theories are similar in that they all try to explain how to be an effective leader. Effective leaders help create effective organizations that are achieving shared goals to align the organization with its environment.

There are several major categories of leadership theories. Discussing the leadership theories in chronological order reflects how leadership thought has evolved over time and continues to evolve today. The major leadership theory categories include trait theories, behavioral theories, contingency theories, transactional theories, and transformational (or contemporary) theories (**FIGURE 9.1**). The following

sections provide a brief discussion of each of these major categories and corresponding theories.

Trait Theories

Trait theories are the oldest leadership theories and date back to the mid-19th century. These theories focused on understanding the personal characteristics or traits that leaders possessed.[2] Historians developed the **Great Man Theory**, the earliest leadership theory, by studying prominent male, historical figures. These men were believed to be "great men" or effective leaders. The historians concluded that effective leaders were born and that effective leadership was genetic. Therefore, the theory advanced the idea that the children of great leaders would also be great leaders. The fallacy of the Great Man Theory was apparent when the children of great leaders did not turn out to be effective or notable leaders in many cases. The theory was, however, the first leadership theory, which advanced the idea that leaders had a certain set of traits that made them more effective than individuals who did not have those sets of traits.[4]

Psychologists began to conduct studies to identify the traits or characteristics of effective leaders. **Traits** are personal characteristics used to categorize individuals, such as physical characteristics, education, intelligence, and cognitive ability, among others. There are two types of traits—primary and secondary. **Primary traits** refer to personal characteristics that individuals cannot change about themselves like physical characteristics (e.g., age or race). **Secondary traits** refer to personal characteristics that surface in certain situations like an easygoing disposition or anxiety. Individuals can change secondary traits, unlike primary traits. The U.S. military funded considerable research to try to identify what traits effective leaders possessed. However, scholars never found a universal set of leadership traits. Research indicated that different sets of traits were helpful in different situations.[2,3]

In the 1940s, Stogdill reviewed the literature and identified intelligence, alertness, insight, responsibility, initiative, persistence, self-confidence, and sociability as important leadership characteristics.[5] Stogdill revisited the literature in the 1970s and refined his list

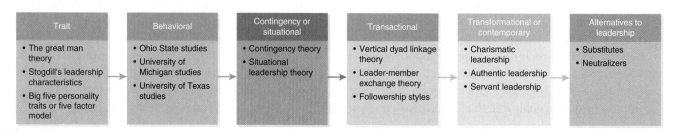

FIGURE 9.1 Major leadership theories and concepts.

of leadership characteristics to include achievement, persistence, insight, initiative, self-confidence, responsibility, cooperativeness, tolerance, influence, and sociability.[6] Advancements in psychology led to the identification of a set of leadership traits in the 1990s that included social intelligence, in addition to those identified by Stogdill.[2] Zaccaro, Kemp, and Bader identified cognitive abilities, extraversion, conscientiousness, emotional stability, openness, agreeableness, motivation, social intelligence, self-monitoring, emotional intelligence, and problem solving as important leadership characteristics.[7] The Big Five Personality Traits or Five Factor Model identified neuroticism, extraversion or surgency, openness to experience, agreeableness, and conscientiousness as a way to classify the five common aspects of personality.[8] Extroversion is strongly associated with leadership emergence and effectiveness followed by conscientiousness, openness to experiences, low neuroticism, and agreeableness.[9] Failure to find a universal set of leadership traits kept researchers searching for what makes an effective leader. This led researchers to study the behaviors of leaders.

Behavioral Theories

Behavioral theories emerged in the 1940s and continued through the 1970s.[10] Scholars turned to conducting studies that explored the behaviors of effective leaders because trait theories had failed to identify a universal set of leader traits. Behavioral theories asserted that leader behaviors were a better predictor of leadership effectiveness. Leader behaviors were important because they were what leaders used to influence followers to do certain things. Researchers began identifying different behavioral styles. These styles provided insight into how leaders acted in different situations and whether those behaviors helped leaders and followers achieve shared goals.

The Ohio State Studies

The Ohio State studies refer to a series of research projects conducted by Ralph Stogdill at Ohio State University in the 1940s. These studies shifted leadership theory from a focus on traits to a focus on understanding how leader behaviors or styles contribute to leadership effectiveness. Leadership styles are a set of related behaviors or recurrent patterns of behaviors leaders use with followers.[2,4] Stogdill advanced the idea that how leaders behaved led to their effectiveness or ineffectiveness as a leader. To test this idea, Stogdill and his research team surveyed thousands of employees in different organizations and asked them to describe leadership behaviors and identify which behaviors were associated with effective leaders.[11]

The research indicated two major categories of leader behaviors or styles called consideration and initiating structure (**FIGURE 9.2**).[6] The **consideration style** of leadership means that leaders have a set of related behaviors that focus on building relationships with followers. Consideration includes to the extent that leaders are considerate of others. Considerate leaders engage, talk, share decision-making, recognize, trust, and respect their followers. The **initiating structure style** of leadership means that leaders focus on getting work tasks done. This leadership style focuses on production and ensuring that everyone understands what tasks need to be completed, when they need to be completed (i.e., work or production schedule), how they need to be completed (i.e., policies, procedures, specifications), and the follower's role in helping accomplish the work.[4,6] Also, the studies revealed that leaders could possess a high or low orientation toward people or tasks and that the orientations were independent of one another. So, how do these leadership styles contribute to leadership effectiveness? Stogdill demonstrated from his research that effective leaders were focused on relationships and being able to work with others to create structures within an organization to accomplish tasks.[6]

University of Michigan Studies

The University of Michigan studies refer to a series of research projects conducted by Rensis Likert at the University of Michigan.[12,13] Likert and Stogdill were engaged in similar studies on leadership behaviors around the same time. The researchers, however, worked independent of one another. Likert surveyed an entirely different set of organizations and respondents. The findings from the University of Michigan studies supported the findings from the Ohio State University studies.[2] Likert and his team found two behavioral

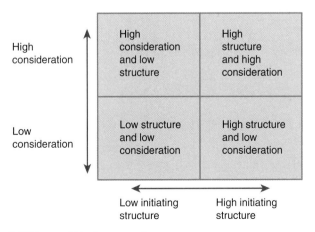

FIGURE 9.2 Ohio State studies.

Reproduced Figure 9-1 from Borkowski, N. (2016). *Organizational Behavior in Health Care.* 3rd ed. Burlington, MA: Jones and Bartlett Publishing.

styles that leaders exhibited called employee-oriented behaviors and production-oriented behaviors. Employee-oriented behaviors were relationship and other-focused behaviors similar to what Stogdill described as consideration. Production-oriented behaviors were task-focused behaviors similar to what Stogdill described as initiating structure and focused on tasks and production performance. Originally, Likert thought that these styles were on opposite ends of a continuum, with employee-oriented behaviors generally being more effective. He ultimately agreed both are important. The University of Michigan studies and the Ohio State studies used two different surveys and samples but arrived at similar conclusions. The conclusion was that there were two dominant leadership styles or sets of leadership behaviors—employee-oriented or relationship-focused behaviors and job-oriented or production-focused behaviors. The most effective leaders utilized a combination of both leadership styles.[10,14]

University of Texas Studies

The University of Texas studies refer to a series of research projects conducted by Robert Blake and Jane Mouton at the University of Texas in the 1960s. The team's research continued through the 1990s and resulted in revisions to the Leadership Grid they developed. The Texas studies were based on the Ohio State

and the University of Michigan studies. Blake and Mouton were trying to verify the findings from the two previous studies. Additionally, the team wanted to see if their studies could more precisely identify and define behavioral leadership styles associated with leadership effectiveness as well as better understand the two broad categories of leadership styles that the previous studies had identified.

The University of Texas studies confirmed the main findings from the Ohio State and the University of Michigan studies.[2] Blake and Mouton found two leadership styles, which they called concern for people and concern for production. **Concern for people** was the term used to categorize leadership behaviors that were relationship focused. The University of Michigan studies termed this employee-oriented behaviors, and the Ohio State studies termed this consideration. **Concern for production** was the term used to categorize leadership behaviors that were task focused. The University of Michigan studies termed this production-oriented behaviors, and the Ohio State studies used the term initiating structure to characterize this leadership style.[15]

The refined measurement helped Blake and Mouton develop the Managerial Grid[16] that later became known as the Leadership Grid.[16–19] The Leadership Grid is a two-dimensional matrix of leadership behavior based on different levels and combinations of the two dominant leadership behaviors—concern for people and concern for production (**FIGURE 9.3**). The

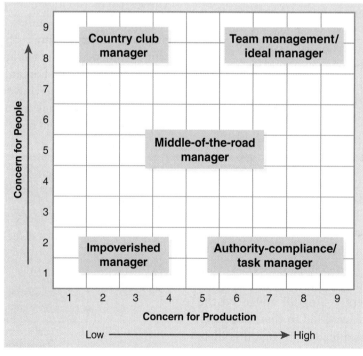

FIGURE 9.3 Blake and Mouton's Leadership Grid.

Y-axis plotted concern for employees and the X-axis plotted concern for production. The Leadership Grid identified five major leadership styles based on different levels of these two dominant categories of leader behaviors. The five categories include the following: (1) country club management, (2) team management, (3) middle-of-the road management, (4) impoverished management, and (5) **authority**-compliance management.[16] The optimal point on the grid is team management. **Team management** characterizes leadership behavior as having a balanced concern for both people and production. This leadership style recognizes that the relationships leaders have with followers impact the work of individuals and teams and, ultimately, whether organizational goals are achieved. **Country club management** characterizes leadership behavior as having a high concern for people and relationships but a low concern for tasks. This leadership style results in strong relationships but can result in a lack productivity or task completion. **Middle-of-the-road management** characterizes leadership behavior as having a moderate concern for people and production. This leadership style finds an optimal level of concern for people and tasks to achieve an acceptable level of organizational efficiency, effectiveness, and stability. **Impoverished management** characterizes leadership behaviors as having low concern for both people and production. This leadership style is often termed "retirement in place" or "checked out leadership" because the leader puts little, if any, effort into the organization. This results in ineffective leadership that can result in a leadership void and underperformance. Finally, **authority–compliance management** characterizes leadership behavior as having a low concern for people but a high concern for production. This style of leadership focuses on efficiently and effectively completing work, and leader–follower relationships suffer as a result.[16-18] The Leadership Grid is still widely used in organizations today. You may be asked in the future to use the grid to assess yourself or others.

The behavioral theories of leadership broadened the understanding of leadership effectiveness beyond a certain set of traits. Effective leaders need to engage in high levels of both relationship and task-focused behaviors. This was a significant contribution to understanding leadership. However, there were leaders who exhibited a high concern for relationships (or people) and tasks (or production) that were not effective. There were also leaders who exhibited a low concern for relationships and tasks that were effective. This led scholars to continue to study leadership to understand the situation or context in which different leadership styles were effective.

Contingency Theories

Contingency or situational theories emerged in the 1960s. These theories sought to understand how leaders behaved in different situations. Contingency theories build on behavioral theories just as behavioral theories build on trait theories. Contingency theories shifted the focus from leader behaviors to the situations that leaders faced, such as the type of task, follower, group, or context.[2] The situations that leaders faced were believed to moderate the relationship between a leader's behaviors and the follower's outcomes. Therefore, there is not one leadership style or a set of behaviors that lead to leader effectiveness in every situation. Leaders must adapt and use different leadership styles based on the situations in which they find themselves. Based on a situation, leaders may need to use a relational style of leadership to be effective. In contrast, leaders may find themselves in a situation where a task-focused style of leadership is most effective. These theories advanced that leadership effectiveness could be improved by considering the situation the leader faced when deciding what behavioral leadership style to use.[10]

Fiedler's Contingency Theory

Fred Fiedler developed the first contingency theory of leadership called the Leader–Match Theory.[20] The goal was to understand the situations that leaders faced and then determine which leadership style best matched the situation. Fiedler developed a way to measure situations and found that what mattered most was situational favorableness. **Situational favorableness** refers to "the degree a situation enables a person to exert influence over a work group."[10(p67)] The leader will be more effective if the leader's behavioral style fits the situation the leader faces.

Fiedler measured situational favorableness based on three dimensions, which include leader–member relations, task structure, and position power.[10,20] **Leader–member relations** consider what the relationship is like between a leader and their followers—good or poor. This dimension looks at whether a leader and followers are able to work together in a positive and cooperative manner. Leader–member relations also reflect how much followers trust and respect the leader and are willing to follow a leader's directions. The second dimension is task structure. **Task structure** refers to how well tasks are defined—structured or unstructured. Structured or well-defined tasks do not require much input from leaders because followers understand how to complete work tasks. In contrast, there is a need for leaders when tasks are unstructured because followers are not sure what to do and need input from the leader. In this case, leaders help followers understand what needs to be done. The third factor is the leader's position power. **Position power** refers to the leader's position within an organization, which can be strong or weak. A leader has more power the higher or closer the leader's position is to the top of the organization. Position power gives leaders the authority to reward and punish followers. Promotions and raises are common examples of how leaders can reward followers. Likewise, leaders can withhold advancement opportunities and can in extreme cases terminate an **employee**.[10] Together, these three dimensions determine how favorable a situation is for a leader or situational favorableness.[20] The model identifies eight different situational contexts leaders face and prescribes the most effective leadership style for each situation (**FIGURE 9.4**).

A drawback of the Leader–Match Theory was the belief that leaders could not change their leadership style but, instead, needed to change the situation or their job to one that better suited their leadership style. Fiedler believed that if a leader was task focused, it would be difficult to change their leadership style to one that was more relationship or follower focused (and vice versa). This limited the ability of leaders to improve their effectiveness. This resulted in the notion that organizations should change leaders to fit the situations that the organization faced. This was not popular among leaders or organizations, and it was not a very feasible approach to improving leadership effectiveness.

However, this theory did point out factors other than leader style that influenced leader effectiveness.

Hersey–Blanchard's Situational Leadership Theory

Paul Hersey and Ken Blanchard developed one of the most widely used contingency theories called Situational Leadership Theory in the mid- to late-1960s and into the 1970s.[21] The team's work continued through the 1990s and resulted in refinements to the Situational Leadership model. The model is still popular and in use today in many organizations.[2] Hersey and Blanchard advanced the idea that there is not one "best" leadership style and that a leader's style should vary based on the situations they faced.[10] They found that a leader's style should depend on a follower's maturity level or readiness level.[21] Maturity level depends on a follower's motivation level, experience, education, and willingness to assume responsibility related to their work. The model identified four maturity levels. The first maturity level characterizes followers who have both a low competence (i.e., experience and education) and commitment (i.e., motivation and willingness to accept responsibility) levels related to their work. The second maturity level characterizes followers who have a low competence level and high commitment level. The third maturity level characterizes followers who have a high competence level and low commitment level. The fourth maturity level characterizes followers who have both high competence and commitment levels.[2] Leaders

Situation	Leader–member relations	Task structure	Leader's position power	Most effect leadership style
1	Good	Structured	Strong	Task focused
2	Good	Unstructured	Weak	Relationship focused
3	Good	Structured	Weak	Task focused
4	Good	Unstructured	Strong	Task focused
5	Poor	Structured	Strong	Relationship focused
6	Poor	Unstructured	Weak	Task focused
7	Poor	Structured	Weak	Relationship focused
8	Poor	Unstructured	Strong	Relationship focused

FIGURE 9.4 Fiedler's contingency model of leadership.

Modified from Lussier R, Achua C. *Leadership: Theory, Application, and Skill Development.* Mason, OH: Cengage Learning; 2016.

vary their directive and supportive behaviors based on the maturity or readiness level of followers.[10] Hersey and Blanchard created a two-dimensional matrix similar to the grids utilized by the behavioral theories and identified four leadership styles (**FIGURE 9.5**).

Situational Leadership Theory developed four leadership styles based on the different follower maturity levels. The four leadership styles are as follows: (1) telling, (2) selling, (3) participating, and (4) delegating.[10] Leaders should use the **telling leadership style** when followers do not possess the knowledge, skills, and abilities to complete a task. The focus here is not on motivation or the relationship between the leader and follower but on acceptable task completion. Leaders spend time telling and showing followers how to complete a task. Leadership should use the **selling leadership style** when a follower needs to receive support and encouragement from leaders to complete a task for which the follower has some of the necessary knowledge, skills, and abilities. With this approach, leaders provide support, feedback, and encouragement to followers. Leaders should use the **participating leadership style** when a follower knows how to complete a task but feels insecure about completing

the task alone. Leaders can involve the follower in planning and decision-making to increase the follower's confidence. Finally, leaders should use the **delegating leadership style** when the followers know how to complete a task and are willing to complete a task. This is a helpful theory to practicing leaders.[2,22] The theory provides leaders with insight into how to change their leadership style based on their followers. This allows leaders to tailor their style to what different followers need based on follower readiness/maturity. This helps improve leader effectiveness because different followers have different needs that require different leadership styles.

Contingency theories are widely used today. These theories help leaders increase their effectiveness by utilizing different leadership styles in different situations. These theories define different aspects of situations that leaders should assess and consider to help them understand what leadership style would be best or more effective. Leaders are able to adapt their leadership style to what followers need to complete their tasks and achieve their work goals. This helps achieve goals at the follower level, which supports goal attainment at the organizational level.

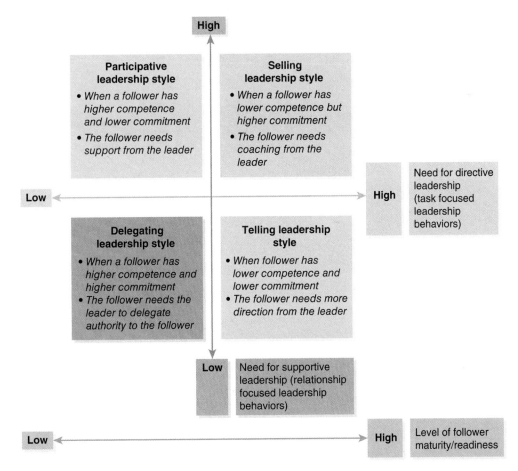

FIGURE 9.5 Hersey and Blanchard's Situational Leadership Model.

Modified from Blanchard K, Zigarmi P, Zigarmi D. *Leadership and the One Minute Manager: Increasing Effectiveness Through Situational Leadership®II*. New York, NY: William Morrow; 2013.

Scholars and leaders have found contingency theories helpful because they are practical and easy to implement in daily interactions between leaders and followers. These theories failed, however, to consider the role of followers in the leader–follower relationship. Scholars began to explore the role that followers played in leadership because followers are an important part of the situations that leaders face. This leads to the next set of theories called transactional theories that focus on the exchanges and relationship between leaders and followers.

Transactional Theories

Transactional theories emerged and shifted the focus from understanding how leaders influence followers to understanding the role of followers and how followers influence leaders. Transactional theories are also called exchange, relationship, interactional, or exchange–relationship theories. These theories focus on the interactions and exchanges between leaders and followers. Trait, behavioral, and contingency theories all provide valuable insight into leadership. However, these theories focus on the characteristics, behaviors, and situations of the leader versus the follower. Transactional theories focus on understanding the reciprocal relationship and influence between

leaders and followers. These theories help leaders consider follower motivation, satisfaction, and performance. Leaders are able to understand how their relationships with followers matter and how they can play a role in improving motivation, satisfaction, and performance.

Vertical Dyad Linkage Theory

The Vertical Dyad Linkage (VDL) Theory focuses on the relationship and the one-on-one interactions leaders have with followers.[23] Based on leader–follower interactions, followers belong to one of two groups, namely, the **in-group** or the out-group (**FIGURE 9.6**).[24] Followers in the in-group have a strong working relationship with the leader and receive more of the leader's attention. These members also receive more support, autonomy, information, benefits, or rewards from the leader. Likewise, these followers are able to exert higher levels of influence on the leader. In contrast, followers in the **out-group** do not have a strong working relationship with the leader and receive less of the leader's attention. These members are also less likely to receive support, autonomy, information, benefits, or rewards from the leader. The leader–follower relationship influences the satisfaction and performance of individual followers. Followers in the

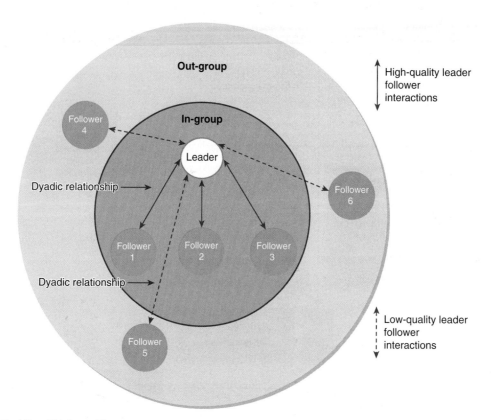

FIGURE 9.6 Vertical Dyad Linkage Theory.

in-group have higher levels of effort, dependability, satisfaction, performance, and overall engagement in the organization. In-group members are committed to the leader and the organization's success. Over time, in-group members receive additional roles and responsibilities. Leaders trust in-group members and invest time and energy in their development and success. In contrast, followers in the out-group have lower levels of effort, dependability, satisfaction, performance, and overall engagement in the organization. Out-group members are not committed to the leader or the organization's success. Out-group members do not receive the same opportunities to advance their role and responsibilities in the organization. An out-group member can become an in-group member. However, moving from the out-group to the in-group takes time, energy, and effort. This could include performing additional roles and responsibilities that the leader notices and values.[23] The VDL Theory is relevant today. Recent research indicates that leaders should minimize or eliminate in-groups and out-groups inside and outside the organization because such differentiations limit information and resource flows, employee engagement, innovation, creativity, and synergy.[15]

Leader–Member Exchange Theory

George Graen and J.F. Cashman proposed the Leader–Member Exchange (LMX) Theory in 1975.[25] Today, LMX is the dominant transactional or exchange theory of leadership. LMX Theory revised and replaced VDL Theory. LMX Theory considers how the leader–follower exchange relationship develops over time and how the exchange relationship influences leader and organizational effectiveness (**FIGURE 9.7**). High-quality leader–member exchanges produce benefits for both leaders and followers. Benefits for followers include better performance evaluations, higher levels of job satisfaction, higher levels of leader satisfaction, increased performance, more promotions, and better work assignments. Benefits for leaders include lower levels of employee turnover, improved retention, increased productivity, and higher levels of employee commitment, engagement, and citizenship behaviors.[2,26-33] LMX Theory encourages leaders to develop high-quality relationships with all followers. Research points to the negative impact that leadership interactions can have if they create in-groups and out-groups.[2]

Followership Styles

Recent leadership research has sought to understand the role of followers and followership styles. A follower has been defined as "a person who is under the direct influence and authority of a leader"[15(p240)] and followership has been defined as "the behavior of followers that results from the leader–follower mutual influencing relationship."[15(p240)] Robert Kelley studied followers to understand different followership styles. Like leadership styles, Kelley based followership style on follower behaviors. He identified five types of followership styles that include the alienated follower, conformist, pragmatic survivor, passive follower, and effective follower[34]

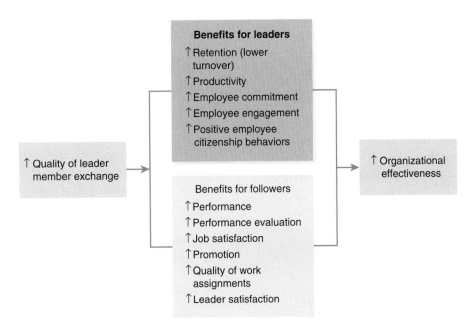

FIGURE 9.7 Benefits of high quality Leader-Member Exchange (LMX).

Based on information from and a modification of Liden RC, Sparrowe RT, Wayne SJ. Leader-member Exchange Theory: The Past and Potential for the Future. *Res Pers Hum Resour Manag.* 1997;15:47–120.

(**FIGURE 9.8**). These styles emerged from different combinations of follower behaviors. For example, some followers were critical thinkers, whereas others were not. Some followers were proactive, whereas other followers were passive. These follower behaviors served as the basis for Kelley's followership styles.[34]

- **Alienated Follower:** The alienated follower is a critical freethinker. The follower is passive and not engaged with the leader, team members, or the organization. The follower has a lot to offer, but remains detached and skeptical. These followers are quick to criticize and point out shortcomings and problems with others and the organization, but they are not interested in being a part of the solution.[34,35]
- **Conformist Follower:** The conformist follower is not a critical or independent thinker. The follower is active and engaged with the leader, team members, and organization. The follower adheres to rules and is not willing to "rock the boat." These followers want to conform to the rules, norms, and expectations of their leader, work groups, and organization. Conformists also do not question rules, norms, or expectations.[34,35]
- **Pragmatic Survivor:** The pragmatic survivor is a chameleon and is constantly changing their follower behavior to match what is happening in their organization. They assess the situation and then adopt the most advantageous follower style. Pragmatic survivors are critical thinkers and proactive when the behaviors benefit them. Likewise, these followers can become passive and not engage in relationships or critical thinking when it does not benefit them.[34,35]
- **Passive Follower:** The passive follower is not a critical or independent thinker or engaged in team or organizational activities. They are able to think critically but do not question the leader very often. These followers are engaged to the point that they "stay off the radar" of the leader and others in the organization. This type of follower does just enough to get by—no more, no less.[34,35]
- **Effective Follower:** The effective follower thinks critically and engages in work relationships, their work, and their leader. Effective followers enhance leadership and organizational effectiveness because these followers are able to function independently and at higher levels within the organization. Leaders are trying to develop effective followers because they exhibit positive organizational behaviors that create value and enhance the work environment.[34,35]

Leaders can use followership styles to better understand the types of followers they are interacting with and work to develop more effective followers.

Transformational Theories

Transformational or contemporary theories emerged in the 1970s. James MacGregor Burns began to look for a way to unite the leadership and followership and studied prominent historical leaders to understand how the leaders garnered support from their followers. He focused on how leaders motivated followers by meeting their psychological, among other, types of needs. He found that transformational leaders use vision, values, ethics, and morals that speak to the followers and give them a sense of purpose, which in turn motivates followers.[36] Today, transformational theories permeate contemporary leadership thought and organizations. These theories focus on how leaders can change or transform followers by inspiring and motivating them to achieve their full potential. In turn, followers are able to transform their organization, which improves leadership and organizational effectiveness.[2] Transformational leadership emerged as a means to inspire and empower employees in response to uncertainty and change. These theories recognize that modern times require continual organizational transformation, which starts with individual followers and their continual transformation. These theories seek to harness the dynamic capabilities within individuals and organizations to meet the dynamic demands of an organization's external environment while appealing to the follower's need for vision and purpose.[10]

Charismatic Leadership

Max Weber, a German sociologist, proposed a theory of **Charismatic Leadership** in the early 1920s.[37] He observed that leaders who had charisma were able to

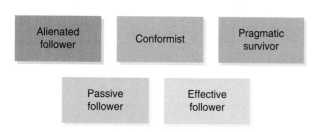

FIGURE 9.8 Followership styles.

inspire and change followers because these leaders were able to use their charisma to make emotional connections with their followers. In turn, this motivated followers and enhanced their personal performance. Charismatic leaders are able to articulate a vision for the future, shape the beliefs of followers, set high aspirational goals for followers, and are willing to make significant sacrifices for followers. Charismatic leaders are able to draw followers in and develop a common purpose with their followers.[38] In 1977, House developed a Charismatic Leadership model based on Weber's work.[39] This theory spoke to how leaders use their personality to influence followers and inspire them. Charismatic leaders are confident and strong communicators. Leaders who possess charisma can **leverage** it to inspire and instill trust in their followers that leads to personal and organizational change.[37]

Authentic Leadership

Bill George developed authentic leadership in the early 2000s.[40,41] This approach focuses on leaders developing authentic relationships with themselves and with their followers. This requires a heightened level of self (intrapersonal) and other (interpersonal) awareness.[2] Characteristics of authentic leaders include purpose, values, relationships, self-discipline, and heart (**FIGURE 9.9**). Authentic leaders have a clear **purpose** they are personally **passionate** about and they want to share with others. They have identified their purpose

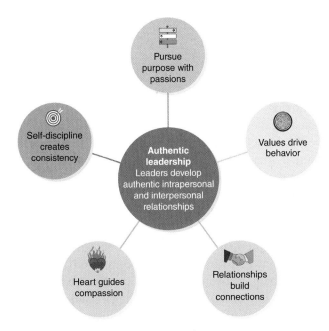

FIGURE 9.9 Authentic leadership characteristics.

Modified from Northouse PG. *Leadership: Theory and Practice.* 8th ed. Thousands Oaks, CA: Sage Publications Inc.; 2019.

and passion through reflection and introspection. **Values** guide the leader's **behaviors** from decision-making to interactions with followers. **Relationships** are important to the leader because they provide an opportunity for leaders to **connect** with their followers. They are open and honest with themselves and their followers. **Self-discipline** keeps the leader moving toward their goals despite the triumphs or setbacks. **Consistency** also helps the leader achieve their goals over time because they are regularly working toward their goals. Followers also know what to expect because an authentic leader's behavior is consistent with who they are because the leader's values, purpose, and passion guide them. Authentic leaders use their **heart** to be aware of their followers' psychosocial needs. They are **compassionate** and able to empathize with their followers. This helps build trust, openness, and an authentic relationship between the leader and the follower.[2,40]

Servant Leadership

Robert Greenleaf popularized the Servant Leadership approach in the 1970s. Servant leadership focuses on service to others and inverts many of the traditional approaches to leadership that are leader-centric. The servant leadership approach focuses on leaders considering what followers need and then the leader works to meet those needs.[42] Greenleaf believed that great leaders were motivated to serve and fulfill the needs of their followers first and then transform followers into servant leaders.[43,44] Greenleaf identified 10 characteristics of servant leaders that include: (1) listening, (2) empathy, (3) healing, (4) awareness, (5) persuasion, (6) conceptualization, (7) foresight, (8) stewardship, (9) growth commitment, and (10) building community[2] (**TABLE 9.1**).

Servant leaders are other oriented. They listen to their followers and desire to develop deep and sincere relationships with them.[45] Research indicates that this approach results in higher levels of trust, organizational citizenship behavior, job satisfaction, positive attitudes, and enhanced team performance.[2,45] Feedback is an integral part of the relationship building between servant leaders and their followers. Listening helps the leader empathize with their followers and understand their unique perspectives and viewpoints. Servant leaders also seek to understand the social, emotional, and professional development needs of their followers. Servant leaders take a holistic view and interest in the health and well-being of their followers. They are concerned with the social, emotional, and professional needs and well-being of their followers. Awareness

TABLE 9.1 Servant Leadership Characteristics Checklist

Place a check mark if the leader you are assessing possess the characteristics	Characteristics	Description
	Listening	Listens to others to build relationships
	Empathy	Strives to understand others and their unique perspectives
	Healing	Promotes healing in all aspects of other's social and emotional health and well-being
	Awareness	Seeks to understand the strengths, weaknesses, values, emotions, and behaviors of themselves and others
	Persuasion	Exerts influence through persuasion versus authority
	Conceptualization	Creates a compelling vision that inspires others
	Foresight	Anticipates future threats and opportunities
	Stewardship	Assures efficient and effective use of resources
	Growth Commitment	Dedicates time and energy to enhance and build the knowledge, skills, and capabilities of others
	Building Community	Strengthens bonds between people inside and outside the organization

Modified from Northouse PG. *Leadership: Theory and Practice.* 8th ed. Thousand Oaks, CA: Sage Publications Inc.; 2019.

helps leaders assess their own strengths, weaknesses, values, and beliefs, as well as those of their followers. Servant leaders are not only aware of their follower's needs but also their own emotions and behaviors and how their emotions and behaviors influence their followers. Awareness helps leaders to use their emotions and behaviors in a way that persuades and inspires others to be servant leaders. This leads to a philosophy of working with and through others versus a more authoritarian approach to leadership. This is important because servant leaders are able to conceptualize big plans that require followers who are ready to mobilize to achieve the leader's vision and mission with the leader. Strong leader–follower relationships develop grand and demanding visions and plans because such plans take time to realize and achieve. Having foresight and the ability to analyze and anticipate the

future also helps enhance decision-making and planning. This can help move followers by minimizing or removing some barriers and challenges that impede reaching the organization's vision, mission, and goals. Foresight helps servant leaders be better stewards of human, financial, and other types of resources. Development needs and personal growth are something servant leaders take seriously and actively work to help followers. This relates to being good stewards of organizational resources and helping followers reach their full potential. Together, the characteristics of servant leaders help build bonds and community. Servant leaders help cultivate communities that are focused on fellowship and followers. This helps build relationships that are grounded in trust, honesty, feedback, and service to humankind, whether inside or outside the organization.[2]

Alternatives to Leadership: Substitutes and Neutralizers

Steven Kerr and John Jermier developed the Substitutes for Leadership Theory that proposed there are alternatives to task and relationship styles of leadership in certain situations.[46] There are individual, job/task, and organizational factors that can either substitute or neutralize task/job and relationship aspects of leadership and enhance satisfaction, performance, and outcomes.[35]

Substitutes take the place of leadership in certain situations and make leadership unnecessary or redundant.[35] *Individual substitutes* include professionalism (substitute for both task and relationship-oriented leadership), training (substitute for task-oriented leadership), education (substitute for task-oriented leadership), and experience (substitute for task-oriented leadership). *Job or task substitutes* include well-designed jobs/tasks (substitute for task-oriented leadership), clear roles and responsibilities (substitute for task-oriented leadership), real-time feedback (substitute for task-oriented leadership), and intrinsic motivation (substitute for relationship-oriented leadership). *Organizational substitutes* include cohesive and high-functioning work teams (substitute for task and relationship-oriented leadership) and formalized goals and plans (substitute for task-oriented leadership).[46–49]

Neutralizers weaken or neutralize the influence of leader behaviors on followers. *Individual neutralizers* include low value of rewards (neutralizer for task-oriented leadership). *Job or task substitutes* include geographic distance (neutralizer for relationship-oriented leadership). *Organizational substitutes* include lower position power (neutralizer for task- and relationship-oriented leadership) and inflexibility (neutralizer for task-oriented leadership). There are no effects for the other potential combinations.[46–49]

Conclusion

Leadership plays an important role in organizations. As a result, scholars have spent decades studying and developing theories to understand and explain what makes an effective leader. Early scholars believed there was a special set of traits leaders possessed. When scholars were unable to identify a universal set of traits, they began to look at how effective leaders behaved. The behavioral theories identified two categories of leader behaviors related to leadership effectiveness, which significantly advanced leadership thought. However, leadership theory evolved again when scholars realized that leader behaviors did not consistently lead to effectiveness. Scholars found that the most successful behaviors leaders used were contingent or dependent on the situation they faced. Transactional theories were developed to focus on the quality of the relationship between the leader and the follower. Followership theory provides insight into how different types of follower behaviors influence leaders. Today, contemporary leadership theories recognize that leadership is a complex construct and that effective leaders are able to transform and inspire followers to work with them to accomplish shared organizational goals.

Discussion Questions

1. What are the key differences between leaders and managers?
2. Discuss the evolution of leadership thought and theories. Compare and contrast the major categories of leadership theories.
3. Compare and contrast the major trait theories discussed in the chapter.
4. Compare and contrast the major behavioral theories discussed in the chapter.
5. Compare and contrast the major contingency theories discussed in the chapter.
6. Explain the role of followership.
7. Compare and contrast the major transformational theories discussed in the chapter.
8. Explain the role of substitutes and neutralizers of leadership.

Learning Activities

1. Write your own definition of leadership. How would you describe and characterize your leadership style?
2. Interview a public health or healthcare leader. Ask the leader to share experiences that have shaped them as a leader. Identify different leadership theories your leader has used. Ensure that you provide examples or support for the leadership theories you identify during your discussion with your leader.
3. Select a leadership theory that interests you from the chapter. Write a leadership case that discusses how public health and healthcare leaders can use these theories in practice.
4. Think about a public health or professional experience you have had. What leadership

styles did you observe? What were the strengths and weaknesses of this style?

5. Strong leaders are continually assessing their professional skills and are committed to being life-long learners. Select a leadership or professional assessment tool. Take the assessment and review your scores. Identify your strengths and weaknesses and develop a professional growth plan for continuing your professional development.

References

1. Kast FE, Rosenzweig JE. *Organization and Management: A Systems and Contingency Approach*. 4th ed. New York, NY: McGraw-Hill; 1985.

2. Northouse PG. *Leadership: Theory and Practice*. 8th ed. Thousands Oaks, CA: Sage Publications Inc.; 2019.

3. Kotter JP. *Leading Change*: Boston, MA: Harvard Business Review Press; 2012.

4. Bass B. *Bass and Stogdill's Handbook of Leadership: Theory, Research, and Managerial Applications*. 3rd ed. New York, NY: The Free Press; 1990.

5. Stogdill RM. Personal factors associated with leadership: A survey of the literature. *J Pyschol*. 1948;25(1):35–71. doi: 10.1080/00223980.1948.9917362.

6. Stogdill RM. *Handbook of Leadership: A Survey of Theory and Research*. New York, NY: Free Press; 1974.

7. Zaccaro SJ, Kemp C, Bader P. Leader traits and attributes. In: Antonakis J, Cianciolo AT, Sternberg RJ, eds. *The Nature of Leadership*. Thousand Oaks, CA: Sage Publications, Inc.; 2004:101–124.

8. Goldberg LR. An alternative "description of personality": The big-five factor structure. *J Pers Soc Psychol*. 1990;59(6): 1216–1229. doi:10.1037/0022-3514.59.6.1216.

9. Judge TA, Bono JE, Ilies R, Gerhardt MW. Personality and leadership: A qualitative and quantitative review. *J Appl Psychol*. 2002;87(4):765–780. doi:10.1037/0021-9010.87.4.765.

10. Johnson JA, Rossow CC. *Health Organizations: Theory, Behavior, and Development*. 2nd ed. Burlington, MA: Jones & Bartlett Learning; 2019.

11. Schriesheim CA, Bird BJ. Contributions of the Ohio state studies to the field of leadership. *J Manage*. 1979;5(2): 135–145. doi:10.1177/014920637900500204.

12. Likert R. *New Patterns of Management*. New York, NY: McGraw-Hill; 1961.

13. Likert R. *The Human Organization: Its Management and Value*. New York, NY: McGraw-Hill; 1967.

14. Wren DA, Bedeian AG. *Evolution of Management Thought*. 6th ed. Hobokan, NJ: Wiley; 2009.

15. Lussier RN, Achua C. *Leadership: Theory, Application, and Skill Development*. 6th ed. Boston, MA: Cengage Learning; 2016.

16. Blake RR, Mouton JS. *The Managerial Grid: Key Orientations for Achieving Production Through People*. Houston, TX: Gulf Publishing Company; 1964.

17. Blake RR, Mouton JS. *The New Managerial Grid*. Houston, TX: Gulf Publishing Company; 1978.

18. Blake RR, Mouton JS. *The Managerial Grid III: The Key to Leadership Excellence*. Houston, TX: Gulf Publishing Company; 1985.

19. Blake RR, McCanse AA. *Leadership Dilemmas: Grid Solutions*. Houston, TX: Gulf Publishing Company; 1991.

20. Fiedler FE. A contingency model of leadership effectiveness. *Adv Exp Soc Psychol*. 1964;1:149–190. doi:10.2307/255636.

21. Hersey P, Blanchard KH. Life-cycle theory of leadership. *Train Dev J*. 1969;23(5):26–34.

22. Borkowski B. *Organizational Behavior, Theory, and Design in Health Care*. 2nd ed. Burlington, MA: Jones & Bartlett Learning; 2016.

23. Dansereau F, Graen G, Haga WJ. A vertical dyad linkage approach to leadership within formal organizations: A longitudional investigation of the role making process. *Organ Behav Hum Perform*. 1975;13(1):46–78. doi:10.1016/0030 -5073(75)90005-7.

24. Graen GB. Role-making processes withing complex organizations. In: Dunnette MD, ed. *Handbook of Industrial and Organizational Psychology*. Chicago, IL: Rand McNally; 1976:1202–1245.

25. Graen GB, Cashman J. A role-making model of leadership in formal organizations: A developmental approach. In: Hunt JG, Larson LL, eds. *Leadership Frontiers*. Kent, OH: Kent State University Press; 1975:143–166.

26. Liden RC, Sparrowe RT, Wayne SJ. Leader-member exchange theory: The past and potential for the future. *Res Pers Hum Resour Manag*. 1997;15:47–120.

27. Liden RC, Wayne SJ, Stilwell D. A longitudinal study on the early development of Leader-Member Exchange. *J Appl Psychol*. 1993;78(4):662–674. doi: 10.1037/0021-9010.78.4.662

28. Graen GB, Uhl-Bien M. Relationship-based approach to leadership: Development of Leader-Member Exchange (LMX) theory of leadership over 25 years applying a multi-level, multi-domain perspective. *Leadersh Q*. 1995;6(2):219–247. doi:10.1016/1048-9843(95)90036-5.

29. Gerstner CR, Day DV. Meta-analytic review of leader-member exchange theory: Correlates and constructs issues. *J Appl Psychol*. 1997;82(6):827–844. doi: 10.1037/0021-9010 .82.6.827.

30. Atwater L, Carmeli A. Leader-member exchange, feelings of energy, and involvement in creative work. *Leadersh Q*. 2009;20(3):264–275. doi:10.1016/j.leaqua.2007.07.009.

31. Harris KJ, Wheeler AR, Kacmar KM. Leader–member exchange and empowerment: Direct and interactive effects on job satisfaction, turnover intentions, and performance. *Leadersh Q*. 2009;20(3):371–382. doi:10.1016/j.leaqua.2009.03.006.

32. Volmer J, Spurk D, Niessen C. Leader–member exchange (LMX), job autonomy, and creative work involvement. *Leadersh Q*. 2012;23(3):456–465. doi:10.1016/j.leaqua.2011 .10.005.

33. Ilies R, Nahrgang JD, Morgeson FP. Leader-member exchange and citizen behaviors: A meta-analysis. *J Appl Psychol*. 2007; 92(1):269–277. doi:10.1037/0021-9010.92.1.269.

34. Kelley R. *The Power of Followership: How to Create Leaders People Want to Followers and Followers Who Lead Themselves*. New York, NY: Doubleday Business/Currency; 1992.

35. Daft RL. *The Leadership Experience*. 7th ed. Boston, MA: Cengage Learning; 2018.

36. Burns JM. *Transforming Leadership: The New Pursuit of Happiness.* New York, NY: Grove Press; 2003.

37. Ledlow GR, Stephens JH. *Leadership for Health Professionals: Theory, Skills, and Applications.* 3rd ed. Burlington, MA: Jones & Bartlett Learning; 2018.

38. Weber M. *The Theory of Social and Economic Organization.* Henderson AM, Parson T, trans-ed. New York, NY: Free Press; 1947.

39. House RJ. A 1976 theory of charismatic leadership. In: Hunt JG, Larson LL, eds. *Leadership: The Cutting Edge.* Carbondale, IL: Southern Illnois University Press; 1977:189–207.

40. George B, Sims P. *True North: Discover Your Authentic Leadership.* San Fransico, CA: Jossey-Bass; 2007.

41. George B. *Authentic Leadership: Rediscovering the Secrets to Creating Lasting Value.* San Fransico, CA: Jossey-Bass; 2003.

42. Greenleaf RK. Essentials of Servant-Leadership. In: Spears LC, Lawrence M, eds. *Focus on Leadership: Servant-Leadership for the 21st Century.* New York, NY: John Wiley & Sons, Inc.; 2002:19–26.

43. Sendjaya S, Sarros JC. Servant leadership: Its origin, development, and application in organizations. *J Leadersh Organ Stud.* 2002;9(2):57–64. doi:10.1177/107179190200900205.

44. Russell RF, Stone AG. A review of servant leadership attributes: Developing a practical model. *Leadersh Organ Dev J.* 2002;23(3):145–157. doi:10.1108/01437730210424.

45. Spears LC. Introduction: Tracing the past, present, and future of servant-leadership. In: Spears LC, Lawrence M, eds. *Focus on Leadership: Servant-Leadership for the 21st Century.* New York, NY: John Wiley & Sons, Inc.; 2002:1–18.

46. Kerr S, Jermier JM. Substitutes for leadership: Their meaning and measurement. *Organ Behav Hum Perform.* 1978;22(3):375–403. doi:10.1016/0030-5073(78)90023-5.

47. Howell JP, Dorfman PW. Leadership and substitutes for leadership among professionals and nonprofessional workers. *J Appl Behav Sci.* 1986;22(1):29–46. doi:10.1177/002188638602200106.

48. Howell JP, Bowen DE, Dorfman SK, Kerr S, Podsakoff PM. Substitutes for leadership: Effective alternatives to ineffective leadership. *Organ Dyn.* 1990;19(1):21–38. doi:10.1016/0090-2616(90)90046-R.

49. Podsakoff PM, MacKenzie SB, Bommer WH. Transformational leader behaviors and substitutes for leadership as determinants of employee satisfaction, commitment, trust, and organizational citizenship behaviors. *J Manage.* 1996;22(2):259–298. doi:10.1177/014920639602200204.

CHAPTER 10

Controlling and Budgeting in Public Health Organizations

LEARNING OBJECTIVES

After reading this chapter, you should be able to:

- Define the controlling management function.
- Discuss the steps in the control process.
- Explain the benefits and costs of organizational controls.
- Discuss characteristics and design considerations of organizational controls.
- Explain the levels of controls and the types of controls.
- Compare and contrast different types of financial statements and budgets.
- Explain the role of quality and behavioral controls.

▶ Introduction

The **controlling function** refers to the process of monitoring and evaluating organizational performance and adjusting organizational activities, if necessary, to accomplish an organization's performance plans and goals. Robbins and Judge define controlling as "monitoring activities to ensure they are being accomplished as planned and correcting any significant deviations."[1(p7)] Daft defines organizational control as "the systematic process of regulating organizational activities to make them consistent with the expectations established in plans, targets, and standards of performance."[2(p660)] The purpose of the controlling function is to provide feedback to help an organization understand how it is performing based on its established plans and goals. Managers use this information to reinforce desirable progress and performance or adjust organizational plans or performance goals if needed. Analyzing control feedback also helps the organization understand what types of adjustments may be needed.[3]

The controlling function links all the managerial functions (i.e., planning, organizing, staffing, and coordinating/leading) and relates to the technical subsystem described by Kast and Rosenzweig.[4] The technical subsystem refers to the methods, procedures, techniques, and processes to transform organizational inputs into outputs. Controls, especially managerial controls, help link organizational planning to operations and, ultimately, performance. Managers are responsible for coordinating an organization's subsystems and corresponding processes to produce outcomes by the most efficient and cost-effective means possible.[5] This function reveals how an organization is a system with subsystems that have defined and interdependent transformation processes. The controlling function gives managers at all levels of an organization the means to influence an organization's transformation process to optimize output and meet organizational goals. This function also emphasizes the importance of organizations having measurable goals. Managers continuously monitor an organization's key performance indicators and progress toward its goals. Evaluating organizational performance gives managers an indication of how well an organization's plans and performance are progression. This provides insight into what the organization needs to do to move forward. Often, the controlling function is challenging for managers and organizations. Managers can find controlling difficult because an organization has underdeveloped plans and poorly stated goals. Controlling can also be difficult because it requires implementing organizational change and motivating employees to participate in change. Controlling, however, is a critical aspect of management in order to achieve organizational goals.

▸ Control Process

Generally, the controlling process consists of four steps that help compare actual performance to planned performance and reveals if there is a need for corrective action. The control process consists of the following steps: (1) establish performance standards, (2) measure actual performance, (3) perform a variance analysis, and (4) plan and implement corrective action, if necessary.[2] **FIGURE 10.1** outlines the control process.

■ **Step 1: Establish Performance Standards**—This step consists of an organization establishing measurable performance standards or targets based on its organizational goals and business activities. This step is critical to managers and their ability to control organizational performance and take needed corrective action in the future. Organizations have different standards and different units of measurement based on organizational goals and the nature of the organization's activities. Public health organizations provide services and often have operational, time, monetary, quality, and satisfaction standards. Many organizations are not well versed in establishing standard measures and, as a result, often establish one measure for a certain set of activities. This measure then becomes the sole measure of performance for an individual **employee**, team, department, or manager. This is the reason why measuring performance can be stressful for managers, departments, and individual employees. Managers

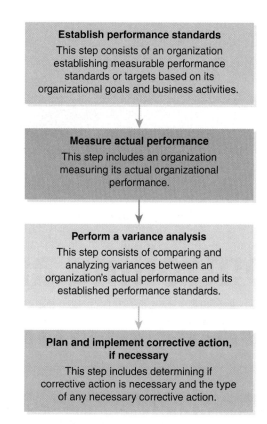

FIGURE 10.1 Control process.

Modified from Daft RL. *Management*. 12th ed. Boston, MA: Cengage Learning; 2016.

and organizations should try to establish multiple standards, if possible, for organizational activities. This helps provide a more complete picture of an organization's performance. This can also help reduce stress and provide more insight into what, if any, corrective actions are needed.[5]

■ **Step 2: Measure Actual Performance**—This step includes an organization measuring its actual organizational performance outcomes. A process has to be developed to guide how an organization plans to collect performance information based on the performance standards that were established. This step requires organizations to think about how they are collecting information related to their daily activities. Also, this step again illustrates that the controlling function is intentional and must be thoughtfully designed and embedded within an organization.[1,5]

■ **Step 3: Perform a Variance Analysis**—This step consists of comparing and analyzing variances between an organization's actual performance and its established performance standards. Managers can compare performance on a daily, weekly, monthly, quarterly, or annual basis. Often, an organization makes comparisons at multiple time intervals to understand performance trends. This allows the organization and managers to evaluate their performance and ask a series of questions. Did the organization or department achieve the desired performance target? If yes, we (the organization or department) need to keep doing what we are doing and see if successful practices could work in other areas of our organization. If not, why did we not achieve the target? What needs to be changed to meet the established performance standard? These are the types of questions managers are able to ask themselves about an organization's performance at this step in the control process. This provides managers with informative and actionable information on how to maintain or improve performance.[2,5]

- **Step 4: Plan and Implement Corrective Action, If Necessary**—This step includes an organization determining whether corrective action is necessary and the type of any necessary corrective action needed. Organizations and managers that rely on one performance measure may find it challenging to determine what type of corrective actions are needed. Managers who use multiple measures may find it easier to identify problem or underperforming areas and develop targeted actions to improve performance. This can help limit unnecessary organizational change, which can enhance employee motivation and participation in change activities. Organizations and managers often fail to devote sufficient time to understanding what is limiting performance and developing a corrective action plan. As a result, managers take different types of corrective actions to try to address the performance problem. This can waste time and organizational resources if reactionary responses versus thoughtful plans are implemented. Additionally, poor problem recognition and corrective action plans can frustrate and fatigue employees, which can lead to demotivation and additional performance issues.[1,5]

► Control Characteristics

Managers should keep in mind characteristics of desirable controls when they are developing control measures and processes. Liebler and McConnell identified important characteristics of organizational controls. **Time and timeliness** are important to the controlling process and function. An organization's controls should quickly detect and report deviations from established performance standards, so that corrective actions can be taken promptly. Managers should minimize **costs**, to the extent possible, when developing control processes,

measures, and tools. Integrating controlling activities into existing workflows, processes, and systems helps reduce the need for additional steps and additional costs. Controls should be as **comprehensive** as possible. Measures should allow a manager and an organization to report on the performance of workers, equipment, and processes. This helps provide a holistic view and assessment of performance. Comprehensive means there is a measure or set of measures designed for key steps and activities in a business process. This allows managers to detect deviations from the performance early in the process. This also helps reduce waste and expenses. **Specificity and appropriateness** help ensure that controls are measurable and appropriate for the type of business activities an organization performs. Control measures should be **objective** and something that an organization, auditors, and external reviewers can reasonably observe and measure. Controls should also reflect **responsibility**. All levels of an organization—from individual employees to managers to executives—should have a set of measures related to the activities for which they are responsible. This promotes responsibility and accountability for performance and reveals at what level corrective action is needed. Finally, **understandability** is important for controls. Control measures, processes, or tools will not be used if managers and individual employees do not understand them or if they are too complex and cumbersome to use. Organizations with strong control measures, processes, and tools are able to optimize performance, as well as enhance organizational decision-making and planning.[3]

► Benefits and Costs of Controls

The controlling function has a number of costs and benefits to consider. The controlling function looks different for every organization. All organizations use some form of controls; however, organizations can select the types and the number of controls that are utilized. This means that there is a controlling continuum for organizations. Organizations weigh the costs and the benefits of controlling activities to determine the level of control they believe is right for their organization.

Benefits of Controls

There are a number of benefits associated with controlling activities.

- Controls monitor organizational efficiency and effectiveness. **Efficiency** refers to monitoring an organization's internal processes to help ensure that the organization is putting its resources to the most productive use possible. **Effectiveness** refers to satisfying the external needs, wants, and desires of customers.[2,6]

- Controls help enhance organizational quality.[3] Monitoring helps detect any process problems or inefficiencies, which help reduce defects and waste. Financially, an organization with minimal defects wastes fewer organizational resources, both financial and nonfinancial. From a customer perspective, satisfaction will be higher when processes produce goods and services that are free of defects or inefficiencies.
- Organizational controls can help improve communication. Controls that are specific and clearly delineate responsibility help provide clarity to organizational activities and to employees. This helps enhance collaboration and coordination, which help improve performance.[7]
- Financial stability is a significant benefit of controlling activities. Looking at how revenues and expenses are changing helps managers ensure profitability and financial health for their organization.[8]
- Legal compliance is often ensured through the controlling function. Compliance ensures that an organization is adhering to all applicable laws and regulations. The compliance process documents that the organization is, in fact, following laws and regulations. This helps organizations avoid costly lawsuits and **litigation**.[3]
- Organizations with strong controls are able to enhance and decentralize decision-making.[6] Controls that are diffused throughout an organization can quickly signal whether organizational processes are meeting or exceeding established performance standards. In turn, employees and teams at all points in the process across the organization are more autonomous, invested, and empowered to make decisions regarding how to adjust the process and their contributions to it.
- Control activities provide objective measures of performance that an organization can use in recognizing top performers. Controlling can be a way to recognize individuals, teams, and departments for meeting their performance goals or for making significant improvements. Recognition helps improve employee morale, satisfaction, and productivity.[6]

Costs of Controls

There are a number of costs associated with controlling activities.

- Controlling takes considerable time and resources. Complex and cumbersome performance systems require a significant amount of an employee's or manager's time, which impacts an organization's efficiency and productivity.[3]
- Organizational controls may be poorly designed and may not accurately report performance results. Organizations must remember to measure what matters and measure it in multiple ways. Organizational priorities and goals are outlined in an organization's strategic plan, which should inform an organization's approach to controlling.[7]
- Organizations that exclusively focus on performance metrics can create organizational cultures that are overly competitive or toxic. Strong organizational performance takes strong processes and people. Managers play an important role in communicating how people and processes are interconnected and designing controls that recognize the need to balance and value both people and processes.[6]
- Corrective action plans can be poorly implemented and fail. This can result in organizational conflict and poor customer service or quality. Departments or employees can begin blaming others for failed plans, which is counterproductive.[3,6]
- Controls hold individual employees, managers, and departments accountable for their performance. As a result, comparing expected performance to actual performance carries a risk of identifying underperforming areas. Organizational members may be reluctant to collect or analyze performance information based on the risk of being "found out" or identified as an underperformer. Some employees may try to exaggerate or even falsify performance information to avoid negative consequences.[5]

▶ Designing Organizational Controls

Designing organizational controls varies across organizations. Organizations must consider how formal control systems should be in their organization. **Formalization** refers to the degree to which regulations, policies, rules, and guidelines structure the work completed in an organization.[9] Formalization is an easy way to control what activities are being performed in an organization, how the activities are being performed, who is performing the activities, and at what level and in what areas the activities are being performed. A high degree of specification or formalization exerts a high degree of control over employees and processes, which promotes consistency in organizational outputs. A low degree of specification exerts a low degree of control over employees and processes within an organization, which can result in inconsistency in organizational outputs. Highly formalized organizational controls are associated with punishments when regulations, policies, rules, and guidelines are not met.[10] **Specialization** refers to the degree organizational tasks are divided into specific jobs and is related to the concept of formalization.[11] Specialization often stems from the degree of formalization within an organization. A high degree of specialization can produce consistent and high-quality performance because an employee is able to hone a specific skill set based on the types of tasks performed in their job. A low degree of specialization can produce inconsistent and average- to low-quality performance because an employee is completing a broad range of tasks that require a diverse skill set. A diverse skill set can result in employees with lower levels of proficiency in completing certain tasks because they do not regularly complete the task to become highly skilled. Specialization can produce consistent results, which enhances control within an organization.[10] Teams can develop specialized skill sets like individual employees.

Organizations should consider the advantages and the disadvantages of formalization and specialization when designing organizational controls. An advantage of formalization is that it promotes consistency across an organization. Formalized policies, rules, and guidelines make it easier to communicate what activities need to be completed and how these activities need to be completed. A lack of policies, rules, and guidelines can contribute to confusion, and can reduce efficiency and control. Likewise, specialization provides individual employees with clarity on the tasks they are responsible and accountable for completing. A disadvantage of formalization is that it may restrict innovation, collaboration, and teamwork. Likewise, specialization can lead to few transferable skills and cases where an employee may become obsolete because they possess an out-of-date set of very specific skills. An organization with overly formalized controls may not perform well in dynamic environments. Dynamic environments require continual organizational change so that organizations can adapt to their environment. Formalization can make change difficult, if not impossible, in extreme cases, which will negatively influence an organization's performance and, ultimately, its survival. Employees with specialized skills may find it difficult to perform new tasks that are needed to align with the environment because they possess a limited skill set.

This could slow and limit an organization's response to environmental changes.[10,12]

The degree of centralization and decentralization in an organization is important to consider when designing organizational controls. **Centralization** reflects an organization's preference for organizational decision-making at higher levels of the organization.[10,11] **Decentralization**, in contrast, reflects an organization's preference for organizational decision-making throughout an organization and across its many levels.[10,11] An organization is considered decentralized if operational decisions are primarily made at lower levels of an organization, such as departments or teams. Today, organizations continue to move from centralized to decentralized structures, designs, and decision-making approaches. Professionalism influences the degree of centralization or decentralization in an organization. Highly educated professionals are accustomed to making their own decisions and tend to prefer a higher level of decentralized decision-making. Decentralization is preferable when organizations are operating in a dynamic environment and must make decisions quickly.[13]

Organizations should consider the advantages and disadvantages of centralization and decentralization when designing organizational controls. An advantage of centralization is consistency in decision-making. This helps enhance coordination across an organization. However, too much centralization can result in an organization that is unable to respond to environmental changes, which could disadvantage an organization in adaptation. An advantage of decentralization is that it allows departments, teams, and individuals to have higher levels of autonomy, which is associated with higher levels of motivation and job satisfaction. This approach could also allow an organization to respond to environmental changes by tapping into a diverse set of skills and experiences when deciding how to adapt. This can help spur innovation and inspire creativity.[11] However, decentralization can result in a lack of consistency and a lower level of organizational performance if departments, teams, and individuals are making decisions that do not support the overall strategic plans and goals of the organization.[9,10] Employees may not take responsibility for decision-making when it is delegated to them.[13]

▶ Levels of Control

There are different levels of organizational controls. Robert Anthony identified three broad levels of control that include strategic control, management or tactical control, and operational control.[14] These control levels correspond to the level of the organization and associated plans previously discussed. **Strategic control** is defined as "the process of deciding on objectives of the organization, on changes in these objectives, on the resources used to obtain these objectives, and on the policies that are to govern the acquisition, use, and disposition of these resources."[14(p24)] The strategic control function relates to an organization's strategic management activities, strategic plan, and, ultimately, the organization's vision, mission, and values. These controls ask the question of how well the organization is doing within the environment or the context in which the organization finds itself based on its strategy. The strategic plan is the broad framework or overarching plan for an organization and outlines strategies for achieving the plan's stated goals. All organizational activities should align with the strategic plan and coordinate resources in ways that work toward the attainment of the plan. Therefore, strategic controls provide aggregated insight and status updates as to how the organization's strategy is working or not working. This provides insight into adjustments or corrective actions that may be required. Strategic controls require an organization that is operationally strong and functioning well.

Managerial or tactical control is defined as "the process by which managers assure the resources are obtained and used effectively and efficiently in the accomplishment of the organization's objectives."[14(p27)] This control function is carried out regularly and includes controlling activities and projects, such as budgeting, programming, job functions, and tasks at the department or business unit level. Control at this level centers on ensuring that tactical or departmental goals are being achieved. Middle managers are involved in controlling at this organizational level and bridging an organization's strategic and operational controls.

Operational controls are concerned with internal efficiency and the details of an organization's processes and systems are working. Operational control is defined as "the process of assuring that specific tasks are carried out effectively and efficiently."[14(p69)] Operational controls complement strategic controls and provide insight into the internal workings of an organization and the processes, systems, and individuals that are executing the organization's strategy on a day-to-day basis. Operational control looks at the day-to-day outcomes of teams or specific individuals. Team and shift leaders are involved in controlling at this organization level. Managers focus on shift, daily, weekly, monthly, or quarterly performance outcomes to assure they meet standards.

▶ Types of Organizational Controls

The overall goal of the control function is to optimize organizational processes and operations to enhance organizational performance. There are three types of organizational controls that managers should be familiar with: feedback control, concurrent control, and feedforward control.[2] **FIGURE 10.2** highlights these controls. These controls are not mutually exclusive. **Feedback control** refers to collecting information about a completed process to determine how well an organization's process produced a desired result (i.e., output) and how the process can be improved in the future. This approach is retrospective and results in lagged feedback and potentially suboptimal performance outcomes for a period of time. A drawback of this type of control is that problems may persist over the life of a process and result in poor performance during that period. This feedback can be used to address any problems or suboptimal performance at a later date when the process is repeated. However, this could mean that organizational resources have not been efficiently used, which could be costly to the organization in the short-term. In contrast, **concurrent**

Feedback control	Concurrent control	Feedforward control
• Feedback control refers to collecting information about a completed process to determine how well an organization's process produced a desired result (i.e., output) and how the process can be improved in the future. • This approach is retrospective and results in lagged feedback and potentially suboptimal performance outcomes for a period of time.	• Concurrent control refers to collecting real-time information about processes and providing that information back to organizational members to enhance organizational operations and performance during these processes. • This approach is real-time information so that corrective action be taken immediately to improve performance outcomes.	• Feedforward control refers to detecting a disturbance that could affect an organizational outcome and adjusting the process before the factor impacts what an organization is producing or providing. • This approach is proactive and enhances performance and, at the same time, safeguards organizational resources from waste.

FIGURE 10.2 Types of organizational controls.

control refers to collecting real-time information about processes and providing that information back to organizational members to enhance organizational operations and performance during these processes. The advantage of this approach is that managers are able to take corrective action immediately to improve performance. This helps to resolve problems quickly versus letting them persist and influence outcomes. This real-time feedback helps employees or teams enhance their performance, which can enhance motivation and satisfaction. This control type supports learning, growth, and development among organizational members. A drawback to this approach is that it can require more time and resources to provide continuous monitoring and feedback. Additionally, this approach can be disruptive to the operation of processes if changes need to be made while the process is underway. **Feedforward control** refers to detecting a factor that could affect an organizational outcome and adjusting the process before the factor impacts what an organization is producing or providing. This type of control is also referred to as a preventive control. It is proactive and significantly enhances performance and, at the same time, safeguards organizational resources from waste. Feedforward control anticipates operational problems and solves them before they can impact performance. Feedback, concurrent, and feedforward are all types of control that can be exerted throughout the organization. Finances, quality, and behaviors are key areas for implementing organizational control.[5]

▶ Financial Controls

The general purpose of financial control is to ensure that an organization's resources are properly allocated to meet its goals and objectives. Financial controls are an important aspect of the controlling function that managers need to understand. There are two primary types of financial controls that managers use: financial reporting and budgeting.

Financial Reporting

Many managers see the reporting of financial results, or financial reporting, as the ultimate financial control. Put simply, financial reporting is the creation of key financial statements, which include the statement of net assets and statement of activities, and some additional statements that are beyond the scope of this chapter. Managers are especially concerned with financial statements because external stakeholders use these statements to evaluate the financial position of an organization and make critical decisions based on the information. Usually, when one thinks of financial reporting, they think of shareholders of companies listed on a public stock exchange. However, virtually every organization has external stakeholders that relies on financial reporting. For example, local health departments must share financial information with state and federal departments and agencies in order to obtain grants and fulfill **audit** and reporting requirements. Taxpayers can use financial information to measure the effectiveness and efficiency of public services and public entities. Donors can use financial information to evaluate the need for and impact of their gifts. Managers also have a very important personal stake in these results as stakeholders may also use them to measure their performance. The following sections discuss financial reports typically used by state and local public health departments and by (i.e., taxpayers, governmental officials) control purposes.

Statement of Net Assets

The statement of net assets or position, which is similar to a balance sheet in non-governmental organizations, measures three key metrics that include assets, liabilities, and net position at a point in time. The statement of net assets is usually prepared on a periodic basis such as a month, quarter, or annual (or fiscal) basis (**FIGURE 10.3**). In simple terms, assets are what the organization "owns," such as cash, receivables (i.e., amounts owed to the organization), property (i.e., buildings and furniture), and equipment (i.e., computers and laboratory equipment). Liabilities are what the organization "owes" to outside entities, and net position is simply the difference between the two. For example, if an organization has cash and other assets worth $3 M, and has outstanding debts of $2 million, the organization's net position is $1 million.

The advantage of using metrics from this report is that the numbers are fixed at a point in time and are relatively easy to compare from period to period. One can easily see how much cash is on hand, compared to liabilities, and how the organization's financial position has changed over time. One disadvantage of the statement of net assets is that it is a relatively simplified view of the organization, and additional information is usually needed to evaluate the effectiveness of an organization. For example, an organization may have a lot of cash on hand and low debt since the management team is unable to identify investment opportunities to expand the organization. The next year, the same organization may have lower cash and a higher debt level because a new management team successfully identified a growth opportunity that required a

Statement of Net Assets

Assets 2018

Current Assets

Cash	$	3,500,000
Prepaid expenses	$	200,000
Receivables	$	7,500,000
Due from Government	$	14,000,000
Inventory	$	500,000
Total Current Assets	$	25,700,000

Non-current Assets

Capital Assets Net of Depreciation	$	5,000,000
Total Non-current Assets	$	5,000,000
Total Assets	$	30,700,000

Liabilities

Current Liabilities

Accounts Payable	$	900,000
Accrued Payroll (i.e., wages that are due to employees)	$	1,800,000
Due to government	$	150,000
Bonds and notes payable	$	2,000,000
Total Current Liabilities	$	4,850,000

Non-current Liabilities

Bonds and notes payable	$	10,000,000
Total Non-current Liabilities	$	10,000,000
Total Liabilities	$	14,850,000

Net Position

Invested in Capital Assets	$	5,000,000
Restricted	$	7,000,000
Unrestricted	$	3,850,000
Total Net Position	$	**15,850,000**

Note: The financial statement has been simplified for educational purposes.

FIGURE 10.3 Statement of Net Assets.

Modified Gaspenski L. Public Health Finance Tutorial Module V. Public Health Finance & Management. http://www.publichealthfinance.org/media/file/PHFM_Finance_Tutorial_V.pdf. Accessed September 4, 2019. and Tri-County Health Department Financial Statements (December 31, 2018). Tri-County Health Department. https://www.tchd.org/DocumentCenter/View/6235/2018-Annual-Financial-Report-. Published May 24, 2019. Accessed September 4, 2019.

short-term loan. For example, a public health organization may make a significant investment in a communications system that will be used during disasters. In summary, the importance of this report cannot be understated, but one must obtain additional details before making a judgment based on this report alone.

Statement of Activities

The statement of activities, which is similar to an income statement, measures revenue of the organization against expenses over a period of time (**FIGURE 10.4**). Revenues are money coming into the organization, and expenses represent money going out of the organization. Different revenue sources may be listed, as well as different categories of expenses. Revenues for public health organizations consist of federal, state, and local budget allocations, grant funding, insurance reimbursement (primarily Medicaid), service contracts, and support from donors. Expenses include payroll/salaries, benefits, supplies for specific programs (i.e., maternal health, family planning, immunizations, etc.), vehicles, wireless communication devices and plans, among others. Revenues minus expenses provides an indication of how on organization is doing financially. If an organization's revenues exceed (or are more than) its expenses, the organization has a positive fund or ending balance or surplus. This is a favorable financial position. If an organization's revenues are less than their expenses, the organization has a negative fund or ending balance. This means the organization is losing money and may not have the ability to cover its expenses. This is not a favorable financial position if it continues and it can threaten the ongoing viability of the organization or programs.

Statement of Activities

Revenues 2018

Service Charges	$	13,000,000
Appropriations (i.e., city or state)	$	19,356,000
Operating Grants	$	1,500,000
Other revenue (i.e. donations)	$	2,000,000
Total	$	35,856,000

Expenditures

Public Health Services	$	33,118,000

Net Assets

Beginning Net Assets	$	13,112,000
Change in Net Assets	$	2,738,000
Ending Net Assets	$	15,850,000

Note: The financial statement has been simplified for educational purposes.

FIGURE 10.4 Statement of Activities.

Modified from Gaspenski L. Public Health Finance Tutorial Module V. Public Health Finance & Management. http://www.publichealthfinance.org/media/file/PHFM_Finance_Tutorial_V.pdf. Accessed September 4, 2019. and Tri-County Health Department Financial Statements (December 31, 2018). Tri-County Health Department. https://www.tchd.org/DocumentCenter/View/6235/2018-Annual-Financial-Report-. Published May 24, 2019. Accessed September 4, 2019.

As the name suggests, the statement of activities is an effective tool for evaluating an organization's operational effectiveness. Metrics from the report are often used to evaluate managers. The statement can easily be matched to the operational goals of an organization. For example, if a manager aimed to increase revenue by $1 million over the last year, the manager can determine whether this goal was achieved by evaluating the income statement. There may also be areas where efficiency is measured from this report. The organization may have an efficiency goal of keeping payroll at last year's level. The statement can be used to evaluate payroll expenses to determine whether this goal was achieved. While this report is extremely important, one should recognize that, like the statement of net assets, understanding underlying information is equally as important. Too often, we hear of organizations that made poor long-term decisions by managing purely according to the results of this financial report. This is not to understate the importance of the income statement, but to emphasize that one must also obtain details and information from multiple sources before making decisions based exclusively on this report.

Budgeting

The development and **administration** of budgets are an essential part of the management function. Ross explains that, "A budget is a department's or organization's operating plan expressed in monetary terms."[8(p5)] An organization's budget reflects and communicates its vision, mission, values, and goals. The budgeting process helps align an organization's resources with its organizational strategies and goals. Therefore, an organization's strategic plan should guide the budgeting process. Budgets also help educate and inform organizational members about how resources are allocated throughout the organization.[8]

Budgets are generally developed at the program, department, and organizational level based on an organization's strategic plan and goals. Most public health managers are nonfinancial managers. This means these managers are outside the finance and accounting department and are responsible for an organization's operations or support functions. These managers may have little to no formal training in finance or accounting, which can make budgeting an overwhelming and even intimidating task to many. Often, public health managers receive a budget from the organization's financial officer or department. The budget is based on past expenditures and activities and serves as a starting point for revising the budget for the next year. Managers usually revise their budgets and make budget requests on an annual basis to reflect the future activities they expect their unit to undertake to achieve their unit's goals. Budget time can be a contentious time in organizations as departments compete for organizational resources. Programs and departments spend time trying to justify why they need certain resources and how the resources will help them achieve their organizational goals.

The Budgeting Process

A simplistic view of the budgeting process is forecasting or predicting projected revenues and expenses based on an organization's plans and goals. **FIGURE 10.5** provides a flowchart of budgeting activities. The first step in the

Future (prospective)	**Present** (concurrent)	**Past** (retrospective)
Estimation of budget year revenues and expenses Resources that should be consumed	Facilitation and control Resources being consumed	Evaluation (accountability and incentives) Resources consumed
Beginning six months before the start of fiscal year	Twelve months, the fiscal year	Concluding six months after the end of the fiscal year

FIGURE 10.5 Simplified budgeting process.

Modified from Cleverley WO, Cleverley JO. *Essentials of Health Care in Finance.* 8th ed. Burlington, MA: Jones & Bartlett Learning; 2018.

budgeting process is **planning**. Organizational goals and strategies drive an organization's budget. Budgeting helps provide the resources organizational units need to carry out organizational plans. The next step in the process is the **programming stage**. During this stage, the organization determines what work needs to be completed, how it needs to be completed, and when the work needs to be completed. This provides the basis for estimating revenues and expenses incurred through business activities. Next, the organization determines if it has sufficient resources to carry out the planned activities. Leaders will need to revisit organizational plans and make any necessary adjustments if the organization does not have sufficient resources. If sufficient resources exist, the budget is disseminated to operational units or departments. Managers receive plans, goals, and resources that they use to control operations and organizational performance. Managers receive **feedback** based on the financial control measures the organization has selected to use throughout the year. Managers generally receive monthly reports that provide feedback on how their unit or department is performing from a financial standpoint. Units or departments are on budget if they are meeting their financial performance measures and do not have significant variances or differences between budgeted and actual financial results. **Variance analysis** helps determine what type of corrective actions is needed, if any. At the end of the year (or year-end), units or departments are evaluated to determine whether they have met their performance and financial goals. The budgeting process then begins again with the planning process.

Types of Budgets

Managers use different types of budgets. Each budget has a different purpose and, therefore, is a different way of considering and controlling an organization's financial performance. Operating and capital budgets are the two primary types of budgets that managers use.

Operating Budget

An **operating budget** is a forecasting tool that focuses on a relatively short time period or operating cycle, generally one year. The budget is developed by projecting revenues and operating expenses for the coming year and then determining if revenues will cover expenses in the case of public and nonprofit organizations. For-profit organizations would be concerned that there is an adequate profit in addition to ensuring revenues exceed expenses.[8] There are several methods to forecast operating expenses. Each method has its advantages, depending on the circumstance under which the budget is created.

Static Budget. A static budget is a fixed budget that does not change over the course of the operating period. The incremental budget process is commonly used to develop static budgets. In this process, the budget is developed using the current year as a base, and then numbers are adjusted up or down based on predetermined factors, such as anticipated revenues and inflation. Other factors, such as efficiency and regulatory changes, may be forecasted and factored in accordingly for the new budget cycle (or period). An organization that expects revenue and expenses to be consistent may simply take the current year's results and use an inflationary multiplier to extrapolate **expense** data.

Static budgets are usually used in organizations and departments where the revenues and expenses are consistent and reasonably predictable. They are ideally suited in administrative departments where the cost may not change based on the output of the organization. This budget is not very resource intensive to develop, and the resulting budget allocation is immediately known and easily communicated to relevant personnel. However, this budget may also be a disincentive to promote efficiency within a department. The resources allocated to the department are the same over the budgetary period, no matter the output, which may result in unnecessary spending by managers to deplete their allocations so these are not reduced in the next year's budget.

Flexible Budget. A flexible budget is one where expenses are ultimately combined into a cost per-unit of output. This requires a high level of operational detail and an understanding of which inputs are driven by outputs. Due to the amount of detail, lower-level managers are usually tasked with determining the costs for their unit or department. A flexible budget is very useful for organizations whose major expenses are related to the volume of output produced and there is a consistent history from which to extrapolate projected expenses. During the budgeting process, operations and administrative managers determine which resources a medical clinic needs, such as medical supplies, staffing, and overtime needs. The costs of these items are consolidated into the cost of an output, such as a clinic visit. This type of budget decentralizes the process and directs managers' attention to the costs they incur, as well as holding them accountable for actual results compared to budget. The flexible budget may also alleviate some administrative burdens. Since the budget is based on volume, a manager may not be required to seek upper-management approval for additional expenses, such as overtime as volume increases. While it is simple to assess the efficiency of operations based on cost-per-output, this is a very simplistic measure and any major deviation from projected volumes might negate the usefulness of the budget, as there is usually a fixed expense component in the cost-per-output. Compared to a static budget, the numbers on a flexible budget frequently change, making it difficult for a manager to quickly assess the efficiency of their department.

Zero-Based Budget. A zero-based budget does not allow managers to carry over budgeted expenses from year-to-year or from one budget period to another. This budgeting approach asks the question, "Should an activity be continued in the future?" Managers must start from zero and must justify each expense for the next budget period or cycle. These expenses are accepted or rejected by upper management based on the budget justification a manager provides. Realistically, organizations may use zero-based budgeting every couple of years because this budgeting approach is too complex and time consuming to complete on an annual basis. This approach strives to get departments or units to think about what they are doing, how they are doing it, and if there is a more cost-effective way to operate. Zero-based budgeting can create competition

within organizations over resources. Units that are more productive often receive more resources, whereas underperforming areas receive fewer resources. The thought is that this will encourage the underperforming areas to think of alternative ways to increase their efficiency. Higher-resource allocations go to units that are operating efficiently as a reward for being able to use organizational resources in a more effective way.

The zero-based budgeting approach has many advantages and disadvantages. An advantage of this approach is that it questions the status quo and challenges organizations to think of alternative ways to produce goods and services. Competition for resources can be a powerful motivator that promotes collaboration, innovation, and creativity. This approach also tries to get the entire organization involved in day-to-day operations, particularly to think of ways a unit or department can operate more efficiently. A disadvantage of this approach is the time and amount of paperwork it requires. Managers also need some basic budgeting skills to start at zero. There is always the chance that managers may not possess sufficient budgeting skills and default back to prior budgets. The zero-based approach can also be gamed by managers trying to make their unit or department's output look more attractive than it really is in order to secure more organizational resources.[8]

Program Budget. Program budgeting is designed to help organizations fulfill their mission. This approach forces an organization to prioritize what it wants to do and focus on it. This approach centralizes budgeting activities in contrast to the previous budgeting approaches. Units or departments do not drive the budgeting process; rather, the mission and goals of the organization drive the process. This more centralized approach to budgeting tries to achieve synergy and efficiencies across an organization as opposed to organizational units or departments that work independent of one another. Budgets can create silos within organizations that restrict organizational collaboration and efficiency. Public agencies, especially the military and national health systems, use a program approach to budgeting. This approach helps to keep an organization focused on its priorities and allocates organizational resources to priority areas and activities. This helps to keep organizational goals and resources flowing to priority projects and activities.

The program budgeting approach has many advantages and disadvantages. An advantage of this approach is that it focuses on what the organization wants to accomplish or organizational priorities. Organizations are competing for resources with other programs or governmental entities, which keeps the organization focused on trying to demonstrate value in a range of monetary and nonmonetary outcomes (e.g., clinical outcomes and number of clinic visits). A disadvantage of this approach is that setting and agreeing on priorities may be difficult. This approach considers both monetary and nonmonetary outcomes. Nonmonetary outcomes are difficult to establish objectively, in contrast to monetary outcomes that are easier to articulate and measure. Government resources are dependent on tax revenues, which can increase or decrease with economic booms or busts.[8]

Capital Budgeting

Capital budgeting is a process whereby an organization determines the capital investments (e.g., machines or equipment, computers, vehicles, software or information systems, acquisitions, building expansion, and property purchases) required to ensure the long-term needs and strategic goals of an organization are met. These are usually very expensive, often multimillion-dollar investments, that have a life span of several years to decades. There are generally three kinds of capital investments that include mandatory investments, replacement of current equipment, and organizational expansion. **Mandatory investments** are those necessary to meet regulatory requirements to keep the organization in compliance with applicable laws and requirements. Examples include required safety equipment or improvements needed to bring a building up to building code requirements. The **replacement of current equipment** usually involves the replacement of obsolete equipment, such as a Computerized Tomography (CT) scanner or laboratory machine. **Organizational expansion** relates to increasing the ability of the organization to produce more of its current outputs, along with adding new programs and services. For example, a public health clinic providing new services, like obstetrics and gynecology services, or expanding the organization into new markets or geographic areas would require equipment.

The first step in the capital budgeting process is to determine the goals of the organization, and then the investments necessary to meet those goals. Once the necessary investments are identified, the cost of each investment should be evaluated against future cash flows (usually increased revenue or cost savings) resulting from the investment, while accounting for borrowing costs and the time value of money referred to as return on investment (ROI). Investments are then ranked by a combination of ROI and other factors, including nonfinancial ones, depending on the

organization. Since many investments are multiyear, investments can be regularly evaluated to ensure they align with an organization's goals and are producing the anticipated results. The capital budgeting process is accomplished by an organization's board of directors and executive leadership team. The executive team may seek input from managers and individual employees. However, this process is the responsibility of senior management.

▶ Quality Controls

Quality is an important topic for any organization and industry, particularly for public health and health care. **Quality control** refers to organizational processes and people who strive to ensure zero product or service errors. Quality is particularly important in health care because the consequence of poor quality can be disability or even death. Poor quality and outcomes can result in costly lawsuits and litigation. Problems with healthcare quality were revealed in two seminal publications from the Institute of Medicine (IOM) (now called the National Academy of Medicine), *To Err Is Human: Building a Safer Healthcare System*[15] and *Crossing the Quality Chasm: A Health System for the 21st Century.*[16] The reports looked at poor health outcomes the U.S. health system was producing and provided recommendations on how to improve quality. The IOM defined healthcare quality as the "degree to which health services for individuals or populations increase the likelihood of desired health outcomes and are consistent with the current professional knowledge."[17(p21)] This definition and subsequent IOM reports that were published linked healthcare outcomes to system and organizational processes. The reports indicated that the U.S. healthcare system and organizations did not have adequate quality controls in place to prevent adverse and often fatal health outcomes. This resulted in poor performance outcomes for the system collectively as well as for individual organizations.

The **Continuous Quality Improvement (CQI)** approach was popularized in the 1980s and embraced by healthcare organization following the IOM reports highlighting the poor quality of health care in the United States. The concept of CQI is defined as "an organizational process in which employee teams identify and address problems in their work processes."[7(p155)] The approach adapts and applies many Total Quality Management (TQM) principles to health care. This approach builds on Donabedian's Structure-Process-Outcome Quality of Care Model.[18] This model helps healthcare delivery organizations promote quality through organizational structures and processes. An organization works to ensure quality by designing or redesigning systems and processes, so that they minimize errors or mistakes and maximize quality. With CQI, an organization adopts a culture of continuous change because it recognizes there are always ways in which an organization's operations can be improved. This approach tries to address issues before they occur. When issues occur, managers, employees, and the organization as a whole have a common language, approach, and tools to assess these issues to improve quality and, more importantly, the processes and systems around organizational activities.

▶ Behavioral Controls

Employees are important to organizational performance. As described in Chapter 7, managers work to correct and shape employee behavior to be consistent with an organization's rules, policies, procedures, values, and performance expectations. Managers want to cultivate and reward employee behavior that supports organizational performance. Motivation, rewards, and discipline are controls that managers can use to shape employee behavior. Managers want to motivate employees because it brings about positive or desirable employee behavior and performance, such as attachment, attendance, organizational citizenship, satisfaction, and minimized deviant behavior (i.e., lying, stealing, and fraud) and poor performance. How do managers motivate employees? Rewards, benefits, recognition, and relationships are incentives that managers can use to motivate employees. Coaching, counseling, and ultimately discipline may need to be used if motivation and rewards are not working to encourage employees to behave in ways that meet organizational expectations. Discipline involves sanctioning employees to correct an employee's behavior or performance. A detailed discussion of behavioral controls can be found in Chapter 7.

Conclusion

The controlling function links all of the managerial functions. The controlling function provides feedback on whether or not organizational plans and goals have been achieved. The control process provides a step-by-step guide to how organizations can establish organizational controls that can then be used to assess organizational performance. This process also provides insight into the types of corrective actions that are necessary. Common organizational controls include financial, quality, and behavioral controls.

While controls provide many benefits, they come at a cost. Organizations have to evaluate the costs versus benefits of control processes. This includes making decisions regarding the extent of strategic, tactical, managerial, and operational controls that are used. Likewise, decisions must be made regarding the degree of formalization versus specialization and integration versus decentralization, and the extent to which feedback, concurrent, and feedforward processes are designed into the controls. Common organizational controls include financial, quality, and behavioral. Financial controls focus on the use of multiple types of financial statements and budgets. Quality controls are essential to health related organizations because of the human consequences of their outputs. Behavioral controls intersect with all of the other approaches to control because they deal with the behavior of people in the control process.

Discussion Questions

1. What is the managerial control function?
2. Identify and discuss the steps in the control process.
3. Discuss desirable control characteristics that managers should keep in mind when designing controls.
4. Explain the benefits and costs of organizational controls?
5. How do formalization and specialization influence organizational controls?
6. How do centralization and decentralization influence organizational controls?
7. What are the levels of organizational controls?
8. What are the types of organizational controls?
9. What are financial controls? What are the two main types of financial controls that managers use?
10. Define operational and capital budgets.
11. Compare and contrast the financial statements used for financial reporting and control.
12. Compare and contrast different budgeting approaches discussed in the chapter.
13. Explain why quality control is of particular importance in public health and health-related organizations.
14. Explain the relationship of behavioral control to the other organizational control approaches.

Learning Activities

1. Interview a public health professional about the different types of organizational controls their organization uses. What are the costs and benefits associated with the controls the organization uses?

2. Develop a public health or healthcare case study that illustrates how managers can use the control process discussed in the chapter. Ensure that you can clearly identify each step in the process and include information in your case that provides a clear example of how the process can be used.

3. Identify a public health or health organization that interests you. Interview a public health manager about the financial statements and budgets their organization uses. Discuss challenges with completing the budgeting process. What advice does your manager have for early career professionals or professionals who do not have a lot of experience working with financial information or budgets?

4. Identify a public health or health organization that interests you. Interview a public health manager about the quality controls and measures the organization uses. How does the organization ensure continuous quality improvement? What advice does your manager have for public health professionals related to designing quality controls?

References

1. Robbins SP, Judge TA. *Organizational Behavior*. 14th ed. Upper Saddle River, NJ: Pearson Prentice Hall; 2011.
2. Daft RL. *Management*. 12th ed. Boston, MA: Cengage Learning; 2016.
3. Liebler JG, McConnell CR. *Management Principles for Health Professionals*. 7th ed. Burlington, MA: Jones & Bartlett Learning; 2017.
4. Kast FE, Rosenzweig JE. *Organization and Management: A Systems and Contingency Approach*. 4th ed. New York, NY: McGraw-Hill; 1985.
5. Merchant K, Van der Stede WA. *Management Control Systems*. 4th ed. Harlow, UK: Pearson Education Limited; 2017.
6. Merchant KA, Van der Stede WA. *Management Control Systems: Performance Measurement, Evaluation and Incentives*. 4th ed. Pearson; 2017.
7. Buchbinder SB, Shanks NH. *Introduction to Health Care Management*. 3rd ed. Burlington, MA: Jones & Bartlett Learning; 2017.
8. Ross TK. *A Comprehensive Guide to Budgeting for Health Care Managers*. Burlington, MA: Jones & Bartlett Learning; 2019.
9. Burton RM, Obel B. *Strategic Organizational Diagnosis and Design: The Dynamics of Fit*. 3rd ed. New York, NY: Springer; 2004.
10. Burton RM, Obel B, Håkonsson DD. *Organizational Design: A Step-by-Step Approach*. 3rd ed. Cambridge, UK: Cambridge University Press; 2015.
11. Borkowski B. *Organizational Behavior, Theory, and Design in Health Care*. 2nd ed. Burlington, MA: Jones & Bartlett Learning; 2016.
12. Tolbert PS, Hall RH. *Organizations: Structures, Processes, and Outcomes*. 10th ed. London, UK: Routledge; 2016.
13. Miner JB. *The Management Process: Theory, Research, and Practice*. New York, NY: Macmillian Publishing Company; 1973.
14. Anthony RN. *Planning and Control Systems: A Framework for Analysis*. Cambridge, MA: Division of Research, Graduate School of Business, Havard University; 1965.
15. Kohn JT, Cooigan JM, Donaldson MS. *To Err Is Human: Building a Safer Health Care System*. Washington, DC: National Academies Press; 2000. doi:10.17226/9728.
16. Institue of Medicine. *Crossing the Quality Chasm: A New Health System for the 21st Century*. Washington, DC: The National Academies Press; 2001. doi:10.17226/10027
17. Institute of Medicine. *Medicare: A Strategy for Quality Assurance, Volume 1*. Washington, DC: The National Academies Press; 1990. doi:10.17226/1547
18. Donabedian A. The quality of care: How can it be assessed? *JAMA*. 1988;260(12):1743–1748. doi:10.1001/jama.1988.03410120089033.

Suggested Readings and Website

The National Association of County and City Health Officials (NACCHO) has a learning portal called NACCHO University that provides training on a wide range of topics for public health managers and professionals. The training provides a number of resources related to financial management under the Leadership and Management topical area. Visit NACCHO University at https://www.pathlms.com/naccho.

CHAPTER 11

Ethics for Public Health Managers and Workforce Diversity

LEARNING OBJECTIVES

After reading this chapter, you should be able to:

- Describe principles of ethics used in public health organizations.
- Better understand the moral basis for ethics in public health.
- Discuss the special nature of ethics in the public sector.
- Describe the ethics-focused organizational culture.
- Be familiar with different codes of ethics that help guide public health managers.
- Discuss ethics in the decision-making process.
- Define and describe diversity as it pertains to the public health workforce.
- Discuss the benefits of having a diverse public health organization.
- Discuss cultural competence.

▶ Introduction

Many historians trace the development of ethical theory back to Plato (427–347 BC) and Aristotle (384–322 BC). In fact, the word **ethics** has its root in the Greek word *ethos*, which means customs, conduct, or character. Ethics is concerned with the kinds of values, morals, and behaviors an individual, profession, or society embraces as desirable or appropriate. Furthermore, ethical theory provides a system of rules or principles that serve as guides to making decisions in a particular situation. Ethical issues are either implicitly or explicitly involved in any decision made in the public health arena, including those made by public health managers. This is reiterated in Johnson's *Meeting the Ethical Challenges of Leadership: Casting Light or Shadow*. These principles include the following: respect, service, justice, honesty, and community.[1]

In any of the positions and roles mentioned in previous chapters, a public **health professional** could be in a **leadership** position. Leaders are not limited to management roles. In public health agencies, there are team leaders, project leaders, program leaders, community leaders, task force leaders, committee chairs, and so on. In fact, most public health professionals will be called upon to be in a leadership position at some time in his or her career. The leader's ethical responsibility to serve others is derived from the concept of *beneficence*, which is in the Hippocratic tradition of making choices that *benefit* patients. For public health managers, this can be extended to all being served, including coworkers and people in the community. Specifically, public health ethics involves developing processes for policies that ensure the opportunity for input from community members; incorporating a variety of approaches that anticipate and respect diverse values, beliefs, and cultures; collaborating with a wide variety of agencies and professional disciplines; and implementing policies that enhance the physical and social environment. Within the communities being served, there is a strong relationship to social justice, and within public health organizations, both ethics and social justice necessitate the embrace and practice of workplace diversity.

▶ Principles of Ethics in Public Health

As described in James Johnson and Caren Rossow's *Health Organizations: Theory Behavior and Development*, 2nd ed., ethics is a set of values and moral principles that help form a consensus about what is right and wrong. There are four common branches of ethics to be considered: descriptive ethics, normative ethics, moral psychology, and applied ethics.[2]

Descriptive Ethics: also called comparative ethics, describes how people behave when confronted with ethical choices.

Normative Ethics: also called prescriptive ethics, specifies what people should do or not do when confronted with an ethical dilemma and choices.

Moral Psychology: examines how people form moral reasoning as they develop intellectually. Moral reasoning begins at birth and advances with age through adulthood.

Applied Ethics: also known as practical ethics or professional ethics, uses ethical theories, codes of ethics, and moral reasoning to problem solve and guide behavior. The **American Public Health Association (APHA)**, American Medical Association (AMA), American Nurses Association (ANA), American College of Healthcare Executives (ACHE), and many other professional societies have used applied ethics for this purpose. Likewise, other examples of applied ethics used in public health are *bioethics* and *organizational ethics*, both of which will be explored.

Since the description of ethics provided by Johnson and Rossow includes moral principles, values, and moral psychology, it is useful to identify some of these that directly pertain to the roles and responsibilities of public health managers and others working in public health. Ruth Gaare Bernheim at the Institute of Practical Ethics and Public Life provides a list of moral considerations in *Essentials of Public Health Ethics*, as shown in **TABLE 11.1**, which are instructive and can serve to frame the ethical practice of public health management.[3]

According to Johnson and Rossow, there are four overarching principles that guide public health ethics: autonomy, beneficence, non-maleficence, and social justice.[2]

Autonomy is often defined as self-determination, making one's own decision and often used in reference to informed consent, decision-making related to diagnosis and treatment, as well as community-level interventions that should involve the affected citizens.

Beneficence is rooted in the Hippocratic Oath and includes acting in a positive manner for the benefit of the patient or client with kindness and charity.

Non-maleficence is the obligation to first do no harm or to avoid unnecessary harm. This principle is often cited when discussing physician-assisted suicide and euthanasia; it also can be useful in many environmental health decisions.

Social Justice is defined in many ways; often, it is about what is fair, being treated equitably, or in fairness of distribution of services. This will be explored further in this chapter in the section titled Social Justice.

All four ethical principles are used by intuitional ethics committees (IEC), as well as by public health administrators and managers when confronted with ethical dilemmas to aid in decision-making. To add clarity, the Public Health Leadership Society (PHLS), in consultation with public health professionals from across the United States, promulgated a set of principles that have been adopted or endorsed by the APHA and nearly ten other national associations.[4] These principles are presented in **EXHIBIT 11.1** and effectively serve as a code of ethics for public health practice. As explained in Shi and Johnson's *Public Health Administration: Principles of Population-Based*

TABLE 11.1 Moral Considerations for Public Health Managers

1. Producing benefits

2. Avoiding, preventing, and removing harms

3. Producing the maximal balance of benefits over harms and other costs (often called utility)

4. Distributing benefits and burdens fairly (distributive justice) and ensuring public participation, including the participation of affected parties (procedural justice)

5. Respecting autonomous choices and actions, including liberty of action

6. Protecting privacy and confidentiality

7. Keeping promises and commitments

8. Disclosing information as well as speaking honestly and truthfully (often grouped under transparency)

9. Building and maintaining trust

EXHIBIT 11.1 Principles of the Ethical Practice of Public Health by Public Health Leadership Society

1. Public health should address principally the fundamental causes of disease and requirements for health, aiming to prevent adverse health outcomes.
2. Public health should achieve community health in a way that respects the rights of individuals in the community.
3. Public health policies, programs, and priorities should be developed/evaluated with community members' input.
4. Public health should advocate and work for the empowerment of disenfranchised community members, aiming to ensure that the basic resources and conditions necessary for health care accessible to all.
5. Public health should seek the information needed to implement effective policies and programs that protect and promote health.
6. Public health institutions should provide communities with the information they have that is needed for decisions on policies or programs and should obtain the community's consent for their implementation.
7. Public health institutions should act in a timely manner on the information they have within the resources and the mandate given to them by the public.
8. Public health programs and policies should incorporate a variety of approaches that anticipate and respect diverse values, beliefs, and cultures in the community.
9. Public health programs/policies should be implemented in a manner that most enhances the physical and social environment.
10. Public health institutions should protect the confidentiality of information that can bring harm to an individual or community if made public. Exceptions must be justified based on the high likelihood of significant harm to the individual or others.
11. Public health institutions should ensure their employees' professional competence.
12. Public health institutions and their employees should engage in collaborations and affiliations in ways that build the public's trust and the institution's effectiveness.

Management, the consideration and adoption of a statement of broad ethical principles, like the PHLS code of ethics, are only a first step for public health agencies in developing an ethics program. Public health leadership must also encourage managers and their staffs to integrate ethics into training, management, supervision, and decision-making processes.[5] As Bernheim describes it,

This process requires both a bottom-up and top-down process of active participation and discussion by professionals throughout the agency. For public health agencies, this code of ethics can provide important guidance and a foundation for ethics discussions about all public health activities, from disease surveillance and outbreak.

Investigations to determining appropriate interventions to conducting research and program evaluation. The most important impact of adopting this code may be that it can serve as a catalyst for management and staff reflection and deliberation about the ethical dimensions of their day-to-day activities in public health and about ways they can continually improve their practices and policies to reflect ethical values.[3]

▶ Ethics in Public Organizations

As was shown in Chapter 6, the culture of the organization plays a very significant role in how it executes its mission and lives its values. In many ways, the public health manager sets the ethical tone for the agency. Described by Johnson and Rossow, "An **ethics-focused culture** is woven in the organization's policies, procedures, administrative practices, performance measures, and modeled by management and associates alike. Being ethically attuned starts with establishing an ethical culture of shared values based on ethical guidelines, codes of ethics, ethics statements, and procedures."[2] This begins with recognizing ethical ramifications and building an infrastructure of ethical resources that decision-makers can use when uncertainty arises. To help ensure ethical behavior in their organization, the World Health Organization (WHO) requires that every **employee** fully embrace its ethical standards and ethics-focused organizational culture. The primary obligation of all WHO staff is set out in the Oath of Office and Loyalty, which is signed by the WHO staff members.[6] The oath states:

I solemnly swear (undertake, affirm, promise) to exercise in all loyalty, discretion, and conscience the functions entrusted to me as an international civil servant of the WHO, to discharge those functions and regulate my conduct with the interests of the WHO only in view, and not to seek or accept instructions in regard to the performance of my duties from any government or other **authority** external to the Organization.

This code incorporates the basic principles of ethical behavior and standards of conduct applicable to all WHO staff. The following basic principles of ethical behavior must be followed at all times:

- **Integrity**
- **Accountability**
- **Independence and Impartiality**
- **Respect** for the dignity, worth, equality, diversity, and privacy of all persons
- **Professional commitment**

This is supported by ongoing training of staff and managers and is incorporated in policy development, decision-making, and human resource management.[6]

All public health managers in settings from the global to the local have an opportunity to develop their own organizations in a similar way through policy and training.

At the federal level in the United States, the governmental health agencies, including **Centers for Disease Control and Prevention (CDC)**, **Food and Drug Administration (FDA)**, Health Resources and Service Administration (HRSA), National Institutes of Health (NIH), and all other units of HHS, must comply with the Government Code of Ethics shown in **EXHIBIT 11.2**.[7] States and local governments have their own codes to guide employees and managers.

Many of the state and local government agencies follow ethical guidelines promoted by the American Society of Public Administration (ASPA).[8] Category IV **Promote Ethical Organizations** in their code specifically addresses the organizational culture to strengthen organizational capabilities to apply ethics, efficiency, and effectiveness in serving the public. ASPA members are committed to:[8]

1. Enhance organizational capacity for open communication, creativity, and dedication.
2. Subordinate institutional loyalties to the public good.
3. Establish procedures that promote ethical behavior and hold individuals and organizations accountable for their conduct.
4. Provide organization members with an administrative means for dissent, assurance of due process, and safeguards against reprisal.
5. Promote merit principles that protect against arbitrary and capricious actions.
6. Promote organizational accountability through appropriate controls and procedures.
7. Encourage organizations to adopt, distribute, and periodically review a code of ethics as a living document.

EXHIBIT 11.2 U.S. Code of Ethics

1. Public service is a public trust, requiring employees to place loyalty to the Constitution, the laws, and ethical principles above private gain.
2. Employees shall not hold financial interests that conflict with the conscientious performance of duty.
3. Employees shall not engage in financial transactions using nonpublic Government information or allow the improper use of such information to further any private interest.
4. An employee shall not, except pursuant to such reasonable exceptions as are provided by regulation, solicit or accept any gift or other item of monetary value from any person or entity seeking official action from, doing business with, or conducting activities regulated by the employee's agency, or whose interests may be substantially affected by the performance or nonperformance of the employee's duties.
5. Employees shall put forth honest effort in the performance of their duties.
6. Employees shall make no unauthorized commitments or promises of any kind purporting to bind the government.
7. Employees shall not use public office for private gain.
8. Employees shall act impartially and not give preferential treatment to any private organization or individual.
9. Employees shall protect and conserve federal property and shall not use it for other than authorized activities.
10. Employees shall not engage in outside employment or activities, including seeking or negotiating for employment, that conflict with official government duties and responsibilities.
11. Employees shall disclose waste, fraud, abuse, and corruption to appropriate authorities.
12. Employees shall satisfy in good faith their obligations as citizens, including all just financial obligations, especially those—such as federal, state, or local taxes—that are imposed by law.
13. Employees shall adhere to all laws and regulations that provide equal opportunity for all Americans, regardless of race, color, religion, sex, national origin, age, or handicap.
14. Employees shall endeavor to avoid any actions creating the appearance that they are violating the law or the ethical standards promulgated pursuant to this order.

U.S. Office of Government Ethics. www.afsa.org/sites/default/files/Portals/0/us_exec_ethical_code.pdf. Accessed May 02, 2019.

Some professional associations, such as ASTHO, provide ethics training for public health professionals and others, like NACCHO, provide online training opportunities. Since 2010, NACCHO has partnered with the CDC Public Health Ethics Unit to provide public health ethics education and training for local health departments.[9]

▶ Ethics in Decision-Making

Public health managers are continuously having to make decisions on a daily basis. This is reflected in the many programs they manage and in decisions pertaining to staffing, resource allocation, strategic planning, community engagement, and the myriad activities in which they may be involved or for which they may be responsible. While knowledge, data, and information are essential in the decision process, so too are ethics. However, managers often face ethical dilemmas with no easy answers, no matter how much information is readily available in a given situation. This is where ethical principles can be helpful. In fact, a thorough analysis of the situation can lead to insight that raises ethical issues and can serve as inputs into the decision process.[5] A framework, as presented in

EXHIBIT 11.3, to guide the necessary analysis can be used to (1) analyze the ethical issues in a given situation, (2) evaluate the ethical dimensions of various options, and (3) provide justification for a particular public health action.[5]

▶ Workforce Diversity

One of the areas to be considered in promoting the ethics-driven organizational culture of a public health agency or program is diversity within the workforce, which includes public health managers, specifically as it pertains to the workforce—in all areas from recruitment to retention. Many of the human resource functions were discussed in Chapter 7; however, within the context of this chapter's focus on ethics, it is important to further explore the human resource environment to help the manager ensure that core values and principled practices are maintained.

Diversity and inclusion are explicit goals supported by, among others, the APHA, AMA, ASPA, ASTHO, Academy of Medicine, ACHE, and various clinical practice societies. Several racial and ethnic groups, most notably African Americans, Latinos, and Native Americans continue to be significantly underrepresented in

---

EXHIBIT 11.3   Framework for Analysis of Ethical Issues in Public Health

Analyze the ethical issues in the situation.
- What are the public health risks and harms of concern in this particular context?
- What are the public health goals?
- Who are the stakeholders, and what are their moral claims?
- Is the source or scope of legal authority in question?
- Are precedent cases or the historical context relevant?
- Do professional codes of ethics provide guidance?

Identify the various public health options and evaluate the ethical dimensions of those options.
- Utility—Does a particular public health action produce a balance of benefits over harms?
- Justice—Are the benefits and burdens distributed fairly (distributive justice), and do legitimate representatives of affected groups have the opportunity to participate in making decisions (procedural justice)?
- Respect for individual interests—Does the public health action respect individual choices and interests (autonomy, liberty, privacy)?
- Respect for legitimate public institutions—Does the public health action respect professional and civic roles and values, such as transparency, honesty, trustworthiness, keeping promises, protecting confidentiality, and protecting vulnerable individuals and communities from undue stigmatization?

Provide justification for one particular public health action.
- Effectiveness—Is the public health goal likely to be accomplished with this option?
- Proportionality—Will the probable benefits of the action outweigh the infringed moral considerations?
- Necessity—Is it necessary to override the conflicting ethical claims in order to achieve the public health goal?
- Least infringement—Is the action the least restrictive and least intrusive?
- Public justification—Can public health agents offer public justification for the action or policy that citizens, particularly those most affected, can find acceptable?

Adapted from Lee LM. Public health ethics theory: review and path to convergence. *J Law Med Ethics*. 2012;40:85–98.

---

the health professions workforce compared with their representation in the general U.S. population. Demographic trends will result in an older and more racially and ethnically diverse general population.[2]

As described by Johnson and Rossow, the data from the HRSA support these significant changes in the healthcare makeup of the United States.[2] The most compelling argument for a more diverse health professions workforce is that it will lead to improvements in public health. The HRSA examined the evidence addressing the contention that health professions diversity will lead to improved population health outcomes. They specifically examined, reviewed, and synthesized publicly available studies addressing four separate hypotheses[2]:

1. The *service patterns hypothesis*: that health professionals from racial and ethnic minority and socioeconomically disadvantaged backgrounds are more likely than others to serve racial and ethnic minority and socioeconomically disadvantaged populations, thereby improving access to care for vulnerable populations and, in turn, improving health outcomes.

2. The *concordance hypothesis*: that increasing the number of racial and ethnic minority health professionals—by providing greater opportunity for minority patients and clients to see a practitioner from their own racial or ethnic group or for patients with limited English proficiency to see a practitioner who speaks their primary language—will improve the quality of communication, comfort level, trust, partnership, and decision-making in patient–practitioner relationships, thereby increasing use of appropriate health care and adherence to effective programs, ultimately resulting in improved health outcomes.

3. The *trust in healthcare hypothesis*: that greater diversity in the healthcare workforce will increase trust in the healthcare delivery system among minority and socioeconomically disadvantaged populations, and will thereby increase their propensity to use health services that lead to improved health outcomes.

4. The *professional advocacy hypothesis*: that health professionals from racial and ethnic minority and socioeconomically disadvantaged backgrounds will be more likely than others to provide leadership and advocacy for policies and programs aimed at improving health care for vulnerable populations,

thereby increasing healthcare access and quality, and, ultimately, health outcomes for those populations.[1]

Diversity and inclusion continue to be issues on the mind of many public health leaders. A group of interested organizations, including the National Association of Public Hospitals and Health Systems, are calling for the elimination of health disparities.[10] Their goals are to increase the collection of race, ethnicity, and language preference data; increase cultural competency training for clinicians and support staff; and increase diversity in governance and management. The **coalition** stated, "Addressing disparities is no longer just about morality, ethics and social justice: It is essential for performance excellence and improved community health."[10] Some commonly agreed upon concepts have been instructive. They include the following:

- Representation—reflecting employees, patients/clients, and communities.
- Inclusiveness—in welcoming, listening, mentoring, training, and benefits.
- Cultural competency—being respectful and responsive to cultural backgrounds and their impact on health outcomes.
- Broader definitions of diversity—encompassing thought, education, skills, gender identity, and age.

The word *diversity* means different things to different people. For some, it represents differences between human beings related to race or ethnicity. To others, it means the uniqueness of each individual. Yet, for others, and this is increasingly the case, it is an expansive concept that fosters inclusion very broadly. For the public health agency and workplaces generally, a useful tool for encompassing most of what diversity represents in the early part of the 21st century is the "Diversity Wheel" developed by the Johns Hopkins University Leadership Council (**FIGURE 11.1**).[11]

In the future with the advent of artificial intelligence robots, transhumanism, genetic engineering, and various unforeseen developments, the current definitions and thus the diversity wheel could change.

As defined by the Society for Human Resource Management (SHRM), inclusion is "the achievement of a work environment in which all individuals are treated fairly and respectfully, have equal access to opportunities and resources, and can contribute fully to the organization's success."[12]

This assertion by SHRM and the components of the diversity wheel illustrate that diversity must be viewed across different dimensions, those being human, cultural, and systems diversity. The human dimension of diversity includes such factors as race, sexual orientation, gender and gender identity, ethnicity, physical ability, age, and family status. In short, *human diversity* includes the attributes that distinguishes us as human beings. Most workplace definitions of diversity include human diversity as a minimum. *Cultural diversity* encompasses a person's beliefs, values, family structure practice (nuclear or extended family, independent living), and mind-set as a result of his or her cultural, community, and environmental experiences. Cultural diversity is sometimes seen as a secondary dimension, but it can have a powerful impact on how a person behaves in the workplace. Cultural norms vary from one culture to another and influence how individuals interact with their work environment. *Systems diversity* relates to the differences among organizations in work structure and pursuits, including teamwork, reengineering, strategic alliances, military experience, empowerment, quality, education, and innovation. Systems diversity also deals with systems thinking and the ability to recognize how functions in the work environment are connected.[2]

Managing diversity is not necessarily an easy task, as a number of barriers, including biases and prejudices, can get in the way of achieving a harmonious working environment. Some of these barriers, which revolve around the diversity dimensions, can be a great source of tension and conflict. For instance, a person's culture can be a barrier to a work team when other members of the group are not respectful or understanding of the person's values, beliefs, or even clothing, all of which may reflect that person's cultural background.

Population health management requires coordination among a range of health providers and public health agencies, along with the ability to identify and address broader community health factors. Diverse leadership is often better equipped to engage the community and establish the network of partnerships necessary for population health management.

Cultural competence may be defined as a set of complementary behaviors, practices, attitudes, and policies that enable a system, an agency, or individuals to effectively work and serve pluralistic, multiethnic, and linguistically diverse communities.[2] Different from cultural sensitivity, cultural competence is about action, doing something that creates and delivers culturally competent services. Cultural competence is the ability of public health organizations to effectively deliver services and programs that also meet the social, cultural, and linguistic needs of the community. A culturally competent public health system can help improve health outcomes, quality of services, and can contribute to the elimination of racial and ethnic health disparities. Examples of strategies to move a public health agency toward these goals include providing relevant training on cultural competence and

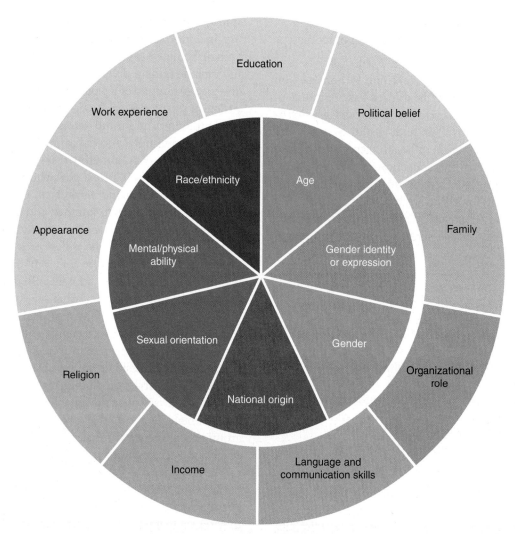

FIGURE 11.1 The Johns Hopkins diversity wheel.
Data from Health Resources and Services Administration.

cross-cultural issues to public health professionals. Likewise, public health managers can develop policies that reduce administrative and linguistic barriers. The demographic makeup of this country will continue to change, and cultural competence and sensitivity to diversity issues will be expected from current and future public health professionals.

The rationale and organizational necessities for aggressively creating and supporting a diversity program include, but are not limited to, the following[2]:

- *Reflection of the service population.* The public health organization should mirror the diversity of the population of the communities being served. Toward this end, the agency should attract and take advantage of the talents, skills, and growth potential of minority professionals within the community.
- *Workforce utilization.* Diverse employees have a lot to contribute to the agency. Public health managers should recognize this fact and should be open to, sensitive to, knowledgeable about, and understanding of the cultures, mind-set, and

practices of the organization's diverse workforce. Doing so will not only enhance staff productivity, effectiveness, and overall performance but also boost morale within the organization.

- *Work–life quality and balance.* Public health managers should recognize that work and personal activities are interrelated, not separate, preoccupations. Both are performed on the basis of necessity, practicality, efficiency, and sometimes spontaneity.
- *Recruitment and retention.* Attracting and retaining a diverse workforce have a lot to do with the emotional and professional quality of the workplace. Public health managers should create an environment in which everyone feels included, professionally developed, and safe.
- *Bridging of generations.* Generational differences in expectations, education, and values exist between younger and older staff. Such gaps should be acknowledged, and attention should be paid to the physical, mental, and emotional well-being of all staff at all ages, regardless of backgrounds.

- *Cultural competence.* This competence is an in-depth understanding of and sensitivity to the values and viewpoints of culturally diverse staff and community members. Public health managers should master the skills necessary to work with and serve these groups and should provide training to all employees.
- *Organization-wide respect.* Public health leaders and managers should create an organizational environment in which the differences in title, role, position, and department are valued and respected but not held too high above others. Each employee, regardless of his or her level within the organization, should be viewed as integral to the overall success of the agency.

One of the generational challenges that can be seen in any multigenerational workforce, which public health certainly is, has to do with different workplace needs, values, work styles, and perspectives. In the United States, we see primarily Baby Boom, Generation X, and increasingly Millennials in the workforce. **EXHIBIT 11.4** explores some of the characteristics of this latter generation.

The following is an interview with a public health manager to gain insight into and experiences in a diverse workforce (**EXHIBIT 11.5**).

EXHIBIT 11.4 Millennials in the Workplace

Joseph Adam Johnson, B.Ed., M.L.A., teacher

Generations have a vast number of similarities and differences. For example, it is easy to find the many differences when comparing the Baby Boomers to Millennials. Of course, many factors are responsible for these generational variances, and the task of comparing the generations is quite complex, but rather the objective of this commentary is to focus on Millennials in the workplace—their needs, motivators, and special interests. As a Millennial myself and having conducted research on the topic, I will describe several ways to better serve employees of this generation.

According to an extensive study by Bentley University's Center for Women and Business, motivation in the workplace is facilitated by the Millennial employee's need for personal fulfillment that aligns with their individual values and aspirations. The Millennial worker no longer views career accolades and advancement over the idea that they serve a larger purpose and that they "are making a difference in the world."[1] In other words, employment in no longer about climbing the corporate ladder, instead fulfilling one's desire to make a change in the world.

Another motivating factor for the Millennial worker is the work environment. Many Millennials would sacrifice income to ensure a better work place. According to Ashira Prossack, a journalist for Forbes whose expertise is Millennials and Gen Z leadership and careers wrote that "a positive work environment where employees feel a sense of camaraderie" is essential to the Millennial workforce.[2]

Furthermore, it is imperative for feedback to be consistent and meaningful from managers. Millennials desire frequent feedback about their work, and in many cases, they want the feedback to be made public. This need for regular feedback breaks for the more traditionally "annual reviews" from the boss.[3] However, considering this generation was raised with immediate, public critiques on their lives via social media, the desire for frequent feedback in the workplace is understandable. In addition, regular and open communication allows the employee to collaborate with their managers and senior staff give them a chance to voice their opinions and participate in setting goals, thus giving the employee a greater sense of ownership over the work.

Essentially, Millennials are seeking comfortable work environments where the free-flow of ideas and opinions are accepted and encouraged. Additionally, the importance of the work to the individual is critical to the tenure of the employee. Millennial workers will change jobs at a quicker pace than previous generations if the work or work environment does not meet their expectations. Furthermore, pay and accolades are not as important to Millennial workers. They hold family and quality of life as a higher priority over employment. However, that is not to say that Millennials do not regard employment as being important, they are often more selective with their career choices while not being hesitant to change jobs. This is especially true in public health with the many changes in the health needs in the country there will be expanded opportunities to work in a wide range of public health programs. In fact, my own father, Dr. James Johnson from the Baby Boomer generation is a medical social scientist and my brother, Dr. Allen Johnson who is Generation X is an epidemiologist.

1 CWB Millennial Report, Scribd, 2011. https://www.scribd.com/doc/158258672/CWB-Millennial-Report?secret_password=2191s8a7d6j7shshcctt. Accessed February 18, 2019.
2 Ashira Prossack, "How To Make Your Workplace Millennial Friendly," Forbes, July 30, 2018. https://www.forbes.com/sites/ashiraprossack1/2018/07/29/how-to-make-your-workplace-millennial-friendly/#5d6a7f57409d. Accessed February 18, 2019.
3 Steinhilber, B. Give millennials some credit; They're changing the workplace for the better. *NBCNews.com.* https://www.nbcnews.com/better/business/7-ways-millennials-are-changing-workplace-better-ncna761021. Accessed February 18, 2019.

EXHIBIT 11.5 Public Health Manager Interview[14]

Jennifer Crawford, MSA, CHES, CPC-M, Prevention Coordinator, Saginaw Chippewa Behavioral Health, Mt. Pleasant, Michigan

Interviewed by Dr. Mark Minelli

(Q): What are some of the most challenging roles in working with diverse groups?

Ms. Crawford: Whether you are working with individuals who are of different ethnic backgrounds, age, or socioeconomic status, it is imperative to be able to relate to each and every person. So often, curricula or programs are designed with one type of person in mind. Therefore, it is up to us as the facilitators to peel back the layers or enhance with information to make it real for our specific audience. We simply cannot rely on "cookie-cutter approaches" if we want the strategies to work with our specific group.

When working with populations different than ourselves, we need to be sure to take the time to gain as much knowledge as possible about the cultures and traditions within that group. By doing so, we are able to learn about appropriate and inappropriate ways to communicate with the community members in order to establish and maintain respect. It is important to identify key individuals within the group who can help you identify your role within the community, while teaching you at the same time. The process of gaining access and respect from those within a community different from oneself takes time and is never-ending, but is so worth it when achieved.

(Q): What advice would you give others in working with diverse groups?

Ms. Crawford: The advice that I would give someone working with diverse groups is to be respectful at all times, even if a belief of the group contradicts something that you believe in. We can certainly respect and show support for the beliefs of others, while maintaining our own values and traditions. Having a mutual respect and openness allows us to learn so much more about one another and ourselves. We should appreciate, embrace, and celebrate the many unique qualities and traditions of the diverse populations with whom we live and work.

(Q): What are things to stay away from in working with diverse groups?

Ms. Crawford: When working with diverse groups, it is imperative to not cast judgment on others for beliefs, traditions, or customs different from one's own. Doing so would certainly hamper any relationships and ability to effectively work with the members of the community.

Another tip would be to not force oneself on the community. Identifying and establishing a relationship with a key community leader who could then help introduce you to the community at an appropriate pace would be the most beneficial. By working with a trusted member of the community, one would be more apt to be welcomed and trusted by others.

(Q): Please describe some advantages of working with diverse groups in a community health setting.

Ms. Crawford: There are many advantages to working with diverse groups in a community health setting. First and foremost, having the opportunity to learn about and work with other cultures is amazing and rewarding and should, therefore, be regarded as a privilege. There are many health issues that affect different populations in unique ways; so, it proposes a challenge to learn new strategies for various target groups, enhancing the skill set of community health workers. Another advantage is the ability to utilize strategies with certain populations that may not be seen as mainstream, depending on the target audience. For example, utilizing cultural norms and traditions, such as language or ceremonies, may not be seen as a typical community health strategy. However, when doing so reinforces a tradition that incorporates healthy decision-making on many different levels, it is a great supplemental community health tool.

Conclusion

In this chapter, we explored ethics and its importance in public health. The various codes that help shape ethical behavior and choices were presented as well. Diversity in the public health workforce was discussed and a broad definition was presented. The importance of a diverse workforce in public health was presented and the role of the public health manager in promoting diversity was discussed. Cultural competency was also described as a critical skill set for public health managers.

Discussion Questions

1. Discuss the concept of ethics and explain why it is important in public health organizations. Give examples.
2. How can a public health manager help promote an "ethics-focused" organizational culture? Discuss any potential barriers.
3. How do codes of ethics help public health managers make better decisions?
4. What is the broadest concept of diversity you can think of? Identify all of the elements and populations represented in your concept.
5. Why are diversity and inclusion important in the public health workforce? How does this help when working in the community? Give examples.
6. What are the core elements of ethical behavior expected of employees at the WHO? Why do you think this is essential in the kind of work they do?

Learning Activities

A. Exercise in Forming a Diverse Public Health Team.

A large community grant was just awarded to form a community coalition to fight alcohol and opioid abuse. The participants are in two counties and have unique populations they serve. Both counties have a large African-American population; one county has a Native American Indian Tribe and the other has a university campus.

As these are different service populations, describe how you would develop a leadership team to represent each unique group. How would you select the team members (i.e., one per group, population based, and health providers versus community individuals)? Your final analysis should provide:
- Rationale statement for your team selection
- Number of group members
  ◦ Composition of group members
  ◦ Frequency of meetings and place
  ◦ Team goals/objectives

Discuss your process and conclusions in class. Ask for suggestions and ideas from classmates.

B. Community Initiative Exercise

Identify a community-based public health initiative in your local area (either in your home town or in the university's area) and find out through interviews and reading the program's printed material and website how it went about getting involvement from the community (inclusion). Where are diverse populations involved? Were there any ethical issues that needed to be resolved? If so, how was this done? Share what you found with the class and discuss how you might enrich the initiative or program with your own ideas and suggestions.

References

1. Johnson CE. *Meeting the Ethical Challenges of Leadership: Casting Light or Shadow.* 6th ed. Thousand Oaks, CA: Sage Publications; 2018.
2. Johnson JA, Rossow CC. *Health Organizations: Theory Behavior and Development.* 2nd ed. Burlington, MA: Jones & Bartlett Learning; 2019.
3. Bernheim R, et al. *Essentials of Public Health Ethics.* Burlington, MA: Jones & Bartlett Learning; 2015.
4. Public Health Leadership Society, Principles of the Ethical Practice of Public Health. https://www.apha.org/-/media/files/pdf/membergroups/ethics/ethics_brochure.ashx
5. Shi L, Johnson J. *Public Health Administration: Principles of Population-Based Management.* 4th ed. Burlington, MA: Jones & Bartlett Learning; 2020.
6. WHO. Code of Ethics and Professional Conduct. https://www.who.int/about/ethics/code_of_ethics_full_version.pdf?ua=1
7. U.S. Code of Ethics. http://www.afsa.org/sites/default/files/Portals/0/us_exec_ethical_code.pdf
8. American Society of Public Administration (ASAP). Code of Ethics. https://www.aspanet.org/ASPA/About-ASPA/Code-of-Ethics/ASPA/Code-of-Ethics/Code-of-Ethics.aspx?hkey=fefba3e2-a9dc-4fc8-a686-3446513a4533
9. NACCHO. https://www.naccho.org/programs/public-health-infrastructure/ethics
10. HRSA Speech on National Public Hospitals Association (NPHA). https://www.hrsa.gov/about/news/speeches/2010/2010-03-09-public-hospitals.html
11. https://essentialhospitals.org/
12. Johns Hopkins Diversity Leadership Council. *Diversity Wheel.* http://web.jhu.edu/dlc/resources/diversity_wheel/index.html
13. SHRM. https://www.shrm.org/
14. Reigelman R, Kirkwood B. *Public Health 101.* 3rd ed. Burlington, MA: Jones & Bartlett Learning.
15. Johnson JA. *Introduction to Public Health Organizations, Management, and Policy.* Clifton Park, NY: Delmar-Cengage; 2013.

Suggested Reading and Websites

American Society for Public Administration (ASPA). Code of Ethics. https://www.aspanet.org/ASPA/Code-of-Ethics/ASPA/Code-of-Ethics/Code-of-Ethics.aspx?hkey=5b8f046b-dcbd-416d-87cd-0b8fcfacb5e7

ASTHO. http://www.astho.org/

Bernheim RG, et al. *Essentials of Public Health Ethics*. Burlington, MA: Jones & Bartlett Learning; 2017.

Johns Hopkins Diversity Leadership Council. http://web.jhu.edu/dlc/resources/diversity_wheel/index.html

Society for Human Resource Management (SHRM). https://www.shrm.org/

U.S. Government Ethics Office. www.afsa.org/sites/default/files/Portals/0/us_exec_ethical_code.pdf

© KTSDESIGN/Science Photo Library/Getty Images.

CHAPTER 12

Public Health Emergency Preparedness and Crisis Response

▶ Introduction

With the possibility of natural disasters seeming to always be present and man-made ones, such as terrorism looming in our collective psyche, it is imperative for all public health organizations to focus on community and organizational preparedness. Additionally, organization development, education, and training are necessary, as are interorganizational exercises and partnerships across all sectors, federal, state, local, and private.

A successful, comprehensive public health emergency management program of preparedness, response, and recovery will help the agency through what could be its most difficult challenge. The public health manager will be center stage during these trying times and can expect to be pulled in many directions by political leaders, clients, employees, and their own families. If ever there is a time for multitasking, this will be it. However, those managers who have an organization-specific disaster response plan will do much better. As we all know, a plan is only as good as its implementation. There will be a need to modify decisions on the ground and adjust accordingly. This is a kind of *organizational improvisation* that will call on all the skills and knowledge previously addressed.[1] Overall damage can be minimized with adequate planning, preparedness, and response.

▶ Crisis and Disaster Planning for Public Health

Contingency plans are important for public health organizations and managers to identify, assess, mitigate, and respond to risks to the organization and those it serves. The World Health Organization (WHO) defines contingency planning as "[…] part of a cycle in which the identification and regular monitoring of risks, vulnerabilities and capacities informs the planning and implementation of measures to mitigate the risks and prepare to respond."[2] From oil spills to vaccine shortages to bioterrorism attacks to storms to seasonal outbreaks, public health organizations must plan and be prepared for a wide range of potential events. Contingency plans are one element of the emergency preparedness process. Public health constantly faces risks; therefore, public health organizations and managers should ensure that contingency planning is a regular and recurring part of the organizational planning process. The goal is to identify, mitigate, and respond to risks to protect life, health, and well-being. These plans recognize that organizations are constantly facing changing circumstances and that organizations must be flexible. The contingency planning process helps organizations, managers, and employees anticipate and prepare for events that could reasonably happen. The plans identify and integrate response roles and responsibilities. Plans provide opportunities to communicate and test communications used during a response. Overall, contingency plans help ensure a prepared workforce, organization, and response partners.[16] The WHO developed a guide, as shown in **FIGURE 12.1**, with steps that organizations and managers can use to develop contingency plans for a wide variety of risks.

Agencies develop contingency plans for each risk an organization identifies. Public health organizations identify risks related to infectious diseases, seasonal outbreaks, weather events, or water safety. The first step in the contingency planning process is to conduct a **risk analysis**. Public health managers facilitate and participate in identifying potential risks or scenarios that their organization could face. A risk is something that if it does occur, it would threaten the health and well-being of the organization or its stakeholders. Public health organizations and managers often engage in scenario-based planning as a tool to identify risks. Scenarios help identify different scenarios that could happen in the future and require contingency plans. Public health organizations generally rank potential risks in terms of their severity and the probability of occurring. The second step in the process is to **mitigate**

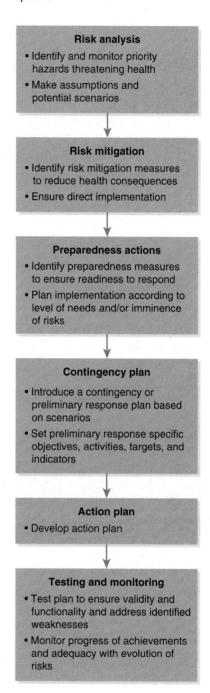

FIGURE 12.1 WHO hazard-based contingency planning flowchart.
Reprinted from WHO guidance for contingency planning, World Health Organization. http://apps.who.int/iris/bitstream/handle/10665/260554/WHO-WHE-CPI-2018.13-eng.pdf?ua=1.

potential risks. There are certain measures or steps that organizations can take to reduce the impact of risks. Managers review the current measures that the organization uses, and they identify new measures that the organization can use to mitigate a risk. This step focuses on what the organization is currently doing and what the organization could do differently in the future to reduce the chance of a risk occurring. This process is a gap analysis that identifies current operations and future changes an organization may need to make to mitigate risks. Managers should collaborate with their staff to identify multipronged approaches to managing and reducing an identified risk. The third step is to identify **preparedness actions**. This step identifies ways to reduce potential risks and put those ideas and plans into action to enhance an organization's preparedness. The fourth step in the process is to develop a **contingency plan**. The organization develops the best and the worst-case scenarios. Many organizations choose to think about the probable case, which is somewhere between the extremes. The contingency plan uses the probable case as the basis for contingency plans. The fifth step in the process is to develop an **action plan**. Action plans contain details about the how an organization will respond if the probable case occurs. The plan should clearly identify response activities, resource requirements, personnel requirements, partners, costs, and timetables. Plans must prioritize response activities to provide order and coordination. For example, if employees do not know what to do first, then they could not respond as well and overwhelm their capabilities. Communication, medical supplies, food, water, and rapid response teams are priority activities in a number of different emergencies versus purchase of a logics supply system. The logics supply system is something that an organization has already put in place, thanks to the contingency plans. The final step in the process is to **test and monitor the plan**. Testing the plan through coordinated exercises or drills provides an opportunity to see if the plan provides the intended response. This aspect of planning needs attention, especially across public health organizations. Regularly exercising contingency plans ensures that they are an appropriate response to an identified risk. Exercises provide an opportunity for personnel and partners to understand their roles and responsibilities in certain situations. Additionally, exercising a plan identifies weak areas that need to be addressed, so that breakdowns do not occur in real time. Therefore, conditions should be as realistic as possible for testing. Adjustments and enhancements should be made following an exercise. Managers should sign off on plans after a plan has been developed and tested. Regularly reviewing, exercising, and updating contingency plans help ensure that responses are accurate, effective, and familiar to those with roles and responsibilities.

The **Centers for Disease Control and Prevention (CDC)** generally follows the contingency planning process outlined by the WHO. The CDC does emphasize a few elements of contingency plans beyond what the WHO outlines. The CDC emphasizes identification of essential organizational systems, functions, and personnel, plan notification and activation, recovery operations, and returning to normal operations. These are important areas for public health managers to discuss and include in contingency plans. For example, clearly identifying individuals who can officially activate a plan is important to ensure clarity and a coordinated response. The plan should also outline recovery operations and steps for deactivating a plan. **EXHIBIT 12.1** presents a generic overview with key elements for consideration in plan development and implementation. There will be wide variation in the plans according to local culture, political structure, and economics.[1]

EXHIBIT 12.1 General Preparedness Plan

Address the following areas in the plan:

- A collaboration plan, including area health care; public health; veterinary, physician, and medical group practices; and law enforcement with specific preparation action steps (stockpiling appropriate levels of material, training, etc.) and with the local hospital(s).
- Reporting of incidents and possible incidents and how the reporting will be done.
- Infection control practices and procedures and decontamination procedures.
- A postexposure management plan for employees (prophylactics, vaccines, and a plan to prevent secondary infections).
- An off-site contingency operation plan.
- An education plan (prospective and concurrent to an attack) and a public relations plan.

Components of an Effective Response

- Establish protocols.
- Establish a response command and control structure where critical decisions can be made (should be community based).
- Develop and implement a training and awareness program with local health care, public health, and law enforcement officials.
- Ensure surveillance systems are in place.

(continues)

EXHIBIT 12.1 General Preparedness Plan   (continued)

Cost Considerations (when preparing a budget)

- Cost of detection devices
- Cost of personal protection devices, such as masks and body covering
- Cost of vaccines and prophylaxis (antibiotics, etc.)
- Cost of training: training professionals, resources, and personnel hours
- Cost of constructing evacuation avenues, decontamination sites, and "safe rooms"
- Cost of temporary or permanent loss of business and government functionality
- Cost of securing substitute personnel in case of temporary or permanent loss of regular personnel

Modified from Johnson JA, Rossow CC. *Health Organizations*. 2nd ed. Burlington, MA: Jones & Bartlett Learning; 2019.

Crisis Communication Plans

Crisis communication plans are vital to public health organizations and the public. A crisis communication plan "describes the process of providing facts to the public about an unexpected emergency, beyond an organization's control, that involves the organization and requires an immediate response."[3] A large part of public health is responding to crises, which requires communication plans. The CDC developed the Crisis and Emergency Risk Communication (CERC) manual that utilizes evidence-based communication strategies to help public health professionals develop crisis communication plans to communicate during a public health emergency or disaster. The crisis communication plan provides a general overview of how a public health organization will respond in the event of an emergency. Managers have to adapt the plan to the types of crises their organization could face. The CDC also has checklists that managers can use to develop crisis communication plans. The CDC's CERC planning guide states that successful communication plans should clearly identify the following[3]:

- Support from top management and leadership
- Identification of a communication team and assignment of communications roles and responsibilities
- Designation of a spokesperson
- Steps for verifying information regarding a crisis
- Plan for how to handle crises during the regular work week, after hours, and on weekends
- Steps for how information will be released to employees and the public
- Media contacts that should be notified at the local and state levels
- Contacts for local, state, and federal departments and agencies
- Procedures on how to engage the Joint Information Center and Emergency Operations Center and contact a designated communications person
- Communication resources

- Messages for certain types of crises (i.e., infectious diseases, bioterrorism, chemical and natural disasters, man-made disasters, and radiation)

The best way for managers to develop crisis communication plans is to understand the phases of a crisis (**FIGURE 12.2**). Different messages and responses will be required at different phases of the crisis. The CDC identifies a communication rhythm that corresponds to the different phases of a crisis (**FIGURE 12.3**).[3]

The **precrisis phase** is where a significant amount of planning takes place to prepare plans for communicating during a crisis. This phase identifies a core communications team and a spokesperson. The communications team develops messages and communication systems that upper-level management review and approve. This is the time to identify a number of contact lists, such as experts, media, and organizational partners. The organization should train any spokespeople during this phase. The **initial phase** of a crisis requires the communications team to obtain and communicate details about the crisis. This phase

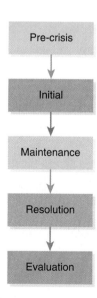

FIGURE 12.2 Crisis phases.

Modified from CERC: Crisis Communication Plans, Centers for Disease Control and Prevention. https://emergency.cdc.gov/cerc/ppt/CERC_Crisis_Communication_Plans.pdf.

Engage Community • Empower Decision-Making • Evaluate

Preparation	Initial	Maintenance	Resolution
• Draft and test messages • Develop partnerships • Create plans • Determine approval process	• Express empathy • Explain risks • Promote action • Describe response efforts	• Explain ongoing risks • Segment audiences • Provide background information • Address rumors	• Motivate vigilance • Discuss lessons learned • Revise plan

FIGURE 12.3 The crisis and emergency risk communication rhythm.

Modified from CERC: Crisis Communication Plans, Centers for Disease Control and Prevention. https://emergency.cdc.gov/cerc/ppt/CERC_Crisis_Communication_Plans.pdf.

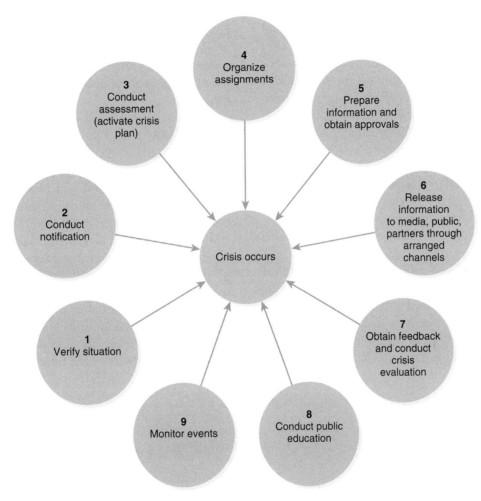

FIGURE 12.4 Nine steps in crisis communication implementation.

Modified from Nine Steps in Crisis Communication Implementation, Centers for Disease Control and Prevention. https://emergency.cdc.gov/cerc/cerccorner/article_071516.asp.

is active and requires continuous communication regarding the following:

- What happened?
- Who was involved or impacted?
- When did it happen?
- Where did it happen?
- How did it happen?
- How is the situation or crisis being addressed?

The CDC identifies nine steps to implementing communication plans when a crisis occurs (**FIGURE 12.4**). The steps correspond to aspects of planning that managers and organizations should consider. The steps provide insight into how to determine if a crisis has occurred and is active. First, confirm that a crisis has occurred from creditable and reputable sources. The crisis communication plan should outline a procedure for collecting and confirming crisis-related information. Second, notify the appropriate organizational and legal contacts. Third, activate the crisis communication plan and assign roles and responsibilities based on the plan. Fourth, assign communications team members specific roles and responsibilities. Fifth, prepare information about the crisis and secure approval for sharing the information. Sixth, the communications team will release information and determine what communication methods and channels are the best for getting information out to the public. Messages should be coordinated with media outlets and other important organizations. Seventh, review the organization's communication plan and make any adjustments based on how the crisis develops or depending on feedback received from key stakeholders and audiences. Eighth, conduct public education about the crisis to help them understand what is happening, how they can be safe, and how they can be prepared for the next crisis. Finally, monitor the situation. The communications team will continue to collect and share information until the crisis is over.

The **maintenance phase** requires continual monitoring and updates about the situation. Circling back to the what, who, when, where, and how questions are important during this phase. These questions provide an opportunity to place the situation in context. The **resolution phase** communicates what happened and how the situation was resolved. Communication should acknowledge what went right and what went wrong. This is also a great time to communicate how the public can be prepared in the future for similar events. The **evaluation phase** provides an opportunity to review how the crisis communication plan worked in practice. Reviewing the plan provides an opportunity to understand what went right and what went wrong with the communication plan. The plan should identify, debrief, and address any deficit areas.

▶ Preparedness and Response

Preparedness goes beyond planning in that it is primarily focused on building capacity for a timely and effective response to public health emergencies. **FIGURE 12.5** presents one model that illustrates the capabilities as they relate to the 10 essential services of public health previously discussed in the first chapter of this text.[4]

There are many organizations involved in public health emergencies, and they certainly are not all public health entities. There are also schools, law enforcement, fire departments, businesses, faith-based organizations, transportation, and governments at all levels. However, there are certain key organizations that are often involved. **TABLE 12.1** provides a list of many of these and a brief description of their functions.[5]

The phases that are likely to be seen are illustrated in **FIGURE 12.6**.[6]

Several critical success factors for all communities should be considered by public health managers. As described by Johnson and Johnson[7] and further asserted by Rossow and Johnson,[8] these factors include training and education; mitigation of confusion, fear, and panic; time management; building response capacity; and economic empowerment.

Leaders of public health organizations must take responsibility for addressing concerns about the possibility of any of the disruptors described in this chapter. These leaders should inform all of their key stakeholders, including their boards and staff, that preventive as well as response policies and programs are underway. This may take place in the form of briefings, in-service

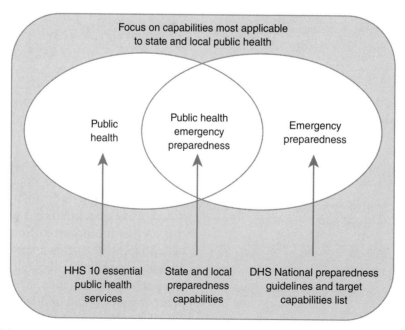

FIGURE 12.5 Public health emergency preparedness capabilities.

TABLE 12.1 Key Disaster Response Entities

Organization	Functions and Definitions
Public Access System	Enables public to communicate response needs, typically through the 911 phone system
Fire Department	Finds and extricates victims; often provides on-scene incident management
Emergency Medical Services (EMS)	Assesses scene for medical needs, initiates triage of patients, assesses individual patients for status and treatment needs, initiates life-sustaining first aid and medical care, determines treatment destination, and transports patients to definitive care
National Response Framework	Defines principles, roles, and structures of U.S. national response to disasters
National Incident Management System (NIMS)	Comprehensive model for managing emergencies in the United States
Emergency Management Agency (EMA)	A state or jurisdictional agency tasked with preparedness and response for disasters and other emergencies; sometimes called the Office of Emergency Preparedness (OEP)
Department of Homeland Security	The coordinating agency for all federal agency responses to disasters
Department of Health and Human Services (HHS)	The federal action agency charged with lead responsibility for supporting health officials in disaster response
Assistant Secretary for Preparedness and Response (ASPR)	Offices have leadership roles in carrying out support functions for health and medical services as delegated by HHS
Centers for Disease Control and Prevention (CDC)	One of 13 major operational components of HHS; within the CDC, the Office of Public Health Preparedness and Response coordinates and supports CDC's response efforts
Federal Emergency Management Agency (FEMA)	Responsible for emergency management at the scene of a disaster through preparedness, mitigation response, and recovery activities
Emergency Support Function 8 (ESF#8)	The public health and medical function of the National Response Plan provides coordination between HHS operating divisions and ESF#8 interagency partners
National Disaster Medical System (NDMS)	A multiagency response system coordinated by the U.S. Public Health Service OEP with responsibility for responding to overwhelming medical needs in a disaster-struck state or territory
Disaster Medical Assistance Team (DMAT)	A trained unit of medical response personnel available to respond with the NDMS to a disaster scene
Office of the Surgeon General (OSG)	Deploys teams that carry out responsibility of ESF#8
American Red Cross (ARC)	Private voluntary national organization tasked by government to provide mass care and shelter to disaster victims
Private Volunteer Organization (PVO)	National and local volunteer groups that carry out response; groups have a broad range of functions and structures

Reproduced from Shi L, Johnson JA. Novick and Morrow's Public Health Administration. 3rd ed. Burlington, MA: Jones & Bartlett Learning; 2013.

FIGURE 12.6 The four phases of disaster.

workshops, simulations and mock exercises, security enhancements, and coordination with other agencies, along with medical facilities. Public health organizations with their community partners will want to develop disaster plans and crisis management initiatives that help victims and their families remain in the information loop or in some cases to evacuate affected areas. Additionally, local businesses will need to have contingency plans and backup systems as well. There are several "critical success factors" for a public health

organization to consider, and these should include the following[8]:

1. Workforce training
2. Mitigation of confusion
3. Time management (time is critical)
4. Building response capacity
5. Economic constraints
6. Coordination with other agencies
7. Mitigation of fear and panic

Training and Coordination

Training is essential for all public health staff. This could be in the form of awareness enhancement or actual training in disease/agent detection and early intervention. **TABLE 12.2** identifies core competencies needed by the public health workforce. Additionally, the training of "disaster coordinators" will be important.[4] These individuals can serve as a resource person, advisor, counselor, or organizer. They also could have the responsibility for staying informed and maintaining contact networks. Ideally, this coordinator would receive continuing education for periodic updates on skills and knowledge

---

TABLE 12.2 Emergency Preparedness Core Competencies for All Public Health Workers

All Public Health Workers must be competent to

- Describe the public health role in emergency response in a range of emergencies that might arise (e.g., "The department provides surveillance, investigation, and public information in disease outbreaks and collaborates with other agencies in geological, environmental, and weather emergencies.").
- Describe the chain of command in emergency response.
- Identify and locate the agency emergency response plan (or the pertinent portion of the plan).
- Describe his/her functional role(s) in emergency response and demonstrate his/her role(s) in regular drills.
- Demonstrate correct use of all communication equipment used for emergency communication (e.g., phone, fax, radio).
- Describe communication role(s) in emergency response—within the agency using established communication systems, with the media, with the general public, and personal (with family, neighbors).
- Identify limits to own knowledge/skill/authority and identify key system resources for referring matters that exceed these limits.
- Recognize unusual events that might indicate an emergency and describe appropriate action (e.g., communicate clearly within chain of command).
- Apply creative problem solving and flexible thinking to unusual challenges within his/her functional responsibilities and evaluate effectiveness of all actions taken.

Public Health Leaders/Administrators must also be competent to

- Describe the chain of command and management system ("incident command system") or similar protocol for emergency response in the jurisdiction.
- Communicate the public health information, roles, capacities, and legal authority to all emergency response partners—such as other public health agencies, other health agencies, and other governmental agencies—during planning, drills, and actual emergencies. (This includes contributing to effective community-wide response through leadership, team building, negotiation, and conflict resolution.)
- Maintain regular communication with emergency response partners. (This includes maintaining a current directory of partners and identifying appropriate methods for contacting them in emergencies.)

- Ensure that the agency (or the agency unit) has a written, regularly updated plan for major categories of emergencies that respects the culture of the community and provides for continuity of agency operations.
- Ensure that the agency (or agency unit) regularly practices all parts of emergency response.
- Evaluate every emergency response drill (or actual response) to identify needed internal and external improvements.
- Ensure that knowledge and skill gaps identified through emergency response planning, drills, and evaluation are addressed.

Public Health Professionals must also be competent to
- Demonstrate readiness to apply professional skills to a range of emergency situations during regular drills (e.g., access, use, and interpret surveillance data; access and use lab resources; access and use science-based investigation and risk assessment protocols; identify and use appropriate personal protective equipment).
- Maintain regular communication with partner professionals in other agencies involved in emergency response. (This includes contributing to effective community-wide response through leadership, team building, negotiation, and conflict resolution.)
- Participate in continuing education to maintain up-to-date knowledge in areas relevant to emergency response (e.g., emerging infectious diseases, hazardous materials, and diagnostic tests).

Public Health Technical and Support Staff must also be competent to
- Demonstrate the use of equipment (including personal protective equipment) and skills associated with his/her functional role in emergency response during regular drills.
- Describe at least one resource for backup support in key areas of responsibility.

Data from Bioterrorism & Emergency Readiness Competencies for All Public Health Workers, Centers for Disease Control and Prevention, 2003.

needed to be effective in this role. **EXHIBIT 12.2** describes the minimum qualifications for a typical emergency preparedness and response coordinator.[4]

Mitigation of Confusion

Mitigation of confusion is a critical success factor in managing any public health crisis. The natural tendency of humans in a state of confusion is to panic. If this occurs, more harm is likely to result. Training, preparedness, and prior discussion of the range of possibilities and response scenarios all help to mitigate confusion. Fast, clear communications to all staff is essential along with the development of roles and responsibilities that are clearly understood and communicated widely.

Time Management

Time is critical in all matters pertaining to infectious diseases and other potentially life-threatening agents. Early signs, early diagnosis, early warning to the non-infected or nonexposed groups, and early intervention all have positive implications for the decreased spread and eventual decreased impact of the disease or harmful substance.

Response Capacity

Response capacity may be in the form of a trained workforce, along with needed equipment and supplies.

It also includes working with local health agencies and other organizations to develop a quick response to a crisis. There are financial considerations, such as cost of training, supplies, equipment, and downtime, that should be part of **capacity building** within the health organization. Some might even consider budgeting a "health crisis reserve" for contingency planning.

Mitigation of Fear and Panic

It is important to decrease stress and anxiety in anticipation of a possible disruptive event and, likewise, control for panic by putting in the requisite time and resources to properly train the workforce and educate the larger community. This should include the design of a crisis-control command center where all communications originate. When there are but a few people directing the response, it tends to minimize confusion and maximize effective distribution of information.

As shown in this chapter, public health has a natural role in disaster preparedness and response and all other public health emergencies. State departments of health, with responsibility as a major directing unit overseeing the public's health, already work in partnership with local health departments (LHDs) and other appropriate federal, state, and local agencies regarding other health challenges. Thus, the multisector coordination and communication channels are in place to be deployed for emergency and crisis response purposes.

EXHIBIT 12.2   Qualifications for Emergency Preparedness and Response Coordinator

Relevant knowledge, skills, and abilities for public health emergency response coordinators include the following:

- Skill in organization and planning techniques
- Skill in public relations and public speaking
- Skill in computer and communication equipment operation
- Knowledge of basic budget development and fiscal management
- Knowledge of public health and epidemiology
- Ability to establish and maintain effective working relationships with other government and public health officials, employees, agencies, volunteers, and the public
- Ability to communicate effectively, verbally, and in writing
- Ability to learn the principles, practices, and techniques involved in the emergency management
- Knowledge of the principles and the practices of governmental and public health agency structures and resources
- Minimum qualifications call for the equivalent of a master's degree in public health, biologic sciences, community health, emergency management, planning, hazard assessment, business or public administration, or other related field; and 2 years of emergency management, community planning, or other related work experience. Selected applicants are subject to and must pass a full background check. In addition, emergency response coordinators generally are required to possess a valid state driver's license. Other organizations may require 5 years of responsible experience in public administration, research, and finance, including 3 years of emergency management experience and a master's degree in public or business administration, government management, industrial engineering, or a related field. Other combinations of experience and education that meet the minimum requirements may be substituted.

Reproduced from Turnock BJ. *Essentials of Public Health*. 3rd ed. Burlington, MA: Jones & Bartlett Learning; 2016.

Conclusion

The role of public health managers in dealing with disasters and other crises is a central part of their responsibility. Likewise, they must ensure that the workforce is trained and prepared. This chapter offered examples of the planning process and emphasized the need for capacity building as part of preparedness. Core competencies of the workforce were identified, and a description of the role and capabilities of a disaster response coordinator was provided. Key agencies that may be involved were identified and a description of what might be expected was discussed in a phase model of crisis.

Discussion Questions

1. Why is planning such an important part of preparedness? Give examples.
2. What are the recommendations of the WHO as they pertain to emergency planning?
3. Describe the disaster response coordinator's role. What are his or her qualifications?
4. What are the phases of disaster preparedness and response?
5. Identify core competencies that all public health workers should have.
6. What is crisis communication and why is it important?
7. What is the role of the local health department?
8. What other agencies and organizations are involved?

Learning Activities

1. Find a public health disaster or emergency in the news. Develop a crisis communication plan using an organization involved in the story based on the CDC's Nine Steps in Crisis Communication Implementation.
2. Volunteer at your local Red Cross and participate in their disaster training program.
3. Find out what your university has planned for the following: (1) a major weather event, (2) a mass shooting, and (3) a disease outbreak.
4. Watch the YouTube video of a lecture presented by Dr. James Johnson, available at https://www.youtube.com/watch?v=n93tBVqAnl4
5. Discuss these two topics in class: (1) organized improvisation and (2) all-hazards approach. Give examples from the lecture and, if possible, from your own experience.

References

1. Johnson JA, Rossow CC. *Health Organizations*. 2nd ed. Burlington, MA: Jones & Bartlett Learning; 2019.

2. WHO guidance for contingency planning. http://apps.who .int/iris/bitstream/handle/10665/260554/WHO-WHE-CPI -2018.13-eng.pdf?ua=1

3. CDC. CERC: Crisis Communication Plans. https://emergency .cdc.gov/cerc/ppt/CERC_Crisis_Communication_Plans.pdf

4. Turnock BJ. *Essentials of Public Health.* 3rd ed. Burlington, MA: Jones & Bartlett Learning; 2016.

5. Shi L, Johnson JA. *Public Health Administration: Principles of Population-Based Management.* 4th ed. Burlington, MA: Jones & Bartlett Learning; 2020.

6. Johnson JA, Stoskopf C, Shi L. *Comparative Health Systems.* 2nd ed. Burlington, MA: Jones & Bartlett Learning; 2019.

7. Johnson JA, Johnson A. Community preparedness and response: the Katrina experience. *Soc Sci Perspect J.* 2006;(1):20–27.

Suggested Websites

CDC. Crisis and Emergency Risk Communication. https: //emergency.cdc.gov/cerc/index.asp

Johnson lecture on preparedness and response after Hurricane Katrina. https://www.youtube.com/watch?v=n93tBVqAnl4

WHO. http://apps.who.int/iris/bitstream/handle/10665/260554 /WHO-WHE-CPI-2018.13-eng.pdf?ua=1

Public Health Organizations and Their Websites

1. Agency for Toxic Substances and Disease Registry (ATSDR), https://www.atsdr.cdc.gov/
2. American Public Health Association (APHA), https://www.apha.org/
3. American Society of Tropical Medicine and Hygiene (ASTMH), https://www.astmh.org/
4. Association of State and Territorial Health Officials (ASTHO), http://www.astho.org/
5. Association of Schools of Public Health (ASPH), https://www.aspph.org/
6. Centers for Disease Control and Prevention (CDC), https://www.cdc.gov/
7. Council on Education for Public Health (CEPH), https://ceph.org/
8. Council of State and Territorial Epidemiologists (CSTE), https://www.cste.org/default.aspx
9. Food and Drug Administration (FDA), https://www.fda.gov/AboutFDA/default.htm
10. Health and Human Services (HHS), https://www.hhs.gov/
11. Health Resources and Services Administration (HRSA), https://www.hrsa.gov/
12. National Institutes of Health (NIH), https://www.nih.gov/
13. National Association of County and City Health Officials (NACCHO), https://www.naccho.org/
14. National Association of Local Boards of Health (NALBOH), https://nalboh.site-ym.com/
15. National Environmental Health Association (NEHA), https://www.neha.org/
16. National Institutes of Health (NIH), https://www.nih.gov/
17. Pan American Health Organization (PAHO), https://www.paho.org/hq/index.php?lang=en
18. Public Health Accreditation Board (PHAB), https://www.phaboard.org/
19. The Public Health Foundation (PHF), http://www.phf.org/Pages/default.aspx
20. World Health Organization (WHO), https://www.who.int/

Glossary

Contributed by Amanda Okufer, MPH

A

Access (physical) The ability to get doctors, facilities, and information. Hospitals, clinics, and other resources must be located where they can be reached and designed without barriers.

Access (to health care) The ability to obtain health care. Access includes available physicians and facilities, transportation, acceptance by the facility, and a means of payment.

Access control The ability and responsibility of a healthcare organization to control and account for access to medical records and other protected health information.

Account An arrangement between a buyer and a seller in which goods or services are exchanged and payment is made later.

> **closed account** An account upon which full payment has been made.

> **open account** An account upon which not all payments have been made.

Accountability The duty to provide, to all concerned, the evidence needed to establish confidence that the task or duty for which one is responsible is being or has been performed and describe the way that the task is being or has been carried out.

Accreditation A process of evaluation of an institution or education program to determine whether it meets the standards set up by an accrediting body, and if the institution or program meets the standards, granting recognition of the fact.

Accredited Formally recognized by an accrediting body as meeting its standards for accreditation.

Action plan A listing of specific steps to be taken to accomplish a specified goal. An action plan is usually accompanied by a timetable for each step.

Ad hoc committee A temporary group convened for the accomplishment of a specific task, after which it is disbanded.

Administration Actions taken to achieve organizational goals.

Affiliation needs The human need to belong to a group and be highly regarded by members of that group.

Affirmative action A program implemented by an employer that includes specific steps to increase minority representation in the workplace; positive actions taken to eliminate job discrimination in all phases of employment.

Agency for Healthcare Research and Quality (AHRQ) The lead federal agency for research to improve the quality of health care, reduce its cost, and broaden access to essential services; a component of the Department of Health and Human Services (DHHS).

Agency for Toxic Substances and Disease Registry (ATSDR) The ATSDR performs specific public health functions concerning hazardous substances in the environment. It works to prevent exposure and minimize adverse health effects associated with waste management emergencies and pollution by hazardous substances.

Agenda A list or outline of things to be considered or done.

Agenda setting The process by which ideas or issues bubble up through the various political channels to wind up for consideration by a political institution, such as legislature or courts.

American Public Health Association (APHA) The national association that embraces all public health professions.

Americans with Disabilities Act (ADA) Federal legislation that requires that facilities and services be accessible to persons with temporary or permanent disabilities; ensures that disabled persons are not discriminated against in employment practices.

Applicant pool The group of individuals seeking to be appointed to a vacant position.

Audit An independent review and confirmation that financial reports are accurate and that standard accounting procedures were used to prepare the reports.

Authority The power and responsibility to make decisions or control the behaviors of others; the right to make decisions.

Autocratic leadership A leadership style based on authority and issuing of orders. Autocratic leadership involves little or no consultation in pure form and is more task oriented than people oriented.

B

Balance sheet budget Expected or actual financial status at the end of the fiscal year.

Baseline measures Preintervention data; collected data used for comparison purposes to determine the effect of a new program.

Bottom-up management Management style that encourages delegation of authority and participation of all employees.

Brainstorming A group procedure used to solve problems by generating many possible solutions before any solution is evaluated.

Budget A fiscal plan that estimates projected revenues and how they will be spent.

Bureaucracy A form of organization where regulations and controls predominate; a form of organization based on logic, systems, and rules.

Burnout A condition in which formerly conscientious workers have ceased being effective, usually as a result of cumulative stress. Work is no longer meaningful.

Bylaws A legal document formulated by the board of a not-for-profit organization. The bylaws govern the structure and function of the organization.

C

Capacity building Activities that enhance the resources of individuals, organizations, and communities to improve their effectiveness in acting.

Cash budget A type of budget that projects cash availability and cash utilization, rather than the year-end balance.

CD/ROM A computer device (a compact disc in read only memory format) that electronically stores and makes available on demand educational, music, video, and other types of information.

Centers for Disease Control and Prevention (CDC) An agency within the Department of Health and Human Services (DHHS), which is responsible for monitoring and studying diseases that are controllable by public health measures. The CDC is headquartered in Atlanta, Georgia.

Centralization Retention of decision-making by top management.

Certification The issuance of a certificate, which gives evidence that its recipient (an individual, facility, or device) meets certain standards for which testing has been done by the certifying body.

Chain of command The supervisor–supervisee flow of authority that specifies who reports to whom.

Change agent A person who views creating change as an important part of his or her responsibility. A change agent can be an employee or an external consultant.

Charismatic leadership A leadership style that is based on energetic, highly personal management traits.

Chief executive officer (CEO) The top paid administrator. The CEO of a company is often the president, although many other titles are used.

Chief financial officer (CFO) The person whose responsibility for the budget is exceeded only by the responsibility of the chief executive officer. The CFO is often a vice-president or controller, although other titles are commonly used.

Chief medical officer (CMO) The person (usually a physician) responsible for the medical affairs of a corporation or organization. The actual duties will vary widely, depending on the context. This person is sometimes called the chief medical director.

Chief operating officer (COO) The person in charge of the internal operation of the organization. The CEO, while responsible for the internal operation of the organization, also has external responsibilities with the governing body, with the community, with other institutions, and so on.

Claim (finance) The usage in which the word is employed to describe one form of asset.

Claim (insurance) A request for payment of insurance benefits to be paid to or on behalf of a beneficiary.

Claim (legal) An allegation of legal liability and an accompanying demand for damages (money) or other rights due.

Claims processing The procedure by which claims for payment for services are reviewed to determine whether they should be paid and for what amount.

Coalition A group of organizations that have created an alliance to enhance the members' power and influence.

Collective bargaining The formal process of negotiating and administering a written signed agreement between labor and management. Collective bargaining usually covers wages, working conditions, and fringe benefits, and the agreement, once signed, has the force of law.

Committee A group of people set up for a specific purpose: to consider or investigate a matter, to report on a matter, or to carry out certain duties.

Compensation Wages and salaries paid to employees and other benefits, such as insurance coverage.

Confidentiality Exists when there is a link between personal information and the person's identity, but that information is protected from others.

Conflict of interest A situation where a person (or organization) has two separate and distinct duties owed concerning, or interests in, the same thing, and therefore cannot act completely impartially with respect to that thing.

Consortium An alliance between two or more parties to achieve a specific purpose.

Consultation (management) Advice from an expert given after a study of a situation or problem presented by the individual obtaining the consultation. In the public health field, such consultation often concerns organization, management, and strategic planning.

Contingency planning The incorporation of a margin of error into plans to accommodate unforeseen events.

Contract An agreement between two or more parties, which gives legally enforceable rights and duties to both. A contract need not be in writing to be enforceable unless it is a certain kind of agreement, such as one for the sale of real estate.

Corporation A legal entity, which exists separately, for all legal purposes, from the people or organizations that own it. To take advantage of legal advantages (limitation of liability and tax benefits, for example), a corporation must observe certain stipulations required by law, such as meetings, minutes, and filing of annual reports and tax returns.

> **for-profit corporation** A corporation whose profits (excess of income over expenses) are distributed, as dividends, to shareholders who own the corporation (in contrast to a nonprofit corporation, in which the profits go to corporate purposes rather than to individual shareholders).

> **nonprofit corporation** A corporation whose profits (excess of income over expenses) are used for corporate purposes, rather than returned to shareholders or investors (owners) as dividends. To qualify for tax exemption, no portion of the profits of the corporation may inure to the benefit of an individual

Cost allocation An accounting procedure by which costs that cannot be clearly identified with any specific department are distributed among all or some departments.

Cost analysis A group of analyses from the discipline of economics, which can be applied to a variety of public health interventions.

Cost-benefit analysis A method of evaluating alternatives by comparing the costs of action and its benefits.

Cost containment Efforts to prevent increase in cost or to restrict its rate of increase.

Criterion A measurable indicator of job performance.

Cross-functional A term used in quality management teams to indicate that more than one department is involved.

Cultural competence Possession of the knowledge, skills, and attitudes needed to provide effective services for or working with diverse populations, considering the culture, language, values, and reality of the community.

D

Database A collection of information. A computer database may be a small personal database stored in a microcomputer or a very large database stored in a mainframe computer.

Decentralization Delegation of a great deal of authority to lower levels of management.

Delegation The downward transfer of authority from one position to another.

Democratic leadership A leadership style that emphasizes group decision-making.

Department of Agriculture (USDA) The department of the executive branch of the federal government in charge of a variety of programs dealing with the environment, food production, and natural resource use and preservation.

Department of Commerce (DOC) The department of the executive branch of the federal government in charge of the business and economic sector. It is also responsible for such other issues as weather reports and the census and includes the National Technical Information Service (NTIS).

Department of Defense (DOD) The department of the executive branch of the federal government in charge of the military and national defense.

Department of Education (DOE) The department of the executive branch of the federal government in charge of educational policy.

Department of Energy (DOE) The department of the executive branch of the federal government in charge of energy policy. Its stated mission is "to foster a secure and reliable energy system that is environmentally and economically sustainable, to be a responsible steward of the Nation's nuclear weapons; to clean up our own facilities and to support continued United States leadership in science and technology."

Department of Health and Human Services (DHHS) The department of the executive branch of the federal government responsible for the federal health programs in the civilian sector. The following agencies are under the direction of *DHHS*:

> *Office of the Secretary of Health and Human Services (OS)*

> *Administration for Children and Families (ACF)*

> *Administration on Aging (AoA)*

> *Agency for Healthcare Research and Quality (AHRQ)*

> *Agency for Toxic Substances and Disease Registry (ATSDR)*

> *Centers for Disease Control and Prevention (CDC)*

> *Centers for Medicare and Medicaid Services (CMS)*

> *Food and Drug Administration (FDA)*

> *Health Resources and Services Administration (HRSA)*

> *Indian Health Service (IHS)*

> *National Institutes of Health (NIH)*

> *Substance Abuse and Mental Health Services Administration (SAMHSA)*

Department of Justice (DOJ) The department of the executive branch of the federal government, which enforces certain federal laws. The Department of Justice is headed by the U.S. Attorney General.

Department of Labor (DOL) The department of the executive branch of the federal government in charge of administering federal employer/employee policies and regulations.

Director (management) An operating officer. The title director is used by many institutions for their officers and executives.

Disbursement Paying money to take care of an expense or a debt.

Division of labor Use of narrow job descriptions and repetition to increase efficiency and effectiveness.

E

Economic system The way in which goods and services are produced, distributed, and consumed.

E-mail Electronic mail distributed over a computer network.

Employee A person who works for and is paid by another (the employer) and who is under the control of the employer. An employee is to be distinguished from an independent contractor, who works for himself.

Employee assistance program (EAP) A workplace program that focuses on employee problems, such as substance abuse, burnout, fiscal problems, emotional problems, and marital problems.

Employee health benefit plan An organization's plan for health benefits for its employees and their dependents. The term generally refers to the benefits that are provided. Such plans are not part of the employee's salary. The employees may or may not contribute to paying the cost by deductions from their salaries.

Entrepreneurism A leadership style that emphasizes new initiatives.

Environmental Protection Agency (EPA) The federal agency that monitors compliance with and enforces water, air, noise, and toxic waste pollution rules.

Equal Employment Opportunity Commission (EEOC) The federal agency responsible for enforcing antidiscrimination rules in the workplace. Discrimination based on race, national origin, gender, religion, sexual orientation, disability, or veteran status is prohibited.

Esteem needs The human need to feel competent and to have one's achievements recognized by others. Esteem needs are included in Maslow's hierarchy of needs.

Ethics A system or code that lays out what is good, right, and honorable.

Executive An individual who is a high-level manager and who has authority to make significant decisions. Similar authority is implied by use of the terms employed for corporate officers, such as president and vice-president. The trend is to use these terms in public health organizations where formerly such persons might have been called administrators.

Executive branch In a government with a separation of powers, the part that is responsible for the applying or administering the law.

Executive budget The budget document for an executive branch of government that a jurisdiction's chief executive submits to legislature for review, modification, and enactment.

Exit interview Brief structured interview required of employees who are leaving a company.

Expense The using up of an asset (as in depreciation), or the cost of providing services or making a product during an accounting period. The subtraction of expenses from revenue gives the net income.

Extrinsic rewards Payoffs granted to an individual by other people, such as incentives in a motivation program.

F

Fax machine An electronic device that sends and receives facsimiles of documents over phone lines.

Federalism A system of governance in which a national, overarching government shares power with subnational or state governments.

> **Cooperative federalism** The notion that the national, state, and local governments are cooperating, interacting agents jointly working to solve common problems, rather than conflicting, sometimes hostile competitors pursuing similar or conflicting ends.
>
> **Dual federalism** Federalist theory in which the functions and responsibilities of the federal and state governments are distinguished and separate from each other.
>
> **Marble-cake federalism** Concept that the cooperative relations among the varying levels of government result in an intermingling of activities; in contrast to the traditional layer-cake federalism, which holds that the three layers of government are almost totally separate.
>
> **New federalism** Republican efforts beginning in the Nixon era to decentralize governmental functions by returning power and responsibilities to the states. This trend continued into the 1990s and culminated in the "devolution movement."
>
> **Picket-fence federalism** The concept that bureaucratic specialists at the various levels of government exercise considerable power over the nature of intergovernmental programs.

Federally Qualified Health Center (FQHC) A local, community-based organization that provides preventive, primary care and other services to those who might not otherwise have access to health care; sometimes called a community health center (CHC). To be considered an FQHC, the heath center must have the following features:

Is tax-exempt nonprofit of the public.

Is located in or serves an underserved community.

Provides comprehensive primary healthcare services, referrals, and other services needed to facilitate access to care, such as case management, language translation, and transportation.

Serves everyone in the community, regardless of ability to pay.

Is governed by a community board with the majority of members being patients of the health center.

Fee-for-service (FFS) A method of paying physicians and other healthcare providers in which each service carries a fee.

Food and Drug Administration (FDA) An agency within the U.S. Department of Health and Human Services (DHHS) responsible for protecting the health of the nation against impure and unsafe foods, drugs, cosmetics, biological substances, and other potential hazards. A major part of the FDA's activity is controlling the sale, distribution, and use of medications and medical devices, including the licensing of new drugs for use by humans.

First-line manager A supervisor who is responsible for workers but not for other managers.

Fixed costs Ongoing costs that change little from year to year, such as personnel, insurance, lease, utility, and debt service costs.

Flat organizational structure An organizational structure characterized by wide spans of control and few hierarchy levels.

Flex time An employee scheduling system that permits employees to vary their work schedule to accommodate personal needs, such as child care and transportation.

Formative evaluation Assessment during a project's development and early implementation for improving the project in later stages.

Fringe benefits Elements of an employee's compensation package other than wage or salary. Fringe benefits typically include vacation time, a retirement pension, and insurance coverage.

G

Gatekeeper The person responsible for determining the services to be provided to a patient and coordinating the provision of the appropriate care. The purposes of the gatekeeper's function are to improve the quality of care by considering all of the patient's problems and other relevant factors, to ensure that all necessary care is obtained, and to reduce unnecessary care (and cost). When, as is often the case, the gatekeeper is a physician, she or he is a primary care physician and usually must, except in an emergency, give the first level of care to the patient before the patient is permitted to be seen by a secondary care physician.

Gateway (organization) An organization or system that provides a single point of access to a given universe of products or services. A gateway organization usually provides service directly or, if it does not offer the desired service, makes sure that the consumer or client reaches the proper destination.

Grant (1) A sum of money given by the government, a foundation, or other organization to support a program, project, organization, or individual. (2) An assistance award in which substantial involvement is not anticipated between the federal government and the state or local government or other recipient during the performance of the contemplated activity.

Grapevine Informal channels of communication.

Gross domestic product (GDP) The market value of all goods and services produced by labor and property within the United States during a particular period of time. Income from overseas operations of a domestic corporation would not be included in the GDP, but activities carried on within U.S. borders by a foreign company would be.

Gross national product (GNP) The market value of all goods and services produced by labor and property supplied by residents of the United States during a particular period of time. Income from overseas operations of a domestic corporation would be included in the GNP.

H

Halo effect The tendency to rate an employee well, based on past performance, rather than on current performance.

Hawthorne effect The tendency of individuals who receive special attention to perform up to expectations. Employees who are being monitored work better than those who are not, because employees desire to meet expectations.

Health maintenance organization (HMO) A healthcare providing organization that ordinarily has a closed group of physicians (and sometimes other health professionals), along with either its own hospital or allocated beds in one or more hospitals. Individuals (usually families) join an HMO, which agrees to provide the medical and hospital care they need, for a fixed, predetermined fee. Each subscriber is under a contract stipulating the limits of the service.

Health professional A comprehensive term covering people working in the field of public health or health care who have some special training and/or education. The degree of education, training, and other qualifications varies greatly with the nature of the profession, and with the state regulating its practice.

HIPAA The Health Insurance Portability and Accountability Act of 1996 (HIPAA) is a federal legislation whose primary purpose is to provide continuity of health care coverage. It does this partly by providing limitations on preexisting condition exclusions, as well as prohibiting discrimination against individuals based on health status. The law also guarantees that insured workers will be eligible to keep their insurance if they leave their jobs. It created the medical savings account (MSA) to help individuals pay for their health care. HIPAA also made amendments to other legislation, including the Employee Retirement Income Security Act (ERISA), the Internal Revenue Code (IRC), and the Public Health Service Act. HIPAA also contains a section for requirements for the electronic transmission of health information.

Horns effect The tendency to rate an employee poorly, based on past performance rather than current performance.

Human resources management The function of an organization where the focus is on job analysis, performance appraisal, recruitment, and selection. The human resources domain of public health management ultimately serves to promote healthy workplaces, thus keeping with the foundations and fundamentals of public health.

Humanistic approach A management style based on the belief that managers get things done through people. This approach emphasizes worker participation and worker satisfaction.

I

Indian Health Service (IHS) An agency within the Department of Health and Human Services (DHHS) whose goal is to ensure that comprehensive, culturally acceptable personal and public health services are available and accessible to American Indian and Alaska Native people. The IHS manages a comprehensive healthcare delivery system for more than 561 federally recognized Indian tribes in 35 states. IHS provides services to approximately 1.8 million members in urban areas, as well as on reservations.

Incremental budgeting A method of budget review that focuses on the increments of increase or decrease in the budget of existing programs.

Incremental changes Minor adjustments to keep the organization moving toward its goals.

Incremental funding The provision of budgetary resources for a program or project based on obligations estimated to be incurred within a fiscal year when such budgetary resources will cover only a portion of the obligations to be incurred while completing the program of project.

Information overload A condition that occurs when managers have so much information available that they have difficulty making decisions and determining what information to disregard.

Insurance A method of providing for money to pay for specific types of losses that may occur. Insurance is a contract between one party (the insured) and another (the insurer). The policy states what types of losses are covered, what amounts will be paid for each loss and for all losses, and under what conditions.

Insurance coverage Generally, refers to the amount of protection available and the kind of loss that would be paid for under an insurance contract.

Internal audit A review of financial records by a financial division employee to check for accuracy and adherence to procedures. The main purpose of an internal audit is to determine if fraud or other undesirable practices are occurring.

Internet A term used to describe the interconnection of hundreds of computer networks in such a way that allows them to communicate with each other and allows the user to search them all simultaneously, sometimes called the information superhighway.

Interpersonal communication Verbal and nonverbal transmission of messages, usually in a face-to-face setting.

Intrinsic rewards Self-granted and internally experienced payoffs.

J

Job enrichment The addition of responsibilities to a position, so that the work is more meaningful to the position holder. It is often used to increase satisfaction with jobs that are monotonous.

Job specifications Requirements of a position, including education, work experience, certifications, and skills.

K

Knowledge-based management Management practices and decisions supported by valid data.

L

Leadership The process of influencing an organization and its employees to move toward goals and objectives.

Letter of transmittal Cover memo that accompanies documents being mailed, such as grant applications.

Leverage Financing by borrowing.

    capital leverage See *financial leverage*.

    financial leverage The ratio of total debt to total assets. Financial leverage is also called capital leverage. An institution uses financial leverage when it believes it has *positive* leverage, that is, it can use the money obtained by debt financing (see *financing*) to earn more money than it costs to borrow the money (interest and taxes). Should the cost of borrowing exceed the added revenue, the situation is one of *negative* leverage.

    negative leverage See *financial leverage*.

    operating leverage The ratio of fixed costs to variable costs (see *cost*). When it takes very little added labor or materials to provide added units of service or products, the operating leverage is high (and the marginal cost of added units is low); a greater volume brings accelerated profits, once the break-even point is reached. The higher the proportion of the costs that are variable (that is, the lower the operating leverage), the greater an increase in units of service or products will be required to increase profits.

    positive leverage See *financial leverage*.

Leveraged Financed largely by borrowed funds.

Liability (legal) An actual or potential responsibility to do something, pay for something, or refrain from doing something. Liability is used to refer to a legal duty or other obligation, often one which must be enforced by a lawsuit.

> **corporate liability** Legal responsibility of a corporation rather than of an individual.

> **joint liability** The responsibility of more than one defendant to share in legal liability to a plaintiff.

> **product liability** An area of law that imposes legal responsibility on manufacturers (and in some cases, distributors and retailers) of goods that leave the factory in an unreasonably dangerous condition and that, in fact, cause harm to someone because of that condition.

> **professional liability** A legal duty, which is the result of performing (or failing to perform) something that one does (or should have done) as a professional.

Liability (financial) In finance, a liability is an obligation to pay.

> **current liability** A liability due within 1 year.

License A legal term that represents a specific right to do or use something or to refrain from it.

Licensure A method used to ensure that persons who provide services are adequately qualified. The licensure law will often define the scope of practice for that profession, and anyone performing services within that scope must first have a license to do so.

Limited liability company (LLC) A form of organization that allows all owners and managers to have limited liability for the debts of the company or organization but also favorable tax treatment that avoids traditional corporate taxation.

Line-item budget The classification of budgetary accounts according to narrow, detailed objects of expenditure used within each agency of government, generally without reference to the ultimate purpose or objective served by the expenditure.

Litigation Lawsuits and other legally filed complaints that claim violation of laws and regulations.

Lobbying Attempts to influence the passage or defeat of legislation.

Local health department A unit of local government that implements local, national, and state public health policy. It typically carries out some clinical services, environmental services, and support services. Clinical services may include, for example, dental health, occupational health, nursing, maternal and child health, family planning, communicable diseases, and Women, Infants, and Children's Programs (WIC). Environmental services may include general environment, vector control, animal control, and pollution control. Support services may include, in addition to administration, vital statistics, laboratory, and health education.

M

Macroeconomics The economic theory that pertains to forces which determine the decisions and actions of populations, rather than of individuals; the latter theory concerning individuals is called *microeconomics*.

Maintenance Organizational function responsible for the fiscal, physical, and human resources infrastructure of the organization.

Managed care Any arrangement for health care in which someone is interposed between the patient and physician and has authority to place restraints on how and from whom the patient may obtain medical and health services, and what services are to be provided in a given situation. Managed care was originally designed to control costs, encourage efficient use of resources, and ensure that care given is appropriate.

Management A word that refers both to the people responsible for running an organization and to the running process itself; the use of numerous resources (such as employees and machines) to accomplish an organizational goal. Permeates all other functions and subsystems of the organization. It involves those in charge of all of the other functions.

Management information system (MIS) A system, typically computer based, that provides managers with information needed for decision-making.

Manager Any individual who is responsible for directing the activities of an organization or one of its components.

Medically underserved area A rural or urban area that does not have enough healthcare resources to meet the needs of its population or whose population has a relatively low health status. The term is defined in the Public Health Service Act and is used to determine which areas have priority for assistance.

Medically underserved population A population group that does not have enough healthcare resources to meet its needs. The group may reside in a medically underserved area or may be a population group with certain attributes; for example, migrant workers, Native Americans, or prison inmates may constitute a medically underserved population. The term is defined in the Public Health Service Act and is used to determine which areas have priority for assistance.

Mentor A person who has accepted the role of introducing a new employee to the organization and the complexities of the position; an experienced employee who has agreed to guide an inexperienced employee. Mentors are frequently used to prepare individuals for career advancement.

Merit pay A form of performance incentive; a salary or wage increase granted for outstanding achievement. Merit pay may be a permanent increase or only for the period it was granted (a one-time-only bonus).

Mid-level manager A manager below the level of vice-president who supervises other managers.

Motivators Factors such as achievement, recognition, responsibility, and advancement that acts as incentives to improve job performance.

N

National Institutes of Health (NIH) The nation's premier biomedical research organization. The NIH is an agency within the Department of Health and Human Services (DHHS). Based in Bethesda, Maryland, the NIH consists of 28 separate institutes and centers. The institutes carry out research and programs related to certain specific types of diseases, such as mental and neurological disease, arthritis, cancer, and heart disease. There is an institute for each of the categories of disease for which NIH has programs, and a number of other components not specific to any disease categories.

Net worth Assets minus liabilities.

New public administration An academic advocacy movement for social equity in the performance and delivery of public services; it called for a proactive administrator with a desire for social equity to replace the traditional impersonal and neutral bureaucrat.

New public management A disparate group of structural reforms and informal management initiatives that reflect the doctrine of managerialism in the public sector.

Nongovernmental organization (NGO) Legal entities created by private individuals, private organizations, publicly traded organizations, or in some combination where government influence, supervision, and management are removed, or at least greatly minimized, from the NGO's strategic and operational mission.

Nonprofit An entity whose profits (excess of income over expenses) are used for its own purposes, rather than returned to its members (shareholders, investors, and owners) as dividends. To qualify for tax exemption, no portion of the profits of the entity may inure to the benefit of an individual.

Nuisance complaints Minor legal actions. Nuisance complaints are sometimes filed by disgruntled former employees or clients.

O

Occupational Safety and Health Administration (OSHA) A federal agency responsible for developing and enforcing regulations regarding the safety and health among workers in the United States.

Organization A structured social system consisting of groups and individuals working together to meet agreed upon objectives.

Organizational awareness The ability to understand and learn the formal and informal decision-making structures and power relationships in an organization or industry. This includes the ability to identify who the real decision-makers are and the individuals who can influence them, and to predict how new events will affect individuals and groups within the organization.

Organizational behavior The study of individual and group behaviors in organizations, analyzing motivation, work satisfaction, leadership, work–group dynamics, and the attitudes and behaviors of the members of organizations.

Organizational culture The pattern of shared values, beliefs, and norms—along with associated behaviors, symbols, and rituals—that are acquired over time by members of an organization. It is the historically developed sense of the institution's "legacy"—what it is and what it stands for—that permeates throughout the organization and is known to all who work for it.

Organizational development An approach or strategy for increasing organizational effectiveness. As a process, it has no value biases but is usually associated with the idea that effectiveness is demonstrated by integrating the individual's desire for growth with the organizational goals.

Organizational theory A sociological approach to the study of organizations focusing on topics that affect the organization, such as organizational environments, goals and effectiveness, strategy and decision-making, change and innovation, and structure and design.

Outcome Refers to the "outcome" (finding) of a given diagnostic procedure. It may also refer to cure of a patient, restoration of function, or extension of life. When used for populations or the healthcare system, it typically refers to changes in birth or death rates or some similar global measure.

P

Peer review Review by individuals from the same discipline and with essentially equal qualifications (peers).

Performance The actual carrying out of an activity. To be able to evaluate performance accurately requires considerable sophistication in the collection and the analysis of data about the performance demonstrated.

Performance appraisal The formal methods by which an organization documents the work performance of its employees. Performance appraisals are typically designed to change dysfunctional work behavior, communicate perceptions of work quality, assess the future potential of an employee, and provide a documented record for disciplinary and separation actions.

Performance data Data that are developed from the activities of an individual or institution. More sophisticated performance data can be developed from ongoing information systems, which can describe patterns.

Performance management The systematic integration of an organization's efforts to achieve its objectives.

Performance measure Something used to gather data on and evaluate activities and outcomes.

Planning The analysis of needs, demands, and resources, followed by the proposal of steps to meet the demands and needs by use of the current resources and obtaining other resources as necessary.

> **community-based planning** Planning where the attempt is made to have the planning initiative within the local community, rather than external to the community.

> **comprehensive health planning** Planning that attempts to coordinate environmental measures, health education, health care, and occupational and other health efforts to achieve the desired results in a community.

Policies Formally approved rules, regulations, and guidelines for action.

Public health The science and art of preventing disease, prolonging life, and promoting physical health and efficiency through organized community efforts for the sanitation of the environment, the control of community infections, the education of the individual in principles of personal hygiene, the organization of medical and nursing services for the early diagnosis and preventive treatment of disease, and the development of the social machinery that will ensure every individual in the community has an adequate standard of living for the maintenance of health.

Public relations Efforts to promote a program or organization. It usually involves but is not limited to media campaigns.

Q

Quality control (QC) The sum of all the activities that prevent unwanted change in quality. This usually involves the identification of any problems or opportunities for improvement, and prompt corrective action, so that the quality is maintained.

Quality improvement (QI) The sum of all the activities that create desired change in quality. This often involves an analysis of patterns in order to identify opportunities for improvement.

Quality management (QM) Efforts to determine the quality of the service being rendered to develop and maintain programs to keep it at an acceptable level, to institute improvements when the opportunity arises, or the quality does not meet the standards, and to provide the evidence required to establish confidence that quality is being managed and maintained at the desired level.

R

Recruitment The process of seeking, locating, and hiring acceptable employees.

Resources Human, fiscal, or technical assets available to be used in achieving goals and objectives.

Revenue Increase in an organization's assets or a decrease in its liabilities during an accounting period. This is in contrast with *income* which refers to money earned during an accounting period.

> **marginal revenue** The addition to or subtraction from total revenue resulting from the sale of one more or one less unit of service or product.

Risk (financial) A chance of monetary loss.

Risk (health) The likelihood of disease, injury, or death among various groups of individuals and from different causes. Individuals are said to be at risk if they are in a group in which a given causal factor is present.

Risk management The process of minimizing risk to an organization at a minimal cost in keeping with the organization's objectives.

S

Sexual harassment Unwanted sexual attention that creates an offensive or intimidating work environment.

Stakeholder (1) Any individual or group that might be affected by the outcome of something. All decisions have their stakeholders. (2) The affected individuals or communities along with those who are influential in developing a plan to address the problem in question.

Standard (threshold) A measure of quality or quantity, established by an authority, by a profession, or by custom, which serves as a criterion for evaluation. It is a threshold, below which one should not fall. This type of standard is distinguished from a standard that is simply a "norm."

Strategic planning A process through which senior staff decide on goals, objectives, and strategies to accomplish the mission of the organization.

Systems thinking A way of thinking and practice that incorporates systems science and its various tools to improve organizational and health outcomes and processes.

SWOT analysis A review of an organization's Strengths, Weaknesses, Opportunities, and Threats. The review of strengths and weaknesses provides an internal assessment for the organization, whereas the review of opportunities and threats provides the organization with an analysis of the external environment. The SWOT analysis is generally used in the strategic planning process.

T

Time management The body of knowledge that emphasizes the efficient use of time.

Transformational leadership Leadership that strives to change organizational culture and directions. It reflects the ability of a leader to develop a values-based vision for the organization, to convert the vision into reality, and to maintain it over time.

U

United States Public Health Service Commissioned Corps (USPHS) One of seven uniformed services of the United States. The USPHS is under the direction of the Surgeon General within the Public Health Service. Its mission is to protect, promote, and advance the health and safety of the American people. The USPHS has approximately 6000 officers.

V

Vision A view of an organization's future. The purpose of strategic management is to transform the vision into a reality.

Vision statement The identification of objectives to be achieved in the future.

W

World Health Organization (WHO) The division of the United Nations (UN) that is concerned with health. Headquartered in Geneva, Switzerland, the WHO came into being in April 1948 when the United Nations ratified the WHO's Constitution. Its objective is the attainment of the highest possible level of health by all peoples. It is governed by the World Health Assembly, which meets annually.

Z

A process emphasizing management's responsibility to plan, budget, and evaluate. **Zero-based budgeting** provides for analysis of alternative methods of operation and various levels of effort. It places new programs on equal footing with existing programs by requiring that program priorities be ranked, thereby providing a systematic basis for allocating resources.

Index

Page numbers followed by *f*, *t*, *b*, and *e* indicate figures, tables, boxes, and exhibits.